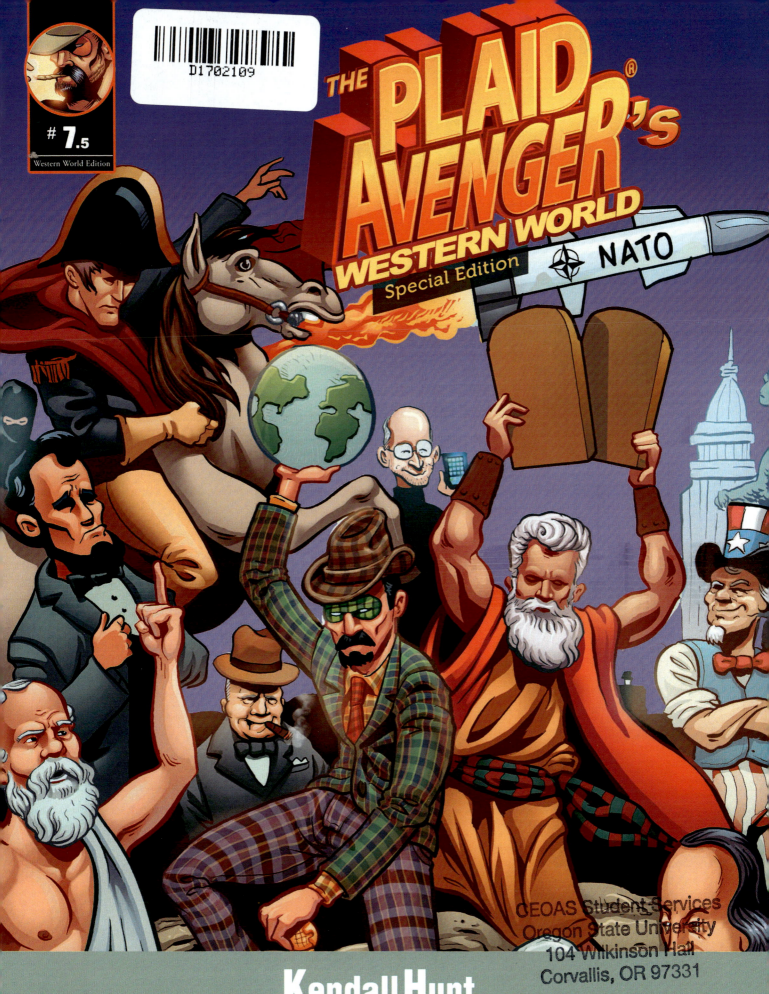

Illustrations on the cover and cartoons throughout book created by Klaus Shmidheiser.

Kendall Hunt
publishing company

www.kendallhunt.com
Send all inquiries to:
4050 Westmark Drive
Dubuque, IA 52004-1840

Copyright © 2012, 2014 by John Boyer

ISBN 978-1-4652-5808-3

Kendall Hunt Publishing Company has the exclusive rights to reproduce this work,
to prepare derivative works from this work, to publicly distribute this work,
to publicly perform this work and to publicly display this work.

All rights reserved. No part of this publication may be reproduced,
stored in a retrieval system, or transmitted, in any form or by any
means, electronic, mechanical, photocopying, recording, or otherwise,
without the prior written permission of the copyright owner.

Printed in the United States of America

Introduction ix

PART ONE
UNDERSTANDING THE PLAID PLANET

1   A Plaid World Intro   2
2   World Population Dynamics   15
3   The State of States   35
4   The Plaid World Economy   61
5   Developed or Developing?   81
6   International Organizations   101

PART TWO
THE REGIONS

7   North America   125
8   Western Europe   149
9   Eastern Europe   169
10   Russia   193
11   Australia and New Zealand   227
12   Latin America   241
    Conclusion   263

Acknowledgments

Contributing Writers: Steven Rich, Flash Clark, Josette Torres, Amber Zoe Smith, Alexander Reniers, Nicholas Reinholtz, & Jason Hushour

Chief Editor and Zen Master of the Red Pen: Josette Torres, aka girlinblack

Editors: Josette Torres, Stacy Boyer, Chris Drake, & Lauren Beecher

Image Acquisitions: Katie Pritchard

Graphics Creation: Katie Pritchard

Film Critic: Steven Rich

Content Editor: Andrew Shears

Personal Assistant to the Plaid Avenger: Katie Pritchard

And a special thanks to the most awesome plaid artist on the planet:
    Cartoonist: Klaus Shmidheiser

A whole book on the world of the West? Count me in, partners! Yeehaw!

Introduction

A GEOGRAPHY OF THE WESTERN WORLD

Just what is the "Western World" anyway? You may have heard this term before but not known what it refers to. As we'll see, it's complicated and depends a bit on your perspective—something that's going to be essential to our use of geography this term. More about "perspective" later . . .

For now, it's enough to know that "western" can mean a direction, a region, or a location (the western part of the United States), a genre (as in cowboy movies or music), and even a cultural framework or a mode of thought. These multiple meanings might have you confused over what this class is going to cover—not the western U.S., or cowboys, but roughly half of the world divided between the "West" and the "non-West."

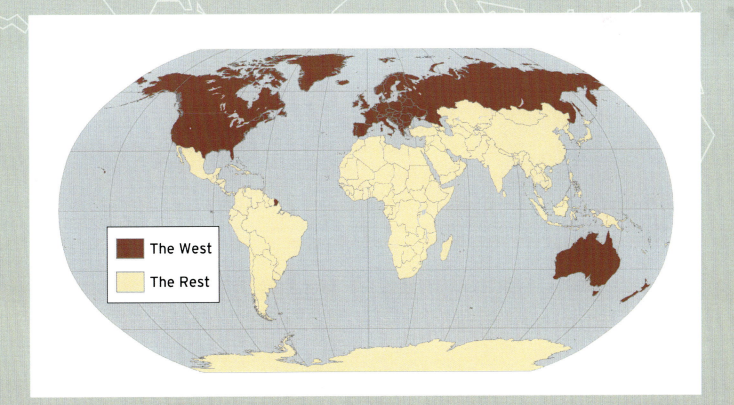

Plaid Avenger's World
INTRODUCTION

What makes something "western" then? As we'll see, this terminology comes about through its use in defining parts of the ancient world as separate from each other, specifically the "East," or the Orient: the Middle East, North Africa, and Asia, from the Occident: Europe. At one time, people generally thought that Europe was the western boundary of the world, thus Europe was "the West." These terms were further institutionalized during the governing of the Roman Empire between eastern and western areas, for example, and they came to stand not just for a place but for a whole set of ideas about the world.

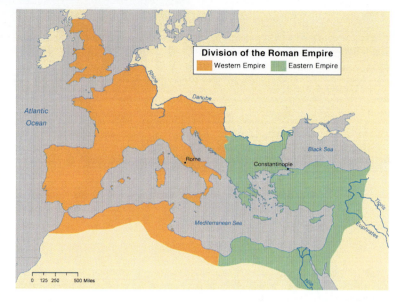

We now know of course that the world is round—if you keep going west, you'll ultimately never stop, but that doesn't mean that these terms are not still important. As people began to more thoroughly globalize—to spread over the earth, linking individuals, households, villages, towns, and eventually cities together in networks of trade, communication, and more, some parts were more heavily influenced by European immigration and conquest. This is why our "Western world" includes North America, Russia, Australia/New Zealand, and even Latin America along with Europe.

Even though we will challenge these distinctions later, at the moment it may be easier to think about "west" and "non-west" as a dualism, or a binary (0 or 1, this not that, etc.), that uses not just Europe, and not just places affected by Europe (because you can argue that everywhere is affected by Europe to some extent), but parts of the world that retained large numbers of people, culture, ideas, and so on. And despite plenty of supporting evidence that this "Western world" is not, and never has been, completely unified (the foreign policy difference between Russia and the U.S. is just one in any number of examples), we will use this "taxonomy" (a way of artificially classifying something) to make sense of this big, complicated world that we live in.

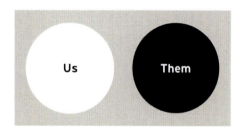

But wait a minute—we don't consider ourselves "European" here in the U.S., right? Mostly not. We have our own identity, systems of governance, culture, economy, etc., some of it very different from the Old World. Yet it would be very difficult to argue that we weren't heavily influenced by European immigration, especially before the 1970s and the 1980s, after which the majority of migrants began to come from Asia and Latin America. Whether we realize it or not, there are remnants of Greek philosophy and ideas from the Renaissance in our systems of government, inventions by Old-World thinkers in our technologies, and the imprint of agricultural and industrial revolutions everywhere. The fact that this is written in English is a taken-for-granted connection to the Occident. In many other ways, we have been and continue to be influenced by Europe, culturally, politically, economically, and so on.

Does this mean that we are not influenced by the Orient aka 'the East'? Of course not. In fact, one point that will be made clear throughout the term is the influence of other places on Europe, and on us. This is the challenge of a course or framework that seeks to create a geographic taxonomy—to break the world into parts in order to understand it better. This process tends to downplay the connections, interactions, and linkages between people, places, and ideas. Despite this challenge, we will use a "Western" versus "non-Western" distinction as a tool to try and learn a bit about roughly half the world, knowing its limitations, shortcomings, and potential problems in advance. We will attempt to adopt the perspective, even temporarily, that we are all in some ways "Westernized," some perhaps more than others.

PERSPECTIVE

One very important term or concept we will use is the idea of "perspective." It might be easier to provide an example. . . .

What do you see in this black and white image? A woman? How would you describe this woman? Young? Old? Hopefully you'll get to the point where you can see both: a side profile of an old woman with a large nose and chin, and a young woman looking off to the right with what appears to be a feather in a hat. (If you don't see both, keep working on it, you'll eventually get there.)

This optical illusion is used in a variety of different ways and contexts, often in books or lectures about subjects like art or psychology. And while some may even suggest which woman you see first says something about the state of your mind (if you see the young woman, you think in a youthful way, for example), for our purposes this graphic serves as an excellent example of perspective. If you looked at it and only saw one woman, let's say the old woman, without any indication that there was more to the picture, you'd probably assert that this was a picture of an old woman. You might even be willing to argue that, in fact, this is a picture of an old woman and even make decisions based on this. Your perspective, or perception, is that this is a picture of an old woman. Yet, as you now know, there are two women.

This is a great example of perspective for a few key reasons. First, in certain terms, what you see, hear, touch, feel, etc., is what you believe. Our senses drive our experiences; our experiences influence our thinking, decision-making, and so on. However, we may not always see everything, like when you didn't know there were two women in the image. So the second key point, and one that is essential to your success in this course, is that your perceptions—the ideas you have about the world already—is likely incomplete. In fact, a critical justification for a course like this is to point out some of the things you may not already see about the world you live in. If you are open to this idea, you will likely experience a shift in perspective—one that will help you not just learn more about the world in this course, but that will allow you to continue learning well beyond this short academic term.

Therefore, it is necessary, here in the very beginning of this course, to adopt the "perspective" that our perceptions—yours, mine, everyone's—are incomplete, limited, and even biased. An implicit goal is to be introduced to information, ideas, theories, concepts, and more that will help you see more of the picture, knowing in advance (of course) that in our incredibly complicated world we will never be able to see everything at once. Furthermore, it will probably help at the outset to recognize that all of the information in this course—readings, lectures, videos, etc.—are coming from multiple, partial perspectives.

GEOGRAPHY

What about the other word in the title of this course: "Geography?" It's very likely if you are a product of the American educational system, public or private, that you had very little geography in school. This is largely the result of a nearly universal misconception that geography is a descriptive exercise—mostly memorizing places on a map, such as cities, rivers, countries, etc. This is not only misunderstanding what geography is, it's often incredibly boring.

You're going to learn a lot more about what geography means in this course. For now, think of it in literal terms: "Geo-graphy" means to study or to write about the Earth. Yes, nearly anything we learn about can be considered geography: physical processes like glaciation or erosion; social, political, and economic ideas and institutions like banking, or the Occupy Wall Street movement; historical processes; technological advances; philosophies, ideologies, and even culture: food, music, fashion, and more. Nearly everything can be analyzed using a geographic lens.

So what makes something geography versus another discipline? Perspective! In a sense, geography is not so much a discrete academic discipline as it is a perspective that can be used to analyze or understand nearly anything.

Here is a very important phrase that I want you to try to remember: Geography can be thought of as "why things are the way they are because of where they are." Any time we're learning about something, there's always a where. Even in cyberspace, or in someone's imagination, there's a "spatial" component, for our purposes a "where-ness." Think about this: Can there be any individual or event studied in history that is not geographical? Time and space are linked (you might learn more about this in a physics course). Yet history—something no one seems to need to explain the utility of—is the study of space-time emphasizing time, or the

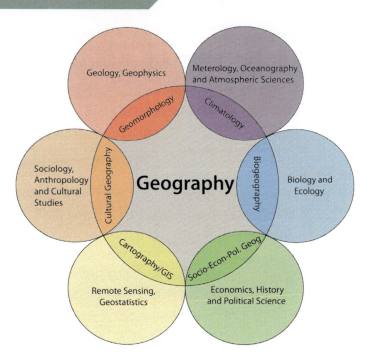

temporal dimension. Geography, then, is looking at space-time, emphasizing where, or the spatial dimension.

Our perspective this term will be to look at roughly half of the world, emphasizing how where things are might show us aspects we may not already see. It might be the only time you experience geography taught this way, and it might be challenging for you, particularly if you're not open to re-shaping your own mental map of the world. But I guarantee it will be more interesting than an exercise in memorization.

THE PLAID AVENGER'S WORLD

Speaking of interesting, other than in this introductory chapter and the brief conclusion, the perspective in this textbook is provided by The Plaid Avenger, a comic book character dreamed up and constructed by John Boyer who teaches geography at Virginia Tech. Unlike every other regional geography textbook in existence, Boyer set out to make the study of the world not only interesting but engaging.

The Plaid Avenger's approach is to focus on events, issues, and processes that help us try and make sense of our complicated, interconnected world. The first six chapters break down and explain general concepts, themes, and issues, things like "globalization," "population," and "development," which are happening everywhere, albeit in different ways. The idea is that we need to know a little bit about these concepts and broad trends before we can understand how they are playing out in specific places.

The rest of the chapters, except for the conclusion, focus on specific "regions," parts of the world that are (somewhat arbitrarily) separated from each other. This is an attempt to reduce the "scale," or the level of analysis, in order to better understand each individual part. Again, the specific regions in this book are chosen because they are meant to represent "the Western World."

We'll start with Europe, the most "Western" as it is generally considered the core of "the West," followed by North America (the U.S. and Canada), Russia, Australia and New Zealand, and ending with Latin America. Finishing with Latin America is deliberate, as this part of the world, perhaps more than the others chosen, is Western in some ways but also not-Western. In fact, as we'll see, there is an ongoing debate about where Latin America fits in the world between experts that are supposed to be able to make decisions about this sort of thing. Ending with a region that fits in some ways and not others should help us both understand and challenge the categorization process of breaking the world into pieces, and it will likely leave you with more questions than answers.

A FINAL WORD ABOUT PERSPECTIVE

My approach to this course is probably different than that of any of your other classes. We will certainly explore concepts, facts, and information about individuals, events, and places. However, this is not a class about being clearer about a subject or a topic. In fact, you are likely to be more confused about the world at the end than at the beginning. Believe it or not, this is the goal!

The reality is that we live in an incredibly big, complex, and dynamic world, one that is sometimes beautiful and sometimes terrible, and often incomprehensible in its diversity, intricacies, and changes. The idea that you can learn everything about our planet, or even half of it, in one academic term is laughably ambitious. Still, we will try our best.

A big part of this is your willingness not only to learn (to read, write, think, question, etc.), but to accept the inevitable destruction of your old models, or maps, of the world that you rely on, and to understand that, for this term (and likely for the rest of your life) learning means accepting new maps and models.

If you feel upset or offended by information in this book, lectures, films, supplementary materials, or anything else in this class, remember that this is all from different perspectives. I don't intend that you accept or agree with any of it to be successful in the course. I do expect that you keep an open mind about the legitimacy of these other perspectives, which is a cornerstone of our democratic system.

Got thrones? Game on!!!

If you do have an issue with any of the course information, it is my wish that you talk to me about it rather than allow it to fester and become a barrier to your learning. I have had many productive conversations about differences of opinion and encourage these to become a part of the course more generally.

Overall, I hope that you gain a tremendous amount of knowledge about the world through this course. More important, I hope that you also gain wisdom, which to me means seeing something from many different angles.

It's obviously a risk to teach the course this way, to discuss and use controversial subjects and materials. It'd be much safer to use a well-regarded textbook that lists descriptive information about each part of the world and hopes that your rote memory is strong enough to make it to the cookie-cutter exams provided in the teacher's edition. I find that type of reading good for taking naps, and not for much else. Instead, I hope you'll find that the effort undertaken to gain what you can from this class is a risk worth taking.

Got it? Good. Game on. . . .

PART ONE
UNDERSTANDING THE PLAID PLANET

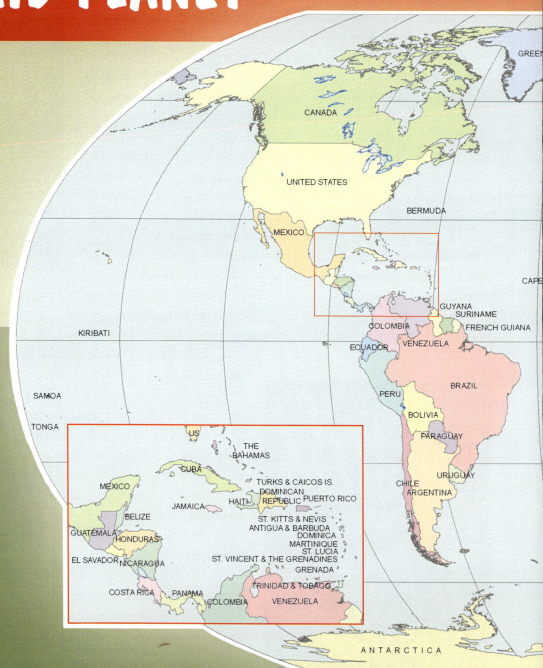

CHAPTER OUTLINE

1. Age of Globalization
2. A Wealth of -ations
3. What Is Geography
4. What Is a Region?
5. A Matter of Scale
6. So Who the Hell Is the Plaid Avenger?

A Plaid World Intro

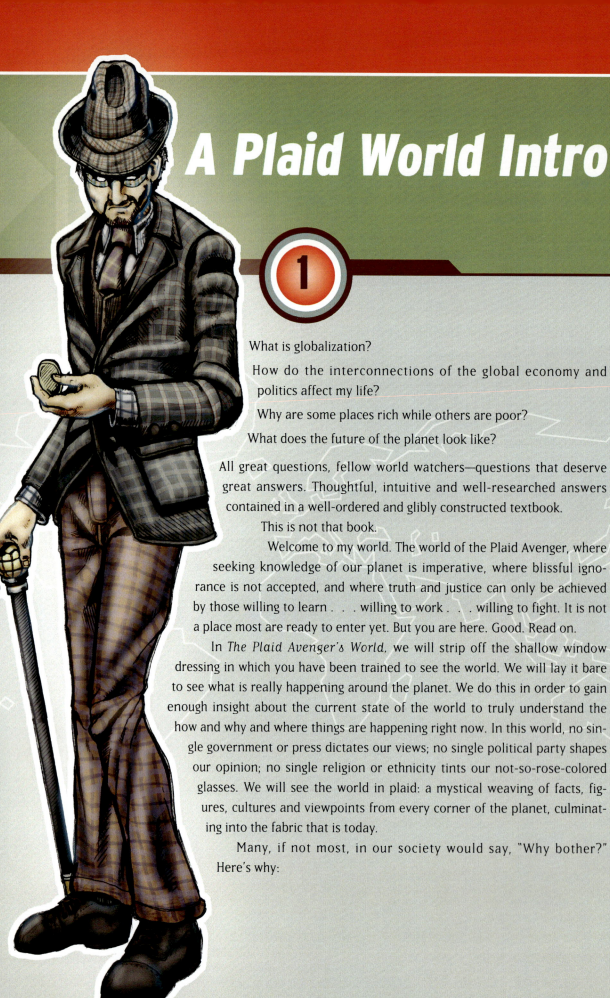

1

What is globalization?

How do the interconnections of the global economy and politics affect my life?

Why are some places rich while others are poor?

What does the future of the planet look like?

All great questions, fellow world watchers—questions that deserve great answers. Thoughtful, intuitive and well-researched answers contained in a well-ordered and glibly constructed textbook.

This is not that book.

Welcome to my world. The world of the Plaid Avenger, where seeking knowledge of our planet is imperative, where blissful ignorance is not accepted, and where truth and justice can only be achieved by those willing to learn . . . willing to work . . . willing to fight. It is not a place most are ready to enter yet. But you are here. Good. Read on.

In *The Plaid Avenger's World*, we will strip off the shallow window dressing in which you have been trained to see the world. We will lay it bare to see what is really happening around the planet. We do this in order to gain enough insight about the current state of the world to truly understand the how and why and where things are happening right now. In this world, no single government or press dictates our views; no single political party shapes our opinion; no single religion or ethnicity tints our not-so-rose-colored glasses. We will see the world in plaid: a mystical weaving of facts, figures, cultures and viewpoints from every corner of the planet, culminating into the fabric that is today.

Many, if not most, in our society would say, "Why bother?" Here's why:

AGE OF GLOBALIZATION

Globalization: what is it and what does it mean to me? Economically? Technologically? Politically? Socially? Culturally? Morally?

We constantly hear about how the world is getting smaller—is it? Pure poppycock! The world is the same size it has always been . . . *but* it is becoming more connected and more interdependent than ever before. Goods and services and information are exchanged in our local stores from every nook and cranny of our cram-packed planet. For the first time ever, we can travel to any part of the world virtually overnight. Corporations move capital and jobs from one country to the next in a matter of days. News of international significance is reported seconds after it happens. We can communicate in real time with any part of the globe. The world is now one system . . . mostly.

We are the first generation of humans who enjoy foreign travel as a casual part of life, who communicate by direct-dialing to any country on all continents, who receive instant news of world happenings, who expect to work overseas or work for a company that deals overseas. Let me reiterate that—expect; it is not an exception. This is a really important concept, especially to you—the first generation that is living in the postindustrial, highly interconnected age.

Many, if not all of you, will work for multinational companies whose business is all over the world. Many, if not all of you, will work and live outside the United States at some point in your careers. Businesses and jobs are internationalizing as we speak—almost all jobs, not just the fancy ones. You guys are the people who are going to be running the world. You guys are the decision makers—when all is said and done, I'm just a single superhero out thwarting international intrigue. But *you* will be the ones building the bridges, and electing leaders, and stabilizing governments, controlling monetary exchange rates; you may even be setting up all sorts of private, national, or even international businesses/programs/projects that will shape the world and its population.

Make no mistake about it, the AIDS rate in Africa *does* affect you, the increasing coal consumption in China *does* affect you, an earthquake in Japan, and the price of cocaine in Colombia *does* affect you. (allocation of your tax dollars, your jobs, the price you pay for goods, global pollution which affects your health, etc.) Globalization is pretty much a one-way street. We are not going back to medieval times, no matter what isolationists say, do, or think. Ignore the rest of the world at your own peril—you won't be hurting anyone but yourself. How did this globalization happen anyway . . . and how has it shaped our planet?

Understanding the Plaid Planet

PART ONE

A WEALTH OF -ATIONS

Of all the organisms hanging out on this blue marble we call Earth, us human-types have been the biggest modifiers, movers, shakers, benders and breakers of our fair planet. We grow food, we congregate in cities, we move around, we plan, we build machines, we communicate, we educate, we procreate . . . and do it faster and more thoroughly year after year after year at a larger and larger scale that has inevitably consumed the world. The idea that globalization is merely a modern phenomena is pure poppycock; all of human history can be seen as a relentless drive to expand our tribe to every nook and cranny of the planet, and to increase the non-stop interactivity between peoples, for better or for worse. Think about it. Civilization, migration, urbanization, industrialization, modernization, communication: all have served to organize, spread, and interconnect us. What a wealth of -ations that all feed into one grand scheme of globalization!

You probably have learned about a lot of these -ation terms in other classes and coursework, but I want you to think about them again for a few minutes in the context of this globalization concept. Without getting into too much tedious detail, I tell you that humans have been doing this globalizing gig since the birth of the species (or since a naked dude and a naked dudette were plopped down in a garden, if you prefer). **Migration** of humans started when the first modern *Homo sapiens* started

Take a bite of this apple, and let's get this globalization ball rolling!

trucking their tribal units to new turf outside of Africa over 70,000 years ago. Humans subsequently spread to all continents and all major islands, and this process of movement and interconnection is still going strong today.

Humans used to migrate in order take advantage of new unpopulated lands, untapped resources, or to follow game; in today's world, they migrate for jobs, for security, for a better life in a richer place. Wait a minute—is there a difference between those migration motivations? Maybe not. Did you really think that "illegal" Mexican migration to the US or African migration to Europe was some new thing? Ha! We've been on that route forever. But let's be civilized about this, which brings me to . . .

Civilization, a process that wildly impacted the human experience. See, we used to be the ever-expanding, ever-migrating, hunter-gatherer types living in small unconnected bands scattered across the planet, but around 12,000 years ago, some folks stumbled upon agriculture, and that was a game changer. Humans did a radical lifestyle shift from hunters to farmers. From that point forward, we hairless ape types turned into peeps who were developing cooler and cooler tools, growing more and more food, congregating together in bigger and bigger pools. It was human civilization, fools!

Specifically neolithically, we refer to this slow cumulative process that occurred independently in many different locations between 10,000BC and 3,000 BC as **The Neolithic Revolution**. The nifty Neolithic! Neo for "new" and -lithic for "stone." The New Stone Age! And those humans were totally new-rocking it out!

The Migratory Circle of Life is nearly complete.

Early iPad prototype: the iPetroglyph.

See, all that extra food surplus as a result of growing plants in a predictable cycle led to folks settling down in a permanent place. Then some smart peeps who did not have to waste their whole lives just finding food began to pursue their passions . . . and thus they invented the **domestication** of animals, the wheel, pottery, tin-smithing, the Bronze Age, written languages, architecture, engineering, legal structures, religious institutions . . . you starting to get the picture here? Oh yeah, 'cuz they would have been painting pictures as well.

That's what the extra food is really important: it increasingly allowed people to do their own thing . . . to specialize their skills and inventions. This in turn created even better tools/technologies, specialization of work, and increasingly complex societies and cultures which encouraged trade and cooperation. And not just trade within a single society, but between different ones in different places.

Aha! That was the evolution of intentional interconnections between populated areas in an effort to trade not just goods and services, but ideas and technologies and peoples themselves! Globalization game on! They call this stuff "outsourcing" and "economic activity" and "technology transfer" in today's world . . . but it's all the same stuff as way back when. From the Flintstones to Futurama: Same shizzle, different millennium.

This civilization gig also transforms the geographic organization of human life: we go from small bands of folks out in the wild to hanging out with each other in bigger in bigger numbers in things called villages, and then towns, and then cities. The first major civilizations that popped up 6,000 years ago in China, Indus Valley, Mesopotamia, Egypt, et al. began a perpetual process of population growth and **urbanization** that continues unabated to this day. Translation: humans have increasingly chosen to live in big population clusters in built-up areas that we call cities as opposed to hanging out in the sparsely-populated rural areas we refer to as "the sticks." Humankind reached a milestone in 2009 when, for the first time in human history, over 50% of the world's population now lives in an urban area. That percentage is growing bigger, faster than ever.

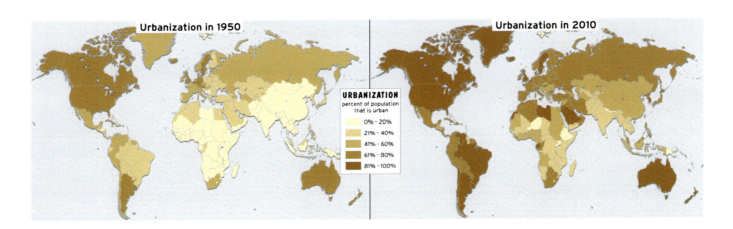

This urbanization has intensified human interaction exponentially over time; interaction which has accelerated the creation and transfer of ideas and technologies. New ideas, new inventions, new stuff! Which prompted **industrialization,** of course! Did you ever stop and wonder how it is possible for so many people to now cram themselves into cities, thus not being able to grow their own food or collect their own water or hunt their own bison? Because we invented machines to do the heavy lifting that used to require all our labor, and we discovered energy sources to fuel those machines. Bottom line: one dude on a tractor can grow enough food to feed a million people in the city; ten kids in a sweat shop can make clothes for that million, and oil-powered big machines can build skyscrapers and sewer systems and water lines for that million people. What the heck is left for those city folks to do?

Much like at the beginnings of the Neolithic Age, they have moretime to think. To interact. To create. To be inventors, doctors, artists, engineers, scientists, industrialists, priests, rock stars, and whatever else we come up with. That's how we got electricity, the polio vaccine, the Hoover Dam, mobile phones, and computers. Unfortunately, with so much free time and such diverse and bizarre human motivations, we also have nuclear weapons, mustard gas, lawyers, and Sham-Wow. Such is the yin and yang of life. But I digress. This urbanization/industrialization combo has served to link up the globe like never before: more humans compacted into bigger, concentrated urban areas has caused even more interaction within the city, but also increasingly between cities worldwide. Cities are both the engines and the nodes of globalizing forces; the conduit for transfers of ideas, money, technologies, and power, everywhere, all the time.

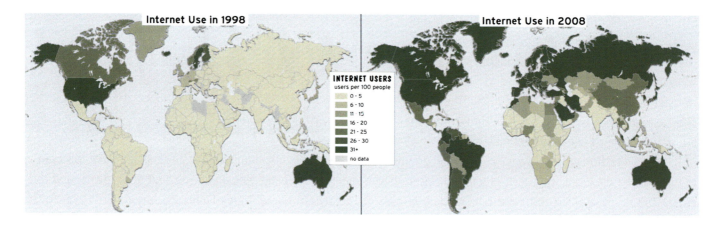

This "connectedness" is now happening at light speed, thanks to advances in transportation and **communication.** Yep, our last -ation is really the power-booster icing on this globalizing cake. From smoke signals to the Pony Express to trans-oceanic telegraph cables, we humans have spent a lot of time and effort figuring out how to better transmit information to each other across the planet. Let me be the first to tell you, my brothers and sisters: we have almost reached the end-game on this one. With mobile phones, the Internet, and satellite TV/radio, we can pretty much transmit any type of information almost instantaneously to any part of the globe. It's totally insane if you think about it.

More ideas, more information, more interaction between more people than *ever* before. Twittering every second of our collective experience! And more folks are jumping into the system faster than ever before as well. Just look at the figure above to see the speed at which the world is hooking up on-line!

We have essentially set ourselves up as a single huge worldwide computer, wherein all the humans attached to this systems are interacting to solve problems, sell goods, provide news, and everything else! You can chat with friends in Uzbekistan, watch a live news report from Brazil, vacation at the Vatican, have business transactions with South Africa, and share research ideas via Skype with associates in Switzerland. That, my friends, is global connection. That is globalization, made possible by all the other -ations of note in this section.

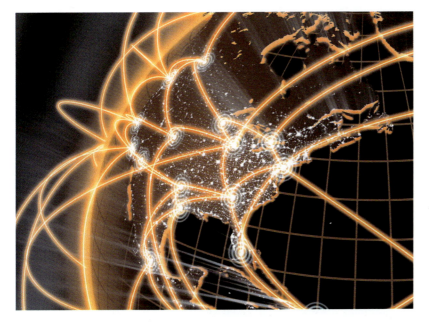

What does it all add up to? A more fully connected world in every sense of the word, in which the actions of any one person affects the lives of everyone. All of the aforementioned -ations have gone from local, isolated or internal concepts to completely planetary themes in scope and practice. In this increasingly populated and interconnected world, it is becoming clear that all "local" problems are actually "global" problems, from the movement of narcotics, to an outbreak of an infectious disease, to environmental pollution, to the existence of nuclear weapons, and so on.

And there are global problems a'plenty on our poor little planet! However, the solutions lie within this connected framework as well. See, this globalization is neither bad nor good. It just is, and will continue to be. Will globalization result in a homogenization of culture? In a modernization of all societies? In a pacification of the planet? In a disintegration of the concept of the sovereign state? Oh, my oh my, what a delicious stew of other -ation possibilities that I will leave to you to debate . . . and we will return to the tensions of the local versus the global in the final chapters of this book, to see how globalization is playing out in the 21st century plaid world.

For now, I just wanted to spill some of that crazy globalization knowledge on your skullcap to see the sparks fly.

Knowledge is power, or at least empowerment. The more you know about the globalizing world in which we live, the more power you have. It's good to have at least a minimal geographical understanding of our planet. What's that? You don't know what geography is?

An all-inclusive neural network now . . . from a nebulous Neolithic nucleus!

Understanding the Plaid Planet
PART ONE

WHAT IS GEOGRAPHY?

Geography is one of those words, and subsequently one of those fields of study, which has become so generic that it seems to have lost its own definition in the modern world. The term is so truly holistic in meaning that many other social sciences, as well as a lot of the physical ones, are actually sub-branches of it, as opposed to geography's current designation as a sub-branch of one of them. What am I talking about? Consider for a moment the origin of the word and the discipline; **geography** has its roots in the ancient world, roughly translated as "describing the Earth," and every culture and society with a written record has done just that—described both physically and culturally the environment around them as they understood it.

Be it Greek philosophers calculating the size of the known world in the 2nd century BCE, Chinese diplomats considering trade ties with Southeast Asia in the 11th century, military strategists planning the Boer War in Africa, or American scientists assessing the impact of the loss of Brazilian rainforest on world climate in the 21st century—all are geographers in the sense that they are studying the physical and/or cultural components of their environments to gain understanding and make decisions—just as all of us do every day in our own lives. How do I get from here to there? Should I buy an American car to support the American economy, even though their fuel efficiency is worse than imported cars? What is the foreign policy of the political party I support? Should I donate money to alleviate hunger in Ethiopia? Is this neighborhood I'm in a high-crime area? Paper or plastic? All questions require us to consider economic, social, political, and environmental knowledge and repercussions of that knowledge on the world around us.

We are unique!

I am intentionally pointing out here that the world around us, every place on the planet no matter where you are, has both physical traits and cultural traits that make it unique. Every place has a certain climate, particular landforms, and some kind of soils, vegetation and animal life. These are its **physical** traits, much like every human has some natural hair color, skin color, a certain height and weight, and particular physical abilities—maybe to run fast or jump high. At the same time, every place has languages being spoken, religious practices, economic activities, political organizations, and human infrastructure like roads and buildings. These are the **cultural** traits of the place, just like a human has certain religious beliefs, spoken language, a job, a learned skill like archery, and a favorite flavored ice cream. Just like every human in the world, every place in the world is unique in its own right, kind of like snowflakes. Defining any place in the world, or any region of the world, involves looking at both of these aspects, as well as their interaction with each other.

Every place on the planet is unique in that even when many of these factors are identical—say between two small towns in the Midwest located only five miles apart—there will still be tangible differences. Each town has a different history. The weather may be pretty much the same, but one will get more rainfall than the other. The people may all be of the same religion, but there will be different churches that do things just slightly different. The economies may both be based on corn, but there will be different business names, and different storefronts. There will be at least one Chinese restaurant in both towns, but they will definitely have different tasting General Tso's chicken. Like human identical twins, no matter how much is the same, there are always distinguishable differences upon closer examination. To understand our world, we will look at the physical and cultural traits of regions of the planet, how these traits converge to form a distinct region, and perhaps more importantly for our assignment, how these regions interact with each other.

So what the heck is a region?

WHAT IS A REGION?

The world is just too darn big and filled with a heck of a lot of things going on and way too many facts and figures and images and names and places for us to know and comprehend everything all of the time. You can't possibly even know all the facts and histories and physical variables of your own home town, much less your county, your state, or your planet. There's just too much, and the story is added to and updated daily. But don't give up hope! Nil desperandum, my dear friends! Across the desert lies the promised land! The human mind has a coping mechanism for this overflow of knowledge, which of course has gotten much worse with the advent of global communications and the 24-hour news cycle: We assess importance. We filter. We generalize. We are going to do the same geographically for the planet. By synthesizing and systematizing vast amounts of information from parts of the world and making pertinent generalizations, we create a unit of area called a **region.**

Regions are areas usually defined by one or more distinctive characteristics or features, which can be physical features or cultural features, or more often than not, a combination of both. We could identify a strictly physical region such as a pine forest, the Sahara Desert or the Mississippi drainage basin. Conversely, we could form up an area that we would identify culturally like the Bible Belt, a Wal-Mart store service area, or even Switzerland (defined by human-created political borders). However, since we have already pointed out that every part of the planet has both types of traits, most regions are identified as a combination of physical and cultural characteristics, such as the regions we refer to as the Midwestern US, tropical Africa, or Eastern Europe. These names typically make one think of both physical and cultural traits simultaneously, and may actually be meaningless in a context of just one or the other. This last type of world regional delineation is what we will mainly utilize in our journey.

That is a good jumping off point for what we will consider a region for our global guidebook. A region has three components:

1. A region has to have some area.
2. A region has to have some boundaries—although these boundaries are typically fuzzy, or imperfectly defined. Where does the Middle East stop and Africa start?
3. A region has to have some homogeneous trait or traits that set it apart from surrounding areas. This is the most important component to consider!

The user (that is you!) defines what trait is homogeneous. You can define any place on earth as being in an infinite number of regions, depending on what trait you pick. Your current exact position could be described as in a distinct political region like Charleston, California, or Canada. Or perhaps you're in a distinct physical region like the Everglades or the Appalachians or the Badlands. Simultaneously you may be in a distinct socially defined region like the Bible Belt, the Rust Belt, or the "The Beltway"—what region do you think you are in right now? Play this exciting "name your region" game with all your friends, and you will be the toast of the town. Or perhaps a big geek. But I digress.

Here is a quick breakdown of the world regions we will be examining:

FIGURE 1.1 WORLD REGIONS AS DEFINED BY THE PLAID AVENGER

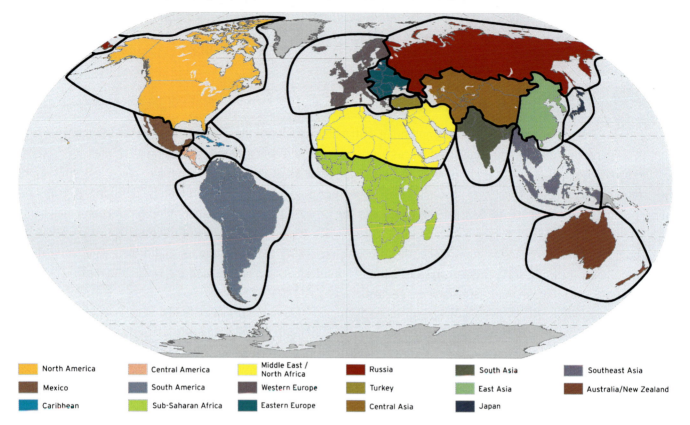

Why these areas? Why these borders? Why these regions? Because they are defined by homogeneous traits as picked by me. These are the Plaid Avenger's world regions. The bulk of this book will be explaining these regions and their homogeneous traits. Your world regional map may be different than mine depending upon what traits you want to focus on. Don't like my regions? Then go write your own blasted book!

A MATTER OF SCALE

When we are being geographers, or defining regions, or even just trying to get from point A to point B, we must always keep the **scale** of our endeavor in mind. How much area are we talking about? Are we examining someone's backyard in Australia, or the entire Australian Outback? That is a big shift in scale! Does this description of the environment in my hometown scale apply to a larger scaled area like my state or country? It rarely does. Thus, we must always be wary about how far we can push our analysis. Changing scales typically calls for reassessment of the area being considered.

The other reason to pay attention to scale is because it plays an important component of our definition of regions. Since we have already expressed that regions have some sort of homogeneous factor that defines them, we must consider at what scale does this homogeneity apply—because the scale itself defines it. Let me give you an example.

A couple presidential elections ago the USA, by majority, elected Barrack Obama—a Democrat—to the presidency. Since more than half voted Democrat, we could say that the US, at the country scale, is a Democratic region, based on that singular homogeneous trait. However, if we looked at the state of Texas, it voted predominately Republican—so at a smaller scale, you are looking at a Republican region. The city of Austin, a smaller region within Texas, is a hip liberal art-sy town that voted predominately Democrat, thus, in that smaller region, you are back to a Democrat-defined area. Maybe most of the people in a certain city block in Austin, a smaller region still, voted Republican, so at the block scale you are in Republican territory again. Thus, defining regions based on voting preferences *demands* that you state the scale of focus. Most importantly, the larger the region you define, the more exceptions to your homogeneous trait you will find within your region.

This is what generalizations are all about—we are going to discuss and define our regions with *generally homogeneous* traits within the region, knowing full well our generalization won't apply to everyone and every place. For example: by any definition, the Middle East region would be identified as an area dominated by Islam. Oops, except for a radical and extremely important exception—that of the Jewish state of Israel. For our travels, we will be pointing out and elaborating mostly on those homogeneous traits which define our regions, but will also include those glaring exceptions to the rule when they are of particular significance to today's headlines. The other main goal of this guide is to describe each of the world regions' interactions with each other, and their role in the world at large. This is a tall order to be sure, but a goal worthy of pursuit by the mightiest of global superheroes, the Plaid Avenger.

SO WHO IS THE PLAID AVENGER?

Yes, it seems that everything is growing into a singular world system. We speak of a world economy in which goods and services and businesses move all over the planet; they even have a club for everyone: the WTO. We have a great global transportation network that can transport us faster than ever to any point on the planet. We have the United Nations: a world legislative body that sets standards and rules for conduct on the planet (and I've heard rumors that they are also supposedly peace-keeping enforcers of these rules . . . although I won't swear to this). Thanks to mass media and global telecommunications, we can even speak of movement towards a more homogeneous world culture—where in the world can you *not* talk on your mobile phone while you watch MTV and sip on a Coca-Cola?

But wait, there seems to be something missing. Hmmm. . . . Global leadership . . . check. Global legislature . . . check. Global economy . . . check. Global judicial system . . . Global judicial system . . . Global justice??? Bueller . . . Bueller . . . Bueller? Where is it? I knew something was missing! No justice to be found!

Just as the world continues to become more interconnected, and every event across the globe becomes more pertinent to our daily lives, we also gain more knowledge about inequalities and unfairness around the planet. This comes at a time here at the dawn of the 21st century when conflict proliferates around the globe, multinational corporations grow unchecked and unhindered by law, diseases have the capacity to truly create an unprecedented planetary epidemic, and trade in guns, drugs, and people continue unabated. Yes, even the trade in people . . . you know, slavery. Global inequality may be reaching a new zenith; that is, the gulf between the rich and the poor widens as every day passes, and those poor folks are growing in numbers. You heard of the "Occupy Wall Street" movement? You may live to see an "Occupy the Globe" movement as well!

The Plaid Avenger is a product of this age. Somewhere at a major university on the eastern seaboard of the US, a meek but smartly dressed college professor by day, he toils in an effort to educate the youth of America about the wider world, and their role in it. By night, he roams the planet fighting organized international crime, abusive multinational corporations, and corrupt governments, wherever they may be. The Plaid Avenger: international equalizer and educator. A fighter for truth, global justice, and the international way, he also possesses an unstoppable urge to bring plaid back into fashion.

That brings us to your first assignment: Your first mission to become globally literate—that is, smart—and know the locations of the states of the world. Most Americans call them "countries," but you should start calling them "states" now and just get over it. Look back to Figure 1.1, and get to work. The reason? While I'm not an advocate of memorizing every town, district, and province on the map, we do need to have a working vocabulary to discuss things intelligently. Not that you need to be able to draw a map from memory, but you will be amazed how much more intelligent you appear when you are in a discussion about a news event and you know with authority that Senegal is in western Africa, not in Central Asia. Trust me, your date will dig it.

Understanding the Plaid Planet
PART ONE

Perused an atlas or wall map and now know all the states of the world? Got them all down? Then look at the following figures. A straight-up matching game with some sassy style. As the Plaid Avenger must often work undercover around the planet, he has an endless array of outfits to help him blend into the local environs he is investigating. He also

A

B

C

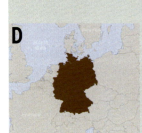
D

E

F

1

2

3

A Plaid World Intro
CHAPTER ONE

frequently has to foil dastardly plots at famous local landscape.. Study the costumes, maps and photos below. Your mission: match the appropriate highlighted country map to the outfit the Plaid Avenger would be wearing and the appropriate undercover agent he would be meeting there. Good luck, and see you in Chapter 2.

a

b

c

4

5

6

d

e

f

CHAPTER OUTLINE

1. Intro to People aka World Sex Ed 101
2. Regional Differences in Population
3. How Population Is Changing
4. How/Why/Where Population Is Changing: The Demographic Transition
   - 4.1. Demographic Transition Stage One
   - 4.2 Demographic Transition Stage Two
   - 4.3 Demographic Transition Stage Three
   - 4.4 Demographic Transition Stage Four
5. Population Pyramids
   - 5.1 The Classic Pyramid
   - 5.2. The Column Shape
   - 5.3. Inverted Pyramid . . . You Mean It's Upside Down?
6. It's Hard to Stop Having Babies
7. A Prickly Problem of Skewed Sexes . . .
8. Some Final Thoughts on People . . .

World Population Dynamics

2

BEFORE we get to the regions, we will focus on several topics that are better approached at the global scale; they involve traits that all regions possess equally, like people or religions, or that all regions participate in as a singular global unit, like the world economy or international organizations. Since people create, define, and operate all the cultural aspects of our planet, let's start with them.

INTRO TO PEOPLE AKA WORLD SEX ED 101

People, people, people, all over the world. Old ones, young ones, rich ones, poor ones, black ones, white ones, Asian ones, and even plaid ones. Some places got lots of people, while others have just a few. Are there too many people? Perhaps not enough in some places? Some states have growing populations, while other states actually have shrinking populations. What's that all about? Although there are great differences around the world in numbers of people as well as growth rates of populations, it is best to approach the subject by looking at it systematically. That is, we can look at how human population dynamics operate as a whole, because the rules are essentially the same anywhere you go on the planet. Let's get to know how it works, and then you can apply your knowledge to understand what's happening in any state or region of interest. Game on!

For starters, you should know that we just crossed over the 7 billion mark in terms of how many peeps are currently alive on the planet. This has not always been the case. In fact, numbers this huge for human population are actually quite recent. Consider Figure 2.1.

As you can see, for most of humankind's existence, population totals have been relatively small. It took approximately one million years, from the beginning of time until about the year 1800, for the first billion humans to appear on the earth at the same time. From then, it's roughly

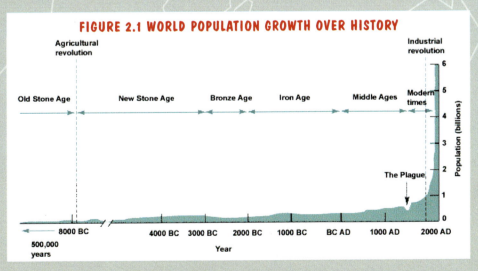

- 1927 that the second billion showed up
- 1960 saw the crossing over to 3 billion
- 1974 picked up number 4 billion
- 1987 flipped the pop-odometer to 5 billion
- 1999 the predawn of the 21st century we reached 6 billion
- And Happy Halloween! On that costumed holiday in 2011, 7 billion peeps were alive for the tricks and treats!

What you may be detecting here is a radically accelerated population increase in the last fifty years. The time it takes to add another billion people gets shorter every cycle, with the 8 billion mark already rapidly approaching. Why is this happening? Population growth is exponential, not mathematical. Adding ten more fertile females to the population pool doesn't equate to adding just ten more babies, but more like one hundred babies. Each woman has the potential to spawn many more offspring, who in turn can produce many more offspring themselves down the road. Get it?

CHART 1: TOP 20 POPULOUS STATES

COUNTRIES RANKED BY POPULATION: 2014

Rank	Country	Population
1	China	1,361,000,000
2	India	1,240,000,000
3	United States	317,000,000
4	Indonesia	250,000,000
5	Brazil	201,000,000
6	Pakistan	185,000,000
7	Nigeria	173,000,000
8	Bangladesh	152,000,000
9	Russia	143,000,000
10	Japan	127,000,000
11	Mexico	118,000,000
12	Philippines	99,000,000
13	Vietnam	90,000,000
14	Ethiopia	86,000,000
15	Egypt	86,000,000
16	Germany	80,000,000
17	Iran	77,000,000
18	Turkey	76,000,000
19	DR Congo	68,000,000
20	Thailand	66,000,000

As a result of this exponential growth in the human population, many folks believe that the planet is already overpopulated. Is that true? I can't give you an answer for that, because it is a relative question. Where are we talking about? Siberia? It's certainly not overpopulated. Calcutta, India? Yeah, maybe they have maxed out on the peeps. Maybe. Many assume that Africa as a whole is overpopulated, but given the size of the place and its current population totals, it is actually quite sparsely populated, particularly if you compare it to a place like Western Europe. And if Western Europe is overpopulated, why do many of its governments encourage their citizens to have more babies? Hmmmm . . . things get complicated fast. Plaid Avenger rule of thumb: a place seems to be considered truly overpopulated only when not enough resources exist to supply the people who live there. Thus, the 70 million people in Ethiopia may all agree that their country is overpopulated, but the 80 million people in Germany would probably not consider themselves so, even given that Ethiopia is roughly three times the size of its schnitzel-eating friend.

But enough for now on the theme of over- or underpopulation. Let's look at where people are in the first place.

REGIONAL DIFFERENCES IN POPULATION

Where are people, and where are they not? In some parts of the world, harsh climates and terrains are too formidable for large numbers of humans to hang out in. The cold Arctic areas in Canada and Russia, the great desert and steppe regions in North Africa and Central Asia, and the high Andes and Himalayan ranges serve to keep population numbers low. Humans tend to proliferate in well-watered areas and along coastlines. Generally speaking, human settlements favor the mid-latitudes; there are far more people in Eurasia and North America than in tropical areas. Draw on your own experiences to figure out this trend. Would you like to live in a tropical rainforest, a desert, or a mountain top? Why or why not?

FIGURE 2.2 POPULATION DENSITY, MAJOR CENTERS

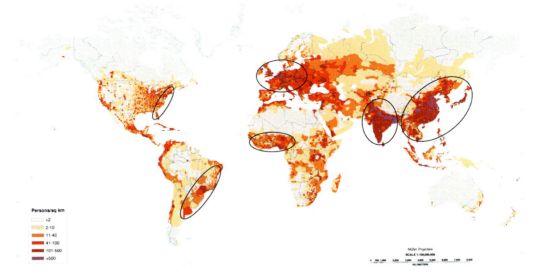

People have adapted to living in just about every extreme environment on our planet—just not in great numbers. What is the deal with the great numbers? It has a lot to do with history, culture and current population dynamics, which we'll get to in just a second. First, a few points about the map in Figure 2.2. As you can see, I've circled just six big population clusters on the planet for our discussion, but of course there are others . . . that you should discuss amongst yourselves. I can't do it all!

For starters, over half the world's population are found in Eurasia, particularly a people-packed arc from Japan to Eastern China, through Southeast Asia to South Asia. The common perception is that China is far and away the most populated state with over a billion people. But watch out! India has a billion people as well, and, more importantly, is growing at a faster rate than China, which means that it will certainly become the top slot within a couple of decades. Don't forget India's neighborhood—Pakistan and Bangladesh are both members of the top ten most populous states in the world as well.

The monstrous Asian population centers are, in large part, a product of history. People in these areas have been getting busy—in more ways than one—for thousands of years since the innovation of agriculture and the birth of civilization as we know it. They have existed as stable civilizations for long periods of time. They also happen to be in physically conducive environments—well-watered, mid-latitude lowlands. This also helps to explain why the cradle of Western Civilization—Mesopotamia, which is just as old—did not form huge populations over time. Its physical environment is more arid and unable to support large numbers of people.

However, due to great leaps in technology during the Industrial Revolution, including lots of technologies that helped keep more humans alive longer, Europe's population boomed wicked fast in the last several hundred years. And now they are another significant center for people-packing on the planet. By contrast, the Americas have historically had low population numbers, pre-contact. When Europeans did arrive in the New World, they brought diseases that wiped out a vast number of people, thus leading to even lower numbers on our side of the planet. But the Western Hemisphere has now been going and growing for long enough to have significant population concentration in eastern USA, along with the mega-cities area of eastern South America centered in southern Brazil. History, technology, and the physical world have a lot to do with where most people are today.

Two more global population points of interest: Africa, largely believed to be overpopulated, is a ginormous place with half the population totals of South Asia or East Asia, but note the large concentration of peeps in West Africa, centered around Africa's most populous state of Nigeria. My favorite population fact deals with Russia and the US, the two Cold War adversaries. Look again at the map and realize this: these two regions account for less than 10 percent of the world's population, but have effectively shaped the political and economic fate of the other 90 percent during the last 50 years. Interesting, isn't it? Okay, maybe not, but it certainly was during the Cold War. Yes, those rascally Ruskies used to be a world power, but now Russia is a state currently in population decline. Which brings us to our next point: where are populations growing, where are they shrinking, and why?

HOW POPULATION IS CHANGING

To complicate matters further, not just total population but also **population growth rates** are unevenly distributed around the world. Population growth rate refers to how fast or slow a group's population total is expanding . . . or shrinking, when referring to our Cossack friends. When you see a number like 3.5 for a population growth rate, it indicates that, by this time next year, the population total for that country will be 3.5% bigger than it is right now. A negative number is the inverse: population growth of −0.5 means that population total for next year will be 0.5% smaller than it is presently. Check out Figure 2.3 below for some insights . . .

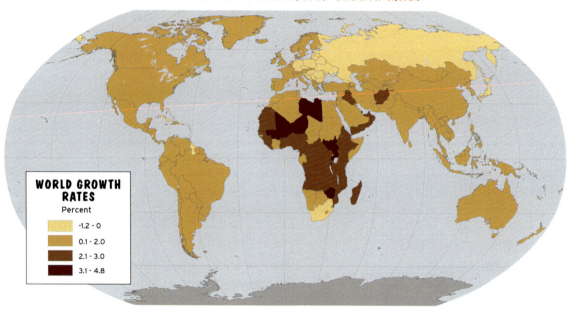

FIGURE 2.3 WORLD POPULATION GROWTH RATES

Source: CIA World Factbook 2014

Look! Ethiopia and Yemen's population total is expanding very quickly, which means those countries have a high population growth rate. Both the US and China's total population gets bigger every year, but not by much percentage-wise; the countries have a moderate to slow growth rate. Russia and Japan's population totals are getting smaller every year—a negative growth rate. You may have also identified a major trend: the highest growth rates typically occur in states that we consider underdeveloped, a.k.a. the poor ones. Say again? You mean the poorest areas of the planet are where more people are being added faster than ever? That is correct. The developed, or richer, states all seem to have low growth rates. So the places that could afford to provide for more kids, have less kids? Yep, that's true as well. Why is this so? Good question. Answer: the Demographic Transition.

HOW/WHY/WHERE POPULATION IS CHANGING: THE DEMOGRAPHIC TRANSITION

The Demographic Transition is a lovely little model that goes a long way in explaining lots of things about human population change around the world today. Be forewarned: it is just a theory, but man, it makes a whole lot of sense when applied to just about anywhere, anytime. It helps us understand why population is booming in the poorer parts of the world while it shrinks in richer areas, and even why women in Laos may have ten kids, when women reading this book here in America may not want to have kids at all.

The model is based on the experience of the currently, fully developed states, which underwent a population surge on a smaller scale beginning about 1700 in Europe, and then later stabilized. Other states—typically ex-colonies of Western European powers such as the United States or Australia, or states in close proximity to Western European powers, such as Russia—followed suit in the last several hundred years. Every other place on the globe can be seen as somewhere in the transitional process that these states have gone through.

Generally speaking, this "transition cycle" begins with high birth rates and high death rates, passes into a high birth rate/lower death rate period for a variety of reasons, and ends with low birth rates and low death

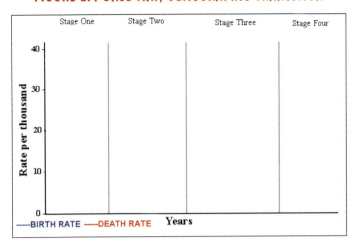

FIGURE 2.4 BASE MAP, DEMOGRAPHIC TRANSITION

rates. The total population at the beginning and end of this cycle is stable or has a very low, perhaps even negative, growth rate. However, it is the massive increases in population during the middle phases that makes the model so compelling, and explains so much about what is happening in today's world. But I'm getting ahead of the story. Let's take it one step at a time.

For the rest of this discussion, **birth rate** refers to how many children are born every year per 1000 people. To give you some context, the birth rate in the US right now is about 14/1000 every year. **Death rate**, of course, refers to how many people kicked the bucket that year per 1000 people. The US death rate is currently around 8/1000. Now, on to the transition.

DEMOGRAPHIC TRANSITION STAGE ONE

This whole concept hinges on the idea that all societies want to go *from* premodern, hunter-gatherer, stick-collecting goobers *to* postmodern, latte-sipping, Vespa-driving goobers. It does seem to make sense. Given the option anywhere in the world, I think most folks would choose the latte; that is, most societies are striving to become industrialized, richer, and all-around better off. You don't have to buy my theory, because quite frankly, I'm not selling it. There are those that argue that we would all be a lot better off living in grass huts somewhere weaving baskets from giraffe hair, because that would be true sustainable development in harmony with Mother Earth. Good luck with that one. Give anyone a chance not to live on a dirt floor, and I'll bet they pack their bags, set the giraffes free, and head out to a better life for themselves and their kids. But I digress. Where were we? Ah! Stage One . . .

STAGE ONE of societal development finds us making baskets from giraffe hair. We typically associate this stage with premodern times; most folks are hunter-gatherers, living solely by collecting food naturally occurring out in, um . . . nature. This is pretty much the way things were for a great number of humans for a good long time in human history. Small groups of folks on the move, searching for food, waiting around for civilization to pop up. Of note for our model is that both the birth rates and the death rates are extremely high and erratic. Essentially you have a situation where lots of kids are born per 1000 people, and lots of people die per 1000 people, with some years being really good, and others being really bad. Why would that be?

Why the high death rates? Because this lifestyle is hard, and it sucks! It's easy to die from just about anything: lack of health care, food shortages, poor food containment so things go bad fast, lack of regular clean water, lack of sewage disposal or worse yet, your sewage disposal plan involves your drinking water source, animals that want to eat you, animals that just want to kill you, animals just having fun with

Some Stage 1 hold-outs: Kalahari Bushmen in Namibia.

I liked your Granny too. She was delicious.

you, diseases of all sorts, simple infections you could contract from a hangnail . . . ew, this sounds like no fun at all. **Infant mortality**, the number of children that don't make it to their first birthday per 1000, is also high because of lack of immunizations and/or adequate diet. **Life expectancy**, or the average age to which the population is expected to live, is low. Old people get sick more easily, can't pull their own weight out picking berries and therefore don't eat as much, and in general, are slow enough to get caught by the animals that want to eat them. Poor Granny. I really liked her. Now she is cheetah food.

Why are the birth rates high? The same reasons that they are high in parts of today's underdeveloped world. For starters, it's a mindset; if you expect half your kids to die before they reach adulthood, then you should have twice as many. Makes sense. Also, children are often seen as a resource in these societies: maybe Junior starts picking berries at an early age to help out the fam. More kids = more labor = more food = good. Plus, no health care = no health education = no sex education = no contraceptive usage. Well, I guess people could always just abstain from having sex . . . yeah, right.

Why are the rates so erratic? For the simple fact that some years are good, while others years are bad. A drought or a plague would cause births to drop and deaths to rise. A very good, wet season with lots of food available would cause the spikes to move in the opposite direction.

Because both birth and death rates are extremely high, they offset each other, equating to a total population that is low and a population growth rate that is slow or stable. Looking back at Figure 2.1, you can see that for most of human history, population growth rate has been very slow, or stable, right on up to the Industrial Revolution. Before we leave this rather boring phase, just a quick note: there really are no more societies like this left anywhere on the planet. You have to dig deep into the Amazon rainforest, the remote savannas of tropical Africa, or into the highlands of Papua New Guinea to find folks still living this lifestyle. Even then, they will be very small numbers of people in isolated pockets. No state economy on the planet today would be classified in Stage One.

FIGURE 2.5 DEMOGRAPHIC TRANSITION STAGE ONE

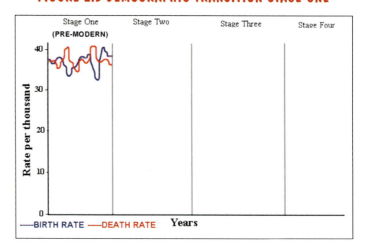

DEMOGRAPHIC TRANSITION STAGE TWO

STAGE TWO is the trickiest phase to consider, because we are going to pack a veritable smorgasbord of different human experiences under this single banner. They occur over long periods of time, but have this one big Stage Two result: the death rate declines while the birth rate remains high and stabilizes. Fewer people die; same amount of people being born. What happens to the total population numbers in such a situation?

Before we answer that, let's define the stage a little more. I said it is fairly all-inclusive of the human development spectrum, and I meant it. Stage Two includes the transition of humans from hunter-gatherers to agriculturalist to factory workers. Yes, this is a long stretch of time that also entails the formation of what we call technical innovation, civilization, and urbanization. Essentially, dudes figure out that staying put in one place and growing food is more productive than moving around and hunting all the time—an agricultural revolution. With increases in technology, so much extra food is

World Population Dynamics
CHAPTER TWO

FIGURE 2.6 DEMOGRAPHIC TRANSITION STAGE TWO

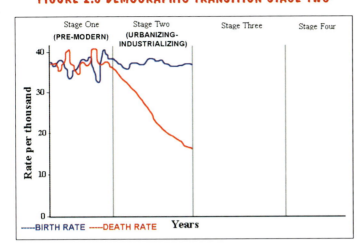

produced that not everybody has to be farmers. Some become blacksmiths, butchers, priests, traders, artists, and inventors—that's specialization. This leads to the formation of villages, towns and eventually cities where larger and larger groups of dudes hang out and exchange products and services with each other—that's urbanization. Further technological advancements lead to the creation of machines to automate our work, which leads to the creation of machines that make stuff, and even make other machines—that's industrialization. Eventually taken to its logical extreme: robots that make robots that kill all the humans. Yikes! The Terminator! This is worse than the Granny-eating cheetah! But that is for a future textbook, so let's stick with Stage Two for now. . . .

What's all this got to do with people having kids? During this part of the societal transition, death rates absolutely plummet. Why? Remember how I told you that everything sucked in Stage One? In Stage Two, everything gets way better. Increases in food production and increases in food storage technology allow for a steady, stable food supply. There are no more "bad" food years or, at the very least, not as frequent as they were in Stage One.

Technological advances in water resources, sewage treatment, and health care, all based on growing scientific knowledge, serve to keep more people alive for longer periods of time. Child mortality drops and life expectancy rises. We have developed the shotgun to ensure that Granny is not eaten by the cheetah. More important, however, is the fact that more kids stay alive than ever before; young children become an increasingly bigger percentage of the total population. Education across the board, at all levels, also significantly increases quality of life and survivability.

During this vast sweep of progress, death rates drop and birth rates remain solidly high and even stabilize high. What is going on here? Basically, people are caught in a mental time warp and old habits die hard. If Mom had ten kids, and her mom had ten kids, and her mom had ten kids, it is highly likely that you would be of the mindset to have ten kids as well. It's just what people do. The society as a whole, and certainly not the individuals within it, does not understand that it is going through a transition. The mentality that producing large numbers of kids is good because half of them are going to die and the rest will help gather berries remains the same, even though conditions have changed. At the end of a Stage Two society, half the kids are now NOT going to die; maybe only one or two of them will die, maybe none at all. Granny had ten kids and only five survived. Mom had ten kids and seven survived. I had ten kids and . . . holy crap in the kiddie pool, all these little brats are still here!

This mind warp is called **cultural lag**. Conditions have changed, but the culture is lagging behind. Folks with Stage One mentality are thinking "Wow, this is just a good year," without realizing that it is a good year after a good year after a good year, but they are still having kids like it's a boom-and-bust cycle. Result: **population explosion!** More kids beget more kids, and people just don't die like they did in Stage One. Mo' peeps having moo' peeps having mo' peeps.

Stage 2 Shenanigans: A Heaping Helping of Historical Human Activities

FIGURE 2.7 CULTURAL LAG

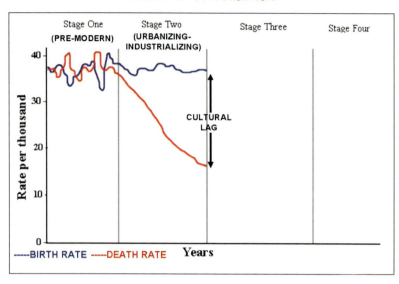

Stage Two main points: death rates decrease, while birth rates remain the same, total population explodes, and the structure of the total population becomes more youthful. This last point is the most important for the rest of this story, as we have more potential baby-makers entering the scene. Many states in the world may fall into the later fringe of Stage Two, mostly in Africa, Central America and parts of Southeast Asia. These states are still heavily reliant on agricultural production as a main economic activity. They also may have their death rates drop more from foreign external aid, importation of life-saving technologies, and humanitarian relief than from true upward evolution of the society. An important note: all of these things will help the death rate drop immediately, which means the period of cultural lag will likely be longer, significantly increasing total population overall. Angola and Guatemala are examples of states in Stage Two.

DEMOGRAPHIC TRANSITION STAGE THREE

As we move to **STAGE THREE,** we approach more familiar ground. Stage Two ends with the beginning of the industrialization of the society. Stage Three takes us the rest of the way through it, ending with what we refer to as the "mature industrial phase." Most states on the planet are currently located here, with varying degrees of development that can be quite radically different, depending upon whether they are early Stage Three or late Stage Three.

At this time, the Stage Three state continues down the modern industrial path. This is marked particularly by a shift in what the majority of folks do for a living. It is at this point that the scale gets tipped; more people are working in the processing, manufacturing and service sectors than are working as farmers. This development is significant because this typically means that agricultural technology has superseded the need for vast amounts of human labor in the fields. This

So long farming! We are manufacturing minions now! As we also shift to services. . . .

equates to less farmers, which equates to more people leaving the countryside and heading to the big city to get a job—increasing urbanization.

Even today, agriculture is still the number one job on the planet. However, states in which agriculture is not the predominant occupation are further down the development road. That is, they are typically richer than states that still rely heavily on the agricultural sector to employ people. Food for thought—pun intended.

We're just getting warmed up with the impacts of this stage (agriculture-to-industry, and rural-to-urban shifts). What happens to the ideas about having lots of kids when this shift occurs? Plenty! Life in the big city is more costly. Having more kids to feed costs more money. Plus, you've got to clothe them and house them and buy school books for them and throw birthday parties for them and eventually buy them cars. Wow! This is starting to suck as bad as Stage One. But it gets worse! The value of kids has changed as well. Junior used to be an asset picking berries and plowing the fields. Now Junior is an added cost who only picks his nose and plows the family car into the side of the garage. The cultural lag is over thanks to you, Junior! No more kids for us!

In addition to these changes, several other things of note are on the rise. Health care technology and accessibility continues to increase, and especially with regards to increasing knowledge about birth control and contraceptive use in general. Increasing education across the board helps more and more people, but I want you to think more specifically of the education of women and its impact on the whole equation: more educated women = more women entering the workforce = more contraceptive use = more women delaying family formation = fewer kids.

Educating the women of any society decreases **fertility rate** instantaneously. Okay, maybe instantaneously is a bit strong, but it's a HUGE factor in affecting the fertility rate in today's world.

Fertility rate is simply how many kids on average one woman will have in her lifetime in a particular state. The fertility rate of the US is about 2.1. In Italy, the fertility rate is about 1.3. But in Mali, the fertility rate is about 7.5. The average woman in Mali will have seven kids and one half, say from the waist down. In the US, a woman will have two kids and a leg.

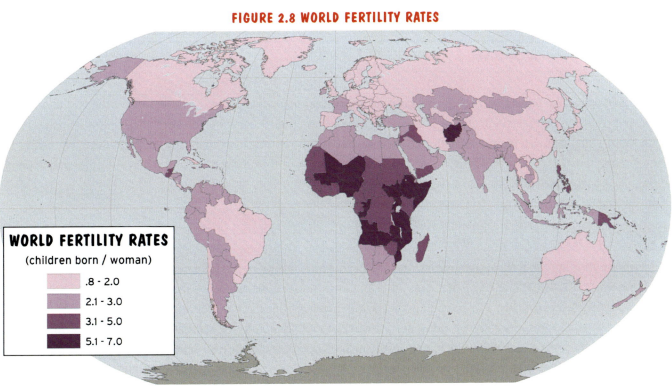

FIGURE 2.8 WORLD FERTILITY RATES

WORLD FERTILITY RATES
(children born / woman)
- .8 - 2.0
- 2.1 - 3.0
- 3.1 - 5.0
- 5.1 - 7.0

Source: CIA World Factbook 2014

For our international readers, that is what we call a joke. Actually, the US figure is a quite important fertility rate; that number also happens to be something called the **replacement level**. A fertility rate of 2.1 is exactly what it takes to "replace" the current population. See, two people have to get together to create kids (at least still for now, thankfully) and if two people produce 2.1 kids, then when the parents die, there are still two humans they've created to take their place. Sweet! We'll return to this idea in a little bit.

Back to Stage Three. The result of increases in health care, technology, childcare and education serve to knock the death rates down even further. However, there is only so much that modern medicine can do, and eventually that line flattens out. Child mortality decreases and life expectancy increases a bit more, but we all have to die sooner or later, so we'll say goodbye to Granny once again.

FIGURE 2.9 DEMOGRAPHIC TRANSITION STAGE THREE

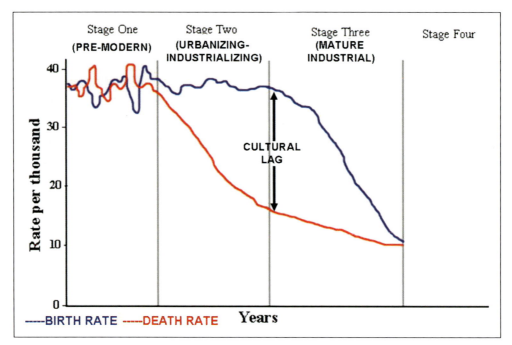

Of a more radical impact, increasing urbanization due to the employment shift, re-evaluation of the cost and benefits of having children, increased education of women (and all that entails) combine to overcome cultural lag causing the birth rate to plummet and meet the death rate. People may still be getting busy, but they are not having the babies like they did previously. After several generations, the fertility rates sink down closer to 2.1, the percentage of young people in the society about equals the middle aged cohort, and the older people as well. Good examples of early Stage Three states would be India and Brazil; late Stage Three, China and Chile.

DEMOGRAPHIC TRANSITION STAGE FOUR

Now we are through the transition, approaching life as we know it here in the fully developed, post-industrial, mostly Western world. **STAGE FOUR** is characterized by population stability, where death rates and birth rates are both low and parallel each other nicely. This post-industrial world is one in which yet another economic shift has occurred; now most folks work in the service sector, not quite as many in the manufacturing sectors, and virtually no one works in agriculture. If these terms are confusing to you, just hang on; we will be delving into economics in the next chapter.

In this stage, the population age structure has become older overall. Technology and education may still be increasing, but only in minute detail can they lower death rates anymore. The population of a Stage Four state is overwhelmingly urban and educated; they use some form of birth control and spend way too much on coffee.

The US, France, and Japan are all great examples of Stage Four states. As a result of expected higher standard of living and higher costs of living, many people will plan to have one or two children at most. Some people will decide not to have any children at all.

This leads us to a possible expansion of the Demographic Transition to a Stage Five, in which birth rates actually dip below death rates. The effect? Net population loss—the state's population shrinks every year, and unless supplemented by immigration, the state would eventually disappear. **Immigration** is when people not born in the state move into it. **Emigration** is just the opposite perspective: when people leave your state, they are emigrating out of it.

These concepts are increasingly critical in today's world, because many Stage Four and Five states rely on immigrants to fill jobs, pay taxes and boost slumping population growth rates. The US is a prime example whose population is increasing partly due to immigration. This is actually more pronounced in Europe where states may be fading away because the locals just aren't having many kids. If any at all.

Of course, the disappearing state thing has never happened before, but there are several states that are currently in this Stage Five category. Russia, Sweden, Italy, and Japan are all losing people. Italy and Japan are both in dire straits, but for different reasons; both have declining fertility rates, but in Italy it's because no one wants to have kids at all, while Japan refuses to allow any immigration into its pristine palace. We shall see how that works out in the long run. Serves them right for creating Pokemon.

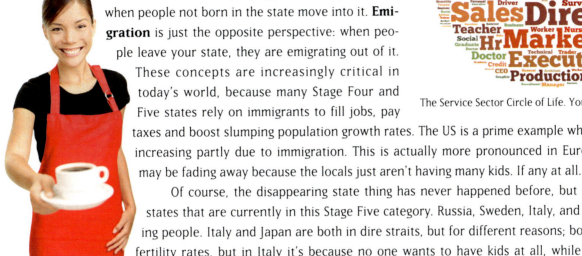

The Service Sector Circle of Life. You will likely live here.

Have another cup . . . and get back to Stage 4 work!

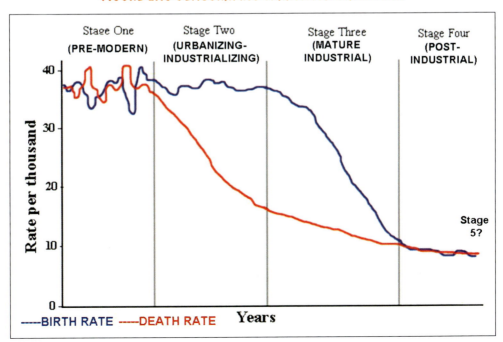

FIGURE 2.10 DEMOGRAPHIC TRANSITION STAGE FOUR

POPULATION PYRAMIDS

A final tool for our consideration of population dynamics on the planet is called a population pyramid. Population pyramids are constructed to show the breakdown of the population for gender and age groups. The x-axis across the bottom displays either a percentage of total population or actual population numbers, and the y-axis shows age cohorts, typically in 5-year increments. The two sides of the pyramid are divided up with males on one side, females on the other. Kind of like your junior high prom dance floor. In the Figure 2.11, you can see that in the rainbow of fruit flavors for Nepal in 2011, there are about 2 million males aged 0–4 years old, about 1.5 million females aged 10–14 years old, and about 0.5 million males aged 50–54.

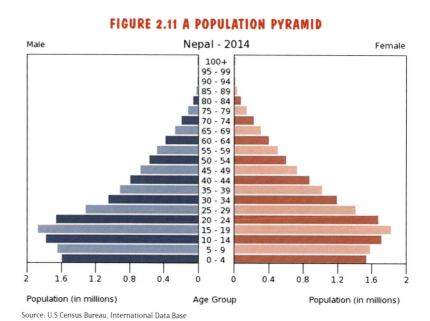

FIGURE 2.11 A POPULATION PYRAMID

Source: U.S Census Bureau, International Data Base

Like I give a crap about how many Nepalese women are over 80 years old! What do these pyramids really tell us? They tell us all sorts of things about a state: current population, current economic conditions, and quite a bit about the standard of living as well. But that's not all! These pyramids tell us a whole lot about what the future will hold and you don't even need a crystal ball. Consider the three basic shapes that these pyramids can take: a **classic pyramid**, a **column** shape, or an **inverted pyramid**.

THE CLASSIC PYRAMID

The classic pyramid shape is, um . . . shaped like a perfect pyramid. The wide bars at the bottom taper up gradually to smaller and smaller bars as age increases, displaying that there are more people in the younger brackets and the size of the group diminishes steadily with age. Broad-based pyramids (Kenya in Figure 2.12 below) are characteristic of popula-

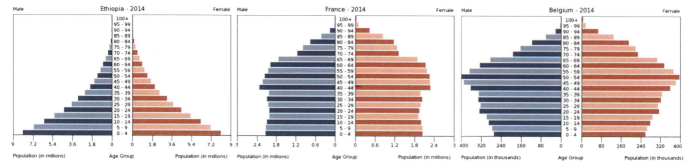

FIGURE 2.12 THREE TYPES OF PYRAMIDS: CLASSIC, COLUMN, AND INVERTED

Source: U.S Census Bureau, International Data Base

tions with high birth rates and lower life expectancies. Why? You already know the answer! Look back at the Stage Two and Stage Three descriptions of the Demographic Transition.

Industrialization and agricultural innovations, as well as increases in technologies across the board, result in advances in food supply and public health overall. This results in recently reduced infant and childhood mortality rates, and slightly increased life expectancy. However, they are definitely in the cultural lag mode, as fertility rates continue to be high. This in turn results in high population growth rates and in many cases, outright population explosion. Each year, the bottom bracket of 0–5 year olds gets wider than the previous year. Of particular significance: the numbers of kids under the age of 15 is larger than the number of folks in the 15–35 brackets.

Why is this significant? Because the under-15 are dependents in the society; that is, they absorb resources. Typically, the 15–35 year olds are the biggest providers in the society, both in economic means as money-makers for the state (gross domestic product, or GDP) and as family sustainers of young people and the elderly. That is, they provide most of the resources. Perhaps now you are starting to see why countries with this type of pyramid are often poorer or less-developed; the dependents often vastly outnumber the providers. More often than not, Stage Two and early Stage Three societies exhibit the pyramid shape demographic. The best examples of this type are any African country.

There is ever so much more we can say about a society with this type of pyramid. It is probably heavily reliant on agriculture or other primary industries for much of its economic earnings. Most people definitely grow some food, either as an occupation, for sustenance, or both. The society probably has lower literacy rates and little to no social safety nets like welfare, and also lacks adequate infrastructure, like good roads or sewer systems. Also, as pointed out earlier, many of the gains in health care, food availability, and life-sustaining technologies may be attributed to foreign aid and humanitarian aid programs. This adds a distinct 21st century dimension to the transition model; no one really knows what impact this will have in the long run for less-developed countries.

THE COLUMN SHAPE

All columns are not created equal, and there can be radical variations on this shape, but the main thing to identify this type of population pyramid is the more overall fuller figure. No, I'm not talking about a waist size here—that's a different book altogether. The real distinguishing mark here is that the size of the 15–50 year cohorts are *roughly* the same size as the under-15 cohorts, giving the overall shape more of a cylindrical look. The older age brackets also grow slightly, and upwards, as more people stay alive longer, adding to the elongated shape.

When this is the case, we realize that the fertility rate must be much lower than in the true pyramid shape, usually hovering between 2.0–3.0. This means that those child-bearing folks (typically between 15–50 years old) are having just two or three kids each, roughly replacing themselves or maybe even just a bit more. Remember that term **replacement level**? Well, the closer a society gets to that 2.1 fertility rate, which constitutes the replacement level, the more perfect the column shape will become. Some examples of this are the US, Lebanon, and Norway.

The operative words in these states is "stability." The total population growth rate is low, or perhaps even zero, with the state adding just a few percentage points of population every year. What else can be said about these countries? They are fully developed industrialized or post-industrialized societies. The highs: GDP per capita, standards of living, health care quality and access, available social programs, life expectancy, education levels, technology levels, urbanization, use of birth control, service sector jobs, and SUV ownership. The lows: fertility rate, infant mortality, illiteracy, farmers, miners, and people who die from infectious diseases.

INVERTED PYRAMID . . . YOU MEAN IT'S UPSIDE DOWN?

Indeed. This is an easy one to describe, because its essential ingredient is that the younger cohorts are smaller than the older ones; child-bearing peoples are creating less people than themselves; and total population is actually shrinking! Fertility rates are under 2.1 and thus the replacement level is not being reached; left unchecked, the population would shrink into nonexistence. This has never really happened before, and is not likely to ever come to its full conclusion, either. To counter this effect, immigration is increased or some other government policy is put into place to encourage fertility rates to rise.

Why does this scenario happen? Perhaps due to several different reasons. The first and foremost explanation is due to the same processes at work which serve to end cultural lag in developing societies. Namely, the higher cost of living in highly urbanized areas, combined with kids becoming a drain on resources, changes attitudes towards family size. Smaller is better in industrialized societies. They only have one or two kids, and invest heavily in them, as opposed to having lots of kids. In some places here in the 21st century, this has gone to an extreme; many people totally opt out of the family thing altogether; they want no children in order to maintain their own high standard of living. End result: fewer or no kids, replacement level for the state is not reached. The best examples of this today are Japan, Italy, and Sweden.

Another reason for declining populations in the world may be due to economic circumstances. Some countries, while considered part of the developed world, have gone through radical changes and economic collapse due to the end of the Soviet Empire. Russia, Belarus, and Ukraine are all in this inverted pyramid category due to lack of resources, jobs, health care, and many other services that the government used to supply. This is particularly evident in some of the measures of well-being for Russia, whose current life expectancy more approximates a poor, underdeveloped African country than a former world superpower. Hard times can also cause fertility rates, and a state's population, to decline as life becomes too difficult and large families too expensive to maintain.

IT'S HARD TO STOP HAVING BABIES

Many of you will look at these definitions and numbers and come up with some puzzling questions. You may wonder how China is the most populous state on the planet, at 1.4 billion people, yet their fertility rate is only 1.73. Or perhaps you may discover that projecting ahead in India, they will continue to grow their population rapidly for some time to come, and indeed will surpass China as the most populous state very soon, but their fertility rate is only 2.73. That's not very much more than replacement level! How is this possible?

Simple. **Population Momentum** is the answer you seek. Consider India for the next 50 years:

FIGURE 2.13 INDIA: THE SNOWBALL GROWS

What these three images from 2000, 2025, and 2050 in India are showing you is the Demographic Transition model in action. In 2000, India was early- to mid-Stage Three, as you can just detect the perfect pyramid starting to round away the edges of the bottom age cohorts in an obvious sign that cultural lag is wearing off and fertility rates are starting to sink from what were highs of four to six kids average per fertile female. We see that, in 2025, this has taken full effect; India is certainly in the column shape as its late Stage Three or early Stage Four industrialization has knocked down fertility rates to a precise 2.1, the replacement level. It's a perfect column. How can population totals continue to expand after this?

Population momentum is like a snowball rolling down a steep hill. Even after fertility rate stabilization, the population pyramid will have to "fill out its figure," as you can see by projecting further ahead to 2050. Everyone may be only having 2.1 kids, but a much bigger number of them are doing it, as represented by those bottom age cohorts back in 2000, where the stabilization actually starts. By the time the snowball reaches the bottom of the hill, it is massive—as will India be by the time its population total flatlines.

A PRICKLY PROBLEM OF SKEWED SEXES . . .

I would be remiss in my duties to fully educate and illuminate on population issues without shining some light upon some more disturbing manipulations of the Demographic Transition which are spelling social and sexual disaster for some states! Of what do I speak? The un-natural selection of the sexes, no less!

Say what? Well, in the natural way of things, boy babies slightly outnumber girl babies at birth, usually on the order of 105 boys to 100 girls. Why is this so? Hmmm . . . maybe it's because boys are crazier, riskier, and the ones that usually go to war with each other and therefore die/kill off each other in greater numbers than girls do. Thus, you need a few more of them around so that after some of them die off, your society will still have enough men to match up with women for the procreation gig. It's like that for most animals, and our species ain't no exception.

But dig this: in some countries around the world there is a significant cultural bias that favors males over females, especially in Asia, but the trend is spreading. Male babies are prized over females because males carry the family name, are a symbol of virulence, get higher paying jobs, are stronger physically for work on the farm, and are seen as the potential extended family providers when the parents get old. In India, it is the traditional role of the bride's family to 'pay' the groom a **dowry** when the couple gets married, so having a daughter actually 'costs' the family all the way up to adulthood. A family stands to gain a lot of money in India if they have a bunch of sons, and no daughters.

"Yo, where are all da ladies at?"

Basically, in these societies men are seen as the continuation of the family lineage and the major breadwinners, but that belief alone is not the problem. It becomes a problem when parents start to skew the sexual ratio on purpose to get more males into the mix. With the advent of sonograms/Ultrasound in the 1980's, coupled with easy access to safer abortion options, there has been a real "gendercide" underway, where female fetuses have been aborted in greater and greater numbers in an effort to get more male offspring . . . and it is starting to radically affect the demographics of the states, in increasingly negative ways. . . .

Particularly in China, India, South Korea, and Vietnam, males outnumber females at alarming rates. Right now in China, there are 35 million more boys than girls. In India, there are only 915 daughters born to every 1000 sons. These ratios are seriously skewed from the natural norm. And while Asian cultures seem to be the epicenter of this syndrome, even they are not alone anymore: the practice has spread to Europe, where skewed sex ratios now can be found in Albania, Armenia, Azerbaijan, Serbia, Bosnia and Georgia.

So there are way too many penises in some countries. So what?

Ummm . . . can you say "life without a wife," and more critically, can you think about the potential problems that will cause? Not enough women for all the men means that an increasing number of males in these societies will not be able to find a wife and start families. That will affect fertility rates for sure (and wedding cake sales), but more importantly it leaves a gigantic pool of unmarried, unattached, uncontrolled, undersexed, and testosterone-fueled males in your country. Whoa! That ain't nothing but trouble!

Indeed! The affects are becoming obvious: there is unrest among young men unable to find partners. Reports are increasing from China and India of antisocial behavior and violence, threatening societal stability and security, as unattached males are more likely to be involved in harassment, gang activity, gambling, and even violent crime. But business opportunities have sprang up to serve the needs of these men as well: prostitution is on the rise, as is the trade in buying foreign wives. A quiet mass 'migration' may be in effect wherein Thai, Vietnamese, and Burmese women are being brought into China as mail-order brides. (Market price for Burmese bride is currently between $600 and $2,400.)

"I don't care if we are out! I want a woman, now!"

So consider the repercussions of this skewed battle of the sexes in these societies, and how it affects not just the demographics, but also the cultures, economies, government policies, social stability, and even immigration policies in these places. All of these states have already outlawed abortions based solely on preferential sex of the fetus, but things like Indian tradition, China's 'One Child Policy,' and current economic situations in the Caucuses trump the law and social convention . . . but with grave repercussions imminent. Penis propensity problems will proliferate!

SOME FINAL THOUGHTS ON PEOPLE . . .

They disgust me! No, I'm joking. I love all the plaid peoples of the planet. What can we say about the future of our plaid population? It shouldn't be too hard to figure out some general trends. Most countries will continue down the development path, and thus we should be able to track what's happening in societies and within population dynamics through the lens of our Demographic Transition model. Everybody in the world wants a good job, a good standard of living, access to health care, and a better life for their kids. It's just the human way.

Having said that, there is nothing to lead me to believe that poorer states won't continue to try and modernize and industrialize like the rich ones have. Is this possible? That's a whole other ballgame we won't get into yet. But what will this mean for the peoples of the planet? The world population total will continue to go up for some time to come, but we can be more specific than that:

- → The least-developed countries are the places where population will truly grow the fastest, and the most. Regions like sub-Saharan Africa, the Middle East, Central America, and parts of Asia will continue to pile on the humans, even though they are the regions perhaps most ill-equipped to handle more.
- → Regions further down the development path, like China, India, Mexico, and South America, will continue to grow, albeit at a slower pace as fertility rates stabilize.
- → Fully developed regions, like Western Europe, US/Canada, and Australia are stabilized populations with no growth, but with the potential to grow bigger mostly through allowing immigration from other regions.
- → Regions that are currently shrinking in populations, like Russia, Eastern Europe, some parts of Western Europe, and Japan, will almost certainly not disappear—but most certainly will encourage folks to have more kids and allow more immigration as well.

→ However, we should never underestimate the power of culture to undo all our tidy demographic transition assessments! Some states in the Middle East and South America are maintaining their high birth rates even despite increased development and climbing costs of living. This is due primarily to powerful religious influences (Islam and Catholicism) which prize large family size. Also, there are folks bucking the trend in places like China, where the state-sponsored One-Child Policy predominated for decades, because the wealthy and growing middle class can now simply afford to have more kids, and want to do so despite government tax penalties. Quite the opposite of anything the model would have predicted. These wacky humans can be so impulsive when it comes to procreation!

This is the current state of the plaid world. This is the future state of the plaid world. How many kids do you want? How many can the plaid world support? All of the factors explained in this chapter combine to create the world population of today. Check out the regional totals in Figure 2.14 to see how these things are reflected in today's world, and know these figures well.

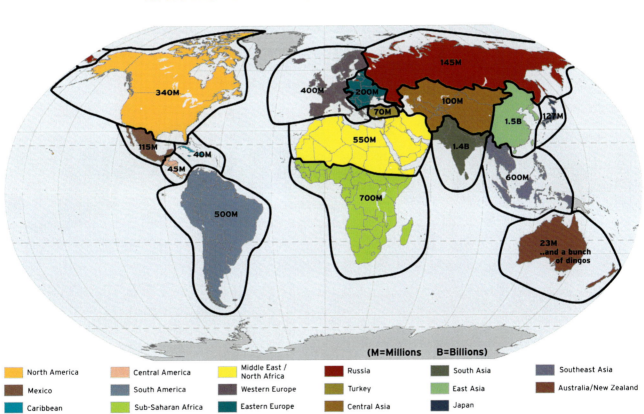

FIGURE 2.14 WORLD REGIONAL MAP WITH POPULATION TOTALS

(M=Millions   B=Billions)

Understanding the Plaid Planet

PART ONE

Now let's see what you've learned about population dynamics, population pyramids, and fertility rates. Help the Plaid Avenger find his way home with his family. Match the Plaid Avenger fertility rate to the appropriate population pyramid and then to the country to which they belong. Be sure to notice the partial children!

Fertility Rate

Country of Origin

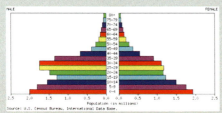 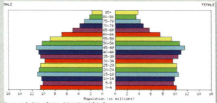 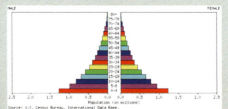

Population Pyramid

Source: U.S Census Bureau, International Data Base

World Population Dynamics
CHAPTER TWO
33

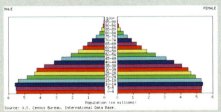 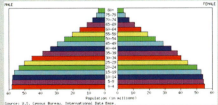 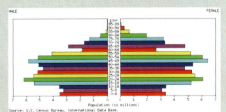

Source: U.S Census Bureau, International Data Base

CHAPTER OUTLINE

1. Idea of a State
2. The Essential Ingredients
   2.1. All You Need Is Love . . . No, I Meant Sovereignty
   2.2. But Sovereignty May Be Redefined
3. Nation, State, or Nation-State?
4. How Many States Are There?
5. Who Controls the State?
   5.1. Anarchy
   5.2. Communism
   5.3. Democracy
   5.4. One-Party States
   5.5. Theocracy
   5.6. Monarchy
   5.7. Military Governments
   5.8. Dictatorship
   5.9. Fascism
   5.10. So Who Is What, and Where?
6. A Final Word on the State of States

How many of these comic caricatures of planetary principles can you peg?

The State of States

3

WE'VE talked about peoples in the world, how fast those peoples are pro-creating, and how those peoples' societies evolve—but, where are they doing all this? Mostly they are doing it in some place we call a **state**. This textbook is all about the regions of the world, and indeed we're going to tackle 18 or 19 of those regions here in a little bit. That's first and foremost how the Plaid Avenger wants you to understand what's going on around the planet. But regions are user-defined, and even as good a user as I am, many edges around regions can be fuzzy. On the other hand, everybody is located in a legally and physically defined entity called a **state**. The borders of a state are not up for debate. What the heck is a state anyway? What's that all about? Where did it come from? Why is it important for understanding the world? Let's state some state facts here, and understand the state of states . . .

IDEA OF A STATE

The idea of a defined territory over which a political entity would rule is a fairly new concept. If you think back, for most of human history there have been kings, or rulers, or leaders of *peoples*, not of geographically defined political *spaces*. Think back to, let's say, the French. I know most of us try not to think about the French, but bear with me for a moment. Throughout most of history, the king or leader has been referred to as the *King of the Francs*, not the *King of France*. Only around the 16th and 17th centuries did the innovation of legally defining a space on Earth evolve—the idea that we're going to define a place on the planet in which those Francs cohabitate and call it "France." In the 18th century, the concept spread to the European colonies and ex-colonies, and then on to the rest of the planet.

FIGURE 3.1 SOVEREIGN STATES BY AGE

SOVEREIGN STATES
Independent since:
- Before 1800
- 1801 - 1914
- 1915 - 1939
- 1940 - 1959
- 1960 - 1989
- 1990 - present

There are some truly old states in the world. China and Persia (Iran), in particular, are ethnically distinct nations of folks who marked the borders of their empires for a good long time. While we can recognize this fact, the idea that these borders are recognized by all other states is the truly European addition to the idea; it is also why most European states are counted among the world's "oldest," even though they may be relatively new in the real scheme of things. One has to look no further than the United States to see how new this concept is; the US is in the "oldest" category of states despite the fact it is truly one of the youngest countries on the planet! We've only been around for 200 years total, but we are one of the oldest continuous sovereign states!

A 19th century wave of "new" states cropped up as European colonies started declaring independence: the countries of Latin America, South Africa, and Australia. Some others popped up as a result of disintegrating empires in Europe: Germany, Italy, Bulgaria, and Romania. Another wave cropped up as the Ottoman Empire, which controlled a large chunk of the Middle East, dissolved in the early 20th century. Sovereignty didn't really get to places like Africa and India and Asia, large chunks of which were European colonial holdings, until they became independent countries—that is, states—in the second half of the 20th century. If we look around the planet, most states in the world are fairly new.

A state, in its basic definition, is a politically and legally and territorially defined geographic area that is recognized by other sovereign states across the planet. Most sovereign states on the planet are fairly new, having been reshaped or declared independent in the last fifty years or so. Maybe we should start defining these terms that the Plaid Avenger is throwing out here. What is a state? What is a nation? What is a nation-state? Before we even get to those, we have to tackle the critical issue of sovereignty, which is one of . . .

THE ESSENTIAL INGREDIENTS

What are we talking about? We hear these terms all the time, but what do they mean? Well, we kind of already hinted at it. A state has something to do with some defined boundaries. That's easy. A **state** is a legally defined and recognized political area on the planet. Legally defined lines are drawn (like a deed to a property), and all the neighbors agree to its parameters—at least for the most part. A few of those lines are still disputed.

But it's not just about a legal description, is it? When we think about the term "**the state**," and if you ask people what was exactly needed to have a state, you would get a wide variety of answers. Many would say you need a government to head up the state, or a military to protect the state, or a fence around the state. Others would say you need an economy, or money, or an official currency, or jobs to have a state. Some might point out that you obviously need some area and some people and some stuff to have a state. Maybe you need roads and buildings and sewer systems and hospitals and McDonalds to have a state. Perhaps you need a constitution, or laws, or courts to have a real state. What do you think a state needs?

I'll give you the real-deal brief answer: you really only need two things to have yourself a state. Number One is sovereignty. The concept is so important, that the Number Two thing you need is also sovereignty. Yeah, I'm a goofball, but now you will always remember the two things you need to be a state: Sovereignty and sovereignty. If you have that, then all of the rest of the stuff doesn't even matter.

> **What state am I in, when I'm in the United States?**
> By the way, the term *state* is what we use synonymously with *country* here in the United States of America. It gets confusing. Here in the US, we say we're in the state of California or New York, but we're not really. We're in the state of the USA. We say *countries* because it makes it easier for us. Country = state, state = country; just use the term **state** when you're dealing with international politics. Everybody understands it better. What state of mind are you in right now as you are contemplating which state of the United States you are in, which of course is a state in its own right, right now. Right?

ALL YOU NEED IS LOVE . . . NO, I MEANT SOVEREIGNTY

So what is this **sovereignty** stuff all about? Well, the concrete definition of sovereignty is really up for grabs nowadays. For the last few hundred years, it has been a concept that everybody has agreed on and understood. However, in the last couple of decades, there's been some serious debate about what it truly means. Times have changed, and it appears the idea of sovereignty is also changing. This redefinition is causing considerable consternation in the world, among big states, small states, and all states in-between—but I'm getting ahead of myself.

First, we want to find out what it *truly* means for an entity to have sovereignty, and thus be called a state. The Plaid Avenger's interpretation is this: when an entity (a government, king, dictator, etc.) has a defined territory on which it exercises TOTAL internal and external control . . . then they gots the sovereignty. No other state can have any power over your territory or the people in it. How can a government demonstrate that it holds real ultimate power over its territory and the peoples in that territory? Kill them. Straight up. If the state can legally get away with that, then it has sovereignty, and it is a sovereign state in the world.

What?

Let me say that again.

In the end game, does the political entity have the ultimate right to do the ultimate deed within its borders? And what is the ultimate deed? The ultimate, beat all, true test of power is the taking of life from its citizens. When you think about it, everything else is quite trivial, isn't it? The right to tax them, to enact laws over them, to jail them, to make inferior products at crappy jobs, or sing sappy national anthems . . . that's all pretty tame stuff compared to death. If you can legally kill people within your state—that is, the leaders and government can kill their own citizens legally and nobody else in the world can do anything about it—then you're in something we call a state that has sovereignty.

People want to say that sovereignty means a system, a government, some leadership, some people who vote, some laws . . . well, you'll have all of that too. But if you want the real test of "Is this place a state?" then find out if they can kill their own citizens. Now that sounds extreme, and . . . it really is! Are we a sovereign state in the US? Can the US pass the ultimate sovereignty test? Absolutely. They kill people all the time; it's called capital punishment. The death sentence.

So the government kills people. They put criminals to death. But that's too easy. Let's take it a step further: How about innocent people? What would happen if the government of this country, or any country, just decided to kill 10,000 of its own citizens? Let's say the FBI or the CIA bungled some information—like that's never happened before—and decided the entire state of New Jersey had to be eliminated by presidential directive, and then nuked it. Millions of lives taken by the state. (On the plus side: no more 'Jersey Shore.') Now, again, that's extreme. Nothing like that's going to happen . . . yet. But let's say it happened. What would France's response be? What would the United Kingdom do? What would China do? What would Angola do?

Save for giving the offender a great big collective hairy eyeball, the answer is . . . they would do nothing (*especially if it were France*). Even though it's an extreme event, and it may be of horrific consequence, the US is a sovereign state. They can legally kill their own citizens, as can all sovereign states. That is an agreed upon principle, and again, it's the extreme. If you can kill someone in your state, then you can pretty much do anything else: tax them, tell them what to do, make some laws, all that stuff. If you can do the extreme, you can do all the lesser stuff, and that's the first big principle rule of sovereignty. The *Number One Rule of Sovereignty* is: Does the state have the ultimate right to do the ultimate deed to its citizens, without the interference of other states? If the answer is "yes," then you're in a sovereign state.

How do you get that status? What if I, The Plaid Avenger, created a Little Plaid Nation over here, and I said, "Well I'm giving myself the authority to kill all people who enter the royal domains of my backyard, which I have christened Plaidtopia." Obviously people would say, "No, you can't do that, man, you are crazy!" Even if Plaidtopia had a constitution, some laws, an economy, some area, a fence, a military, a police force, and a harem of women bodyguards who were trained to kill interlopers on my behalf, it still wouldn't be a sovereign state. The reason that *I* could not do it is because other political entities, namely the other sovereign states, wouldn't agree with it. That's the *Number Two Rule of Sovereignty*.

The *Number Two Rule of Sovereignty* is that all the other states in the sovereign state club have to recognize your sovereignty. You are in the "country club," so to speak, but without the golf benefits. Indeed, the United Nations is kind of the country club, and if all the other sovereign states say, "Yes, you kill your own citizens, and we respect your right to kill your own citizens," then you possess sovereignty. If you are in a legally defined political territory, recognized by other sovereign states, and no other state has power over your territory—as ultimately tested by killing your own citizens—you are a sovereign state. Everything else is inconsequential.

BUT SOVEREIGNTY MAY BE REDEFINED

Why would I suggest that this concept is up for grabs? One of the reasons that today's world is so complicated is because the nature of the world has changed. For centuries everyone has said, "Yeah, you can kill your own citizens. As long as you're not attacking another sovereign state, no one's got a problem with it." That's been the agreed upon, core, central component to sovereignty. Part of the base principle here is **reciprocity**: we will not intervene in your state affairs when you mess with your own citizens . . . and in return, we expect you to respect our ability to mess with our citizens as well. That's the way it all goes. Even today we say, "Hey, the US doesn't like what China's doing to its citizens; we think their human rights are atrocious." But the US is not going to invade. No one's going to do anything about it, really. The US or the UN might protest and say, "Hey! China! Or Russia! You suck for the way you treat people but . . . here . . . be the host of the Olympics anyway." At most, an official condemnation issued from a head of state or perhaps even a trade embargo would be the extent of any disapproval. No active military intervention is going to happen, because that's what it is to be a sovereign state. We respect their sovereignty so that they will respect ours. At least, that is the way it was . . .

Former President Bill Clinton: sovereignty side-stepper.

But it is morphing fast in the 21st century . . . mostly due to the international shenanigans of the US and NATO! How so?

Well, back in March of 1999, during the Clinton administration, the United States led NATO on a bombing campaign of Yugoslavia. Why did the United States and NATO start bombing Yugoslavia, a sovereign state?

Because Yugoslavia invaded the US? No.

Threatened US citizens? Nah.

Because Yugoslavia invaded another fellow NATO country? Nope. Threatened or invaded any other sovereign state? Ummm . . . no.

Because Clinton wanted to defer attention from his White House sex scandal? Mmmm . . . good one, but no.

Does that attack seem important to you? Do you remember hearing anything about it? I doubt it. Let me be the first to educate you on how big a deal it was to sovereign states. Here's an excerpt from the British *Financial Times*: "The enormity of NATO launching its first attack against a sovereign state is not to be underestimated. Unlike Iraq, Belgrade has not invaded another country. Nor is the situation akin to Bosnia, where the legitimate government invited outside intervention. Nor, finally, has the United Nations Security Council specifically authorized NATO to bomb."

Slobodan sez, "I can kill them if I want . . ."

The thing that happened was that this crazy guy, **Slobodan Milosevic**, started killing his own citizens. The who or why or how is not important right this second. What is important is that "killing your own citizens" was one of the baseline agreements of sovereignty. States respect the authority of every other sovereign state to kill its own citizens. You may remember that from seven paragraphs ago. It's the cornerstone. In this circumstance, it was possibly an ethnic cleansing situation, where Slobodan—then leader of Yugoslavia, currently worm food pushing up daisies—may have been persecuting and encouraging his national army to outright kill members of a specific ethnic group. In hindsight, there is not much debate about it. Slobodan was actively pursuing genocide/ethnic cleansing . . . but only against his own citizens. He was the leader of a sovereign state. Should be no problem, but . . .

Apparently, it got to be too much to bear. There was a large outcry about the situation in Europe and even in the United States. Perhaps it was the memory of the Jewish Holocaust that occurred in Europe, or perhaps the instability in this very region that had previously launched World War II, or even as some have pointed out, it was simply because there were white people being slaughtered, and other white people didn't like that idea. (And I include that statement to point out the horrific irony that the US/NATO/UN has stood on the sidelines plenty of times while genocides occurred in Africa and Asia.). For whatever reasons, President Bill Clinton decided to enact a bombing campaign, coordinated with NATO, to stop the genocide. Long story short—the United States bombed Yugoslavia into submission for what it was doing to its own citizens.

Why am I telling this story? Because this changed the whole idea of a sovereign state! As we suggested, this whole "kill your citizens" thing used to be the standard. What a state did to its own people was not up for debate, but apparently this was the straw that broke the camel's back—and it's not an isolated incident. Since the 1999 bombing campaign on Serbia, the US and/or NATO have played an active role in Afghanistan, Bosnia, and Iraq under the umbrella of liberating the locals. Meanwhile, serious genocides have been occurring in Sudan and the Congo, for which many in the international community are calling for invasive action to remedy. Those are on the heels of the now infamous Rwandan genocide of 1994, which no state, international organization, or otherwise, stepped in to stop.

Holy redefining "state"! 2014 Update! Unless you have been hiding in a foxhole under the air-conditioned tent of Muammar Qaddafi, you have heard about the UN-sponsored, US/UK/France/NATO-enacted invasion of Libya! This is a super-gigantic big deal when it comes to the definition of sovereignty, and my friends, I believe it is the last nail in the coffin of the concept in the modern era. Why do I make such bold assertions? Well, why was Libya bombarded by NATO? Because a political protest rose up internally against the government. That's it! There is nothing else to claim here! No genocide, no invasion of another country, no terrorism . . . not even a threat of any of those things! While I have no love of Qaddafi, he had done absolutely nothing to break the old rules of sovereignty . . . which is why I am suggesting that those old rules don't mean diddly-squat anymore.

When Libyans took to the streets to protest against their government, Muammar made the fatal mistake of announcing out loud he would crush the uprising, and apparently even this audible "threat" to civilians has now become the new standard to incite international intervention into a sovereign state! How bizarre! For the first time (maybe ever) you had an entire collective global movement to affect an internal political situation in a state. New stuff. Interesting stuff. But that is a tricky can of worms that has been opened . . . aren't there other states with equally crappy, repressive leaders that harm their citizens? Ummm . . . North Korea? Sudan? Zimbabwe? Will they be next on the list of countries to be invaded on the premise of pathetic leadership? Time will tell. Here in 2014, that debate is currently hottest regarding what to do about the situation in Syria; will 'Team West' pull another intervention, or will classic sovereignty be upheld with the help of Russia and China? Still too close to call as of this writing . . . and the Syrian Civil War rages on. . . .

All of the listed above are actions, or inactions, based upon unacceptable sovereign state behavior in dealing with their own citizens. Again, it used to be the hallmark of what defined a sovereign state; now it's totally up for grabs. How much misbehavior will the international community allow before intervening even when that misbehavior is confined inside a single state?

This is causing a lot of consternation on the planet. If the golden rule for what defines a sovereign state is up for question, then what exactly is a sovereign state? Sorry, my friends, the Plaid Avenger doesn't have an answer for you right now, because nobody does.

With the current movement of UN troops around the planet, and unilateral actions by the United States and/or NATO in today's world, we don't really know. You can see this in today's news as a major point of contention particularly with the Chinese, and a lot of times with the Russians. Why those two? Just because they hate the United States? No, it's got nothing to do with that at all. These two countries, particularly the Chinese, are really big into the classic sovereignty thing because they want to cover their own butts. Remember, forever it's just been: 'don't invade other countries, respect everyone else's sovereignty, and you can get away with whatever you want in your own country.' Well, that's up for grabs now. The Chinese and the Russians think, "We are not really keen with the US involvement in other countries because it is violating the sacred rights of sovereignty to which we've all agreed." The Chinese in particular are very anxious to avoid any outsiders from intervening into what they consider their own sovereign territories of Tibet and Taiwan . . . more on that later. . . .

Sparked by the US/NATO bombing campaign in Yugoslavia (then Afghanistan, then Iraq, then Libya), sovereignty has also been called into question by human rights groups and lots of folks around the planet who say, "Okay, you're right. We're in the 21st century, we cannot allow acts of genocide to occur, even if it is in a sovereign state." While Yugoslavia was the test run for this, in terms of a trial flight on intervening into a sovereign state to protect citizens, it will probably be used more. Indeed, the former Bush administration said, "One of the reasons we went to Iraq was to protect the Kurds and the Shi'ites there from what their own government was doing to them." There are folks around the world who are calling for more action from the UN and the world to stop genocide in other places. Right now, people are saying, "Hey! What's the deal? You guys bomb Serbia to protect *those* guys, and you're currently in Iraq protecting *those* people from their government, so how come you didn't interject in Rwanda? Why aren't you in Sudan or Burma or Palestine right now?" This is a big debate on the world forum right now. It's another reason why, you'll see, that people hesitate big time in the UN to use the word "**genocide**." Why is this?

What's the Deal with Genocide?

Genocide is when a government, or a group of people, kills or tries to completely exterminate another specific group of people, usually based on ethnicity or religion. The worst example of this in modern history occurred during World War II, when the Germans tried to exterminate all of the Jews out of German territory, actually out of all of Europe. This was such a horrific act that, after World War II, the world agreed that we would never allow this to happen again. All the states in the world passed a United Nations law making genocide an international crime. The **Convention on the Prevention and Punishment of the Crime of Genocide** says this: "Any of the following acts committed with intent to destroy, in whole or in part, a national, ethnic, racial or religious group, as such: Killing members of the group; Causing serious bodily or mental harm to members of the group; Deliberately inflicting on the group conditions of life calculated to bring about its physical destruction in whole or in part; Imposing measures intended to prevent births within the group; and forcibly transferring children of the group to another group."

But the old rules of sovereignty were still in play. Things floated along pretty well, until the appearance of possible genocide in Serbia/Yugoslavia, in Rwanda, and in Sudan. Now wait a minute. Didn't we all agree we were not going to let this happen again? Shouldn't we do something?

That is one of the calls on the world stage right now. The reason you did not hear the Rwandan situation referred to as genocide is because the use of that particular word demands a call for action. In other words, as long as everybody in the UN is just saying, "Yeah, well, they've got a civil war," or "They have some sort of internal conflict," or perhaps "They may have isolated acts of ethnic cleansing," (which was said about Rwanda) then there is no need to act. Sovereignty takes precedence. They say these things very intentionally because everyone is scared to whisper, "It's genocide." If everyone in the UN agrees that genocide is occurring, then they have to act. It's their law. "World law" if there is such a thing . . . and that trumps sovereignty.

That's the deal with genocide and why people gingerly dance around the term, particularly at the UN. You also now know how genocide is calling into question the whole sovereignty theme and how the modern definition of sovereignty is being called into question in places where citizens are being persecuted politically even when it is obviously not a genocide. But let's move on to less lethal topics. . . .

NATION, STATE, OR NATION-STATE?

Now we've looked at what constitutes a state. Perhaps now you know more about what constitutes a state than you ever wanted to know. Yeah, me too. But it's my job. However, what about these other terms? What is a *nation*? Is it different from a *state*? If so, then what in the wide wide world of sports is a *nation-state*? It's easy. Let's break it down.

A **state,** you now know, is a legally defined political unit that possesses **sovereignty.** Fair enough. I've beaten you over the head with that for several pages now.

A **nation,** straight up, has nothing to do with a state. You think it does, but it doesn't. A nation is about the people. Remember the intro paragraph of this chapter? It used to be the standard unit of global identity: a leader led a specific group of people. The Romans, or the Huns, or the Aztecs, or the Zulus. It's all about the peoples. A nation has much more to do with the people than any specific area. In fact, some peoples don't even have an area—but I get ahead of myself. A nation refers to a group of people who share a common culture, and who may even want to have their own government, and may want to rule themselves. Common culture could be just about anything, but often it is a combination of a lot of things: a common ethnicity, religion, historical background, diet, shared beliefs and customs, traditional attire, sports and games . . . whatever.

The number of nations in the world is undefined. There could be thousands, nay, millions. It depends on what group of people and on what scale you're looking. Perhaps in every town there's a small nation of people who think that they're different; that they share a common culture, and perhaps would like to form their own country. Again, it's an undeterminable number, but it is all about the people. Let's think about some true examples on the planet that we can all agree are distinct groups of people who share a common culture. This is actually quite easy.

What common cultures are there around the world that are tied to people? How about the French? How about the Germans? Wow, this is easy; let's stay in Europe. How about the Italians? Think of all these guys. They all have distinct common cultures from each other; just think about cuisine or their languages: Germans eat sauerkraut, while the French dine on snails. BTW: ew. The Czechs, the Poles, the Russians are all distinct cultures and peoples. But it can get even more specific. We could look at the UK as a UK culture. Maybe, but there's definitely a Scottish culture within the UK, and an English culture, but we're stuck in the Old World. Is there a Saudi nation? Yes, I believe so. Is there an Argentinean one? That one gets a little fuzzier, but it's possible. Japanese? Yes, definitely. The Japanese are a nation, a distinct group of people and distinct common culture. The Chinese? Yes. The Vietnamese? Yep. Thai, Laotian, Kurds, the Turks, the Cherokee in the US, the Maasai tribesmen in Kenya? Sure. We could go all over the planet and see pockets of common culture,

Distinct nations are all over the place . . . but are they in nation-states?

and an idea of a group of people who share something in common who, may or may not, want to rule themselves, under their own government. That's a nation.

Let's get to the final definition here: what is a nation-state? Simple. Let's just add a **nation** to a **state**, and presto, you got a nation-state. A **nation-state** is a group of people who share a common culture, who want to have their own government and want to rule themselves—a nation—and do so in a defined and recognized political area—a state—which has sovereignty to boot. That is a nation-state. Let's give an example of a nation-state. We look around the world, and see a lot of the ones we've already talked about. Germany: perfect nation-state. This group of people with a common culture in a distinct area that we call Germany. The French: same deal. The Japanese: even better. The Koreans are the best example yet; a 100 percent ethnically homogeneous group of folks with a distinct Korean culture and cuisine. That's it: that's a nation-state.

The list can go on and on, all over the world. Most of the places in the world are close to what we call a nation-state. Of greater significance than listing all the nation-states: let's look at those places in the world that are not nation-states.

FIGURE 3.2 TYPICAL NATIONS WITH STATES

Turks in Turkey, Thais in Thailand. Yep, that's a nation-state!

Which brings up the question: can we have a **nation without a state**? Indeed, we certainly can, and this is one of the causes for conflict on the planet today. There are lots of groups of people with a shared common culture, and a desire to rule themselves in a legally defined territory, but they ain't got their own state. A prime example is the Palestinians in a place called Palestine, which is not yet a state—it might be soon—but who are still largely under the control of Israel. Both parties are working on making the Palestinians a nation-state.

FIGURE 3.3: SOME EXAMPLES OF NATIONS WITHOUT STATES

Nations sans statehood

Let's get more complicated. Places like Chechnya—yeah, that's a good one! A very distinct culture in a place that's called Chechnya, but it's not sovereign. They'd like to be sovereign; they would love to not be part of Russia, because they are not Russian. Or the Kurds: a nation of people scattered across 4 different states. They've been petitioning to become their own sovereign nation-state for decades, but no one wants to give up territory to let that happen.

What about Tibet? You've heard of them. The leader of the Tibetans, the Dalai Lama, is the spiritual leader of the Buddhist movement on the planet. Their spiritual and traditional homeland has been Tibet. Most of the people there share this Tibetan and Buddhist culture, but the area called Tibet is part of China. Thus, they are not a nation-state. It's one that's likely to *never* become a nation-state. That's a little Plaid insider tip for you. Sorry, Lama. China will not let Tibet go.

These are all very good examples of nations without states. Some of these are areas quite active in the world in the terms of conflict, with those people trying to become stand-alone nation-states, and full-fledged sovereign states at that.

Lama has no state.

SO, HOW MANY STATES ARE THERE?

There are an unidentifiable number of nations. Groups of people that are self-defined, and at multiple scales, are all over the place. Every country will have small pockets of folks that consider themselves culturally different. Like the Basque in Spain, the Scots in the UK, or the French in Canada—maybe we should just say the French everywhere. It's impossible to determine the number of nations. Now nation-states, that's a little bit easier, but even that definition gets a little muddled if you think about it too much. Is the US a nation-state? What's our common culture? Besides a shared hatred of Céline Dion, do we share any unequivocal commonality?

However, the number of states we can identify with some confidence. Exactly how many states are there here in 2014? The magic number we're using right now is 195. We're talking about sovereign states in the "country" club. They all recognize each other, and they recognize each other's sovereignty.

Let's get back to the numbers. There are only 194 members of the United Nations. Why 194? Because the Vatican City, which is a sovereign state—and though all the other 194 recognize it as a sovereign state—is not a member of the UN. That's why there's a little confusion here. The Pope and his buddies have said, "Nah, that's okay, the UN is cool, but we're kind of a religious people. We're going to keep to ourselves."

So there are 195 fully recognized states in the world . . . although there are about 10 other geographic entities that have either unilaterally proclaimed themselves as sovereign, or are legitimately working toward sovereign status. Places like Transnistriia, Palestine, and Kosovo are in this nebulous non-state, maybe trying to be a state status.

Pope sez, "Nope" to UN.

In particular, Taiwan for decades has tried to get international recognition as an independent state, and at one point had perhaps half the world's states recognizing it as independent of China; China, of course, considers Taiwan as a 'rogue' entity that is actually part of their state. But times they are a-changing, and as China's economic and political clout has grown in the last decade, the number of other states recognizing Taiwanese sovereignty has dwindled to less than a couple dozen (including such powerhouse players as Palau and Haiti) and you should fully expect that number to continue to shrink, in the mad rush for all countries on the planet to kiss up to China.

While Taiwan is certainly not going to get a sovereign state spot, there have been several new editions to the club in the last few years. The first tag-along is East Timor. It was formerly a colony of the Portuguese—a situation that made it distinct from the rest of the Indonesian territory that was controlled by the Dutch. Over a decade ago, they had an independence movement and the Portuguese finally pulled out, and the Timorese declared independence. Indonesia was not keen on that happening, so it turned into a bloody mess. We won't get into it here, but East Timor has finally come out on top, had its application accepted at the UN, and is fully sovereign now. Same thing is true for "South Sudan," which just voted for succession from Sudan back in 2010, and the Sudanese government peacefully agreed to the split too—well, agreed to it after decades of brutal civil war in the region. It became fully official at the UN in 2011: South Sudan is officially a state as well, despite its wildly uncreative choice of state name. Seriously? South Sudan? That's the best you could come up with? Dudes, you guys should have had a state-naming write-in competition or something.

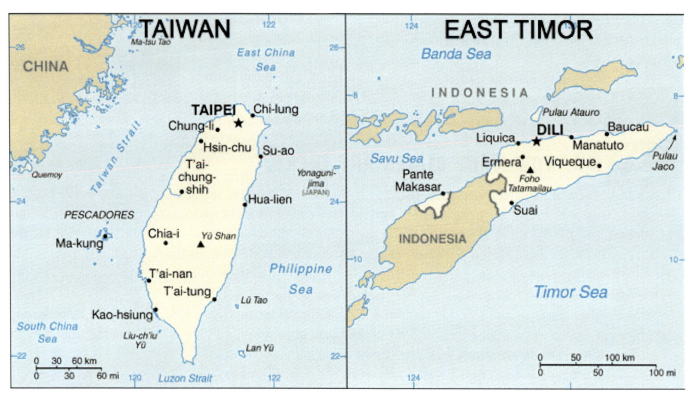

Future statehood? Taiwan out, Timor in!

Number 196 will probably be Palestine. This is a big "IF," since it's the Middle East, and you can't predict its future from one second to the next, much less year to year. For the last decade, there has been a general movement toward true Palestinian independence from the state of Israel. Indeed, given the track record of the last two years, it does seem, with a lot of trouble and turbulence, that they are heading toward that goal. We might be looking at two years out, we might be looking at ten years out, but certainly at some point, it will be a independent state. Maybe.

Speaking of Israel and Palestine, it is also important to note that the recognition of a state is not always a given, depending upon to whom you are asking the question. For instance, while Israel is certainly fully accepted as a state by most governments in the world and the UN, many Arab and Islamic countries continue to shun it; in particular, Iran outright refuses to recognize it at all, as does Saudi Arabia and most other Arab neighbors. But that is not an isolated sovereignly-denying incident. North Korea refuses to recognize South Korea, and vice versa. Turkey refuses to recognize Cyprus. In what can only be called the most un-exciting recognition refusal of all time, Liechtenstein and the Czech Republic refute each other's existence because of some ancient WWII-era decree. What a bunch of boneheads.

The most current, hottest sovereignty showdown erupted in early 2008, when Kosovo declared independence from Serbia, and about 40 countries, including the US and most European Union states, immediately recognized it. This would perhaps be no big deal, like the Taiwan issue is not anymore, but for one small fact: this showdown is pitting major powers against each other. What do I mean? The US, UK, and France all recognize Kosovo, while China and Russia are firmly opposed. Hey, that's a major rift at the UN Permanent Security Council, a topic for later discussion!

One more thing: let me point out a few places that are not states, but are often mistaken for states. Some of them are still colonies of other countries. For example, French Guiana, a fairly big place in South America, is a French colony; it's not a state. Greenland is still a Danish colony. There are some extenuating circumstances and also some strange ones, like Western Sahara, which Morocco is claiming and attempting to absorb legally and politically. It's in some nowhere land status in the middle. Bermuda is an overseas territory of the UK, not a sovereign state. Puerto Rico is not a state, not really an independent territory, and not really a

Kosovo causing consternation.

colonial holding, either. It's just kind of associated with the United States. That's a bit of a muddled situation there as well.

On top of that, you have a lot of nations around the world *without* a state, which are sometimes mistaken for states. Places like Tibet in China we have referenced already, or like the Scots in Scotland. Scotland is a political subdivision of the UK, not an independent sovereign state. It's a nation of Scots, a group of people who definitely think they're culturally distinct. You know, Scottish people, we'd all agree to that—the guys that wear kilts, play noisy instruments, and eat haggis. What the h is that? Haggis consists of a pudding made of onions, oatmeal and sheep's entrails, then stuffed into a sheep's stomach and roasted. Ummm . . . and then they eat it? Ugh, that is definitely a distinct culture—and let's make sure they stay that way. Give them the state status, as long as they keep the haggis!

2014 update: Enough Scots have petitioned to become a separate sovereign state, and the UK has agreed to let them vote on it in 2014! They could possibly join the country club this year, if more the 50% of the Scots vote 'AYE' in the national referendum! New state coming? Stay tuned!

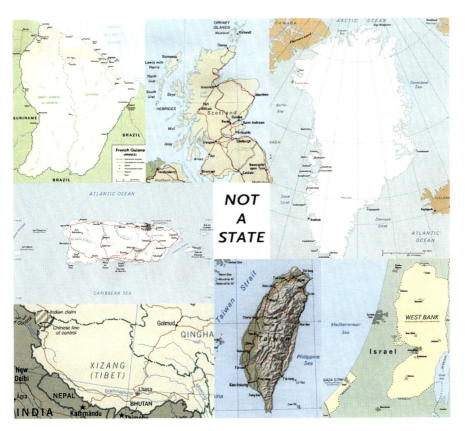

Let me state the obvious: You think it's a state, but it's not a state.

WHO CONTROLS THE STATE?

We talked about what was a state, what is a state, who is not a state, it's all about the state . . . but who controls the state? Well, that's what the rest of this chapter is all about. World governments and world political systems: the peeps in charge of these sovereign entities. Before we get to that, we have to throw out a few terms that we hear all the time, but are wildly confusing to most. And many of these messy and muddled terms refer not to just politics, but sometimes economics and religions and social issues as well. They are terms like the **Left** versus the **Right, Liberal** versus **Conservative, Communism** versus **Capitalism.** We'll get to some of these terms in later chapters, but let's start with the **Left** versus the **Right** for now. Throughout this book, we're going to refer to about 'leftist' governments or 'right-wing' movements, so let's go ahead and flush these things out politically right this second.

What does it mean to be on the **Left** or the **Right** in the political spectrum? Maybe you've heard reference to "lefty commies," or "right-wing fascist" or "leftist guerrillas." So what are these terms referencing? Do I have to be ambidexterous to understand this stuff? Dig this from the get-go: we're talking about the *world* political stage here, not the politics within independent sovereign states. It's easy to get the terms mixed up; you might hear reference to "the liberal Left" or the "conservative Right" in America, but that internal domsetic name-calling stuff doesn't mean the same thing that we are talking about on the world stage.

Check out the world stage, the world political spectrum, from left to right represented across the bottom of these pages. Maybe you're starting to get a sense of what it means. Here's what I want you to know about it: On the extreme **left** would be government styles like communism or anarchy. These are ruling systems where there is (supposedly) little to no central government control. Another way to put it as you head to the left: less government power, more power in the hands of the people. This is best displayed by anarchy, which we think of as a chaotic state, but indeed there are anarchists—political anarchists, that is—and they believe that there should be no government at all. Every single person within every single state in every single society should have the right to do anything they want. That's what true anarchy really means. It's never existed anywhere, and probably never will, but the theory is that the people themselves have *all* of the power. Never mind the bollocks, the government, or the rulers of the state, who have no control over individual people. That's an extreme.

What's on the other side of the political spectrum, on the other extreme? That's on the total extreme **right**, which is just the reverse. All of the power is in government hands, or a single person's hands. Control of the country is in the hands of the few, the people in charge. Most of the population has zero or limited political voice on the extreme right. To think of it in perspective—and extremes are always good to clarify the perspectives—is that the power pyramid is upside

Extreme Left
Anarchy . . .

Communism . . .

Direct Democracy . . .

Representative
Democracy . . .

One-Party State . . .

Power Increasingly Distributed to the Peoples

down in anarchy. The people are on the top; they get everything, and can do anything they want. On the extreme right are fascists like Hitler, who actually said something along the lines of: "*I am the state. An individual person. Me. I am the state. Everyone here in this state of Germany is here at my disposal at my will. You work for me.*" On the left, is just the reverse; the state works for *you*. The state is an apparatus that exists solely for the people. That's a huge difference to consider. That's what the world spectrum is all about. All of the political systems in the world fall somewhere between these two extremes, because—and here's a little insider tip—these extremes don't exist anywhere. In fact, some of these systems hardly exist anywhere at all anymore. Let's go through them really quickly.

ANARCHY

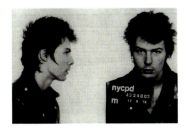

He did it his way.

We'll start on the far left. **Anarchy**, as I already suggested, is essentially no government at all. Maybe the Libertarian party in the United States is close to ideological anarchy, but only in that they want absolute minimal government in terms of taxes, services, and laws. Yeah, Ron Paul partying with Sid Vicious—now there's a good time! No superstructure, no hierarchy of folks that are in control of anything. In an anarchy state, there would be really no government, no taxes, no national defense, no one taking care of roads, or any of that kind of stuff. You're starting to get the flavor of this; high schoolers with punk rock jackets may think that anarchy's really cool, but it doesn't sound too good when you really begin to define what's going on in this type of society. It's pretty much every man for himself. We already know in human society that this deteriorates fairly rapidly into people beating the living daylights out of each other for a cigarette. In the political spectrum, when we're just thinking about this abstract idea politically, it comes down to this: "It's the individual's right to do anything he or she wants." Long story short, anarchy never happened anywhere, and anarchy will never happen anywhere. Not as a legitimate state system. Are there any anarchy states anywhere in the world today? There is perhaps one, but it's not intentional, and that would be Somalia. It is a state that has fallen into chaos—and we typically consider anarchy and chaos synonymous—and indeed, that is the case for Somalia. But they aren't really an anarchy; Somalians didn't intentionally become anarchic; they've just deteriorated into chaos. In the sense of an intentionally instituted system of anarchy, the whole concept humorously contradicts itself, much like Ron Paul running for president. (To be fair, American Libertarianism emphasizes freedom, individual liberty, voluntary association and generally advocate a minimizing of government power . . . not total abolition of it. I think.) But besides the few disintegrating states, there aren't any true intentional anarchic states in the world.

Theocracy . . .   Monarchy . . .   Military Government . . .   Dictatorship . . .   . . . Extreme Right Fascism

Power Increasingly Concentrated into Fewer Hands

COMMUNISM

Communism is another hilarious system because it doesn't exist anywhere either. What a barrel of laughs. The Plaid Avenger wonders if it actually ever did exist anywhere. Why are we talking about it at all if it doesn't exist? Because the ideology is powerful, and it has greatly shaped history, especially the last century. Communism as an idea is still a potent force that shapes judgments of decision makers around the planet. There are several confusing factors about Communism, and before I get to those confusing points, let's just say what it is.

Famous dead communist dudes.

Communism was a concept that had been around forever, but some folks in 19th century Europe, namely Karl Marx and Friedrich Engels, really put it into its modern interpretation. These guys were living in the environment of the Industrial Revolution. They were witnesses to flagrant excesses of capitalism, ruled by monarchs on the throne who controlled all political power, and rich factory owners who controlled the economy. Marx and his crew looked around and said, "This really sucks. We have no power over our lives. We need more power to the people." So they wrote their manifestos and all that jazz, and long story short, came up with this: In a Communist political system there is a government, but the government is solely there (remember the inverted pyramid) to provide everything that the citizens need. To facilitate this provision of economic and political needs, the government would set up small **soviets**: that is, small groups of folks in cities of which every citizen is a member. Everybody is attached to a specific soviet, kind of like voting districts here in the US, but much much smaller. These soviets would debate on every issue that affects the people. In this manner, the government listens to the people directly and distributes resources or makes decisions based on the citizens' needs and requests.

How can a government afford to do that? In this society, there is no private property; the state controls it all. In other words, the government is kind of "by the people, for the people"—we think about that in democracy, but it's even beyond that in theocratical communism. It exists solely to distribute everything as per the needs of the people in the society, and that means economic as well as political power. That's one of the reasons it's extremely confusing. Dig the confusion:

- → Confusing point #1: Communism is both a political and economic term, because it combines politics and economy into one system in which all ownership of property is communal and all resources are controlled by the government; the entire economy and the political system is run by a singular government. It's the only kind of system that works that way. All of the other political systems we'll talk about are just politics, and the economy goes its own way and does its own thing. In true Communism, it's all one big happy family where the government, Big Brother, controls everything.

- → Confusing point #2: When we think about the manifestations of Communism in the world, we typically think of dictatorship. The big one, of course, is during the Russian commie experience: the USSR under Josef Stalin. Or even Chairman Mao. Communism in China turns into Maoist China, a singular leader that ends up being a dictator. Even when it's not a well-recognized singular leader, these systems tend to perpetuate a small group of people in charge of everything.

Indeed, that's exactly what has always happened. During the Russian experience, Vladimir Lenin came to power in 1917 with his commie posse. They were attempting to implement a system that had never been tried before. To become politically Communist meant to be politically and economically Communist. Lenin said, "Well, okay, this has never been done before. We want to get to this utopian society where everybody's equal, and all decisions are made communally, and all property is held communally, and all resources are distributed communally—that's what we're shooting for. But we're not there yet. In fact, we're very far from it. We need to set up a small group of people in order to get from point A to point B. In other words, to get from where we are now to our perfect commie society, we basically have to become an oligarchy/dictatorship . . . just for a while." I'm paraphrasing here. That is not a quote from Lenin. He is not as good-looking as me, although his goatee is stylin'.

Main point: this is supposed to be a temporary thing, a transition, a transitory government in which a few people hold all the power, supposedly just for a brief period of time until everything is 'fixed.' Here's the problem, folks: Of all of the societies that have tried to go down the Communist path, not one single one has actually finished the transition. In other words, they start the transition, and they want to get to this pure utopian society, but it always ends up as a power grab by few people, or typically one person, who we then call a dictator. Some good examples are in the Soviet system, where Josef Stalin became a singular dictator. In the Cuban system, Fidel Castro, who's still there, is a singular man in charge of everything. In China, Chairman Mao, and then his successors, were singular people. It never fully develops into equality for all. Plaid Avenger Tip: Communism will never, has never, and, did I mention, will never work the way it ideally should. Which brings us to. . . .

→ Confusing point #3: There are no Communist countries on the planet right now. They don't exist. Even if we look at places like today's China, or even today's Cuba, these are something closer to what we would call one-party systems, because *purely* political Communist states can't exist—remember, the system is a political and economic combination. It's like peanut butter and jelly or Batman and Robin: they got to happen together. Today, everybody pretty much now has some form of capitalist economies. In other words, the economies of the supposedly "Communist" countries are not communist. Everybody's given up on that (with the possible exception of North Korea, which is a place so bizarre as to not even be claimed by ardent communists). Since Communism in its pure form is both politics and economy, it does not exist. We've got to re-classify everything that *was* categorized as commie in some other category.

Those are the three confusing points about Communism. Let's move onto something more sound, and that is . . .

DEMOCRACY

Now we're getting into familiar territory; this is the stuff that we all get and understand, because we live in it. **Democracy**: *ocracy* = "ruled by" and *demo* = "the people." We are still in this inverted pyramid in which the government is here mostly for the people, as a service for the people, and not the other way around. We are not here to serve the US government, it is here to serve us. It protects us; it does things that are in our interest, not its own interest. That may be up for debate on some issues, but that is the system as it is in the abstract form. **Direct democracy** doesn't really exist anywhere; we don't even have it in the United States. Direct democracy says, "We think everybody's so equal that every single issue and every single person we vote for and every law we enact must be voted upon by every single person involved in democracy, that is, everyone in the state." You can probably figure out why there's not too many of these in the world—because it's impossible. In countries that have

No libation without representation!

millions of people, you can't have millions of people trying to come to a common consensus on what's going on, even if it were something as simple as a dog-leash law. Direct democracy, that is, democracy that involves every single person, really only comes close in one place, and these guys are screwed up on several fronts: Switzerland. I mean, even their cheese is full of holes, so you can't expect too much from the rest of the culture.

The Swiss have the closest manifestation of direct democracy on the planet. All citizens have to spend a large component of their time dealing with all the laws that have to be passed. Sounds like that **soviet** stuff described above, doesn't it? There is a much larger percentage of people who serve in some sort of elected office, like almost all of them. They don't just have a single President, they have a presidential council of like 7 members. I won't say it's a chaotic system because it's not, but it's definitely a time-demanding system that most of the planet is not willing to ascribe. That's why most of the planet is a multiparty state/**representative democracy**.

This is exactly the same as a direct democracy, in terms of the government working for the people. But, instead of every single one of us voting on every single thing, we just vote for a few people and say, "You guys go decide. We will elect you into positions of power, knowing that you are here for our good. If you tick us off, or you do something wrong, we will remove you from your positions by voting for somebody else." That's the way it works, but the main term here is "representative." That is, one person is going to represent our county, or district, or state, and we're giving him or her the power to decide what's best for us. Does that make sense? It should—it's not that complicated.

On a side note: Multiparty states and representative democracy are all the rage on the planet right now. It is the government option of choice for most, and one that is growing. In the last twenty years, since the demise of the Soviet Union, this is the one that all the cool kids do. It is the most accepted, and the most perpetuated by the UN, and by big states like the United States and various European countries. This one is heading up in the numbers column.
Most of the planet is in this category already.

We should also reference another type of democracy that is prevalent throughout the world, but befuddles us Americans because the system still has kings and queens: that would be **constitutional monarchy**. It really is a democracy, but for reasons of tradition (and pompousness), the state has maintained the presence of their royal family as figureheads, most of which have no real power at all . . . but man, they look so cool at fancy frock balls and palace ceremonies! These systems typically have a constitution, a parliament, and a Prime Minister who actually holds the real power, but they will still 'consult' the monarch on vital issues. Mostly all pomp and circumstance. Whatevs. Places still under this Cinderella spell include the UK, Belgium, Sweden, Norway, Denmark, Netherlands, Spain; non-European examples include Bhutan, Bahrain, Kuwait, Malaysia, Thailand, and even Japan, which still has it's antiquated Emperor!

God save the Queen! Fake power must be maintained!

I want to point out another thing under this representative democracy description: How could direct democracy and representative democracy be right next to communism on the political spectrum? This is confusing, and we've already pointed out why the term communism is so confusing. If we are not leftists here in the US, then why are the two systems beside each other on the left side of the spectrum? People in the US don't consider themselves to be leftists, but indeed, if you look at the whole spectrum, you are. That is, you're for power to the people, and that's more liberal, to the left. Liberate the people, freedom for the people, everything's for the people. In that sense, communism, on paper, is right beside democracy. There's just slightly different takes on how to go about getting power in the hands of the people. It's confusing, because communism has never worked. In theory, it's all about people, just like democracy. Now it gets a little simpler, as we're going to start heading to the right side of the spectrum with one-party states.

ONE-PARTY STATES

Hosni and Hu: The only ones to vote for.

One-party states are exactly what they imply: there is only one political party that holds all the cards. Something that looks like elections happen from time to time. Sometimes there are things that look like choices on the ballot, but there's only one real political party that always seems to win. There's only one political party that seems to be in charge. Some of these are in a transition zone from communism, like China and several other Central Asian states that used to be part of the USSR. Some of them are bordering on full-on dictatorship, like what Hosni Mubarak was in Egypt, but have been wise enough to keep in the good graces of Team West by putting on the democracy window dressing. That is, they do have parliaments, and they do have groups of people come together who make laws, but it's pretty much only one group of people or one political party with only one viewpoint of how to run things. In other words, you can go vote at the polls, but there's only one group of folks for which you can vote. Egypt was a great example of this: They had elections for thirty years, and the same guy won every single time, and that was President Hosni Mubarak. Was he that popular? Did people love him that much? Well, perhaps, but maybe it's because he was the only person on the ballot. Hosni's fake-out democracy, one-party state story was the reason that millions of infuriated Egyptians took to the streets and finally forced him from office in 2011, but more on that when we get to the Middle East chapter.

One-party states have the illusion of choice; some of them might have some choices for some of the legislature and parliamentary sections, but it's really one group of folks that kind of have most of the power. They do some things for the people—they are not necessarily completely top-down hard-core, but they are not true democracies. Not all people are created equal, and not all opinions of running the state are heard. It perhaps would only take a nudge to get them closer to true democracy, though. As opposed to theocracy.

THEOCRACY

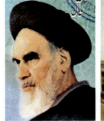 

We are holy, and we are in charge.

Now we're getting to real hard-core rightist politics. Here's where the pyramid now has tipped. Indeed, there are some individual people who rule the state, and they do it for their interest in what they consider the right way to do things with little to no input from the people. This will get worse as we progress right-ward.

Theocracy is fairly straightforward. It's an *ocracy*, "ruled by," *theo*, "religion." Some sort of religion controls the state. Our best examples would be Iran and Vatican City. These are states which are not **secular**. There is no division between the church and the state; in fact, it is one singular unit. The church *is* the state. The person at the top—which in other places we would call the king, or the president, or the head cheese—is a religious person in a theocracy. Like the Pope: he is the head of the Catholic Church, and also the head of Vatican City. In Iran, you have the Ayatollah: a supreme religious leader. He is also the leader of the state; they are one in the same.

Now the Pope has been around for a while, heck, I don't know, like since biblical times I think. But the Iranian theocracy is something quite new on the world stage, and represents a whole new take on how states should be managed. Indeed, most consider the Iranian Revolution of 1979 the last truly revolutionary idea of human history thus far. It's a big deal. The idea that a modern state can be recast and re-organized with religion as the central theme has not been tried lately, if ever. In the past we have had kings or queens or governments that are inherently tied to religion, or that even share power with religion. But this version of theocracy is totally unique in that ALL other power structures are subservient to the religion. It is a new idea, and one that has not totally figured itself out yet, even in the Iranian example, but the concept is finding fertile ground in many Islamic countries around the globe.

As you might expect within these states, religious law or biblical/religious text law is the state's law. This is of particular significance for Muslim states, as there are lots of folks around the planet in Muslim countries who would like to see their countries become theocracies. In doing so, they want to enact religious law as their state law. The Muslim manifestation of this is something called **sharia.** Sharia law is Koranic law: the laws and punishments described in the Islamic holy text, the Koran. The big problem with this, and why I'm pointing this out in this section, is because this is becoming a world issue. There are very few states in the world that have just Muslim people in them, or just *any* single ethnic group, or just *any* single religious group. To adopt the religious law as state law means to enforce that religious law on people who possibly are not of that religion. In their defense, many proponents of sharia would argue that western democracies embrace biblical law as a major component of their legal systems, and that is a valid point. Thou shall not kill, and all those other 10 Commandments is the basis for western law, so what's the difference? We'll look at this in more detail when we look at the Middle East and Sub-Saharan Africa, as this is a particular problem in Nigeria and the **Sahel**. But we need to finish off our political systems. Let's go further right to . . .

MONARCHY

Now these are getting extremely easy. **Monarchies** are the royal families, who, by the blessing of God, are smarter and better than all the peasants within the country that they lead. To be honest, this has been the most important and utilized system of human rule for the better part of human history. The emperors of China, the Shahs of Iran, the Maharajahs of India, the Sultans of the Ottoman Empire: all family lineage positions of leadership. And don't forgot those wacky Euro-duders! This used to be all the rage in Europe; everybody loved their monarchs in Europe. In fact, those

Royal goobers: A dying breed. Sultan of Brunei and King of Saudi Arabia

chip-eating, goober British still love their monarchs so much that they still have them there, hanging out, even though they have no real power (i.e. constitutional monarchies). If you want to get into a good fight in Australia, just make fun of the Queen of England. For whatever reason, there is a strong attachment to this idea, an idea that the Plaid Avenger not only finds preposterous, but quite frankly, revolting. The concept that, at birth, someone is better than me and has the power by the blessing of God to rule me, I find repugnant.

We don't have to describe the system any further; it's simple. The original royal family touched by the divine hand of The Creator and reinforced papal decree, they begat some sons and daughters, creating the kings and queens who are far superior to us mortals. They get to rule until they beget more sons, who beget more sons; and pretty soon, they're all begetting each other, and that's why half of them are insane anyway. What is the power structure of the state? Why, it exists for the frolicking and pomp and circumstance of the crown-wearers, of course! By your leave, your majesty? Yeah, I'll leave you something of great majesty—my plaid boot in your hind-quarters! In states ascribing to monarchy, the royal family has all the political power. Back off, peasants.

There is one important point to make about this government type: it was repudiation and disgust with monarchy that led to the creation of most of those systems to the left of it on our spectrum. The concept of "divine" rights reserved for this elite group of people, particularly the rights to rule the rest of us, became so infuriating to so many on the planet that it became the catalyst for revolutionary thinking—thinking that created a lot of the other government types that we just talked about. Democracy (as we know it today), communism, Marxism, socialism, and probably a handful of other –isms on the left side came about because people were so ticked off and tired of the monarchy system which dominated Europe at the time.

Can anyone think of any examples of this? Oh, how about the United States of America? Yeah, they had a revolution and kicked those tea-sipping suckers out. Later on, the French took their fight one bloody step further than the Americans did by outright killing their royals during the French Revolution. Vladimir Lenin and his commie crew assassinated the royal family as part of the Communist Revolution. Wrap your head around this idea in particular: many of the alternate systems of government around the world today are the rebellious progeny of former monarchies. Before we go any further, let's point out that democracy is an ancient concept; Socrates and the other philosophizing Greeks came up with this stuff long ago. However, democracy in its modern form, in its modern manifestation on the planet, was a result of aversion to monarchy, as was communism. Monarchy is top-down, power-concentrated concept all the way around, but there are some other political systems that leave a worse taste in the Plaid Avenger's mouth, like military governments.

MILITARY GOVERNMENTS

Military governments are exactly what they say they are: governments run by people with guns. Every country on the planet has a military, or something that looks extremely similar to a military. Maybe called a self-defense force, or an emergency reserve, or a ground self-defense force, or a national guard—places like Japan and Costa Rica don't have an "official" military. Whatever name it goes by, the military in most states is subservient to the central government. That is, it's there for national defense, maybe even to internally put down revolts, but it works for, or at the request of, the government. Typically, the head of the state is also the ultimate commander of the military, but is not active militarily. Typically.

My guns are bigger than the politicians!

However, in states run by a military government, the military has actually superseded the political leaders. Often a small group of military elites takes over effective, real control of the government, directly or indirectly, by military coup. The best examples of this on the planet today are places like Egypt, Sudan, and Fiji. In those states, people who are from a military background, or are still active in the military, have wiped out the government for whatever reasons—maybe the government was corrupt, maybe as a move for national security—and have taken control. Does this mean they control everything and everyone at gunpoint? Not necessarily, but the military is the true power in any country.

I know this is confusing. People in the United States might say, "No, not here," but just ask yourself this—if the entire military of the United States wanted to take over the country, could they? Well, obviously, but we have laws and stuff in place here that all of us, including the military, respect. Their role is to serve, and to uphold the law. In other parts of the world, that's gotten a little fuzzy. Governments are taken over by military dictatorships. The government may continue to run as a functional entity, and we would say, "Hey, they've got a senate or legislature; they have courts," but the real power is from a small group of people, and if it's a singular person, we typically refer to them as a military dictator. If it's a group of military people, we would typically refer to them as a **junta**. There are several of these around the world that are still quite active today. Of particular note in current events in Egypt: After the country rose up in the Arab Spring of 2011, they toppled the one-party state of Hosni Mubarak—himself having taken power as part of a military government decades earlier. The people who then took over sucked so bad, a military junta threw them out in 2014! What a political power roller coaster! Other folks like Muammar Qaddafi, the former leader of Libya, may look like kindly old gentlemen, but check out his resumé. Yep, he's only had one job as leader of the military, and then later he picked up the "leader of the country" title. Then in the same Arab Spring alluded to above, he was granted the title of "dead" when his peeps toppled the goverment and took off his head. When military governments get particularly nasty, they can turn quickly into full-on dictatorships.

Muammar: So sad. Such a photogenic dictator, now dust.

DICTATORSHIP

Dictatorships are typically, but not always, started as military governments, where the military has taken over for whatever reason. A central strong figure rises from the ranks, and, sometimes through cults of personality, sometimes through brute force, become the sole leader of the country. A true dictatorship exists when all decision making occurs at one individual's whim.

He has the final say on all laws, all actions, all everything. The state apparatus functions only through him. For example, Hitler said, "I am the state," and he meant it! He

Saddam and Mugabe: They held all the cards!

decided if they were going to invade another country, or what the tax system would look like, or what rights individuals had. It's usually implemented by force of the military, but that's not the defining feature—it's the singular person holding all the cards that sets it apart. It can be military, or it could be religious—these lines get fuzzy. We can say the Ayatollah kind of looks like a religious dictator, and perhaps that's kind of true, but even he has a group of religious folks who work for him that have to come to a consensus on certain things. That does not exist in a true dictatorship, where a single guy has all the power.

The best example of this in the modern world was Saddam Hussein, currently residing somewhere in Hell. He was a single dude, insulated by a cult of personality, who built up and protected his power through use of force. There are other active ones, like the president of Zimbabwe, Robert Mugabe. Mugabe—and again, all dictators are not active military, although he started as a military guy—was a rebel leader who helped fight off the colonial powers, helped liberate his country into independence, and originally was a hero. He was elected, assumed elected power, and then over the years and decades, he consolidated that power and just couldn't seem to get enough of it. After thirty years, he holds all the cards. One man, with all the power; that's a dictatorship. He has refused to give up power, as is often the case in these scenarios, particularly in Africa. Power seems to ultimately corrupt, and the longer you hold on to it, the greater the hunger for it, like "the one true ring" that Bilbo Baggins found. But I digress. Those filthy hobbits always get me off track!

The point here is that dictators can come from a variety of backgrounds, often military, but not necessarily. We might have the tendency to look at Fidel Castro as a dictator. This leads to some questions about a dictator vs. a fascist.

FASCISM

As has already been reflected in the extreme left, anarchy doesn't exist anywhere. **Fascism** doesn't really exist in today's world either. What separates fascism from dictatorship? A very thin line, I suppose. What the Plaid Avenger calls the manifestation of true fascism is that it *is* kind of a true dictatorship, but it's a dictatorship that's not necessarily perpetuated by the use of force. In other words, it's typically a cult of personality. It is a dictator—it is one person with all the cards—but one who has been put there because people like him so much. He's put there by popular mandate.

ANOTHER PLAID AVENGER INSIDE TIP: Neither Hitler nor Stalin drank alcohol. Both were teetotalers in societies well-known for their drinking habits. Think about it.

The State of States
CHAPTER THREE

I am the State!

This is where your best examples are Adolf Hitler and Benito Mussolini, perhaps the only real examples in modern history. While we consider most of their dictatorial actions pretty bad in hindsight, at the time, they were very popular within their countries. They were rulers of the military, but they did not need the military to maintain control, nor to gain power originally. Hitler certainly was the leader of the military, and certainly using that military knocked the living crap out of Europe. But, in his rise to power, he did not hold the Germans under the sway of the gun and say, "I want you to agree to all these policies."

Famous fascists biting off more than they could chew.

Most people just said, "We think you're great, do whatever you want, this is awesome!" Then Hitler got the smack-down, committed suicide in a ditch, and that was pretty much that.

Let's face it: fascism sucks on every level. On the one hand, you have a generally charismatic leader (who is a few fruit loops short of a complete breakfast) who rises to power by mentally mesmerizing a bunch of needy folks who are only looking for a solution to their miserable lives. On the other hand, you have a large population of people who more or less blindly allow their government to get away with ultimately controlling their lives while destroying the lives of others. And that story always seems to have a happy ending. Or not. Ever.

SO WHO IS WHAT, AND WHERE?

Check out the map in Figure 3.4 of current political systems around the globe. Can we detect any patterns? Any problems? Regional variation? As you can see, we have some dominant political systems with some variations on theme from region to region all around our governed globe. . . .

FIGURE 3.4 POLITICAL SYSTEMS OF THE WORLD

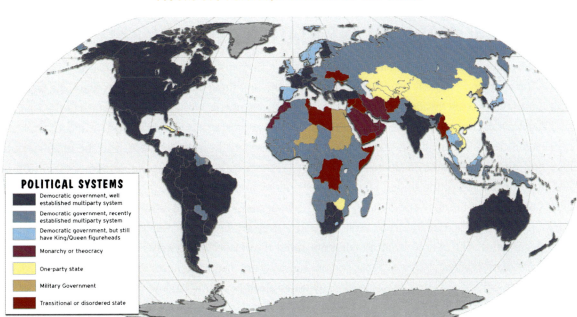

Look at the Americas. All of North America is staunchly democratic with a well-established government. Europe is also staunchly democratic with well-established governments—even the ones that still have kings and queens hanging around. As previously referenced, call them **constitutional monarchies**, but the kings and queens have no real power, they are simply figureheads; old habits die hard. Virtually all of Latin America is also staunchly, long-term democratic. India is the largest democratic nation on the planet, and places like Japan and the UK are considered staunch democracies despite the continues presence of their figurehead monarchs. Don't forget about Turkey, easily the most die-hard democracy on the planet that happens to be totally composed of followers of Islam.

New or newly established democracies on the planet are found in Eastern Europe and Russia. Since the fall of the Soviet Union, they've embraced democracy, but they are still what we call in transition, only about ten to twenty years old. Most of Africa, both in the Middle Eastern sections and sub-Saharan Africa, is sort of in the democracy column, but they are kind of new as well . . . of course with the 2011–12 "Arab Spring" that has occurred across many states of the Middle East, we may see true democracy blooming, but it is still too early to call on how it will turn out. And if we want to summarize the rest of sub-Saharan Africa, there's a little bit of everything going on down there. There are some chaotic states, some military dictatorships, some new democracies, and a couple of old democracies; it's quite the patchwork quilt. The Middle East is characterized by a patchwork quilt of a different flavor: they have most of the theocracies and true monarchies on the planet. Iran is a theocracy, but Saudi Arabia, Yemen, and Morocco have some true old-school kings and queens still in charge.

We get to Central Asia to find a real crapshoot. Some states have put up the new democracy façade, but it's too new and too close to call which way they are going. One of the themes we'll talk about in Central Asia is that they're kind of leaning back toward one-party states. Folks are getting in charge there and hemming up power and staying in control. Of course, we get around to places like Southeast Asia; they've got a little bit of everything. Some places are staunchly democratic, like the Philippines. Some places are in rapid transition, like in Burma where a military dictatorship suddenly broke out into a democracy! And then there's every place in between: some choas in Thailand, some hold-out commies in Vietnam running a one-party state.

In East Asia, we have China, which is definitely a one-party state. I know that the Communist China label is confusing to a lot of people because politically, they have a party called the Communist Party, and that is the party that is in charge, but they are not an economically communist state. Therefore, it's better classified as a one-party state. North Korea is definitely a distinct crazy wacko one-party/dictator state, perhaps better described as a one-psycho state, and South Korea is just the opposite, a staunchly democratic place. That's just a quick summary of what's going on politically in the world. We'll go into more detail about this in each of our regions.

A FINAL WORD ON THE STATE OF STATES

A few general points to consider across the planet here in the dawn of the 21st century:

The number of states is actually growing. That's the first thing to consider. Why is that? The bigger entities are breaking down into smaller ones. Smaller entities perhaps better fit the people within (e.g., the demise of the Soviet Union, the breakdown of Yugoslavia). The best example of all is the division of Czechoslovakia into a Czech state and a Slovak state.

The other main trend to consider is the demise of communism in the global sphere, and the movement away from dictatorships and one-party states to democracies. That is, there is a growing trend of democratization across the planet, something the leaders of the United States are very happy about and promote, of course. You can see this particularly in places like Eastern Europe—the Ukrainian and the Georgian Revolutions, respectively referred to as the Orange and Rose Revolutions. Afghanistan and Iraq? Well, I suppose they are heading towards a democracy, even if it has to be implemented at gunpoint. This whole 'Arab Revolution' thing that is occurring across the Middle East may result in a whole slew of new democracies . . . or at least something different from the autocratic, rightist ruling regimes of the past. Still too early to call on that one, as some like Egypt are already sliding back to military rule, and others like Syria are in full-on civil war.

A minor trend of which you should also be aware: the Iranian experiment with theocracy is both new to the world stage, and being exported abroad. Other states with large Islamic populations may be gravitating towards this system of government. I should say the *people* in those states are interested in some form of theocracy, but certainly not the current governments of those states who like the power structure that has them in the driver's seat right now, thank you very much. One need only look to an extreme manifestation of theocracy, the Taliban in Afghanistan, to see that this idea is not just an Iranian thing. There are also numerous political parties in virtually all Muslim states, from Nigeria to Egypt to Saudi Arabia to Pakistan to Indonesia, which are pushing for a ruling system along the lines of the Iranian model.

The number of states and the number of democracies are on the rise, but we need to know a little more. The Plaid Avenger has put together a little high school yearbook of faces for you to identify, memorize, and be able to recognize if you pass them on the street. These are good people to know—not because they are necessarily good people, but because knowing them will make you a savvy global citizen. This yearbook is certainly not exhaustive, but contains particular faces that will be movers and shakers, newsmakers, and deal-breakers in the year to come. Know them well, my plaid friends, and join the ranks of those in the know, globally speaking. I've provided the names and places. You figure out who is who, and to which type of government they belong. I've provided some superlatives as clues to help you on your way. Good luck!

You simply must know your heads of state to be globally cool.

THE PLAID AVENGER WORLD YEARBOOK

Names	Places	Government Types
Kim Jong-Un	Iran	Established Democracy
Omar al-Bashir	Australia	Young Democracy
Abdullah bin Abdul Aziz Al Saud	Russia	One-Party State
Angela Merkel	South Korea	Theocracy
Xi Jinping	Mexico	Monarchy
Recep Erdogan	Zimbabwe	Dictator
Enrique Peña Nieto	Israel	Anarchy
David Cameron	Afghanistan	Communism
Barack Obama	North Korea	Fascism
Narendra Modi	Tibet	State of Insanity
Dilma Rousseff	Saudi Arabia	
Nicolás Maduro	Germany	
François Hollande	China	
Jacob Zuma	Turkey	
Viktor Yanukovych	Sudan	
Hassan Rouhani	United Kingdom	
Tony Abbott	United States	
Vladimir Putin	India	
Park Geun-hye	Brazil	
The Dalai Lama	Venezuela	
Robert Mugabe	Japan	
Shinzō Abe	France	
Hamid Karzai	Ukraine	
Benjamin Netanyahu	South Africa	

Understanding the Plaid Planet
PART ONE

Most Likely to Fahrvergnügen

Chancellor _____
State: _____
Type of Gov't: _____

Chinese-iest

President _____
State: _____
Type of Gov't: _____

Globally Most Wanted (Arrest Warrant Issued)

President _____
State: _____
Type of Gov't: _____

Fish n' Chipiest

Prime Minister _____
State: _____
Type of Gov't: _____

The Other, Other White Meat

Prime Minister _____
State: _____
Type of Gov't: _____

The Most Popular Politician on the Planet

President _____
State: _____
Type of Gov't: _____

Most Likely to "Curry" Favor with Investors

Prime Minister _____
State: _____
Type of Gov't: _____

Cleanest Linens

King _____
State: _____
Type of Gov't: _____

Most Likely to Lambada

President _____
State: _____
Type of Gov't: _____

Socialist Sledgehammer

President _____
State: _____
Type of Gov't: _____

Most Likely to Run Screaming from a Large Lizard Creature Who was Awakened from Its Underwater Slumber

Prime Minister _____
State: _____
Type of Gov't: _____

Most Likely to Surrender

President _____
State: _____
Type of Gov't: _____

The State of States
CHAPTER THREE

Most Likely to be Mistaken for the Kid from "Up"

Great Successor _____
State: _____
Type of Gov't: _____

Most Mod American Amigo

President _____
State: _____
Type of Gov't: _____

Most Likely to Forgive

President _____
State: _____
Type of Gov't: _____

Most Likely to Eat Vegemite, Crikey!

Prime Minister _____
State: _____
Type of Gov't: _____

Most Moderate and-Modernizing Muslim-

President _____
State: _____
Type of Gov't: _____

Most Likely to Judo-Chop a Bear

Prime Minister _____
State: _____
Type of Gov't: _____

Most Potent Polygamist (Has 20 Kids!)

President _____
State: _____
Type of Gov't: _____

Most Likely to Tae Kwon Do

President _____
State: _____
Type of Gov't: _____

Most Reincarnated

President _____
State: _____
Type of Gov't: _____

Most Kosher

Prime Minister _____
State: _____
Type of Gov't: _____

Most Likely to Instigate an Economic Implosion

President _____
State: _____
Type of Gov't: _____

Most Likely to Not Survive Until the Next Edition of This Book

President _____
State: _____
Type of Gov't: _____

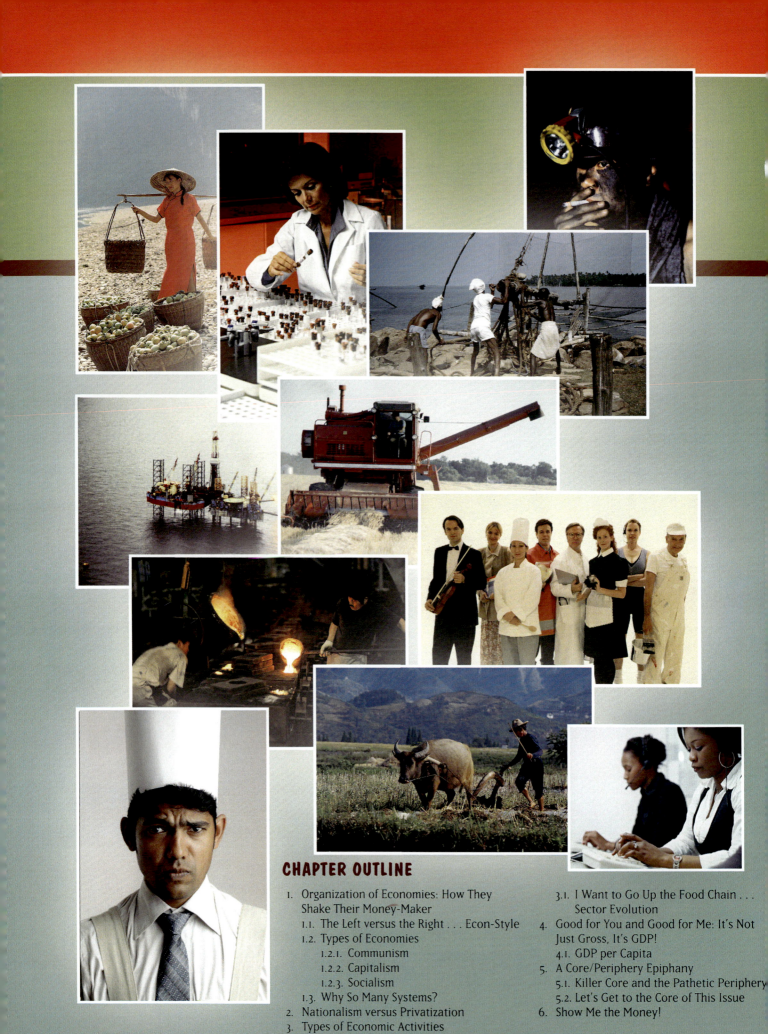

CHAPTER OUTLINE

1. Organization of Economies: How They Shake Their Money-Maker
    1.1. The Left versus the Right . . . Econ-Style
    1.2. Types of Economies
        1.2.1. Communism
        1.2.2. Capitalism
        1.2.3. Socialism
    1.3. Why So Many Systems?
2. Nationalism versus Privatization
3. Types of Economic Activities
    3.1. I Want to Go Up the Food Chain . . . Sector Evolution
4. Good for You and Good for Me: It's Not Just Gross, It's GDP!
    4.1. GDP per Capita
5. A Core/Periphery Epiphany
    5.1. Killer Core and the Pathetic Periphery
    5.2. Let's Get to the Core of This Issue
6. Show Me the Money!

The Plaid World Economy

OK we talked about people on the planet, where they are, how many there are, and how they procreate. We then looked where people live, the state, and how they are ruled within that state. Now let's look at what people do. People like to eat. People like to buy clothes. People like to buy services. People like to buy stuff for the kids. People like to buy stuff for themselves. For all this stuff people want to buy on the planet, they have to have money to do it. All this buying and selling of stuff worldwide makes the economic world go round. So how do people make money in the world? Of course, we don't want to look at each individual person; we want to look at the entire state. How does the state make money? What is going on in the global economy? Let's talk dollars and sense about world economic systems, shall we?

ORGANIZATION OF ECONOMIES: HOW THEY SHAKE THEIR MONEY-MAKER

First, we have to look at the overall organization of the economy within each state, and subsequently each region. We are going to revisit a theme we talked about last chapter: the left versus the right. There's a left and a right in political systems and there's left and right in terms of social idealism; there's also a left and right spectrum when it comes to economies. What does it mean in the economic context when we refer to the left versus right?

THE LEFT VERSUS THE RIGHT . . . ECON-STYLE

Often, you see terms such as communism versus capitalism in the economic spectrum and indeed that's a good place to start. Think about the Cold War. Not only was it the "free" democracies versus the "evil" communist in terms of politics, but was also defined as "free market" capitalism versus communist "command economy."

When we talked about the left versus the right politically, we defined things like communism as a system that was all about the individual, wherein the state was functioning in a capacity to serve the individual: the state exists only to serve the people. The opposite, right side of that politic

Communism

Socialism

Capitalism

← INCREASING GOVERNMENT CONTROL   DECREASING GOVERNMENT CONTROL →

spectrum was exemplified by a person or small group of people at the top that had all the power and the state (the people, that is) worked for them. We can kind of look at this similarly on the economic spectrum by discussing how many/few peeps have the economic power, and how much the government plays a role in manipulating the economy.

TYPES OF ECONOMIES

COMMUNISM

We'll start on the extreme left, just like the last chapter, which makes sense since communism is at once a political system and an economic system all rolled into one. In the economic sense, communism refers to a society where everything in the state is owned, possessed, controlled and operated by the government. What? I thought you just said that 'the left' was all about the people having all the power? I know it is confusing, but dig this: the government in a true communist society simply controls all these things in the name of the people. The commie interpretation is that all the people in the state *are* the state, and thus are the true owners of everything. The government is simply composed of a small group of people that are passing all the stuff out to you, as you need it, because it's your stuff. Bottom line: all stuff is public stuff; no private ownership of anything allowed.

What stuff are we talking about here? All the goods, all of the services, all of the resources, all the land, and all the factories/means of production. Everything. With resources, it's pretty obvious: all the oil, all the wheat, all the coal, all the gold, all the forest, all the land—which is an important one. Means of production include all the factories and processing plants, all the plants that make cars, and tanks, and refrigerators, and light bulbs. Everything is owned and dolled out by the state. This includes all services too . . . the doctors and lawyers and building contractors . . . all those services would also be organized by the state and handed out to the peoples as they are needed. So in the big picture, the farmer grows food that the state redistributes to factory workers and doctors, and the factories make tractors that are given to the farmers to grow that food, and the farmers and factory workers get free health care from the doctors when they need it. Everybody in the society working together as a team, each getting what they need while helping fulfill the needs of others. And the state is in charge of all these transactions.

Again, the state is doing this *for* the people; all the people truly own all the stuff. People, people, people. Why do I keep reiterating that the people own all this stuff in a communist system? Because it don't freakin' work—never has, never will. It's a farce; it's just an abstract idea on how to create a "fair" economy. As we already referenced in the last chapter, communism has never manifested itself truly in this way—in fact, it has never even come close. Every attempt at it has gone awry. A small group of folks have gained power in order to make the transition to the commie utopia, but it has never worked, because money and power ultimately (and sometimes quickly) corrupt the small group of people in charge.

In addition, an entire economy—of even the smallest state—has way too many variables to try to control through a central administration, and winds up being more complicated than any small group can handle. The Russian description of this experience was **command economy**. You can see, just from the words themselves, that the government attempted to control and thus command all aspects of everything. A tall order for even the smartest and least corrupt.

Corruption and complication have combined to make pure communism pretty much an abject failure everywhere it has been attempted. True, pure economic communism is, on paper, possession of everything by everyone. In the real world, it never gets remotely close to that.

Confusing commie points:

→ Communism is both a political and economic term because it combines politics and economics into one system in which ownership of all property is communal.

→ You may think, and correctly so, that Russian communism's political and economic power was very concentrated in the hands of few. This was supposed to be a temporary position while they "fixed" the economy to a true communist utopia. As you now know, they never got it right.

→ Even in today's world you hear references to "Communist China," "Communist Cuba," or even "Communist Vietnam." Make no mistakes about it, my plaid friends: these countries' economies are much more capitalist in nature. Their political leadership may still be called "communist," their economies are def not.

CAPITALISM

Let's head right to the other extreme. On the other side of the spectrum is something of which we are much more familiar: **capitalism**. In capitalist society, all the resources, all the stuff, all the oil, all the land, all the fish, gold, and all the means of production, all the factories, all the car plants, all the doctor's offices are owned by private individuals. **Private ownership** is the key in a purely capitalist society.

Where did this system come from? Capitalism is an amazingly popular and resilient system, mostly because it happens quite naturally. Humans naturally gravitate towards marking off territory and claiming stuff. There is also an inherent agreement that the harder you work and the more risks you take, the more money you should accrue, or at least deserve to accrue. Everybody takes care of themselves, and in doing so, the economy takes care of itself. What this equates to over time is ownership by the few—which reinforces why these systems are on opposite sides of the spectrum. In a communist society, everybody owns everything; in a capitalist one, just a percentage of the population owns things.

Hard-core capitalists would argue for free trade, for free markets, and for minimal government intervention. "Let the market forces run their course" is a mantra of the capitalist. However, in a purely capitalist system in which the government plays no role, it would pretty much be every man for himself. Dog eat dog world. Only the strong, smart, and/or rich survive. Wealth would continue to be further and further concentrated into fewer and fewer hands. That would eventually equate to large segments of the society as destitute, impoverished, uneducated, and perhaps even unemployed. Is that a society that anyone wants? Probably not. Thus . . .

Just like communism, where does true capitalism exist? Nowhere. We live in a predominately capitalist world and capitalism is a popular system on the planet right now. But where does a *purely* capitalist or a *pure* communist state exist? Not anywhere, because virtually every place on the planet is in the middle. What is in the middle? Socialism. That's next.

Confusing capitalist points:

→ We think that all the rich countries, and even many of the poor ones, are pure capitalist societies. Pure capitalism is an extreme in which the central government of the state plays absolutely no part in the economy. This is not true anywhere on the planet, not even in the US which is resoundingly the biggest proponent of capitalist expression on the globe. Even "heavily" capitalist countries like the US or Germany provide some services and benefits to their peeps, and regulate businesses at least a little.

→ Even hard-core capitalist countries end up having anti-monopoly laws for big businesses. Why? Because if businesses and capitalist entities are extremely successful, they will keep getting bigger and bigger and absorbing other businesses until their power becomes unchecked, and uncheckable. Isn't that what pure capitalism is all about? Indeed. But no state wants to become second fiddle to a corporation. And "too big to fail" is becoming too dangerous to be be sustained.

→ We like to think of the capitalist system as the "best" or most equal or even the most catering towards individual rights because everyone has an equal opportunity to own the stuff. However, having the same opportunity does not make for equal, or even fair, distribution of stuff. In the end, capitalism will concentrate wealth into fewer hands—many would say this is appropriately based on how smart you are, level of skill, your hard work, etc. Others say that concentration of wealth perpetuates stagnation in the masses, as idiot-savant kids inherit all the wealth from their rich mommies and daddies (sorry country-clubbers!) and opportunities to access that wealth by the masses becomes diminished. What do you think?

SOCIALISM

Now I know some of you ardent conservatives are saying to yourselves right now, "Blasphemy! There is no such thing as socialism in the US. We're not socialists here in this country; that's a bad word! Socialism is just sommunism in disguise!" But I'm here to tell you that when we're looking at things economically on the planet, virtually everybody is somewhere in the socialist sphere. Having said that, there is a broad range of what it means to be socialist and it goes all the way from close to the extreme left to close to the extreme right. In other words, that's where everybody really is: in a shade of socialism. And there are many, many shades. They all have the root of the word in their interpretation: *social*. In other words, they look out for, or have some role in, the societies over which they rule; societies made up of people.

What is economic socialism? You might have figured this out already: it's somewhere between the extremes. That is, the government (i.e., the state), owns *some* stuff and controls *some* stuff, maybe some lands, industries, maybe some of the resources. At the same time, private interests or private individuals own *some* stuff as well: some oil, some factories, some lands, and indeed, that's pretty much where the world is at this moment in time. Let's delve into this in a little more detail.

Why would the state want to control any of this economic stuff? Short answer: to provide services for its peoples. Even the most ardent capitalist would agree that the state should provide things like an army to defend the country, and maybe road systems or postal systems to facilitate economic growth. Others in a society think that the state should do a whole lot more, like provide social security, welfare systems, and unemployment benefits, maybe even health care. Different states provide different amounts of these things to their peeps.

In either case, how is the state going to pay for these things? Another short answer: by way of resource/industry control or collecting taxes, or some combination of both. Some states are very heavy-handed in this approach, perhaps controlling the most lucrative industry in its entirety . . . like in the state operated oil industries of Saudi Arabia or Venezuela. Other states like the US make some money from resources (mostly by selling the rights to drill to private companies) and some money from taxation. Other states, like Sweden, tax the living daylights out of everybody to make money. Different states have different approaches to making money. Look at the graphic below to see what I'm talking about.

Confusing socialist points:

- Socialism comes in many packages; you may see references to **democratic socialism**, or **social democracy**, or mixed systems which are prevalent in Western Europe and increasingly prevalent in Latin America.
- Socialism can refer to heavy state ownership and control of some industries—the South American model. Socialism can also refer to states that generate revenue by heavy taxation in order to provide lots of services to citizens—the European model.
- The term is often misused by the conservative right in the US who confuse regulation of certain aspects of the economy with government ownership of business—you will see this when any laws are passed which limit big businesses in any way; those on the right will say the US is drifting into socialism. You may also have heard "socialism" used a lot when when the Obama administration was passing its health care legislation in 2010.
- Even though the US and many other states control/own aspects of their economy, we still refer to them as "capitalist" simply because they are more toward the right side of this spectrum. Conversely, places like Venezuela are openly referred to as "socialist" because they are much closer to the left side of the spectrum, as they control many more aspects of the economy. Well, that and the fact that they call themselves socialists.

Let's look at this spectrum from left to right again in terms of some active interpretations of this socialist sphere because really, the entire planet is somewhere in here—albeit in varying degrees.

If we think of all-the-way-left commies like Lenin, we see the attempted manifestation of true communism. He wanted the state to control everything in order to provide all stuff and all services to all the people all the time. He died. Didn't work out so well in the long-term, or the short-term, or really any term in between.

Extreme Left, Full State Control . . .   . . . increasing government control of the economy

The Plaid World Economy

CHAPTER FOUR

Castro is the modern-day Leninist attempt at communism. In Cuba's case, the state does control quite a bit; all of the resources in Cuba are owned supposedly 'by the people' and are administered and controlled by the government 'for the people'. But it's not working out so well, and there is a large underground free-market/black-market economy at work to supplement the services and stuff that is supposed to be supplied by the government, but is not—because they're broke.

King Abdullah and Nicolas Madura are slightly more to the right. Neither embraces communism, and indeed there are a lot of private businesses and private ownership in their countries. However, in both cases, the state controls the extremely lucrative oil industries and uses the profits generated from oil to provide all sorts of services to their people. Saudi Arabia happens to be a little bit better at it right this second, and everything from health care to education is provided to its citizens. Maduro's Venezuela has been trying to duplicate that model, but starting to stumble badly in the process. However, the 'socialist' cause is widely supported by the poor people because of the propaganda, which promises more stuff to the masses.

Hu Jintao's China comes next, even though it is supposedly a communist state that one would assume should be on the extreme left side of this spectrum. Not so. China initiated capitalist reforms for the last three decades and privatization ensued, but the government does still play a heavy hand in many industries and policies, although they continue to move quickly to the left side of this spectrum. Next we see Vladimir "the man" Putin from Russia. What? Russia? They were the center of the commie sphere! How can they be 'right of center' now? Because they fully embraced the capitalist way after the collapse of the USSR, and they did it with such a vengeance that it became a "wild west" of capitalism. Most things went into private ownership, and the government became so broke that it could not provide all those services that it once did. As a result, Russia has since re-taken control of its lucrative oil industry once more, leaning back towards the left side of the spectrum. More on that later. This is the classic example of how the world as a whole is firmly capitalist in outlook, even if the individual states exhibit varying characteristics of socialism.

We can go a little bit further to the right and we get perhaps a lot of European states like Sweden, France, and Norway that—while they don't control a lot of resources outright—heavily tax luxury items like cars in order to raise revenue to supply stuff to their citizens. In Sweden, (I'm picking on Sweden in particular because everybody likes those boxy Swedish cars, the Volvos) almost no one can own a Volvo because the government taxes the heck out of them. Why do they do this? It's considered a luxury good like alcohol or mink furs. They heavily tax those items to raise revenue, because they supply some serious services to their citizens. When a woman has a baby in Sweden, she gets two years off—PAID—maternity leave. Two years? Paid? Wow. In the US, women get like two hours off after having a child. Then it's "Okay, it's out. Get cleaned up, and get back to work! And by the way, those sheets you messed up, yeah, we're gonna have to get five hundred bucks from ya for those. Thanks bunches."

Now we're on familiar ground. The US is certainly much closer to the purely capitalist camp, but through limited resource control and taxation does provide a lot of services to the people. Quite a bit, actually, but not as much as many European states or even Canada, which has free health care. None of the government activities of the developed countries would be considered resource re-allocation, as maybe we would define activities in Venezuela or Cuba, but a lot of stuff is provided to the citizens nonetheless. Ever heard of welfare or retirement benefits, or public shcools?

. . . decreasing government control of economy . . . to the Right, Full Private Control

It is always up for debate in the US between Republicans and Democrats as to how many of these services the government should supply. In fact, it's one of the main dividing lines between these two parties. Republicans are considered as favoring big business because they support free market, free trade, and privatization of perhaps all government services. Democrats are typically associated with wanting the government to provide these services, and maybe even more. This issue is evident in the Republican effort to repeal "Obama-care," which is a heavy state regulation and restructuring of health care in the US . . . but not a "socialist" government nationalization of the entire health care industry, as described by its opponents. This comes on the heels of President Obama partially nationalizing some banks and even auto manufacturers as the economic meltdown unfolded in 2008. Hmmm . . . tricky business for the undisputed champion of free market capitalism.

Adam Smith rounds out our line-up on the extreme capitalist right, and he is here intentionally as the symbol of pure capitalism—he is the dude that wrote *Wealth of Nations* in 1776, the handbook on how and why to keep governments out of the economy altogether. Because as I've already pointed out, pure capitalism doesn't exist anywhere. And Mr. Smith is long since dead, so he doesn't exist anywhere either. No state on the planet does nothing for its people—because that's actually a really good way to get thrown out of office, chucked off the throne, and/or guillotined.

WHY SO MANY SYSTEMS?

Speaking of getting guillotined, (were we?), where did these systems come from? Just like the concentration of political power in the hands of a few was the undoing of monarchy in Europe, there was the same type of impetus in the economic systems. This largely arose because of the Industrial Revolution. The **Industrial Revolution**, as it occurred in the 17th, 18th, and 19th century European experience, enabled a vast concentration of wealth in the hands of the few industrialists—the factory owners—and simultaneously pathetic circumstances for the peasants, the peons—the factory workers.

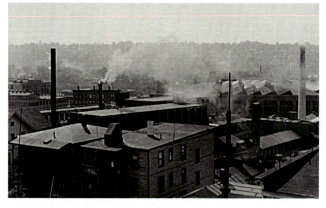
Industrialization: Rise of the Machines. And concentrations of wealth.

During this societal evolution, there were not many laws; in fact, they were nonexistent for things like child labor or workplace safety or minimum wages. The industrialists were all for the 195 hour work week—hey, that sounds good. How about we only pay people a dime a day? That sounds good too! Five-year-olds working in the factory? Why not? Got to give the little people something to do!

What you had was unregulated growth and crappy working conditions that really tested the limits of what societies would tolerate. Needless to say, this really pissed off lots of people and got them thinking about possible alternative systems to unregulated capitalism. Marx and Engels, and then Lenin and others, thought, "Hey, this is unfair. These few factory owners have concentrated wealth and power. And we are powerless." This sentiment was not unlike the active aversion felt by peoples ruled under monarchies at the time as well. Result? Marxism, communism, socialism, and perhaps a few more –isms I don't even know about, were created to offer other options. These new economic systems evolved to offer alternatives to the unchecked power of capitalism—just like alternative government types evolved to counter unchecked power of monarchy at the time. And now, strangely enough, we have come full-circle. Whereas many of these systems originally evolved to check concentration of power and wealth in state systems, the states are now looked to by many to help counter wealth and power which has accumulated somewhere else . . . where would that be? Answer: the corporation!

Corporations are a significant thing to consider, if for no other reason than they've kind of replaced governments as the true holders of real economic power on the planet. You have to understand this; governments were seen as holding all the real power 200 years ago, which fired up enough people who started revolutions to unseat or redistribute that power (e.g., **American Revolution**, **French Revolution**, **Russian Revolution**, etc.). In today's world, multinational corporations are seen as the real powers on the planet and thus we've had a kind of move from protesting against a government or saying, "Hey, this government is unfair, we should change it or do something about it," to "Hey, this

What Is the Deal with . . . Multinational Corporations?

An executive with Dow Chemical recently said, "I have long dreamed of buying an island owned by no nation and of establishing the World Headquarters of the Dow Company on the truly neutral ground of such an island, beholden to no nation or society." Such is the story of multinational corporations. For most of history, the world economy has been controlled by nation-states. They made the rules, set taxes, and imposed regulations and corporations had to follow them. This is changing.

In today's world of globalization, multinationals have become the primary actors in the world economy. Free trade agreements are reducing the barriers for companies to operate in other countries, and the global economy is becoming more interdependent. Many countries want multinational corporations to do business within their borders because they boost the local economy, bring jobs, and pay taxes. Therefore, countries, and even regions of the world, compete with each other to attract multinational corporations by offering tax breaks, lax environmental or labor standards, and improved infrastructure. Multinational corporations may have their headquarters in one country, but they do business in multiple countries of their choosing. In this way, the multinationals now make the rules.

Multinational corporations, which include Exxon, Microsoft, Pepsi, and Nintendo, have become very powerful; some of them have higher revenues than most sovereign states. However, they also have their critics. Nationalists and patriots are suspicious of them because they think that all they care about is making money (corporations would never do that!) and taking advantage of the host country. Antiglobalization protesters claim that the great power the multinationals wield is forcing countries to bend over backwards to please them by doing things like looking the other way when they ruin the environment or take advantage of poor people. There have been arguments that multinationals ruin local culture (so you won't be able to tell Cairo from Tokyo in a few years) and that they destroy local businesses because locals just can't compete with the big multinationals.

Fun Fact: Some consider the Dutch East India Company, founded in 1602, to be the first multinational company.

---

multinational corporation has all the power; they've got more money than our government does and they work outside the laws of our government because they're operating in ten or twelve different countries."

When you see protests against multinational corporations, or outcry against entities like the WTO, you are seeing a reaction to the idea that true power is not held solely by governments anymore. These protesters feel that the new oppressing force on the planet is not any particular state or government, but these powerful economic entities. In their opinion, real threats to human rights and human pursuit of happiness are made primarily by corporations. Now it appears that these multinational corporations are bigger, badder and hold more money than most states on the planet.

The result? People are turning to back state governments to counter the unchecked power of multinational corporations. Confusingly enough, the liberal movement started as anti–big government, and now in most countries is credited with being very pro–big government. How did that happen? Part of that answer lies in how the world has changed in the last few hundred years; 200 years ago, governments were the primary sources of all power, with economic entities like corporations running a very distant second. Is that how it is in today's world? Not hardly. The multinational and even just the national companies in our world have become the major powers, with governments running a close second. In this atmosphere, the liberal attitude has shifted from "liberating" people from an oppressive government to attempting to "liberate" them from the economic powers of today's world. They attempt to do this by using the powers of government to counter those of big business.

NATIONALISM VS. PRIVATIZATION

We need to further define a few terms that we've been tossing around here while describing all of these economic systems. You will see these terms frequently, and they often cause consternation for folks on either side of the economic spectrum. These forces in action have often been the cause of public unrest, strained international relations, and have even been the impetus for invading countries or assassinating leaders. What's the deal?

Nationalization is the state acquisition and operation of businesses previously owned and operated by private individuals or corporations. It is usually done in the name of social and economic equality, often as part of a communist or socialist doctrine. Nationalization of foreign owned property, like the Suez Canal by Egypt in 1958 or the copper mining industry by Chile in 1971, typically attempts to end foreign control of an industry or asset and poses complex problems for international law.

In other words, the state assumes control of an industry, kicks out owners/operators, and starts taking the profits to the state bank account. This seriously ticks off corporations, who in turn usually get their home government to kick up a fuss, take the case to an international arbitrator like the WTO, embargo the nationalizing state, or maybe even invade the country outright to get their stuff back. Sound preposterous? It's happened plenty in the last hundred years. France and Great Britain invaded Egypt to try to regain the Suez Canal, and the US has destabilized or overthrown whole governments in Chile, Guatemala and Cuba to satisfy pressures by corporations who fell victim to nationalization.

As you might have guessed already, **privatization** is just the opposite. Selling of businesses to private ownership after they have been the property of the state is the process of privatizing. Since the collapse of the USSR, Russia and all of its former areas of control have been in a mad scramble to privatize industries. But they are not alone. India and China are fertilized fields for mass privatizations, and the trend is still occurring in the developed world. Western European countries and Japan, who just privatized their postal service, continue to push more government operations to the private business sphere. In the US, the term has often been broadly applied to the practice of outsourcing the management of public schools, prisons, airports, sanitation services, and a variety of other government-owned institutions to private companies. Sometimes this contracting of services does not entail the outright sale of the industry to private hands.

Why the persuasive theme of privatization in the world? The popular argument is that government-run business is like a monopoly—and lack of competition makes the business not-so-productive and noncompetitive and wasteful, and maybe even ripe for corruption. That is certainly a valid point. The other reality is that bigger and bigger corporations have much more leverage than ever before in the past to put pressure on states to privatize. Who funds lobbying groups to persuade congressmen to privatize? Who has money to fund big studies that show that government operations are wasteful? Who would have the money to buy the senator a Ferrari for his teenage daughter's graduation present? And then who would be wealthy enough to bid on the sale of government resources and services that were being auctioned off? Um, maybe massively rich multinational corporations? You can call the Plaid Avenger jaded, you can even call him a leftist, but he is merely a realist. It's the way the world works.

Privatization is the growing theme in the 21st century, but nationalization is far from extinct. Hardcore capitalists and businessmen and multinational corporations across the planet still shudder when they hear the word. Ten years ago, I would have said that nationalization was completely dead and that you wouldn't see this happening much anymore. However, it is making a slight resurgence, particularly in the left-leaning South American region—I should say left-leaning Latin America because it rolls off the tongue much more glibly. You'll also see some of this happening perhaps in Africa in the very near future, but I digress.

NATIONALIZATION ADDENDUM!!! How right I was years ago to include the paragraph above concerning the resilience of nationalization! Since the global economic meltdown started in 2008, governments around the globe have been scrambling to nationalize key industries, even in the hardcore capitalist countries. Forget socialist Venezuela; one need look no further than the US, which partially or fully nationalized a bunch of banks and even some auto manufacturers in an effort to stabilize the crashing economy. Russia and China are following suit, quickly leaning back towards more state control in all things economic in order to prevent the financial chaos which has ensued in the West. Adam Smith is rolling in his grave.

That brings up a confounding question: why would states which advocate free-market capitalism ever stoop to the depths of nationalization? Several reasons crop up. In times of national emergency or war, states often nationalize critical industries like steel or energy in order to ensure national security (they don't have disruptions in bomb and tank production during war time). It can also occur if a state deems the social benefits far outweigh the economic costs, such as running a postal or healthcare system . . . one could argue that having a healthy workforce in your country makes the whole economy work much better, so spending on free health care for everyone brings in a much bigger societal reward. Sometimes it is done for purely economic reasons, i.e. government takeover of a business or industry about to fail, which would equate to lost jobs and revenue for the country.

Put all those reasons together into one big pot and stir, and you have the answer to why US President Barack Obama and many other European leaders are back in the nationalization game right this second. Partial or full government takeover of financial institutions and car companies is being done under the banner of "saving the economy/saving the country" from further collapse and preserving social benefits like jobs, while also alluding to a sense of maintaining national security which would inevitably be threatened if critical components of the economy like the whole banking system were to crash. Interesting stuff.

TYPES OF ECONOMIC ACTIVITIES

No matter what the type of economy, or how far to the left or right in the socialist world they may be, or even if things are being nationalized or privatized, people on the ground are always doing something to make this thing called an economy go forward. What is it those peeps are doing?

I'm not talking about economic structure at the state scale. I'm talking about what real people do on the ground. In real life. What the heck do you do? You chop down trees for a living or do you make toothpicks? What do you do to earn your paycheck? What businesses provide the most jobs in your hometown? What kind of stuff do those businesses make? Now we're on familiar ground here, and this chapter gets exceptionally easy because we can really classify all economic activity that happens in the world into four distinct types of activity.

Why are we doing this? Just so we can call out people and see what level they're on? To point and laugh? Hahahaha—your mama sells seashells by the seashore in the service sector. No! We want to identify these things because it's important to understand what different states are doing and how many people are dedicated to certain activities within the state. This in turn tells us a lot about how the economy operates, why some places are richer than others, and how this is currently changing in different regions around the globe. And it is oh so simple. They all go in order, and it is even numerical. Let us proceed with speed: on to the Primary!

Primary economic activities are as simple as it gets. Literally. This level includes anything and everything that involves natural resource extraction from the Earth. Just taking stuff from Momma Earth and then selling it is a primary activity. The list is short:

- Agriculture production: Cucumbers, cocoa, squash, cows, pigs—I don't care what it is; it's a primary economic activity if it's growing stuff we eat.
- Timbering/logging: Chop down a tree and take it. That's extraction of a raw commodity.
- Mining: Oil, coal, gold, diamonds—mining of everything. That's all simple extraction. Just pull it out of the ground and give it to me.
- Fishing: Yep, just taking a fish out of the water. That's a primary economic activity, even if you use dynamite to do it.

Pretty straightforward, pretty simple stuff. Resource extraction is the key. And that is primary. Now when you hear things like gold or oil, you think, "Oooooweee . . . that is worth a lot of money!" Here is what the Plaid Avenger wants you to know: No it really ain't. Main point: primary activities produce low-value commodities.

Understanding the Plaid Planet
PART ONE

Virtually all primary activities aren't worth squat in the big picture. How can I say that? Oil is worth a lot of money, isn't it? Well, it's critical for everything; it's used for everything . . . but it's worth less per gallon than homogenized milk, and that isn't worth much either, is it? Speaking of milk, what are all agricultural products worth per pound? Per boatload? How about wood? Quick question: would you rather have a business that grew oranges, or made orange juice concentrate? Why? Because one makes more money than the other due to processing of the product, which leads us to . . .

Secondary economic activities involve the processing of everything you got from the primary economic activities. All secondary activity consists of somehow manipulating, altering, refining, making better, doing something to the stuff you got from the primary activities—that is, the raw materials are modified in some way. Here's the main point: modified in such a way so it is worth more money.

You are adding value, and that is something that will continue to happen as you go up this chain of economic activities. As I've suggested earlier, products of primary activity are not worth much. You can cut down a tree, and a tree lying down on the forest floor is worth something, but not a lot. How about if we take that tree, rip off the bark, cut it into planks and then further cut them into boards. That's worth a lot more! Contractors and construction people will pay for boards, not for a tree.

Processing something of a big quantity to a smaller quantity is simple processing, but it still adds value. Then there is also refining. If we take oil out of the ground, it doesn't go straight in your gas tank. It has to be processed. It has to be cleaned up. Taking the oil out of the ground is our primary activity, processing it at a refinery is a secondary activity that adds a lot more value. Further manipulate it into gasoline and it's worth quite a bit more.

This can include a vast array of activities, which you don't often think about. Simple things like roasting coffee beans. Are roasted coffee beans worth more than raw coffee beans? Indeed they are. How about mud? Mud? Mud is just mud—but form it into squares, let it dry out, and now you have bricks. You can't sell mud but you can sell bricks. You've processed it; you've added value. Processing of any raw material counts—including taking a fish and chopping out its guts. Is a gutless fish worth more than a fish with guts? Ask anybody who wants to cook a fish. Most importantly: all "basic manufacturing" items fall into this category: from textiles to furniture to cars to paper to toys. If it is modified or made, it's a manufactured item, and manufactured/factory goods are all secondary activity stuff.

Now let's get up the chain another notch: let's get to tertiary level activities. **Tertiary level activities** are also known as service sector activities, so stage three includes all services on the planet. Perhaps we're going to take some of the raw commodities, or even some finished commodities, and maybe even some manufactured commodities, and do something with them, maybe move them around, further manipulate them, or sell them—provide a service of some sort.

The service sector is what most of us in the developed world are used to and what most of us have done for a living; you really have to go out of your way to find agriculturalists or lumberjacks or people who work on assembly lines in rich countries. But a service sector job? Yeah, we've all done those.

The Plaid World Economy
CHAPTER FOUR

Every hamburger that gets fried, every surgery that gets performed, every used car that gets sold, every fire that gets put out—someone has provided a service. Even simple transportation is a service. Truck drivers are an excellent example of this: taking commodities from one place and simply moving to another place. I'm sorry, what have we done here? We've added value to the commodity! A bunch of lumber sitting in the middle of Saskatchewan, Canada doesn't do a thing for anyone in the United States—but if you put it on trucks and move it to a Home Depot in Des Moines, now you've added value to it. They can use it; it's more accessible; it's worth more. Value has been added.

That's just one division of the service sector. We tend to think of everything from construction to police to doctors to teachers to army people, navy people, air force people, marine people as all providing a service. Perhaps the biggest one you think of is sales. Workers at McDonald's, at the mall, at Walmart, cashiers, wait staff; all these people are providing a service to you. They are moving around stuff from the first two activity levels and getting it to customers and/or increasing the value in some way, shape, or form.

Again, this process entails a ton of different activities, but its main feature is its tendency to increase the overall value of stuff from stages one and two in some discernible manner. Reconsider our hamburger: a cow that we killed in primary activity terms is ground into hamburger during secondary activity—worth more than the cow to be sure, but even raw hamburger is not valuable. Now take it to a restaurant and provide some services in the form of a cook and then maybe a maître d' that seats you at the table and maybe a waiter or waitress that brings you that hamburger. Now you've provided a bunch of services and you will pay a lot more for that hamburger in a restaurant than you will for the raw hamburger at the store and even more than you'll pay for the dead cow somewhere out in the field.

You see, as we progress up this chain we keep providing more, adding more value to commodities. Providing services adds value to commodities. Here's another important thing to consider: how much more do people get paid in the service sector than, say, farmers or lumberjacks or even people who work in a mill? Well, sometimes we have comparative salaries between occupations, but oftentimes as we progress up this chain, people get paid more to do, in real terms, what is a little less. Every level adds value to the commodities themselves, as well as to the salaries of the people who are doing it.

So what's left? **Quaternary sector** is kind of a new one. Some analysts and economists don't even recognize this one yet, due mostly to the fact that these types of jobs have not been on the planet for very long, and don't constitute a big percentage of the labor force. But they are on the rise, and do tell us some important things about the societies in which they occur. Quaternary sector provides something new. Not a natural resource, nor a processed commodity, and not really a service either. In essence, the quaternary sector deals with the creation and manipulation of intangibles—and the main intangible that I am thinking of here is information.

In the technologically advanced countries, an increasing number of people aren't dealing with hamburgers or trees or oil or services so much anymore as they are with the idea of information for information's sake. Computer programming, researchers, lab technicians, even astronauts are all in the realm of data creation, but don't necessarily "provide" a service to anyone. The results of their work may lead to a commodity that is mass produced, but their work in and of itself is neither a commodity nor a service.

To a certain extent, you can even say stock market people are in the quaternary sector because they are not really producing anything. Perhaps they are providing a service, but

it's more likely that they are manipulating information and moving abstract things around to create or add value to them (i.e., stocks).

It's a fuzzy one to be sure, but the reason I like to point it out is because we can make some easy assumptions about any country that has folks working in this sector. How would you describe a state that has a lot of astronauts and archaeologists and research scientists? Hmmmm . . . I don't know much about space travel, but a state that has astronauts must be technologically advanced, rich, and stable. No two ways around it. How much do those folks get paid? Bangin' bank, that's what. What are those products worth? Genetic code, computer programs, cures for diseases . . . are you kidding me? That's real money!

If you can critically examine what economic activities that different countries and regions focus on, you can go a long way to understanding why rich countries are rich, why poor countries are poor, and how the global economy is working. This insight, or should I say sight beyond sight, gives you the inside scoop on the real mechanics of money flow in the world. What? You don't have the sight beyond sight yet? Better call in Lion-O and proceed directly to. . . .

I WANT TO GO UP THE FOOD CHAIN . . . SECTOR EVOLUTION

We can look at any state on the planet, just in terms of their economic activities, to get a fuller picture of what's going on, how rich they really are, and indeed, what their future holds. It's not only about how much money they've got and how much money they are going to make but also what's going on in their society, how developed or developing they are, and lots of other things that we can typically tie to other demographic and cultural factors. And it's easy. Check it:

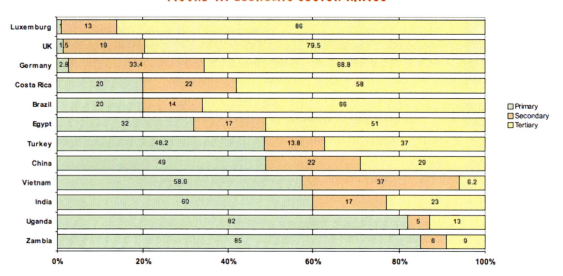

FIGURE 4.1 ECONOMIC SECTOR RATIOS

As you can see in the above graphic, the percentage of people within each state who work in each of these levels of economic activity tells us volumes about what's happening. We can define some obvious patterns between developed and developing countries, as well as explain anomalies to these patterns. First, the trends:

The fully developed countries, that is, the richer countries in the world, have a much greater percentage of their workforce in the tertiary/service sectors than in primary and secondary sectors. Check out Luxembourg, the UK, and Germany on the top of the chart. In fact, primary industries in the developed world account for almost nothing, but that should make sense to you now. Advanced technology and machinery in these countries equates to small percentages of folks needed to grow all the food and mine all the coal.

In the US, just under two percent of the population are farmers, yet those farmers supply the other 98 percent with food, and export tons of food on top of that. They are all the way through the demographic transition; one big tractor in the US operated by one guy can do the work of 1,000 small farmers in Africa—heck, more like the work of 10,000.

Secondary/manufacturing sector jobs are continuing to decrease in the rich, developed world due mostly to the cost of labor. Developed countries have labor unions and health benefits and minimum wage laws; all of which serve to increase the cost of labor. Developing countries typically have none of these things, thus, labor is cheaper. Manufacturing jobs of virtually all things—cars, toasters, toys, luggage, computers—have been migrating from developed countries to developing ones to take advantage of this cheaper labor. What does that leave for everyone to do in the rich states? Service sector employment of some specialized, skilled jobs (doctors, lawyers, firemen) and a lot of un-specialized jobs (clerks, janitors, salespeople). Good money for most. Of course, some of the folks in these societies have the know-how and opportunity to create and manipulate information, leading the world in quaternary level activities as well. In developed regions, there is:

- hardly anyone in the primary sectors,
- typically less than a quarter in the secondary processing sector,
- a majority of the workforce in the service sector,
- and a small but significant number of people in the high-end quaternary sector.

Just the reverse is happening in the developing countries. To point out these major differences, let's start with some of the countries that are the least developed, and subsequently are the poorest parts of the planet. Check out the bottom brackets filled by the African countries in Figure 4.1. They are overwhelmingly primary industry-based, very limited secondary and service sector employment; quaternary is out of the question. What can we say about a place that is almost exclusively agriculture- or fishing- or mining-based? What are those products really worth? As pointed out earlier, not much. In the least-developed regions:

- most folks are in primary—and most of them are farmers,
- less than a quarter are in manufacturing—sometimes much less than that,
- even fewer are in the service sector—with virtually none in quaternary.

Most states on the planet are somewhere in between. The trends do seem to indicate that the more developed a place becomes, the more tertiary and secondary will be gained at the expense of the primary sector. More service, more manufacturing, fewer farmers. End game: more money. We can see this reflected in the chart above. Costa Rica and Brazil are diversified across sectors more in tune with developed countries, and are doing pretty well. We wouldn't think of those countries as impoverished or undeveloped. India and Vietnam are hustling and transforming, but they are still overwhelmingly agricultural-based societies, and as such, are not making the big bank money yet—not per capita anyway. China and Turkey are stable, prosperous societies that are perhaps the most balanced across the board in economic activities. Plaid Avenger inside tip: this balance and diversity will probably serve both these countries well in the future, and you may see other countries try to emulate this approach as opposed to stacking up solely in the tertiary category. Just a hypothesis. But I'm usually right. China has actually stated that they want to keep this diversity in order to maintain their competitive edge in manufacturing.

Confucius say: Get astronaut, but keep farmer. Get scientists, but keep miners. Keep low wage to keep manufacturing sector; make China strong.

He could be onto something.

Now to look at an anomaly. What's the deal with Egypt up there? Looks pretty balanced, perhaps even more developed than Turkey or China. Are they really approaching full development as their economic activity breakdown suggests? Probably not. We have to look at the real world in this case to decipher the truth; Egypt has a low percentage of

Confucius say: Show me the money!

folks in primary sector, not because it's an evolved economy, but because they don't have a lot of agricultural land to farm! It's a desert! Except along the Nile, of course. They have some oil to mine, but not very much, and it just doesn't create many jobs anyway. So, low primary activities. Why high service sector, then? One of the moneymakers for Egypt is tourism. You know: see the Pyramids. How much money are those tourism jobs worth? Again, not too much. We can make sense out of these economic activities on a case by case basis when some of these countries buck our trends.

But the trends do make sense. They do seem to support the concepts outlined in the Demographic Transition Model from Chapter 2. Most states are working toward increasing manufacturing and service sectors, and lessening dependence on the primary sector, because that makes them more money. Currently, most of the value added to primary commodities happens in the developed world—to primary products shipped to them from the developing world. You should be able to see how this puts the poorer countries at a "permanent disadvantage"—they export low value stuff and have to import high value stuff. That's why the more successful countries in the 21st century are trying to catch up, not by producing even more cheap stuff, but by changing percentages in their economic activities sectors. China and India are changing fast and will be making big bucks. Saudi Arabia and Equatorial Guinea are making big bucks on primary sector stuff (oil) but not changing or diversifying internally. Who is going to win in the long term?

GOOD FOR YOU AND GOOD FOR ME: IT'S NOT JUST GROSS, IT'S GDP!

How does what all these folks do for a living in all these different states in the world affect real wealth—that is, real money and real dollars. That something is called GDP. **GDP** is **Gross Domestic Product**. You may have also heard of GNP, or Gross National Product. What's the difference between the two? Are you ready for this? Not much; they are two terms which mean pretty much the same thing. GDP has been growing in popularity and GNP has been falling out of use. Okay, so what do they mean?

GDP is simply all the goods and all the services within any state that are created and sold in that year. What do I mean by all the goods and all the services? Well, everything. Every single thing that is bought and sold. Every transaction in terms of a final sale. Every hamburger that's sold, every car that's sold, every service that's provided, every employee salary at McDonald's, all of it. All of it added together for the year is the GDP.

You do have to put this in context of the *final sale of the commodity* and what that means. For GDP, we only count the final sale and not all the transactions that led up to that final sale. Example: a car. A car gets sold on a lot for $20,000. That $20,000 car transaction is the final sale because it is going to a consumer, who will then "consume" it. That $20,000 goes into the total for GDP for that year. Now the reason we say only the final sale counts is because you can't sell things twice or three times or five times in the case of commodity chains anywhere in the world. The car has tires on it when the guy sold it off the lot. Well, those tires were made somewhere, and then sold to a distributor, who then sold them to a retailer, and then the retailer maybe sold them to a car manufacturer and that's three separate transactions, but you wouldn't count those other transactions because then you would be counting the same tires three times within one year. Only the last sale counts.

However, the car salesman's salary, the distributor's salary, the assembly-line worker's salary—all these services are a part of GDP for the year. The final sale and all worker salaries go into this equation. It doesn't matter if twenty people were involved in the movement, creation and distribution of that car; all their salaries go into GDP.

Now we know what GDP is, but what can we say about patterns of GDP on the planet? Keep your world regions in mind when analyzing the GDP map below. . . .

If we look at the GDP planetary totals, we see that the heavyweights who make the most money on the planet are represented by the developed world, with the United States economy weighing in at number one in the world (for now). Second in line: China has the number two economy on the planet. The third is now Japan, with the European powerhouse of Germany holding steady with the fourth biggest GDP. They all have GDP that total in the trillion-dollar range. That is a million million, or is it a billion million? I can't remember; it's a one with a butt-load of zeros behind it. Over a trillion dollars per year.

But this is where the lines are drawn and we have to stop making comparisons about what we consider to be the developed and developing world based on just GDP. Mainly because China really makes things interesting: China surpassed France and the UK in total GDP in 2008, then bumped the Germans in 2009, and then Japan in 2010 . . . surpassed 3 huge economies in just three years! So is China fully developed? Most would say not. I personally argue the affirmative, but we will get to this in the next chapter. They sure are making the dolla' dolla' bills y'all!

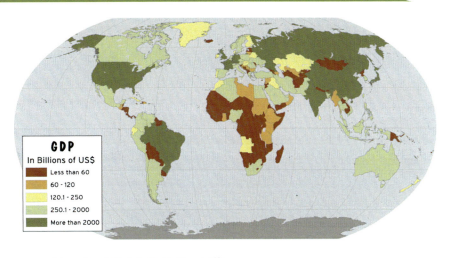

We see that most of the Western European states are still in the high GDP category, and most of Africa and Asia are in the low GDP category, with Latin America, South Asia, and East Asia falling somewhere in between.

I do want to point out a couple things as we look at these totals around the planet. Maybe you are thinking, "Wow, the rich countries—they are really, really rich. The poor countries, they really stink. They don't make squat. I guess everybody's sitting around there not making any money. They're not providing any goods or services. What losers!" Reality check: we have to throw in a disclaimer here. When examining GDP totals, in relations to a state's actual wealth, we have to consider what is *not* included in GDP. Check out the little green box, yo!

What is Not Included in GDP?
We said all the goods and all the transactions of all the goods and all the services are included in GDP—that's everything, isn't it? What would this not include?

First, think of some things that don't have monetary value in an exchange sense, but are actually hard work. This list would include housework, child rearing, any labor done in the home, food grown for home consumption, food gathering, food preparation, firewood gathering, the list goes on. Why would I point this out? Because that's what most of the people on the planet are doing. Every single day. Day in, day out. None of these activities are included in GDP.

Second: anything that the government doesn't know about. Any transaction that occurs between folks under the table. This can refer to anything as innocent as a flea market or a yard sale to items or services traded, bartered or sold between people that is untaxed and therefore not included in the tally. But this also includes anything illegal—stuff the government prohibits and therefore wouldn't be able to tax or know about, including all illicit narcotic production and trade, all moonshining, gunrunning, and human trafficking. All of these activities, which do generate large amounts of wealth, are not included in GDP.

I'd like to point out one example in particular. If we look at Mexico on the map above, we see that they are in the second tier of GDP ranking. Were you to include the illegal drug economy, they would instantaneously be in the top ten nations on the planet for GDP. Don't undervalue the stuff that's not being counted.

I bring this up because when we look at the poorest places on the planet, they're actually working pretty hard—but a lot of the stuff they do doesn't count in the official statistics. GDP is a Western-derived and Western-measured definition of wealth, and simply does not always adequately reflect reality. What do I mean by this? Well, when we look at Africa, it looks like nothing's going on there but indeed, let's face the facts; a whole heck of a lot of work goes on there to keep that place going; it's just not measured.

In summary, anything that's done at home, for home, anything that happens between friends, any type of barter transactions, and any illegal, illicit activities are not counted as part of GDP. That would radically change the map of what's going on here. There's one more thing to consider: the comparison between GDP and GDP per capita.

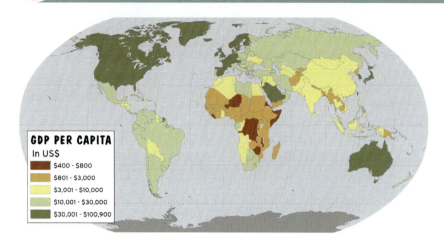

GDP PER CAPITA

Total GDP we covered earlier. **GDP per capita** is simply the total GDP divided by the population total for the state. In other words, it tries to approximate how much wealth there is per person in the society; this is perhaps a much better indicator of how the average Joe is doing in the world. Looking at these two maps side by side offers a contrasting picture of what's happening on the planet in terms of levels of wealth and economic activity. As to be expected, the most developed countries maintain themselves in the highest brackets, and the most undeveloped countries maintain themselves in the lowest brackets of both maps, but look what happens to some interesting places in between.

If we look at total activity, that is, the total GDP map on the previous page, we see total wealth as a singular number that a society or state produces. All these numbers look really big—and wow, would you look at that? China and India are right up there with the developed countries! So is Saudi Arabia! Sweet! They're making bank! They're not doing too bad, right? Brazil, Argentina, they're doing pretty well. Everyone in Saudi Arabia and India and Brazil are rich, aren't they? Eh. Um. Well. Maybe not. How do I know everyone there is not rich?

Well, let's check out a more realistic interpretation in the GDP per capita map. What you see is a bit of a shakedown. India and China in particular have gone from the top classes of total GDP, to the lower classes of GDP per capita, a significant shift when broken down to the individual level. Why does this happen? Well, because they have big populations, and they're producing lots and lots of valuable stuff, *but* broken down to an individual level, it ain't really that much per person. **GDP per capita** is a much better gauge of what's happening in the society in terms of how well the place is really doing. A trillion dollars doesn't really make as much impact if everybody in the society is only getting a buck each. It's even worse if just a handful of people in the society have most of that trillion bucks, leaving even way less to be divided up amongst the penniless masses.

This high GDP/low GDP per capita scenario possibly could be a very equal society, but unfortunately it never happens that way, at least not on this planet. The reality is a concentration of wealth in certain businesses and certain sectors and certain hands, with most people not really cutting much of a piece of the pie. This comparison becomes a much better measure of wealth disparity, and as such, is a much better indicator of how this society or state is really doing.

Sometimes these measures can be skewed radically. In other words, even if a state has a huge number in terms of GDP, and perhaps even when a state has a big number in the GDP per capita category, we still may not be getting the real picture. I'll pick on a few states in particular here. Places like Equatorial Guinea, Saudi Arabia, even Oman; what's happening in these places? High total GDP, high GDP per capita. Are they really so rich? Are they fully developed like the other rich, developed countries?

I think you already know the answers to these questions. Something doesn't add up. Equatorial Guinea, a rich place? Look how much money per person! On the books, they make $50,000 GDP per capita. That makes them one of the world leaders in that category . . . oh, except for the fact that most folks are starving to death under a thieving dictator. Indeed, the majority possess squat and a handful of people own virtually everything. **Wealth disparity** is massive, but the official economic indicator figures remain high because of a double whammy; the GDP total is absolutely massive, and the total population is low, which equates to an exceptionally high GDP per capita . . . on paper.

That's when you have to take the economic sector breakdown of labor in conjunction with GDP and GDP per capita to get a real sense of what's happening in these states. The real deal that's happening in these examples is that these societies have high numbers based on one single thing: the export of oil. They export tons and tons and tons of oil which means they make tons and tons and tons of money, a big number. Even if you divide that by the population, it is still a big number, but all of the wealth is, in reality, in the hands of very, very few people.

Equatorial Guinea is a particularly nasty case where none of these numbers mean squat because most of the people there are impoverished beyond belief, while a single corrupt ruler and his cronies get 100% of the money from the sale of the state's resources. Saudi Arabia, Oman, Iran, and many other OPEC countries fall into similar situations, though not as bad as the Equatorial Guinea extreme. You have to consider other things—looking at the economic sector breakdown of a place in conjunction with its GDP per capita gives us a good sense of what's going on, as well as a good sense of development and standards of living.

A CORE/PERIPHERY EPIPHANY!

Let's add up all of the stuff we have learned so far in this chapter about economic activities and apply it to the singular global economy of which we are all now a part. What do I mean by that? Well, whether you want to accept it or not, the whole human world has been ever-so-slowly moving towards increased global connectivity, with economic activity being the most pervasive and successful system thus far.

Booting up the global economy!

The creation and movement and buying and selling of stuff now happens across the entire globe as a single system. Oil from Kuwait is processed into gasoline in Burma and then fills the tanks of Toyotas in Tokyo. Auto engines made with German parts are constructed in Romania and then shipped to Brazil to be installed in VW Jettas which are sold in Chile. Argentinean leather and Indonesian rubber is sent to southern China to be made into Nike shoes which end up on the shelves of Walmarts in Wisconsin. And that is just the easily identified tangible stuff; there are also billions of dollars worth of services, stocks, investments, and currency exchanges which happen every single day among all the countries of the world. Which brings us to an interesting concept, appropriately named **world-systems theory**, which tries to make sense of the winners and losers of such a global economic scenario.

The development of the current world economy is the result of intensification of world trade, interconnections, and industrialization at a much higher level than in the past. For the last 500 years, the Europeans, and then the Americans (and maybe the Japanese, et al.), have dominated and shaped this global system, and many would argue to their ultimate advantage. Hey, wait a minute! Europeans, Americans, and Japanese . . . that's the rich Team West! You knows this! Through past colonial/imperial activity, coupled with modern industrialization, the Team West core is certainly a huge beneficiary of this world economic situation. *Core* is a great term to use, because it is at the heart of world-systems theory.

KILLER CORE AND THE PATHETIC PERIPHERY

This dude named Immanuel Wallerstein formulated this functional flowchart back in the 1980s, and it continues to evolve even today. He characterizes the world-system as a set of mechanisms which redistributes wealth from the economic **periphery** to the **core**. Another word for periphery would be "edge" or "fringe." In other words, the core gets stuff from the periphery, either resources or money via economic exchanges; in this scenario, the core always gains and the periphery primarily loses, particularly in the long run. Typically, the core country buys the raw resource for cheap, let's say it's steel, from a periphery country. The core makes that steel into a car, and then can sell that car back to the periphery country for a much higher price. Core wins, core wins, core wins!

In Wallerstein's terminology, the core is the developed, advanced, industrialized, rich part of the world, while the periphery is the not-so-developed, raw materials-exporting, poorer part of the world. The free-market and financial systems are the means by which the core exploits the periphery. Maybe some of you think that this is the natural order of things, and that the word "exploit" is too harsh. That's cool. I'm not trying to make a political point here, I just want you to understand how the economy works, and this world-systems approach does do a good job explaining the current flows of wealth in the world, as well as why rich places get richer while poor places mostly get poorer. Pointing out the winners and losers makes the game easier to follow.

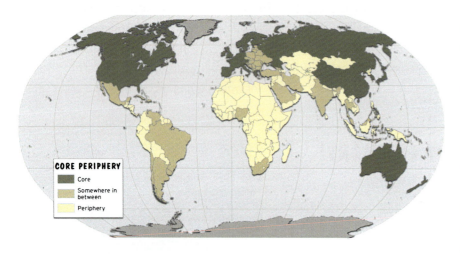

Check out the map to the left, and then let's add some more descriptors to these elements to enlighten even further.

Core states have the maximum level of industrialization and technology, which of course makes them centers for innovation and creation . . . and manipulation of capital; you know, money and credit. Whether you dig this theory or think it's leftist propaganda, there is no disputing that for all of the modern era, the core "Team West" countries have controlled global economic institutions like the IMF, World Bank, Inter-American Bank, the WTO and a host of others. Heck, "Team West" freakin' created all those institutions to begin with! The core runs the show, although that is now starting to change a bit (see G-20 in Chapter 6). The core has the smarts and the industrial capacity to make raw resources into much more valuable commodities. The core also has the cash to reinvest in its own infrastructure and businesses continually in order to keep itself in the top slot. The core is all about keeping free-trade free and opening up new markets to the global system . . . because, of course, all these things benefit them tremendously!

The periphery is the total opposite. They are poorer countries that may lack industrial capacity, financial means, and/or technological savvy to process their resources into finished goods. But they do have natural resources and tons of workers ready to slave away for pennies a day. They end up selling raw resources/cheap labor, which are cheap, and then importing finished goods, which are expensive. You don't need to be a math major to figure out how this story ends. Also, most of the industrial capacity and resource extraction that happens in periphery countries is usually owned fully or partially by multinational corporations from the core, which means that the core countries sometimes benefit economically even from the raw resources too. Ouch! Double-whammy! Most of Sub-Saharan Africa would be the best examples of periphery.

Because they are on the losing side of this equation, periphery countries are often locked into a cycle of never having enough money to invest in their own education systems or businesses in order to break out of this gerbil-wheel. Epic economic fail! When the situation gets bad enough, or when a strong leader comes to power in a periphery country is when you sometimes have things like **nationalization** occur. Remember that stuff from ten pages ago? A charismatic leader like a Fidel Castro or Hugo Chavez or Mohammad Mosaddegh can rise to power under the banner of "kick out the foreign companies and take our country's stuff back." Yep, that's nationalism, and it still may have a role to play in peripheral economies that are ticked off enough to strike back if the game board becomes too stacked against them.

Of course, not every single state in the world falls nicely into one of these two categories. There are those countries that benefit more from their resources, like most of the Middle Eastern states which fully control their oil resources, and there are some places that have effectively nudged their way closer to the core via crafty economic policies and strategic political alignment. Which reminds me to get back to point:

LET'S GET TO THE CORE OF THIS ISSUE

Can a state get to the core if they are seemingly stuck in the periphery? Oh yes, my friends! Things are changing very fast here in the 21st century! While Team West is currently the richest and certainly has an outstanding competitive edge in today's world, this was not always the case. In times past, both India and especially China would have been considered as the economic core of the global system, positions that they are working very hard at reclaiming in the modern era.

China has been strategically controlling its own resources, as well as acquiring cheap resources from other periphery states. They have used these resources along with their massive pool of cheap labor to become the manufacturing "workshop of the world," producing every imaginable industrial and commercial product. They are now core winners. India has taken a slightly different path: investing heavily in service and quaternary sector jobs like computer programming is what is currently pulling them out of the periphery realm.

They are not alone. Some other states have taken alternative paths in an effort to break out of the "poor/loser" category. South Africa, Turkey, UAE, and Brazil are a few examples of up-and-coming regional economic powers whose paths we will look at closer next chapter. Speaking of which, let's get to that. Someone . . .

SHOW ME THE MONEY!

In summary, what people do around the planet and how the economy of the state is structured, in large part, determines how well or how poorly the state is doing—and will be doing in the near future.

We have to look at several more factors to determine the true level of development of a place. Numbers aren't always enough, but we can look around the planet and see some obvious trends. Some of the ones we've already pointed out:

The periphery are the base floor of the wealth of the core!

- → The developed countries and regions are richer, have high GDP as well as high GDP per capita, and have more employment in service sector and quaternary sector activities than primary and secondary ones. Best examples: North America, Western Europe, Japan, Australia
- → The developing countries and regions typically have lower GDP as well as lower GDP per capita. However, in some circumstances, even when GDP total is high, the GDP per capita will still come out on the lower end of the spectrum
- → The developing countries and regions typically have more people employed in the primary and secondary activities than tertiary and quaternary. Examples: Sub-Saharan Africa, the Middle East, Central Asia, Central America, the Caribbean
- → The states and regions that are developing the fastest are changing this equation more successfully than other states who are still heavily reliant on primary activities. Rapidly innovating regions include South America, East Asia, Turkey
- → Some states and regions are currently lagging in GDP not due to economic activity structure, but because of turbulence attributed to shifting economic systems. They are slowly rebounding. See Russia and Eastern Europe

There's a diverse mix of what's going on economically in the world. Know these factors and features and what people are doing for the green, so as to stay keen about what's happening in today's world and which way the states are heading. Who has the money? Who will have the money? Who is developed? Who is developing?

Developed or developing? Hey, that's our next topic . . .

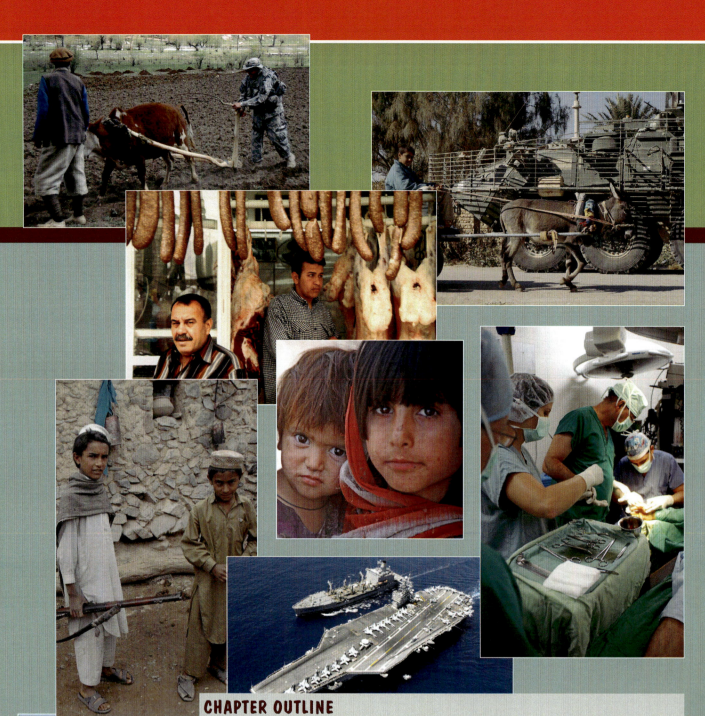

CHAPTER OUTLINE

1. If There Is a Third World, Where Are Worlds One and Two?
2. A Pithy History of the Periphery
   2.1. Colonial Period
   2.2. Into the Modern Era
   2.3. Escape Is Possible!
      2.3.1. Escapees of Note
      2.3.2. Escape Routes
3. Differing Degrees of Development
   3.1. Technologically Speaking . . .
   3.2. Industrially Speaking . . .
   3.3. Economically Speaking . . .
   3.4. Demographically Speaking . . .
   3.5. Socially Speaking . . .
   3.6. How Is Your Health?
   3.7. How Big Is Your Middle?
   3.8. Governmentally Speaking . . .
   3.9. Militarily Speaking . . .
4. The Bottom Line: Who is Developed? Who is Developing? Who is somewhere in between?
   4.1. Plaid Avenger Developmental Rule of Thumb
   4.2. HDI: A UN Take on How Folks Are Doing
   4.3. World at Night: Another Fun Plaid Avenger Measure of How the World Is Doing
   4.4. Avenger Assessment of States' Statuses
5. I'm Developmentally Spent . . .

Developed or Developing?

5

STINKING RICH places. Dirt POOR places. Some states are really well-off, and a whole lot more are struggling day to day to make ends meet. Why are some countries/regions rich, and others poor? As this manual has pointed out, it is not simply a matter of size of the country or the resources it contains. Reality, as always, is much more complicated than that. Before we can even identify traits of these developmental differences around the globe, we should first sort out some basic definitions and terms. Have you ever wondered. . . .

IF THERE IS A THIRD WORLD, WHERE ARE WORLDS ONE AND TWO?

In order to understand these crazy catch-phrases, let's start with a close-up of some other common conundrums. These words and descriptors are often tossed around to describe the state of states—that is, how well off they are, or inversely, how close to being in the global gutter they are.

A **developed country** is one that we would consider first and foremost . . . rich! Most texts, news articles and smart people somehow forget to speak the plain truth and just call a spade a spade. They will describe lots of different variables that account for how a state is rich, without ever outright just saying it. The developed countries are the rich ones! Admit it! Have you heard of a fully developed country that's flat broke? I suppose it's possible, but I've not partied in one yet.

Developed also carries the connotation that these countries are matured, at the end of the cycle, and therefore stable. I think that's a very good way to put it. But what cycle are we talking about? We'll get to that in a bit. You might also hear developed countries called *industrialized countries, more economically developed countries* (MEDC), *fully developed countries*, or even the *First World*.

A **developing country** on the other hand, is perhaps not so rich. However, it may not necessarily be totally poor either, which could be indicated by such measures as GDP and GDP per capita. Most of the planet would be in this category (both numbers of states as well as numbers of people) and, as such, there is tremendous range in the spectrum of "developing-ness." Some states are close to being fully developed. Others are desperately poor and stagnant or not really "developing" at all.

Perhaps developing countries are best described as all the regions that are obviously not fully developed. Is that a nebulous enough description? Yes, but it kind of works. The operative word here is developing, which means that these countries are in transition, are changing, are developing into something newer, better, and richer. No state is actively trying to un-develop are they?

Synonyms for developing countries include *less-developed countries* (LDCs), *least economically developed countries* (LEDCs), *underdeveloped nations, undeveloped nations*, and the most popular term that everyone recognizes: *the Third World*.

The **Third World**. What a hilarious term. Everyone recognizes and uses it, but no one knows what it really means. And it really doesn't mean anything anymore. Here's the real deal: During the **Cold War**, there were two opposing camps: Team 1 was the capitalist democracies led by the US, aka "The West." Team 2 was the communist countries led by the USSR, aka "The Soviet Bloc." They became known, respectively, as the **First World** and the **Second World**. All the other countries were encouraged to join one of these teams, and many did—or at least would allow themselves to be associated with Team 1 or Team 2. In hindsight, it was comparable to siding up with Thing 1 or Thing 2 from "The Cat in the Hat." But I digress.

However, there was a group of holdouts who refused to side up. They wanted nothing to do with the Cold War nonsense, and identified themselves as non-aligned. India, Egypt, Ethiopia, and Yugoslavia led this **Non-Aligned Movement (NAM)**. I point them out by name because their status then, as now, has a lot to do with how the term "the Third World" evolved. Many other similar states joined this movement, and as you might imagine, their poor, less-developed economies became an identifying mark . . . a mark that still sticks today. There is no more Cold War, and there are no more First and Second Worlds, but somehow the Third World is still out there batting. Can someone please tell them the game is over?

But seriously, why was it that these countries were so much poorer than the First and Second Worlds at the time? And why have some of them not changed much since the Cold War era, which is why the Third World terminology has stuck? Ah! I'm so glad you asked! To understand today's world of development, we must travel back in time just for a bit and pick up a theory we introduced at the end of the last chapter. . . .

A PITHY HISTORY OF THE PERIPHERY

Think back to that Immanuel Wallerstein stuff I threw at you in chapter 4. Remember the **world-systems** approach I alluded to? It was that set of mechanisms which concentrates wealth from the economic **periphery** to the **core**. Time to dust it off and take a second look through a historical lens, so that we can more clearly see why places like India and Vietnam and Brazil came to be on the peripheral edges of the world economy prior to the Cold War as well as how the US and Europe were at the core.

In doing so, we can also elaborate on why these descriptions have persisted into the modern era, along with some examples of major changes which are currently underfoot. Ha! Watson, the game is afoot! And Sherlock Holmes' Britain is a great place to start the investigation. . . .

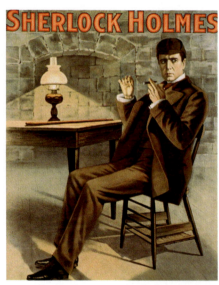

Deucedly developmental deductions, Watson!

COLONIAL PERIOD

In terms of world history, the 1500's to the early years of the 1900's are really a European heyday. Prior to this age, neither European states individually nor the region as a whole made a significant impact on the rest of planet earth. They certainly were not anywhere near the 'core' of a global economy, nor a center of political power, nor a center of technical innovation. You would have had to go to India or China or the Middle East to get those things. Why? Because Europe was a backwater; the US was as of yet "undiscovered"; and Japan was an samurai-infested, isolated state.

But what a difference a few hundred years makes! As the 1500's and 1600's unfolded, European traders, scientists, businessmen, sailors, and military men all increasingly adopted and refined technologies from other societies. Namely, Arab sailing technologies from the Middle East and gunpowder from the Chinese. As a major case in point, the Chinese had invented explosive powder, and employed it for . . . ready for this? . . . fireworks!

Chinese firework make big bang for Europeans!

The Europeans borrow this explosive powder stuff from China and they make . . . guns! I think you may be starting to see how the core/periphery tide was starting to turn already . . .

The Europeans take their newly modified and improved technologies and build grand navies and militaries which inevitably make them masters of the seas, both militarily and for trade. And with that mastery came colonization and imperial takeover. . . you know, the Europeans setting sail and taking over the rest of the planet. North America, South America, Australia, and eventually Sub-Saharan Africa, South Asia, even parts of China et al, come under the direct control and exploitation of the Europeans. Raw resource wealth, wealth from any existing manufacturing, along with wealth created by trade itself, now flowed from the colonized areas back to Europe. Europe is quickly becoming the core.

Tools of the "trade"

Then starting in the 1700's the Europeans are the first to undergo this whole process we now call industrialization. Making machines to do stuff that humans and animals used to do . . . and doing it better, faster, cheaper! Virtually all aspects of agriculture, manufacturing, mining, and transportation are made way more productive and profitable. And this also means that Europe is now the center of innovation and the technology leader . . . which of course makes them richer still. Europe sustains this revolution by fully mastering trade relationships around the globe: absorbing the raw resources of the planet, taking them back home to be processed (thus creating jobs and wealth at home) and then pushing their manufactured goods to their colonies.

Example: UK forces India to stop producing cloth by insisting that they instead sell the UK all their cotton. The UK takes the cheap cotton back to the textile mills in London, produces it into cloth, and then sells the finished goods back to India, at a higher price of course. Buy low, sell high. Europe is now the core and India has become part of the periphery. It is important to note that China undergoes a similar devolution at this time, having their core status severely eroded by European, Russian and even Japanese trade dominance during the 1800's . . . culminating in the catastrophic **1839 Opium Wars** in which the UK totally dismantled Chinese authority altogether in their bid to forcibly sell opium under the banner of "free trade" to China. Wow. Put that in your pipe and smoke it, China. And they did.

Please keep in mind, in this scenario Europe's strong naval presence is perhaps more significant in its successful take-over of global trade systems than it is for its takeover of physical territory itself. Because, inevitably, they will lose those colonies, but the trade dominance remains for some time after that. Here is an equation to consider:

Dominating world trade creates wealth at home = more taxes collected by government = stronger government = government invests more back into technology, infrastructure, military and businesses = stronger military and businesses = more power abroad to colonize and control trade = more wealth = go back and repeat equation. Repeat for centuries.

Not bad for a few hundred years work by folks who previously were groveling in the mud waiting for King Arthur to find the Grail. But changes are coming. . . .

Got Grail?

INTO THE MODERN ERA

Of course, the good old days don't last for the Europeans forever. Independence movements worldwide were kicked off by the American Revolution in 1776, but they didn't happen all at once. It took from 1800 right on up to the 1960's for those European imperialists to lose control of all of their overseas possessions, with many African states the last to shake off the colonial hangover. These movements coincide with the abolition of slavery and serfdom worldwide, and thus the end of free labor, which also put a crimp in the European wealth-generating machine.

In addition, some former colonies and others learned the lessons of European history very well . . . and then duplicated them! The United States in particular underwent its own industrial revolution and rise to global power, and thus entered the core arena itself by the 1900's. Russia and Japan modernized as well, and quickly became core players too, albeit on rockier paths that we will investigate further in later chapters. Australia and Canada followed suit. Point is, the core expanded to include others now in competition with the European masters, and the periphery became even weaker as these new global power players had more economic strength than ever imaginable in the past.

But hang on! Do not interpret this as the end of European economic dominance! Because, as I suggested above, the trade patterns had been well-established for hundreds of years, and they proved to be a much more tenacious beast than simple ownership/control of colonies. Colonial labor may not have been free anymore, but let's face it: former-colony labor remained extremely cheap, as it does into today's world. Basic manufacturing has shifted from the core to the periphery in order to take advantage of this cheap labor, but the profits still go to the core. Same as it ever was.

In addition, while the UK or France or Spain may have officially left the colony of India or Algeria or Chile, they usually left behind multinational corporations under their sponsorship which still controlled and/or profited from the raw resource of the former colony. This is a situation that is still common today. Almost all of the biggest and richest multinational companies of the world originate in Europe or the US, and operate with huge competitive advantage in the "poorer" parts of the planet . . . you know, the periphery! Local yokel companies in Africa or Asia can't possibly compete with the likes of Wal-Mart or Exxon. Core wins!

End result: core countries still import cheap raw resources from the periphery and produce high-value commodities which they then export to the periphery. Core wins! Quite frankly, the equation has not changed much, and neither have the goods traded. The periphery exports cotton, tea, bananas, oil . . . and imports finished goods. The core imports raw stuff and basic manufactures, and exports guns, machines, finished goods, etc. Same as it ever was.

Let's be brutally honest here: the rich, core countries have absolutely no vested interest in changing the system. Why would they? No government or business is going to actively try to change the rules of a game that ensure their own victory. So is economic history finished? Is the system now set forever? Ha! Nothing stays the same forever, and even in the most structured system. . . .

ESCAPE IS POSSIBLE!

As you have now seen in this historical overview, these core/periphery labels are not stagnant statuses my friends! Oh no! China and India in particular used to be core, then were subverted to periphery during the rise of the Europeans, but now they are breaking out again. And speaking of the Europeans: for sure, they are still rich parts of the core . . . but they are starting to slip a bit, and no one here in the 21st century would label Western Europe as a center of innovation or technology anymore. Many analysts are now speculating that perhaps even the top-slotted USA is taking it on the chin from the rising Asian titans. Times are a-changing. However, it is difficult to be dethroned from the core once you are there, so there is no

Let's get the heck out of the periphery!

point to focus too much on the top dogs . . . they will maintain their monopoly for some time to come. More to the point, let's look at those entities that are climbing out of the periphery to join the kings of the core. . . .

ESCAPEES OF NOTE

There are a variety of countries in the world right now that don't fit nicely into the definite core or definite periphery categories. Some states do have significant control over their own resources, or have competitive local industries that do compete on the international stage, or do make more high-valued finished goods for export. Of note, Brazil, Argentina,

Chile, Turkey, South Africa, Mexico, South Korea, Indonesia, Bahrain, and the UAE could all be considered much further down the development path, and I even refer to them as power-players within their respective regions.

With no reservation though, China and India are the future core members to consider. How did they climb out of the core/periphery cycle? Well, both of these countries are unique in that they were previous core members, countries with huge populations, and countries with significant periods of technological innovation and know-how. It's not like they have had to start from scratch. The current re-rise of these Asian giants has more to do with throwing off the yoke of colonial powers and reasserting political, and then economic independence.

India chucked out the Brits in 1947; the Chinese started their modern era after the defeat of their Japanese oppressors in WW2, and their bloody civil war, which ended in 1949. Both states have used their massive pool of cheap labor to increase agricultural production, create a manufacturing sector, and invest in their infrastructure. As pointed out in previous chapters, China has really focused heavily on its manufacturing sector to make a myriad of products for cheaper than anyone else on the globe, and they have done this exceptionally well, to the point of now easily beating the core countries in the competition. Ever see *Made in China* on the tag of any products you own? Ha! You probably can't find anything you currently possess that was NOT made in China!

We take this back now.

With all the massive inflow of wealth, China has invested heavily in its infrastructure, technology and industries to make themselves even more competitive . . . hey! Just like the core countries do! Yep. China is now in the core. India is not quite as far along, and is taking a slightly different path. Instead of focusing on manufacturing, India has been specializing in service sector and high-end stuff like computer programming. Ever call your Dell computer 1-800 help line? Who did you talk to? Yeah, you know it! Someone in India! Their famous technical support centers are even featured in *Slumdog Millionaire*! Oh yeah! Citing Indian specialization reminds me to include this next section. . . .

ESCAPE ROUTES

I have now alluded to different strategies which India and China have taken in order to become more developed, and less peripheral. Let's go ahead and flush these things out totally so you can better assess the strategies that other countries have taken (or will be taking in the future) to attempt to better their situation. There are some major paths that have been followed by poorer peripheral states in order to bust out of the cycle:

1. **Nationalize** a particular resource in the country, focus on efficiency and technology for that one industry, become way more competitive globally for that one industry, and thus reap a bigger percentage of economic benefits. We've talked about this concept already. Middle Eastern countries, and almost all other OPEC members, did the nationalization thing with their oil. It sometimes results in alienation by the core countries, and less competitive and poorly run local industries. But no one would argue that Saudi Arabia, Venezuela, or even Russia is worse off for nationalizing their oil. It has reaped large profits in the modern era, and gained them some measure of control in the global economy. Other states have done it with other commodities as well, even into the modern era.

2. **Import substitution** has been experimented with ever since the **Great Depression** crunched the whole global system. This is a policy in which the government works with private industry to set up production of a variety of higher-valued manufactured goods like cars, washing machines or textiles. The point is not to export them, but sell them to their own citizens, thus decreasing the reliance on importing expensive finished goods from the core. These local goods are given an advantage by the government putting high taxes or **tariffs** on similar goods being imported from other countries, thus making the local goods cheaper and a better deal. More of a short-term fix than long-term solution, but has had mixed successes.

3. **Specialization** on a few commodities which, with government help, can become efficient enough to compete on the export market globally. China focused on making a literal boatload of manufactured commodities at cheap prices, and has done very well. But most other countries usually focus on just a handful of things: India is focusing on service sector jobs and computer programming, while Brazil focuses on an extremely competitive steel industry, as well as military computer applications.

Japan, Taiwan and South Korea all have made trillions focusing on consumer electronics and automobiles. Those country names are just synonymous with high quality products! When a country does something the best, everyone knows it, and everyone wants it . . . especially when they do it the best for the cheapest . . . then that state is making the money! And thus heading out of the periphery, which many of those **Asian Tigers** have done!

Make no bones about it; in all of the examples above, former peripheral states challenged and out-competed core states in these industries, which is why they can't be counted among the totally undeveloped, not-as-developed, or underdeveloped states in the world today. Egads! I have totally lost sight of the development of this chapter! We were supposed to be talking about the developed versus the developing world! Let's get back to topic. . . .

Consumer electronics: Asian Tiger escape route.

DIFFERING DEGREES OF DEVELOPMENT

What are some common measures of the fully developed state versus the fully undeveloped one? The richness versus poorness? Core versus periphery? People in a developed state typically enjoy a high standard of living—i.e., life is good. Food in the fridge, healthy children, bills paid, access to health care, good housing, good environment, and there's even some leisure time to party. Yeah, that sounds about right. And developing? Those folks are probably not eating as much as they should, maybe not getting access to health care, maybe not having clean water or electricity, and their leisure time is otherwise known as "too sick to work."

But we can do even better than that. Let's look systematically at some categories of human life to better compare and contrast the standards of living on our planet. Below is a brief outline of some of the contributing factors of current levels of development in the wider world. This list is not exhaustive, as we have not included all the historic factors that have influenced current state of affairs, or physical resources that these regions possess. However, I want you to think about the bigger developed/developing picture here—if we can understand the mechanics of what is going on in these places, we can better understand the present and better predict the future.

Nukes are high-tech!

TECHNOLOGICALLY SPEAKING . . .

The fully developed state has the highest levels of technology across the board. I'm not just talking about computers here either. Agriculturally, they can grow more food with way fewer people; one big tractor can do the work of hundreds of humans. Industrially, they can produce more and better stuff with machines in factories that typically displace workers as well. Machines do the work; people run the machines. They are also the creators of information; they have the best military technology like nuclear weaponry; they do extreme stuff which requires extreme cash, like space exploration.

The newest and coolest stuff is created in the fully developed world. Infrastructure like roads, bridges, buildings, and communications are at the highest quality and highest safety levels. Emergency and medical services provide lightning response and insane possibilities of keeping people alive. You can reattach an arm? No way! The frontiers of science, medicine, and technology are pushed forward here. The developed world produces all the newest information, is responsible for 99% of new patents, new trademarks, and new copyrights. Meanwhile, *Grand Theft Auto IV* offers mind boggling graphics to thousands of glassy-eyed users.

The developing state does not have all of these technological advances, and some states may have little to none of these things. Agriculture and industry are still labor-intensive, and typically not as productive. Infrastructure is not as good; roads and communication systems may be lacking. When an earthquake or flood occurs, sub-standard buildings crumble. Buildings, sewer systems, and electric grids may be not as safe or efficient as possible; blackouts and back-ups occur regularly. They may possibly be at minimum standards, which means they don't function as well, or for as long. Life-saving technologies and services operate at less than favorable standards. There is no 9-1-1 to call. You will lose the arm.

INDUSTRIALLY SPEAKING . . .

The developed state uses more machine labor than human labor. As such, they have higher **labor productivity**, which means one human can do a crap-load of work. One guy on a tractor can plow a thousand acres. One guy in a semi can move twenty tons of cargo 500 miles in a day. Because of this, they get a heck of a lot more work done per person, but the developed world is also much higher in energy consumption per person; just think of all the energy you use in one day for electricity in your home, at the office, driving your car around, and in making your skinny, half-caff, sugar-free, mocha lattes. In addition, most of the energy produced in the developed world is based on fossil fuels. As a result, there is a high fossil fuel dependency in the developed world: Iraq will have to be invaded . . . hahahahaha I'm joking! (oops, bad example)

The fully undeveloped world can vary greatly in the amount of machine versus human labor. In places where development is low, there is a greater percentage of human labor involved, thereby reducing the rate of productivity in total work done. How many humans does it take to plow that same thousand acres? And how much longer does it take them? Just using elbow grease, the energy consumption per person is significantly lower. Even the type of fuel used changes in the developing world; fossil fuels are too costly, so less efficient fuel sources like coal, wood, and even dried dung are used more often. Dung? Dang.

There is a plus side, though: a lower dependency on fossil fuels, and dried feces is cheap, as it should be. However, those fuels are not very efficient in outputting energy and are overly efficient in outputting pollution. But do realize this little known fact: many oil-exporting countries actually don't use a lot of oil themselves . . . it is too expensive for them! They make too much money exporting the stuff to actually want to burn it! That's why places like Iran are investing in nuclear energy, even though they are a major exporter of oil. How bizarre!

What a load of . . . inefficient fuel.

Looking broadly at the economies of each of these societies, we have to point out that the fully developed world has not only already undergone a full industrial revolution in their society . . . but most of them have now long since left the industrial economy behind. They took full advantage of the technological advances and profits from their industrial/manufacturing era, and are now onto the service and quaternary sector activities. Totally undeveloped states have yet to undergo this revolution, or perhaps only done it in patches . . . mostly due in part to foreign multinational corporations setting up industrial capacity for specific manufacturing purposes. In that scenario, the true benefits of an industrial revolution are never realized. They just get the crappy jobs and the pollution.

ECONOMICALLY SPEAKING . . .

Speaking of those crappy jobs, how do we differentiate the developed and developing states economically? Well, the easy descriptors include what people do for a living, which is the stuff we covered in the previous chapter. It never hurts to summarize again, though.

In the developed state, higher technology and industrial capacity equate to increased labor productivity, which in turn equates to higher salaries. The economy is more diversified. There are more desirable types of labor, more choices of occupations, of typically safer types of labor. You can get a job just using your brain. What a novel idea. More of the economy is focused in the service sector, with some in the quaternary sector as well. Primary and secondary jobs are available, but are not the primary earners of GDP for the state.

More importantly, GDP per capita is high. **Corporate earnings** are higher. The developed state produces value added products which are more expensive. Processed goods and high-skilled services are apparent: computers, cars, lawyers, investment bankers. Exported high-value goods equate to a **positive trade balance** for the state; it sells more stuff than it buys every year. It has a surplus in their economic bank. All of these factors lead to increased investments that are funneled back into the economy and infrastructure, perpetuating the positive cycle.

In the developing state, lower labor productivity usually leads to limited options for everyone economically. Most of the economy is focused in the primary and secondary sectors. Lots of agriculture and basic manufacturing exists, which produces goods of less value. Harder labor, and laxer environmental and safety laws mean more unhealthy/dangerous working conditions. It should also be noted that many developing countries have a very large chunk of their GDP based on a single commodity, like oil or diamonds or copper. This is an extremely risky situation for the state. What happens when the price of oil on the world market plummets . . . sometimes overnight? Yep, that's right: that state loses money, instantly. Makes it hard to plan for the long term. Very volatile economics for the developing state.

Lower salaries, lower corporate earnings, and a special twist—many of the companies operating in the developing states are foreign multinationals, so most profit exits the state and goes back to the multinationals' country of origin. Low value goods are exported, high value goods are imported, resulting in an overall **negative trade balance**. Put it all together and it spells out a lower investment in the infrastructure and economy, less personal wealth, usually less GDP, and almost always less GDP per capita—although we have seen some exceptions to this rule as well.

DEMOGRAPHICALLY SPEAKING . . .

Just to reinforce some concepts from chapter 2, we should also highlight some obvious differences in the demographic makeup of a state based on its level of development. Fully developed states have fully undergone the demographic transition, and both their fertility rates and their population growth rates are relatively low. Fertility rates usually hover around the 2.1 replacement level, and the overall population total is either stable or perhaps even shrinking, as is the case of Japan, Russia, and many Western European states. The column or inverted pyramid shape of the population pyramid indicates that there are typically a smaller number of folks under the age of 15 (dependents) as there are working age cohorts 15 to 55 (the suppliers of labor and wealth).

By contrast, less developed states are somewhere in late Stage 2 or Stage 3 of the demographic transition, and their classic pyramid shape suggests that they are currently in a cultural lag/population explosion scenario. The later in Stage 3 they are, the more rounded the pyramid will appear, especially in the younger age cohorts. Fertility rates remain well above the 2.1 replacement level, usually in the 2.5 to 4 range . . . and the higher the number, the more

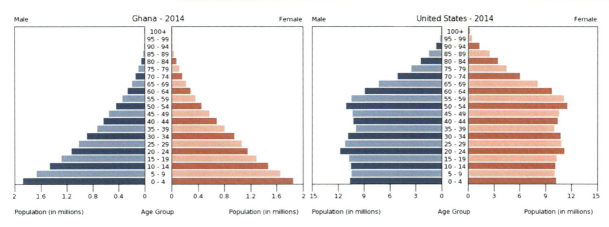

Developing state pyramid . . . develops to . . . a fully developed column state.

explosive the overall population growth. Of particular note, the classic pyramid shape indicates that there are way many more folks under the age of 15 (dependents) than in the working class/provider brackets.

What does this mean in real life, for real families? In the developed world, people have just one or two kids, invest a lot of time and money into keeping those kids alive, healthy, educated, and happy . . . and then eventually pass all their remaining wealth to the kid once mommy and daddy kick the bucket. This type of high investment per kid equates to a huge competitive advantage for children of the developed world. How can they fail? Well, I'm sure some of your fellow students are figuring out new creative ways to fail despite their advantage. We call them slackers.

In the undeveloped world? Large family size means less investment per kid, less resources per kid, and much less wealth to pass on after death. And they don't have that much to pass around to begin with. As total population continues to swell year after year, there are less and less resources to divide up among an ever increasing number of folks. For even an exceptionally smart or gifted child, the climb out of poverty is fraught with major challenges.

SOCIALLY SPEAKING . . .

In the developed state people make decent money. Those folks have higher salaries, which equates to more disposable income, which equates to higher consumption rates of everything and higher rates of saving. It also means people can invest in their own future, as well as provide better health care and education to the next generation. That is crucial. Literacy rates are high. Developed countries heavily invest in education—each generation gets smarter, richer, better, and more cognizant of the Plaid Avenger's World.

The developed world also has higher mobility and social safety nets, like welfare, which increase **risk-taking** and

We ain't so fully developed. This sucks.

increase opportunities. You can risk quitting your job to start a new business or go back to school without your family starving to death. This increases your opportunities for employment and income-making potential. It also makes the country a center of innovation and wealth, as these risk-taking entrepreneurs become successful. Think about it: Could Bill Gates the kid have become Bill Gates the trillionaire had he been born in Uzbekistan or Ethiopia? Doubtful. Infrastructure and education provide a tremendous amount of opportunities that allow the citizenry of the developing world to make their dreams come true.

By contrast in developing countries, less expendable income means less food on the table, less overall consumption, less investment in the future generation, less education, and generally lower literacy rates. Lack of social safety nets leads to less risk-taking, fewer opportunities in employment, and in life. Availability and quality of infrastructure and educational opportunities are generally much lower, thus locking in the cycle of poverty from generation to generation. Focus is on survival, not upward social mobility.

HOW IS YOUR HEALTH?

In the developed state, people should be pretty healthy overall. Increased education, increased access to health care, and increased public hygiene equate to decreased infant mortality, increased longevity, and decreased susceptibility to epidemic outbreaks. You will live longer in the developed world, but what will it eventually get you?

Due to changes in work types, increased consumption, and wider variety of dietary choices, a distinct health shift occurs as a state becomes fully developed. People become more sedentary as they use their brains instead of their brawn to work. They have stress from using their brains too much. People over-consume in caloric intake. In diet, they move from whole grains and fruits and vegetables to processed foods with a radical increase in sugars, fats, and meat. Result? Around 75 percent of people in a developed world die from diseases of the circulatory system (heart disease, stroke) and cancers.

Poorer people eat more grains and veggies. The richer you get, the more your diet sucks!

poor →　rich

In the developing world people are not as healthy. Less education, less access to health care, poor public sanitation and hygiene, and even little or no access to immunizations equate to high infant mortality and lower life expectancy. Epidemics can be catastrophic. Diets consist of basic grains and fruits and vegetables, which is really good, but their caloric intake may not be sufficient for optimal health. Result? 50 to 60 percent of the people will die of an infectious or parasitic disease, or in childbirth. The infectious diseases are easily preventable and curable. What a travesty to be occurring in a world that is medically advanced enough to stop this from happening.

PLAID AVENGER SURE-FIRE WEIGHT LOSS PROGRAM: Move to a developing country. You will certainly eat less than you do now, and likely eat stuff that is actually way more healthier for you when you do eat. And hell-tons of physical labor tends to keep the pounds off too.

HOW BIG IS YOUR MIDDLE?

No, I'm not talking about your waistline . . . we just talked about that in the previous section . . . I'm referring to the size of the middle class. I want you to think critically about this concept, because it ends up being a core component of how most of us now classify the levels of development around the planet . . . especially for those states that do not easily fall into either the full-on developed nor the totally un-developed categories.

In fully developed states, there is much less wealth disparity. That is, there is a roughly equal distribution of wealth across the society. Now, every society and every state has some wealth concentration in the hands of a few rich folks, i.e., the upper class, or aristocracy. And every society and state has a lower, poorer class of folks with not much wealth at all. That is true the world over. However, the percentage of the haves to the have-nots differs wildly from state to state, and I'm suggesting here that fully developed states have a lower percentage of wealth concentration in the hands of the few, with greater distribution of that wealth across the whole society. That's where the middle comes into play.

Poor peeps exist even in rich states, as do the few ultra-rich in poor states. But in the fully developed states, the middle class constitutes the biggest group overall. You know, it's the folks that have a good job, a nice house, a decent car, can go on vacations, and can send their kids to college, and can eventually do this awesome thing called "retire." The ability for a majority of folks in the state to achieve adequate levels of wealth is an extremely powerful stabilizing factor, and one that may be the the newest, best indicator of how developed a state is here in the 21st century. Because as you have seen in previous chapters, a state like Equatorial Guinea has a huge GDP, and even a big GDP per capita figure. BUT, the wealth is totally concentrated in the hands the state dictator and his family . . . while the masses are starving. Therefore, there is no middle class at all. Speaking of which. . . .

In the developing world, there are much greater differences between the haves and have-nots . . . in some societies it may be best described as the few have-all's versus the masses of have-nothing's. **Wealth disparity** is huge. Wealth is overwhelmingly concentrated in the hands of a few, who then, of course, have the power and influence to make sure it stays that way! The impoverished masses have no real competitive avenues to accumulate wealth, and for them "vacation" is another word for unemployed, and "retirement" occurs only at death. Kind of like killing a *Replicant* in movie **Blade Runner**. This makes for an unstable economic and political situation in the state as a whole, which brings us to. . . .

GOVERNMENTALLY SPEAKING . . .

In the developed states, democracy is the undisputed champion. Almost all of the fully developed, rich states on the planet are democracies. The political/economic structure may have varying degrees of socialist policy, but all are staunchly democratic. These systems are more dynamic, more open to change, and they prove it by rotating out leadership in a timely and regulated manner. In addition to their dynamic demeanor, developed states are politically stable, leading to stable economies which actively participate in global trade and investment. This stability is one of the primary reasons that international investment is typically higher in developed countries: because your money and your investment are safe in a stable environment.

In the developing world, most other types of governments can be found. Military dictatorship, theocracy, monarchy, one-party states, and chaotic states abound. It should be noted that many developing states are also democracies, but usually not well-established with long track records. Why is this important to note? Aside from the newer democracies, these systems are more static, or closed to change; some exhibit no possibilities for change at all. The more closed a system is, the more opportunity

Power to the few = revolution overdue.

arises for corruption. This creates an unstable situation in the long term because underlying tensions and forces usually manifest themselves in violent upheaval, civil war, or outright implosion of the state. 2011 Update: See the Arab Revolution across the entire Middle East as your best most modern example of this.

Unstable governments can often lead to unstable economies, and unstable economies are not where international investors put their money. These states are often insular, protecting their industries or economic interest above all, which discourages global trade and investment. As alluded to in the middle class section above, impoverished masses themselves are always a potential flashpoint for total chaos within a state: when conditions get horrific enough, and people have nothing left to lose, they sometimes band together and topple governments. Check out the Haitian or Russian Revolutions for details.

MILITARILY SPEAKING . . .

There's one last category that most people don't really look at to assess development status, but the Plaid Avenger does lots of things that other people don't. I think it's a keen insight into what's happening in the society . . .

In the developed world, military technology is at the maximum. Nuclear capabilities are either possessed or easily acquired. Like in industry and agriculture, most manual labor is done with machines. Soldiers operate big machines and the "death-wielding labor productivity" is very high. Developed states prefer to use their military technology as opposed to large numbers of humans on the ground. Human casualties and injuries are minimized at all costs. A major final point: while total expenditures on the military may be high, in a developed state this expenditure is a fairly low percentage of their GDP total. Check out the box to the right to see what I'm sayin'. (And holy hand-grenades! Be sure to note how many Middle Eastern states are on this astounding arming agenda! We will follow up on that issue in chapter 18.)

In the developing state, military technology can be advanced, but typically is not. They usually buy hand-me-down weapons and last year's camouflage fashion from the developed states, and to be sure, the fully developed states never sell them the top-of-the-line gear. Some states, like India, Pakistan, and China, have nuclear capability, but they are pretty much alone in the developing world in this respect. Lots of other states may want it, but will have to try and buy it, since they lack the infrastructure to develop it themselves.

In developing countries, manpower is still the primary component of the military, and most real action will be dudes on foot, firing guns. China has the largest free-standing army on the planet right now. The last major point: while total expenditures on military expenses may be lower in the developing world, it's a fairly high percentage of GDP and/or the government's budget. Yep. You got it. The less money a state has, the bigger % it usually spends on guns.

MILITARY EXPENDITURES AS A PERCENT OF TOTAL GDP
(THIS IS NOT AN EXHAUSTIVE LIST)

Rank	Country	% of GDP
1	North Korea	33.0%
2	South Sudan	9.4%
3	Oman	8.6%
4	Saudi Arabia	8.0%
5	Israel	5.7%
6	Jordan	4.7%
7	Azerbaijan	4.6%
8	Algeria	4.6%
9	Russia	4.5%
10	United States	4.2%
11	Lebanon	4.0%
12	Yemen	4.0%
13	Armenia	3.9%
14	Angola	3.6%
15	Afghanistan	3.6%
16	Morocco	3.5%
17	Singapore	3.5%
18	Colombia	3.3%
19	Zimbabwe	3.2%
20	Swaziland	3.2%
30	United Kingdom	2.5%
37	France	2.3%
42	China	2.0%

"We got a man down! But military expenditures are way up!"

THE BOTTOM LINE: WHO IS DEVELOPED? WHO IS DEVELOPING? WHO IS SOMEWHERE IN BETWEEN?

Let's get this chapter wrapped up already! Given the terminology, the historical precedent, and the specific categories of comparison, can we now officially point out exactly who the developed and developing countries are? Well, why not? Let's give it a go! Below are a few different systems for classifying these levels of development, and we might as well start is out with the best one . . . namely, mine!

PLAID AVENGER DEVELOPMENTAL RULE OF THUMB

The rich countries are easy to see, so let's not dally on those developed dudes; the rest of the planet is much more interesting to consider. You won't find this theory in a textbook anywhere, besides this one, because it's a Plaid Avenger original. Lots of different states have lots of the developed world features, but still don't seem to be in the fully developed category. Like who?

Pakistan has advanced weaponry and nuclear bombs, but is not fully developed economically or demographically. India has nuclear bombs and is a well-established democracy, but is not fully developed. Saudi Arabia has a huge GDP and free health care, but is not fully developed. China is getting rich as Midas, has high technology, has nuclear bombs, a stable population growth rate, a diversified economy, and even put a man in space . . . maybe they are getting really close, but even they don't seem to be in the fully developed column yet. Okay, maybe they are. Its a close call at this point. So what makes the Plaid Avenger difference?

For me, it's all about how the average dude or dudette is doing. How are most people doing in the society? How much health care or good jobs or education do the *majority* of folks have access to? What is the real GDP per capita of the bulk of the workers? It kind of gets back to that theme I've hit you with about the middle class. There will always be a small percentage of excessively rich folks, and there will always be a lot of poor folks. But how are folks doing in the *middle*? Any country can have any amount of any of the factors listed above, but if it's not accessible to the majority of folks, then I classify the state as still developing. The fully developed states are always marked by the majority of people doing well and having access to all of those great things.

Make sense? That's why places like India may be booming economically right now, may be focused on quaternary computer jobs, have a space program, be a democracy, have a strong military and a huge GDP . . . but most people in India still live on a buck or two a day. And "most" of a billion people is a lot of peeps! India may have lots and lots of trappings of the developed world, but how can you call them fully developed when half a billion people don't have access to health care, or lack a proper diet? My answer: I don't.

HDI: A UN TAKE ON HOW FOLKS ARE DOING

I think the good folks at the UN agree with the Plaid Avenger on this one, too. Here is their take on things:

The UN Human Development Index (HDI) is some sort of complex mathematical formula that takes into account poverty, literacy rates, education, life expectancy, fertility rates, and a host of other factors. It has become a standard

FIGURE 5.1 HDI

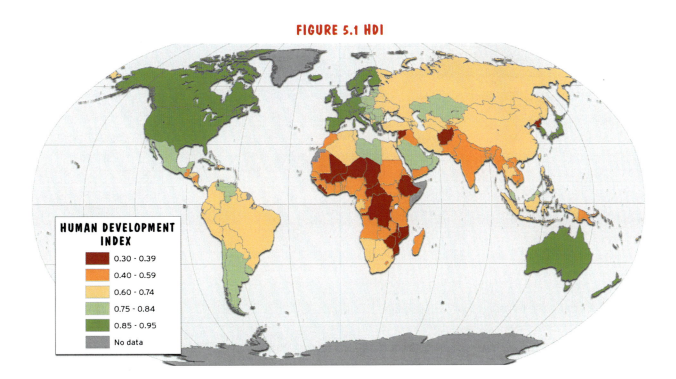

means of measuring overall human well-being. The index was developed in 1990 by a Pakistani economist, which gives it more credibility in the Plaid Avenger's eyes, and is used by the United Nations Development Program in its annual Human Development Report.

As you can see from the map, the closer you are to a perfect score of 1, the better off the humans are in that state. Take what you like from the map, but I just wanted to point out a few trends. Obviously, the developed, richer countries stand out near the top of the spectrum in North America, Europe, Australia and Japan. South America is not in bad shape by this measure, especially the southern states on the continent. Eastern Europe and Russia have slipped; they probably used to be in higher brackets, but factors such as life expectancy in some of these places has plummeted, as has their HDI. China, Central Asia, and some parts of the Middle East and Southeast Asia are also in that bracket, as their fortunes rise while the former states of the USSR fall. As we approach the bottom end of the HDI numbers, we see all of South Asia (esp. India) and big parts of Africa in orange. And finally, the countries in red include swathes of Africa, and failed states the world over.

AVENGER ASSESSMENT OF STATES' STATUSES

So tell us, Plaid Avenger: who is developed? Who is developing? Who is disorganized? Who is darn near deceased? Name the names! Alright then, since you have been so patient and asked so nicely, let's wrap this bad boy up. Here's a final word from the UN about development statuses:

> There is no established convention for the designation of "developed" and "developing" countries or areas in the United Nations system. In common practice, Japan in Asia, Canada and the United States in northern America, Australia and New Zealand in Oceania and Europe are considered "developed" regions or areas. In international trade statistics, the Southern African Customs Union is also treated as developed region and Israel as a developed country; countries emerging from the former Yugoslavia are treated as developing countries; and countries of eastern Europe and the former USSR countries in Europe are not included under either developed or developing regions.

Well, that's nice, I guess. And totally safe. But I'm all about the real deal. Many textbooks and news sources and academics simply lack the spine to actually point things out for what they are. But you know that I will throw down, and I'll tell you the shades of developmental plaid that I view the world in. Consider the following map, as created by yours truly:

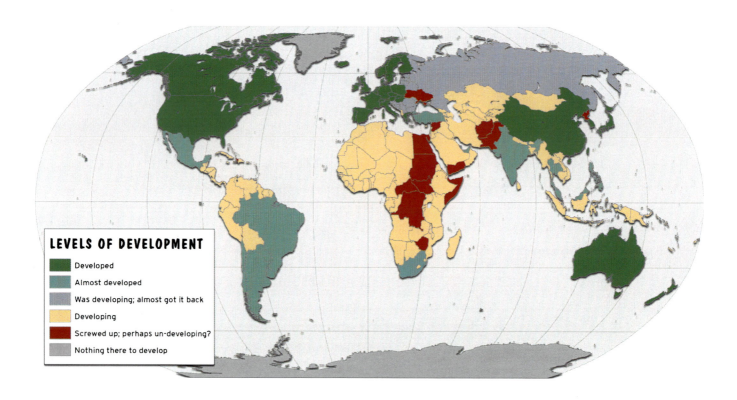

Here's the Plaid interpretation:

Full-on Developed: The easy category. We've beaten these guys down enough this chapter. North American region (US and Canada), Western Europe region, Australia-New Zealand region, Israel, and Japan are the pedal to the metal, full-on fully developed regions/countries. A few others in the club: South Korea, Taiwan, Singapore. Fully developed. No doubts.

You know what? I'm going to go ahead and go out on a limb. Let's pull the tooth and add China to the fully developed category. I know, I know, I know! Most other analysts and books are not ready to do this yet. That's why I'm ahead of my time. China is booming; and Macau, Hong Kong, and Taiwan are already considered fully developed, and are being reintegrated back into China proper. The Chinese have also pulled something on the order of 400 million people above the poverty line since 1980. Nothing suggests that these trends won't continue. High levels of technology, going to put a man on the moon, huge GDP, internal infrastructure investments, growing middle class. . . . Smells like fully developed to me!

Almost developed: This can be a bit tricky, but you can handle it given all you have learned in this chapter. Many South American countries are getting close, like Brazil, Argentina, and Chile. Mexico wavers back and forth—sometimes closer to full development, sometimes falling back to developing status. Check it year to year to see how it's doing. South Africa, Egypt, UAE and Turkey are beating down the door of full development as well. They have most of the features, but their GDP per capita is still fairly low and their middle class still thin in comparison to other developed places. India is booming, but with a much longer way to go, and a much bigger gap to close. The Philippines, Thailand, and Malaysia are our best Asian examples that are rounding out those countries getting close to full developed status.

Was developed, almost got it back: Eastern Europe and Russia are the only players in this category. And a distinct category it is. We don't really consider any place becoming "re-undeveloped," particularly when those places are nuclear powers and former world superpowers. However, the economic and political meltdown caused by the dissolution of the USSR in 1991 has left many of these countries with GDP numbers and life expectancy numbers more similar to impoverished African nations than European states. But they have the know-how, they have the technology . . . and like the six-million-dollar-man . . . they can rebuild it. The Plaid Avenger is assuming that they will: go for it, former commies! Russia could easily jump back to fully developed status soon, especially if they can encourage their declining population to get busy and grow the middle class some more. And one to watch: Poland, which is rocking right now!

Developing: This category still includes a whole lot of countries with a whole lot of people. Comprising big areas of sub-Saharan Africa, the Middle East, Central Asia, South Asia, Southeast Asia and South America, there can be tremendous variability on how far down the path of development they are. Or aren't.

Despite their high per capita GDP, places like Brunei and the Middle Eastern states of Oman, Qatar, and Saudi Arabia are generally not considered developed countries because their economies depend overwhelmingly on oil production and export. This lack of economic diversity is compounded by lack of political diversity; most are old school monarchies and theocracies. However, some of these countries, especially UAE, have begun to diversify their economies and democratize. Similarly, the Bahamas, Barbados, Antigua and Barbuda, Trinidad and Tobago, and Saint Kitts and Nevis enjoy a high per capita GDP, but these economies depend overwhelmingly on the tourist industry.

Many other countries—particularly in sub-Saharan Africa, Central Asia, Central America, the Caribbean, and Southeast Asia—have a patchy record of development at best. Most indicators of progress discussed in this chapter would be on the lower end of the development spectrum. Many have a long way to go, and are not currently traveling that fast on the footpath.

Screwed up; perhaps un-developing? This category is comprised of countries with long-term civil wars, large-scale breakdown of rule of law, or leaders who are totally insane. All could be described as nondevelopment-oriented economies or just outright chaotic systems. You may also see some of them referred to as "failed states." Best examples: Haiti, Somalia, Democratic Republic of Congo, and North Korea. Zimbabwe may be joining them soon if Mugabe continues his dictator antics. I hate to have to do this, but my friends in Pakistan are currently on a serious rocky road which may end catastrophically for them, so they get bumped to this category. Pakistan is not so much focused on developing so much as simple survival right now! Good luck, guys!

WORLD AT NIGHT: ANOTHER FUN PLAID AVENGER MEASURE OF HOW THE WORLD IS DOING

There's a final image to consider. It can show you a lot about the levels of development on the planet. Plus, it's just so awesomely cool.

FIGURE 5.2 EARTH AT NIGHT

From the Visible Earth: A catalogue of NASA images and animations of our home planet:
This image of Earth's city lights was created with data from the Defense Meteorological Satellite Program (DMSP) Operational Linescan System (OLS). Originally designed to view clouds by moonlight, the OLS is also used to map the locations of permanent lights on the Earth's surface. The brightest areas of the Earth are the most urbanized, but not necessarily the most populated. (Compare western Europe with China and India.) Cities tend to grow along coastlines and transportation networks. Even without the underlying map, the outlines of many continents would still be

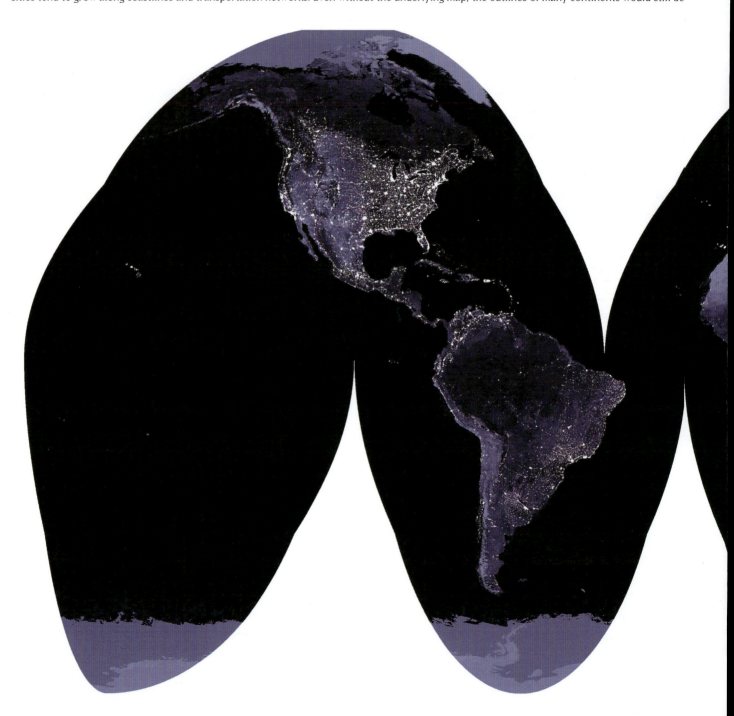

Developed or Developing?
CHAPTER FIVE

visible. The United States interstate highway system appears as a lattice connecting the brighter dots of city centers. In Russia, the Trans-Siberian railroad is a thin line stretching from Moscow through the center of Asia to Vladivostok. The Nile River, from the Aswan Dam to the Mediterranean Sea, is another bright thread through an otherwise dark region. Even more than 100 years after the invention of the electric light, some regions remain thinly populated and unlit. Antarctica is entirely dark. The interior jungles of Africa and South America are mostly dark, but lights are beginning to appear there. Deserts in Africa, Arabia, Australia, Mongolia, and the United States are poorly lit as well (except along the coast), along with the boreal forests of Canada and Russia, and the great mountains of the Himalayas.

Credit: Data courtesy Marc Imhoff of NASA GSFC and Christopher Elvidge of NOAA NGDC.

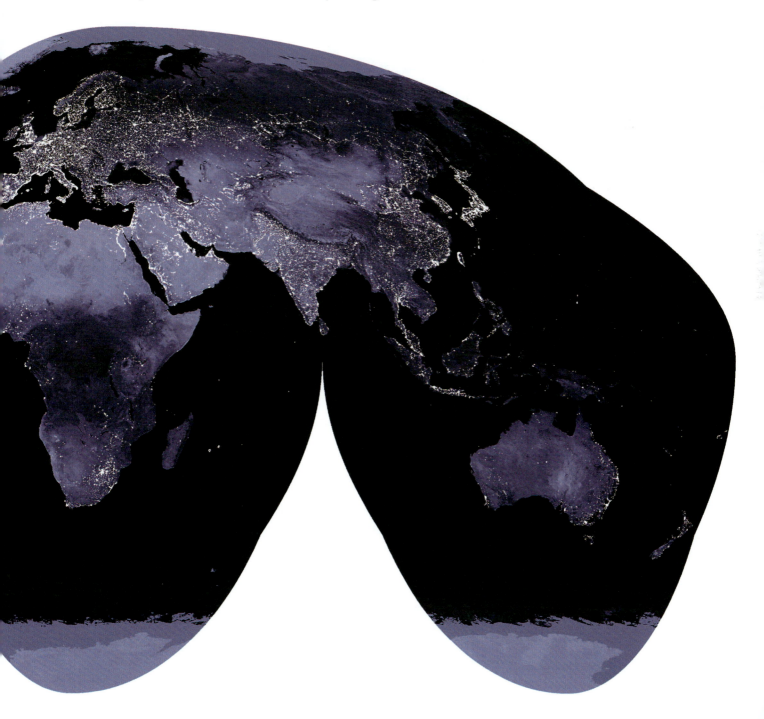

I'M DEVELOPMENTALLY SPENT . . .

There it is. That's the Plaid round-up. Hope you now understand the true differences in what is going on in the world in terms of levels of development, and that you have a better handle on how the world will be changing in the coming decades. I know I do. But dig this reference grid whenever you need a handy guide to assessing a developmental status of a state. It will make you think!

QUICK REFERENCE ROUND-UP

	Developed	Developing
Technology	• Highest levels of technology • Machines work faster and better • Extensively developed infrastructure • Effective emergency response	• Little to no technology • Without machines, people work harder and accomplish less • Unsafe or inefficient infrastructure • Poor emergency response
Industry	• More machine than human labor • High productivity • High energy consumption • Dependent on expensive, efficient fossil fuels	• More human than machine labor • Low productivity • Low energy consumption • Dependent on cheap, inefficient alternative fuels
Economics	• High salaries, high GDP per capita • Diverse economy • Large service sector, some quaternary • Value-added goods and services • Positive trade balance for state	• Low salaries, low GDP per capita • Limited economic options • Large primary and secondary sectors, no quaternary • Low value primary goods • Negative trade balance for state
Society	• Majority of population in middle class • Widespread investment in health care and education; high consumption • Can afford to take risks • Column or inverted population pyramid; fertility rate around 2.1 • Each generation gets better	• Majority of people in lower classes; middle class might exist • Little money to invest in health care, education, or consumption • Can't afford to take risks • True pyramid-shape population; high fertility rates (variable) • Each generation gets more screwed

	Developed	**Developing**
Health	• Decreased infant mortality, increased longevity • Access to effective health care • Sedentary work with mental stress • More processed foods • Most people die from circulatory disease or cancer	• Increased infant mortality and lower life expectancy • Susceptible to epidemics • Physical work with physical stress • Healthy food but insufficient calories • Most people die from preventable and curable disease
Government	• Solid democracy • Politically stable • Open to change protected against corruption • Participation in global trade and investment	• All forms of government found • Politically unstable • Closed to change susceptible to corruption • Insular economies; absent from global trade and investment
Cultural Cues	• Lots of fat people • They eat animals • People go to specific areas named "gyms" in order to stay lean • People have extra time to "recreate" "vacation", and "chill" at malls, parks, beaches, and foreign countries • Some people are so bored that they take drugs for fun • People do this cool thing called "retire" after they have worked for most of their lives	• Mostly skinny people • Animals eat them • People bust ass trying to stay alive 24/7 to stay lean. It's called life • People generally "hang out" only with their families at home or in the village. Most never leave their local area, much less their state • Some people grow drugs for the bored rich people in order to earn money so they can eat • People do this thing called "die" after they work their entire life
Military	• Maximum military technology • Actual or possible nuclear power • Weapons preferred to standing army • Casualties minimized • High military spending is low percentage of GDP	• Typically limited military technology • Nuclear power impossible (with some exceptions) • Standing army is main military power • Higher casualties • Low military spending is high percentage of GDP
Plaid Rule	• Most people are doing pretty well	• No matter what the stats say, most people aren't doing that well
HDI	• Close to score of one	• Close to score of zero
Night View	• Lit up like a Christmas tree!	• Lights out

CHAPTER OUTLINE

1. Economic Entities—Show Me the Money
   1.1. NAFTA
   1.2. DR-CAFTA
   1.3. FTAA (Proposed Only!)
   1.4. EU
   1.5. MERCOSUR
   1.6. ASEAN
   1.7. APEC
   1.8. OECD
2. Defense
3. The United Nations
   3.1. The Real Power at the UN: The UN Permanent Security Council
   3.2. NATO
   3.3. Warsaw Pact—Defunct!
4. New Kids on the BLOC
   4.1. SCO
5. Cultural Organizations
   5.1. Arab League
   5.2. OAS
   5.3. AU: African Union
6. International Oddballs
   6.1. G-7 Group of Seven
   6.2. G-8 Group of Eight
   6.3. G-20 Group of Twenty
   6.4. BRIC
   6.5. WTO
   6.6. IMF
   6.7. The World Bank
   6.8. NGOS
7. The Nuke Group

International Organizations

6

AND now we get to the trendiest world trend of globalization. This chapter consists of brief explanations of some entities that fall outside, or rather across, state boundaries—global players in a global age. We call them **supranationalist** organizations. Above and beyond the national level, these organizations play an increasingly important role in what is happening across our planet. But who are they? Where did they come from? How are we supposed to know this stuff? I don't know, friends. If the Plaid Avenger doesn't tell you these things, who will?

Supranationalist organizations are groups of states working together to achieve a common, or outlined, objective. This is another fairly new concept in human history, as states or nations have spent most of their time doing the opposite: beating the daylights out of each other or undercutting each other at every available opportunity. So why do countries now work together? The Plaid Avenger sees order in the universe; we can classify cooperation into three main classes: economic, defensive, and cultural.

I'll introduce you to the more important and happening entities here, but by no means is this list exhaustive. This chapter will also serve as a functioning reference for you as you progress through the rest of the book; come back often to refresh your memory when you see these acronyms appear in the regional chapters.

ECONOMIC ENTITIES—SHOW ME THE MONEY

Money. Who doesn't want it? Not any of the states of the world, that's for sure. A great way to make more money, if you are a country, is to make some trade deals with other countries. I'll buy all my bananas from you if you buy all of your wheat from me—sound good? On top of that, I won't put an import tax on your bananas, but if any other countries try to sell bananas here, I'll tax the heck out of them. Deal? This is the essence of **trade blocks** which are, as you might have guessed, a dandy vehicle for increasing trade between two countries . . . or perhaps among a whole bunch of countries, depending upon how many new kids are in your bloc.

Many economists believe that **free trade** between countries increases competition, which decreases prices for consumers, which in turn increase consumption of products . . . which ultimately benefits producers and consumers alike! Get governments out of the way, and let the market rule! For this reason, both the United States and the European Union are trying their hardest to promote "trade blocs" or "free trade zones" with neighboring countries, so that they can improve economic performance and increase sales. Even countries in Latin America, Africa and Asia have caught the bug.

However, there is a tug-of-war going on. Independent sovereign states naturally want to protect their own economies, so they are reluctant to sign up for free trade when they think that their local industries may lose the trade game. For example, if Chinese shoe companies make cheaper and better shoes than French shoe companies, France is not going to want free trade in shoes with China. Everybody in France might want to buy the less expensive Chinese shoes, so the French shoe companies would go out of business. Historically, the cheaper imported products are hit with a **tariff,** an import tax, which subsequently makes the price of the product more expensive, and thus the local products can compete better.

Many times, poor countries accuse rich countries of trying to take advantage of them by using free trade agreements. These poor countries argue that free trade isn't equally beneficial for both sides; that it's mostly beneficial for the fully developed, industrialized country because their companies are more competitive. Furthermore, they accuse developed countries of cheating, and they point to agricultural **subsidies** in these rich countries as an example. Farmers in Europe and America produce crap tons of food using lots of big equipment and fertilizers, thus their costs are high, and subsequently the food they make costs more. Farmers in poor countries don't use that expensive stuff and have cheaper labor, therefore their food should cost much less, giving them a competitive advantage in the world market. However, the rich farmers still "win" on the international market because Europe and America give their farmers huge subsidies to offset the higher costs of production they face. Uncle Sam gives American farmers money just to be farmers, and the farmers can turn around and sell their food for cheaper prices and still make money. You dig? And if you dig a lot, maybe you should become a farmer.

Poor countries argue that the only reason that rich countries became rich in the first place is by protecting their domestic industries by using things like tariffs and other forms of **protectionism**. Also, it can be argued that fully developed mega-rich companies from mega-rich countries are so technologically superior that they have a competitive advantage that can never be overcome . . . meaning that the less developed states will always be stuck buying finished goods and selling primary level commodities, thus always losing money. On the other hand, free trade usually does mean more trade, so the less developed countries do stand to sell much more oil or lima beans or flip-flops or beef lips. Poorer countries are torn as to whether or not it is in their best interest to join these trade blocks with the fully developed states.

Perhaps it's on these grounds that we are seeing many new trade blocks springing up that are comprised solely of states in "developing status," with no "rich kids" invited to the party. It certainly is the reason for the foot-dragging with the FTAA, but once again, I have gotten ahead of the story.

Check out these economic entities that you will be hearing a hell of a lot more about, as they will play an increasingly larger role in the way the global economy operates:

NAFTA

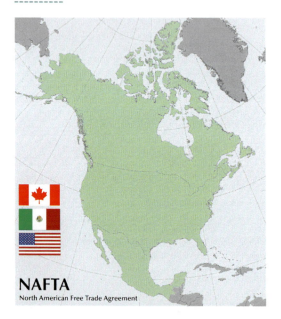

Members: United States, Canada, and Mexico

Summary: NAFTA, which stands for North American Free Trade Agreement, is between the United States, Mexico, and Canada, enacted in 1994. This agreement is meant to gradually eliminate all duties and tariffs on all goods and services between these three countries. However, the three nations are resisting lowering specific barriers that would hurt specific components of their economies. For example, the United States and Canada have been bickering because the United States imposes a duty on Canadian lumber that goes to the United States. The Canadians are accusing the Americans of not sticking to the treaty and are considering imposing duties on American goods to retaliate.

NAFTA has been very controversial in other ways too. Generally, multinational corporations support it because lower tariffs mean higher profits for them. Labor unions in the United States and Canada have opposed it because they believe that jobs will go from the United States and Canada to Mexico because of lower wages there. They were all correct: manufacturing jobs, particularly from the auto industry, migrated rapidly south of the border where wages were significantly lower, but this did make the costs of products cheaper to the consumer as well. American jobs were lost, but Americans pay lower prices for goods. Also, farmers in Mexico oppose it because agricultural subsidies in the United States have forced them to lower the prices on their goods. But make no bones about it: NAFTA has been an incredible plus to the 3 countries, as trade has exploded; more goods and more services now flow between the North American titans than ever before, and it looks set to expand into the future.

Fun Plaid Fact: Chapter 11 of the NAFTA treaty allows private corporations to sue federal governments in the NAFTA region if they feel like that government is adversely affecting their investments.

DR-CAFTA

Members: United States, Costa Rica, Dominican Republic, El Salvador, Guatemala, Honduras, Nicaragua. Currently, the US Administration is pushing hard to get Colombia and Panama into this club as well.

Summary: DR-CAFTA stands for Dominican Republic—Central America Free Trade Agreement and is an international treaty to increase free trade. It was ratified by the Senate of the United States in 2005. Like NAFTA, its goal is to privatize public services, eliminate barriers to investment, protect intellectual property rights, and eliminate tariffs between the participating nations. Many people see DR-CAFTA as a stepping stone to the larger, more ambitious, FTAA (Free Trade Agreement of the Americas).

The controversy regarding DR-CAFTA is very much like the controversy regarding NAFTA. Many people are concerned about America losing jobs to poorer countries where the minimum wage is lower and environmental laws are more lax. Also, some people are concerned that regional trade blocs like DR-CAFTA undermine the project of creating a worldwide free trade zone using organizations like the WTO.

CAFTA members

Fun Plaid Fact: Many Washington insiders see DR-CAFTA as a way of reducing the influence of China in Central America.

FTAA (PROPOSED ONLY!)

Members: *PROPOSED* All of the nations in North and South America, except Cuba. 'Cause the US hates commies. Dirty pinko commies.

Summary: The FTAA, which stands for Free Trade Area of the Americas, is a proposed agreement to end trade barriers between all of the countries in North and South America. It hasn't been ratified yet, because there are some issues that need to be worked out by the participating countries. The developed (rich) countries, such as the United States, want more free trade and increased intellectual property rights. The developing (poorer) countries, especially powerhouse Brazil, want an end to US/Canadian agricultural subsidies and more free trade in agricultural goods.

The key issue here for poor countries is agricultural subsidies. Farmers in the United States, and in rich countries generally, produce agricultural goods at a higher price than poor countries do. However, to keep their goods cheap, and thus competitive on the world market, the government of the United States pays their farmers subsidies. These subsidies make developing countries very angry because they believe subsidies give American farmers an unfair advantage. For this reason, some

Proposed FTAA members

Latin American leaders have stalled the agreement. Former Venezuelan President Hugo Chavez called the agreement "a tool of imperialism" and proposed an alternative agreement called the Bolivarian Alternative for the Americas.

For rich countries, the issue is intellectual property rights, which is best exemplified by copyright laws. Less developed countries sometimes oppose these rights because they believe that if they are enacted, they will stifle scientific research in Latin America and widen the gap between the rich and poor countries in the Americas.

It should be noted, as of this writing in 2014, that this tentative agreement is still stalled by more independent and "leftist" Latin American states that don't want to join a group that the US would likely dominate . . . especially Brazil, which sees itself as the natural true leader of an economically united Latin America. The "leftward swing" of Latin America, that we'll talk about in a later chapter, has seriously squashed the US administration's agenda on this issue.

Fun Plaid Fact: The only country that would not be included in the FTAA is Cuba, because the United States has an economic embargo that prohibits all trade with the communist regime. For this reason, Cuba more fully supports the Bolivarian alternative for the Americas, which is MERCOSUR . . . we will get to that on the next page.

EU

Members: Belgium, Bulgaria, France, Germany, Italy, Luxembourg, The Netherlands, Denmark, Ireland, United Kingdom, Greece, Portugal, Spain, Austria, Finland, Sweden, Cyprus, Czech Republic, Estonia, Hungary, Latvia, Lithuania, Malta, Poland, Romania, Slovakia, Slovenia

Summary: For years, European philosophers and political observers have recognized that the best way to ensure peace on the European continent while also increasing trade is to politically and economically integrate the nations. After the destruction and loss of life caused by World War II, European nations finally began taking small steps toward interdependence. They started by integrating their coal and steel industries in the ECSC (European Coal and Steel Community). What a long way they have come since then! Currently, the European Union, which has 27 member states, has a common market, a common European currency (the euro), a European

Commission, a European Parliament, and a European Court of Justice. The nations of the EU have also negotiated treaties to have common agricultural, fishing, and security policies. More so than any other free trade agreement, the European Union covers way more areas other than just trade.

Consequently, the EU is the most evolved supranationalist organization the world has ever seen—perhaps a "United States of Europe." Free movement of people across international borders of the member states makes it unique in the trade block category. Of greater importance is an evolving EU armed force, a single environmental policy, and increasingly, a single foreign policy voice. That is a very big deal!

However, there has been some resistance to integration within European countries. Some countries, like Norway and Switzerland, have refused to join, and others, like the United Kingdom, have refused to fully adopt the euro: the Brits do use the euro, but maintain their traditional pound as well. Also, in 2005, a constitution for the European Union was rejected by French and Dutch voters, putting the future of European integration into question. Many Europeans simply don't care about the European Union and others see it as a secretive, undemocratic organization that is taking away power from their home countries. Some of the richer countries in Europe are afraid that adding nations with weaker economies will take away money from them just to give it to less productive economies.

But make no bones about it, the EU unification and expansion has made Europe a global power once again. Individually, these European countries are rich places, but none could compete on their own with the likes of the US or even China. However, as a unit, the EU has the largest GDP on the planet. After a serious growth spurt in the last decade, it appears that the expansionism may be played out. Future candidates include Croatia, Bosnia, Macedonia, Albania, and possibly Turkey . . . but Ukraine and Georgia are now seen as too hot to handle for the EU given Russian resurgence of influence in these areas. Russia itself is usually invited to big EU talks as kind of an associate member already, although the idea of Russian ascension into the EU will never happen. Not everybody likes it, but the EU makes Europe a player in the world economy and world political terms. Divided, they are not much. United, Europe still has a big voice.

MERCOSUR

Members: Brazil, Argentina, Uruguay, Paraguay, with the newest addition: Venezuela!

Associate Members: Bolivia, Chile, Colombia, Ecuador, Peru, Guyana, & Surinam.

Summary: MERCOSUR is a free trade agreement between several South American countries that was created in 1991 by the Treaty of Asuncion. Like other free trade agreements, its purpose is to promote free trade and the fluid movement of goods and currency between the member countries. Many people see MERCOSUR as a counterweight to other global economic powers such as the European Union and the United States.

MERCOSUR's combined GDP is only 1/12 of the United States', standing at 1 trillion dollars. But watch out! Brazil is becoming a serious global player with a booming economy, and actually the entire group is prospering. They are further integrating on economic and political decision, and even talking about free movement of workers and a standard labor law throughout the block. Good stuff! However, keep an eye on this one as leftist events unfold in Latin America. It could become a viable force. Already, MERCOSUR has

MERCOSUR (MERCOSUL)

Member states
Associate members

now added all members of the Andean Community (another economic bloc) as "observer states" with the grander goal of uniting the entire continent in super-block called the Union of South American Nations (UNASAR)!!! Wow!

Fun Plaid Fact: I have been watching to see how serious this UNASAR concept is, and the concrete steps taken just in the last few years indicate that it will likely soon supercede MERCOSUR itself, and thus be an added entry in the next edition of this book!!!!

ASEAN

Members: Brunei, Cambodia, Indonesia, Laos, Malaysia, Burma, Philippines, Singapore, Thailand, Vietnam

Summary: ASEAN, which stands for **Association of Southeast Asian Nations**, is a free trade bloc of Southeast Asian countries. Like the European Union, ASEAN may possibly evolve into more than just a free-trade zone; it aims for political, cultural, and economic integration. It was formed in 1967 as a show of solidarity against expansion of Communist Vietnam and insurgency within their own borders. During that time, many countries around Vietnam were turning communist, and capitalist governments were extremely worried that communism might infect them as well. However, even Vietnam has joined ASEAN since then.

ASEAN is significant because of the heterogenous nature of its constituent countries. ASEAN countries are culturally diverse, including Muslims, Buddhists, and other religions. Governments in ASEAN range from democracy to autocracy. The economies of ASEAN countries are also very diverse, but they mainly focus on electronics, oil, and wood.

These guys are increasingly modeling themselves after the EU experiment, too. Even though they remain much more nationalistic than the European countries, the ASEAN group has much bigger goals than to simply be trade block. A common electric grid across the member countries has been proposed; an "open-sky" arrangement is soon taking effect (free movement of all aircraft among member states); and common environmental policies are being adopted across the region. The most interesting ASEAN prospect is now focused on, of all things, human rights! They actually wrote and adopted a legitimate constitution/charter which mentions the idea of protection of equal rights for all. This from a club which, at the time, had the dictatorship of Burma as a member! Interesting Asian times ahead for the ASEAN.

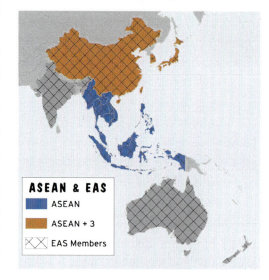

In addition, during annual ASEAN meetings, the three 'Dialogue Partners' (China, Japan, and South Korea) meet with ASEAN leaders . . . and when this happens, it is referred to as **ASEAN+3**. Wow! Those 3 economic titans as semi-associate members of ASEAN? That is a serious economic situation!

And I can do you one better: now ASEAN has become the core of the annual **East Asia Summit** which is the ASEAN+3 plus India, Australia, and New Zealand! The summit discusses issues including trade, energy, security and regional community building. Is this the early formation of an Asian EU? Who knows! But it's a fascinating development!

PLAID ALERT! Holy trade tips! Keep your eyes on this one as well. This could turn into the largest, richest, baddest block on the planet in your lifetime. Booming economies in most member states with more growth in the future. Bigger deal than that: China, South Korea, Japan and India as "associates" members? Are you kidding me? That's like over half of the entire planet's population under one economic umbrella. Watch out! They are going to be hot!

APEC

Members: Australia, Brunei, Canada, Chile, China, Indonesia, Japan, Korea, Malaysia, Mexico, New Zealand, Papua New Guinea, Peru, Philippines, Russia, Singapore, Taiwan, Thailand, United States, Vietnam—pretty much all the guys with Pacific coastline.

Summary: The Asia-Pacific Economic Cooperation trade bloc is a group of Pacific Rim countries that meets with the aim of improving economic and political ties. Like most free-trade blocs, the goal of APEC is to eventually reduce tariffs to nothing. Also, like many free trade agreements, agricultural subsidies have become a point of controversy. The leaders of all APEC countries meet annually in a summit called "APEC Economic Leaders' Meeting" which meets in a different location every year. The first of these meetings was in 1993 and was organized by US president Bill Clinton.

The countries in APEC are responsible for the production of about 80 percent of the world's computer and high-tech components. The countries in many of the Pacific Rim are also significant because the population in many of these countries is increasing dramatically. This trade bloc could possibly become a huge force in the global economy in the near future. Or it could totally be replaced by a proposed Pacific pact being pushed hard by the USA named the TPP. The **Trans-Pacific Partnership**: a very similar economic union that makes even deeper ties between the states, while simultaneously excluding China from the group. Currently only proposed, but being put together at such a frantic pace that it will likely be included in the next edition of this book . . . in which case APEC gets deleted!

OECD

Members: Austria, Belgium, Canada, Denmark, France, Germany, Greece, Iceland, Ireland, Italy, Luxembourg, Netherlands, Norway, Portugal, Spain, Sweden, Switzerland, Turkey, United Kingdom, United States, Japan, Finland, Australia, New Zealand, Mexico, Czech Republic, Hungary, South Korea, Poland, Slovakia

Summary: The Organisation for Economic Co-operation and Development (OECD) is an international organization of countries that accept the principles of democracy and free markets. After World War II, when Europe was in ruins, the United States gave European countries aid in the form of **the Marshall Plan** to rebuild the continent and repair the economy, while also ensuring that European countries remain democracies. The Organisation for European Economic Co-operation (OEEC) was formed in 1948 to help administer the Marshall Plan. In 1961, membership was extended to non-European countries and renamed the OECD. Because it contains most of the richer, more developed states around the world which are all democracies to boot, the OECD is really kind of the core of what I refer to as "Team West" throughout this text.

Like many trade agreements, the purpose of the OECD is to promote free trade, economic development, and coordinate policies. The OECD also does a lot of research on trade, environment, agriculture, technology, taxation, and other areas. Since the OECD publishes its research, it has become one of the world's best sources for information and statistics about the world.

Fun Plaid Fact: While you will still see many references to OECD in news/literature, it has never really been a really pro-active group like the other ones discussed so far, and is of decreasing significance altogether here in the 21st century as regional (specifically Asian) trade blocs have proliferated and dominated.

DEFENSE

Why should countries get together defensively? If they are all on the same team, then they won't fight—right? Well, that's the emphasis of the UN. But perhaps more pertinent are regional defense blocks that have cropped up between countries throughout history. Their thinking is more along the lines of: "I'll help you if you get attacked by an outsider, if you help me if I'm attacked by an outsider." If this sounds like trivial schoolyard thinking, don't laugh; the basis for World War I was a whole host of such pacts between European countries—once one country was attacked, virtually every other country was immediately pulled in as a consequence of defense agreements. Here are the big three that are pertinent in today's world—even though one of them is now gone—plus a fascinating newcomer with tremendous future potential growth. But first, the easy ones . . .

THE UNITED NATIONS

Members: All the sovereign states in the world except Vatican City. There are currently 193 of them. Even the Swiss finally joined a few years ago.

Summary: The United Nations, or UN, was founded in 1945 as a successor to the League of Nations. Like the League, the goal of the UN is to maintain global peace. Unlike the League, no major world wars have happened on the UN's watch. This is not to say that the United Nations has achieved global peace. In fact, UN "peacekeepers" have been on hand to witness some of the most egregious violations of human rights in recent history.

UN Secretary General Ban Ki-Moon

The UN is made up of several bodies, the most important of which is the Security Council (see Security Council section). The second most important body in the UN is the General Assembly where each of the 193 member nations has a representative and a vote. The General Assembly has produced gems such as the *Universal Declaration of Human Rights* and the lesser known *International Convention on the Protection of the Rights of All Migrant Workers and Members of Their Families*. The General Assembly is clearly the home of utopian thinkers, but not of any real international power. This leaves the major world powers like the US and China free to ignore everything that the General Assembly says, without even having to waste the time vetoing it.

The UN also includes hundreds of sub-agencies that you've heard of before, such as the World Health Organization (WHO) and UNICEF. The WHO is in charge of coordinating efforts in international public health. UNICEF (The United Nation's Children Fund) provides health, educational, and structural assistance to children in developing nations. Both agencies are supported by member nations and private donors. UNICEF also receives millions of pennies collected each year by children on Halloween. Just a handful of the hundreds of other UN agency acronyms you may have heard of include the FAO, IAEA, UNESCO, IMF, WMO, and the WTO.

Critics often charge the UN with being ineffective. This is largely true, but the United Nations was never really intended to be a global government. The best way to view the UN is a forum in which nations can communicate and work together. The UN is ill-equipped to punish any strong member for violations. If a member is especially naughty, a strongly worded UN resolution might recommend voluntary diplomatic or economic sanctions. Perhaps after World War III, the United Nations will be once again renamed and given stronger international authority. If there is anything left of us.

THE REAL POWER AT THE UN: THE UN PERMANENT SECURITY COUNCIL

Members: US, UK, Russia, China, and France and 10 other rotating positions.

The Security Council is composed of five permanent members (the United States, the United Kingdom, Russia, China, and France) and ten other elected members serving rotating two year terms. The Security Council is charged with responding to threats to peace and acts of aggression. Basically, for anything to get done, the Security Council has to do it. But things rarely get done because each of the five permanent members has the power to veto and prevent any resolution that they do not like. A single veto from any one of the permanent members kills the resolution on the spot. This group of rag-tag veto-wielding pranksters is currently the ultimate source in interpreting international law. Most of the Cold War saw little to no consensus on anything, as Team US/UK faced off against Team

Russia/China. Whatever one team tried to push, the other team generally would veto. The Frenchies vetoed according to mood and lighting of the room. Even today, votes tend to fall along these same alliance lines.

The other ten rotating members of the Council do not have veto power, but are often used as a coalition building tool to get things done. E.g.: During the build-up to the most recent war in Iraq, the US worked very hard to get as many members of the Council as possible to back the resolution to invade Iraq, knowing full well that China and Russia would veto it. This was a strategic move to show broad support for the war, even though the US accepted up front that the resolution would not be passed.

There is currently speculation that new members may be added to the UN Permanent Security Council. The prime candidates are Germany and Japan. The United States supports their candidacies; maybe because they have over 270,000 military personnel (including dependents of military) in Germany and Japan combined, and they are staunch US allies. There is also talk of including Brazil or India, or even more remotely, an "Islamic member" or an "African member." But seriously, what incentive does the Security Council have to dilute their powers? Remember, all five would have to agree to let a new member in, so while the United States would certainly support the incorporation of Japan, China would be more likely to tell Japan to go commit **Seppuku**, veto-style. However, the four most likely members (Japan, Germany, Brazil, and India) have released a joint statement saying that they will all support the others' entry bids. The best argument for enlargement is that Japan and Germany are the second and third largest contributors to the UN general fund, and thus deserve more power. Regardless, don't count on the Security Council getting any bigger unless serious global strife starts going down, which it will, sooner or later.

NATO

Members: Bulgaria, Estonia, Latvia, Lithuania, Romania, Slovakia, Slovenia, the United States of America, France, the United Kingdom, Iceland, Spain, Portugal, Germany, Italy, Belgium, Switzerland, Luxembourg, Finland, Poland, the Czech Republic, Hungary, Greece, Turkey, Norway, the Netherlands, Denmark, and Canada. New members inducted in 2009: Albania and Croatia!

NATO, which stands for the North Atlantic Treaty Organization, is a military alliance between certain European countries, Canada, and America. It was originally created in 1949 to serve as a discouragement to a possible attack from the Soviet Union (which never occurred). The most important part of NATO is Article V of the NATO Treaty, which states, "*The Parties agree that an armed attack against one or more of them in Europe or North America shall be considered an attack against them all. . . .*" This is called a **mutual defense clause** and basically means that the United States must treat an attack on Latvia the same as it would treat an attack on Tennessee.

Although NATO is a multilateral organization, the United States is clearly the captain of the ship. As a rule, US troops are never under the command of a foreign general. NEVER. Because of this, NATO troops (mainly American) are ALWAYS under American command. The United States also uses NATO countries to base its own troops and station nuclear weapons. Many historians blame the United States for provoking the Cuban Missile Crisis, saying that the Russians only wanted to put nukes in Cuba because the United States had at that time stationed nukes in Turkey (a NATO member).

Since the Cold War, NATO has been looking for a new role in the world. Many of the former Soviet republics have since been admitted to NATO—which, by the way, really ticks off Russia. NATO expansion was promoted as an expansion of democracy and freedom into Eastern Europe. More likely, it was to make sure Russia would never be able to regain the territory. NATO has also been increasingly active in international police work, although there is no real justification for this in the NATO charter. NATO forces were heavily involved

NATO Secretary General Fogh Rasmussen. Don't make him angry. You wouldn't like NATO when he's angry.

in the Bosnia conflict in 1994 and the Yugoslavia conflict in 1999, although in reality these were just American troops under a multinational flag. After September 11th attacks on the US, NATO has also become involved in the anti-terrorism game, even invoking Article V for the first time with regard to Afghanistan. Remember, the war in Afghanistan is a NATO mission, not a US mission. But let's be honest here; the US does most of the heavy lifting, as usual.

And the NATO role continues to become broader and more bullish lately: NATO was the central organizing entity in the 2011 invasion of Libya. Say what? What the heck did Libya do to any NATO country? Answer: Nothing, which goes to show how the entity is rapidly redefining itself here in the 21st century. It appears that NATO is fast becoming the military muscle for the objectives of 'Team West,' wether those objectives are defense, economic, or purely political. Interesting stuff, eh? And infuriating stuff to those not aligned with the NATO countries.

Fun Plaid Fact: The only country in NATO without a military force is Iceland. The Icelandic Defense Force is an American military contingent stationed permanently on the island.

WARSAW PACT—DEFUNCT!

PAST Members: Soviet Union (club president), Albania (until 1968), Bulgaria, Czechoslovakia, East Germany (1956–1990), Hungary, Poland, and Romania.

The Warsaw Pact, or if you prefer the more Orwellian Soviet name—the "Treaty of Friendship, Co-operation and Mutual Assistance," was the alliance formed by the Soviet Union to counter the perceived threat of NATO. The Warsaw Pact was established in 1955 (six years after NATO) and lasted *officially* until 1991 (two years post-Berlin Wall). Much like the Bizarro-Superman to the United State's real Superman, the Warsaw Pact never had the teeth or the organizational strength of NATO. Perhaps this is because many of the members actually hated the dominance of the Soviet Union. Two countries, Hungary (1956) and Czechoslovakia (1961), tried to assert political independence and were subsequently crushed by Soviet military forces in exercises that would make **Tiananmen Square** uprising look like an after school special.

The main idea behind the Warsaw Pact was mutual protection. If the United States attempted to invade any of the Warsaw members, it would guarantee a Soviet response. In this way, the Warsaw countries acted like a tripwire against the expansion of Western-style capitalism and democracy, firmly establishing the location of the Iron Curtain. Shortly after the Cold War, most Warsaw Pact countries either ceased to exist or defected to NATO.

Fun Plaid Fact: The Soviet Union despised American acronyms. Instead of taking the first letter from each word, the Soviets preferred taking the entire first sound. For example, Communist International was "Comintern."

NEW KIDS ON THE BLOC!!!

SCO

Members: China, Russia, Kazakhstan, Kyrgyzstan, Tajikistan, and Uzbekistan

Observer States: India, Pakistan, Mongolia, and Iran

Goodbye, Warsaw Pact! Hello, SCO! Watch this new BLOC! It is evolving fast, with gigantic repercussions for international relations and world balance of power in the future of Asia!

Summary: The Shanghai Cooperation Organization grouping was originally created by 5 member states in 1996 with the signing of the *Treaty on Deepening Military Trust in Border Regions* . . . however with the addition of Uzbekistan in 2001, which brought them up to 6 members, they can't use that wicked cool nickname of "Shanghai 5" anymore. Too bad. But they are are the hottest defense block to keep an eye on, as they are the newest on the scene; so new, in fact, that they have not exactly quite figured out what they are yet. Part military, part economic, part cultural . . . but 100% important to know. Let's just focus on military aspects for now.

Created with that *Deepening Military Trust* issue, they have also agreed to a *Treaty on Reduction of Military Forces in Border Regions* in 1997 and in July 2001, Russia and China, the organization's two leading nations, signed the *Treaty of Good-Neighborliness and Friendly Cooperation* . . . wow,

SHANGHAI COOPERATION ORGANISATION

Member States | Observer States | Dialogue Partners

could they get any more sickening sweet with the descriptors? What an Eurasian love-fest. The SCO is primarily centred on its member nations' security-related concerns, often citing its main threats/focuses as: terrorism, separatism, and extremism. You can easily read into this as a great vehicle for all these governments to help each other crack down on any internal political dissidents as well.

They work together thwarting terrorism and stuff, but they are also quickly absorbing other avenues of cooperation, like in domestic security, crime, and drug trafficking. Over the past few years, the organization's activities have expanded to include increased military cooperation, intelligence sharing, and counterterrorism. Of significant note: there have been a number of SCO joint military exercises, and while it is very early to think that the SCO is a serious strategic military power, please keep in mind that the group is still very young and has a long way to go and to grow. We may just be seeing the beginning of their military prowess. Dig this: both Russia and China are nuke powers, Russia has a ton o' of weaponry, and China has the largest standing army on Earth. So this club could become a serious defensive force, if they put their minds to it.

Is this thing sizing up to be a counterbalance to US power or as an overt anti-NATO? Perhaps. But one thing is for sure: its six full members account for 60% of the land mass of Eurasia and its population is a third of the world's . . . and if you include the observer states, they collectively account for half of the human race. The SCO has now initiated over two dozen large-scale projects related to transportation, energy and telecommunications and held regular meetings of security, military, defense, foreign affairs, economic, cultural, banking and other officials from its member states. No multinational organization with such far-ranging and comprehensive mutual interests and activities has ever existed on this scale before. A combo EU/NATO of Eurasia for this century? Could be! So you gotsta' know the SCO! They are fast becoming a playa'!

CULTURAL ORGANIZATIONS

Some supranationalist organizations form out of a desire to maintain a cultural coherence with like countries, or to promote certain aspects of their culture among their member states. In other words, monetary gain is not the driving force behind the organization, although economics usually sneaks in there as well. Here are three very different such organizations to compare and contrast.

ARAB LEAGUE

Members: Egypt, Iraq, Jordan, Lebanon, Saudi Arabia, Syria, Yemen, Libya, Sudan, Morocco, Tunisia, Kuwait, Algeria, United Arab Emirates, Bahrain, Qatar, Oman, Mauritania, Somalia, Palestine, Djibouti, Comoros

The Arab League is an organization designed to strengthen ties among Arab member states, coordinate their policies, and promote their common interests. The league is involved in various political, economic, cultural, and social programs, including literacy campaigns and programs dealing with labor issues. The common bond between the countries in the Arab League is that they speak a common language, Arabic, and they practice a common religion, Islam. The Charter of the Arab League also forbids member states from resorting to force against each other. In many ways, the Arab League can be seen as a regional UN. It was formed in 1945.

However, the Arab League is better known for their lack of coherence and in-fighting more so than any unifying activities they have had so far to date. In fact, Libyan leader Muammar Qaddafi threatened to withdraw from the League in 2002, because of "Arab incapacity" in resolving the crises between the United States and Iraq and the Israeli-Palestinian conflict. If the Arab League ever gets its act together, it could be a powerful force in the world. Right now, it is not.

Let's get this Arab party started!

Radical Arab League Update for 2012: Holy Middle Eastern Madness! The League finally agreed to something, and that something significantly impacted world events! I am referring to the international invasion of Libya in the early months of 2011, a move that was supported by the Arab League! They voted against one of their own too . . . all the other Arab leaders so despised Muammar Qaddafi that they supported outside intervention to help have him deposed! The Arab League's support of this measure was crucial because US/UK/French/NATO/UN intervention would have likely not happened at all if the League would have voted against it. No western power would have wanted to be seen as a foreign, anti-Islamic, imperialist force invading Libya . . . but once all the other Arab states backed it, then game on! And now the Arab League has united once more: they group is standing with a single opposition voice against fellow Arab Bashar al-Assad, President of Syria currently cracking down brutally on his own people. Saudi Arabia in particular is making plans to arm the Syrian rebels, and the rest of the League will likely support that action! A new era for the Arab group may be dawning.

Fun Plaid Fact: Egypt was suspended from the Arab League from 1979 to 1989 for signing a peace treaty with Israel. Libya has sporadically quit and re-joined the group multiple times depending on how Muammar Qaddafi was feeling at the time. (see more on that in the AU section on next page.) Syria has currently been suspended as well, due in part to the government mass killing of Arabs, aka Syrian citizens.

OAS

Members: Argentina, Bolivia, Brazil, Chile, Colombia, Costa Rica, Cuba, Dominican Republic, Ecuador, El Salvador, Guatemala, Haiti, Honduras, Mexico, Nicaragua, Panama, Paraguay, Peru, United States, Uruguay, Venezuela, Barbados, Trinidad and Tobago, Jamaica, Grenada, Suriname, Dominica, Saint Lucia, Antigua and Barbuda, Saint Vincent and the Grenadines, Bahamas, Saint Kitts and Nevis, Canada, Belize, Guyana

Summary: The OAS, which stands for Organization of American States, is an international organization headquartered in Washington, DC. According to Article 1 of its Charter, the goal of the member nations in creating the OAS was "to achieve an order of peace and justice, to promote their solidarity, to strengthen their collaboration, and to defend their sovereignty, their territorial integrity, and their independence." Other goals include economic growth, democracy, security, the eradication of poverty, and a means to resolve disputes. Historically, the first meeting to promote solidarity and cooperation was held in 1889 and was called the First International Conference of American States. Since then, the OAS has grown, through a number of small steps, to become the organization it is today. Like the Arab League, this organization is a kind of regional UN.

Unlike free-trade blocs, the OAS encompasses many areas other than just trade. For example, it oversees elections in all of its member countries. However, it has also been criticized as a means for America to control the countries in Latin America. For example, when America wanted Cuba kicked out of the OAS, the organization quickly did so. However, many dictatorships that America has supported have remained within the OAS.

But this "US as imperialist" attitude is changing fast in the OAS. US President Barack Obama personally addressed the group in April 2009, pledging to bring more unity to the hemisphere and even hinting at thawing relations with the Cubans. At that meeting, Obama even shook hands with legendary US-hating Venezuelan President Hugo Chavez! The OAS may actually be gaining ground as a legit forum for problem-solving in the Americas. As of this writing, Cuba is being reconsidered for membership, and it appears that things are moving forward rapidly.

AU: AFRICAN UNION

Members: Algeria, Angola, Benin, Botswana, Burkina Faso, Burundi, Cameroon, Cape Verde, Central African Republic, Chad, Comoros, Democratic Republic of the Congo, Republic of the Congo, Côte d'Ivoire, Dijbouti, Egypt, Equatorial Guinea, Eritrea, Ethiopia, Gabon, Gambia, Ghana, Guinea, Guinea-Bissau, Kenya, Lesotho, Liberia, Libya, Madagascar, Malawi, Mali, Mauritius, Mozambique, Namibia, Niger, Nigeria, Rwanda, & Zimbabwe.

Suspended Members: Mauritania

Summary: The Organization of African Unity was established in 1963 at Addis Ababa, Ethiopia, by 37 independent African nations to promote unity and development; defend the sovereignty and territorial integrity of members; eradicate all forms of colonialism and promote international cooperation. This organization changed its name to the African Union in 2002. Institutionally, the AU is very much like the EU with a parliament, a commission, a court of justice, and a chairmanship which rotates between the member countries. The AU is also beginning to deploy peacekeepers, and it has sent over 2500 soldiers to the Darfur region of the Sudan. Every country in Africa is a member of the AU except for Morocco, which withdrew in 1985. Also, Mauritania was suspended in 2005 after a coup d'etat occurred and a military government took power. The new government has promised to hold elections within two years, but many observers are doubtful that it will.

African military problems to be increasingly solved by African troops. How novel!

There are many problems facing Africa such as civil war, disease, undemocratic regimes, poverty, and the demographic destabilization caused by the AIDS epidemic . . . these issues are more than even a rich, well-established regional block could handle, and the AU has thus far proved incapable of positively impacting any of these problems successfully. However, its most successful component to date is their military wing. Major powers from around the globe have hailed the common AU military as the most awesome thing the continent could do, and have supported it whole-heartedly. Why? Because the AU military can thus be tasked with solving African conflicts, without the outside powers becoming directly involved. After the US debacle in Somalia (go watch *Blackhawk Down*) no one wants to send actual troops to stop African conflicts, even in the face of titanic humanitarian disasters like the Rwandan genocide. And maybe now they don't have to! Because the AU has become the choice d'jour for outside support to deal with these issues. While the AU may not get outside support for anything else, look for the military to be bolstered with funding and training from the US, the EU and maybe even China and Russia, in lieu of actual participation in conflicts on the ground.

Fun Fact: The idea of an African Union separate from the OAU came from Muammar Qaddafi, who wanted to see a "United States of Africa." He was sick of developments in the Arab world and publicly gave up on being an Arab. In 2011 he publicly gave up on living, when he was assassinated during the Libyan uprising.

"Up yours, Arab League. I'm African now!"

INTERNATIONAL ODDBALLS

In addition to these, other entities have been formed at the international level for specific functions. Many of these organizations are frequently in the news, so I feel a brief introduction to them is merited. Haven't you ever wondered who the heck is the G7, the G8, the IMF, the World Bank, or the WTO, and what is an NGO?

G-7 GROUP OF SEVEN

Members: Canada, France, Germany, Italy, Japan, UK, and the United States

The **Group of Seven** (or G-7) is the "country club" of international relations. It's a place where the richest industrialized nations go to talk about being rich, form strategies for staying rich, and—like any other country club—figure out how to keep everyone else poor. The leaders from G-7 countries meet each year for a summit. The summits are often widely protested for reasons such as global warming, poverty in Africa, unfair trade policies, unfair medical patent laws, and basically, for a general sense of arrogance.

Originally, the group was called the G-6, which was the G-7 minus Canada. They formed out of the **Library Group** because rich countries were enraged about the **1973 oil crisis**. Then Canada joined the group in 1976, making it the G-7. Even though this group has since evolved into the G-8, the G-7 group still meets annually to discuss financial issues.

G-8 GROUP OF EIGHT

Members: G-7 plus Russia

Same as above, with Russia in attendance. Russia is still a nuclear power, still the largest territorial state on the planet, and perhaps most significantly a major energy resource provider to the world—especially to the G-7 countries. They have to invite the big boy to the party every now and again, or the big boy might feel neglected and go play with China. The G-7 doesn't want that. They need their energy! In 1991, Russia's entry into the group turned it from G-7 to the G-8. Who knows how much longer the G-7 or G-8 will even last given the rapidly changing face of our planet. What do I mean? Well, in our day and age, what point is there to having a meeting of the "biggest" world economies that doesn't include China? Or India? Or Brazil? It's getting to be kind of outdated and pathetically sad for all the old white-boy countries to get together to chat about world affairs without these other up-and-coming-non-white states having input, so we are probably witnessing the end of days of both the G-7 and G-8, although old traditions die hard and they will survive for a bit longer. And the G-8 as a whole maybe be down-graded back to the G-7, as Russia continues to lean more back towards Asian ties over Western ones . . . as evidenced by their more staunch support for the SCO and BRICS (more on that in a minute.)

G-20 GROUP OF TWENTY

PLAID ALERT!!!

Great googly global groups! We have a new international organization titan in our midst, my friends! The G-20 (formally, the Group of Twenty Finance Ministers and Central Bank Governors).

Members: Technically, it is comprised of the finance ministers and central bank governors of the G7, 12 other key countries, and the European Union Presidency (if not a G7 member). Also at the meetings are the heads of the European Central Bank, the IMF, and the World Bank.

The literal translation: the G-8 rich states + Argentina, Australia, Brazil, China, India, Indonesia, Mexico, Korea, Saudi Arabia, South Africa, Turkey + all those aforementioned bank heads. Collectively, the G-20 economies comprise 85% of global GDP, 80% of world trade and two-thirds of the world population. Whoa! That's all the money!

Summary: The G-20 is a forum for cooperation and consultation on matters pertaining to the international financial system which was created in 1999. It studies, reviews, and promotes discussion among key industrial and emerging market countries of policy issues pertaining to the promotion of international financial stability, and seeks to address issues that go beyond the responsibilities of any one organization. The key here is to "promote international financial stability," but I'm thinking they are quickly turning into a whole hell of a lot more. Why would I think that?

Because all the prime ministers and presidents are now showing up for these meetings! A Washington, D.C. summit was held in November 2008 and a London summit in April 2009, which were attended by all the heads of the respective states. Barack was there baby, chillin' with other heads of states! And these folks are truly transforming the power structure of the planet: the G-8 guys realize that they can't fix nothing without the cooperation of titans like China and India. In London, the G-20 adopted a collective approach to solving the global recession, but also are reorganizing the IMF and World Bank to incorporate other non-G8 voices, which have dominated global financial institutions for years. This is exciting stuff!

I truly believe this G-20 unit has now fully superseded the G-7, the G-8, and any other G's as the premier problem-solving institute on earth. The UN is too big and bureaucratic, and the G-7 too white and too exclusive, but the 20 seems to be a great balance of peoples and powers from across the planet. I would speculate that this much more representative and simultaneously streamlined group will be where all sorts of international treaties and agreements will have their foundation stones set; from economic crises to global warming issues to nuclear proliferation problems, look for the talking points to be brought up at these G-20 pow-wows.

This star is new, but shining already. And its future is bright indeed!

Fun Plaid Fact: There actually has been another G-20 gang comprised of an array of developing nations from Africa, Latin America and Asia. Their primary goal has been fighting for trade rights, particularly in the agricultural sector. You probably won't hear much from that group anymore, but just be aware in case you do . . . they are the poor G-20, not this huge rich G-20 described above.

BRICS

Members: Brazil, China, India & Russia

The Avenger has his plaid panties in a bunch about this unofficial "group" because it represents a serious global shift that has started in the last several years: a move to more representative economic and political power on the world stage. You can possibly look at the BRIC as an alternative center of power to the "Team West" rich countries that have run the global show for a century. It is a new, dynamic, and growing coalition which you will hear a lot more about in the future . . . . . just as you will increasingly hear less and less about the G-7 or G-8. So what is this BRIC house all about?

An acronym for the states of Brazil, Russia, India and China combined, BRIC was first coined in 2003 by a financial analyst at Goldman Sachs who speculated that by 2050, these four economies would be wealthier than most of the current major

BRICS 2014

economic powers put together. For sure, China and India will become the world's biggest suppliers of manufactured goods and services, with Russia and Brazil becoming some of the biggest suppliers of natural resources. All four are developing and industrializing rapidly and making bank. Because of their emerging statuses, their increasingly educated populations, and their lower labor costs, the BRIC has also become a magnet for foreign investment, outsourcing, and development of R&D centers.

But this thing has already grown well beyond a simple classification of future rich countries, and this is the deal I really want you to know. It is consistently pointed out that these four countries have not formed a structured political alliance like the EU, NAFTA or NATO . . . . . yet! I'm telling you friends, these guys are thinking about it! They started having face-to-face summits in 2009, and are increasingly agreeing on a whole lot of economic AND foreign policy issues which they then announce to the world under a common voice. Craziness!

What am I spouting about? At the 2011 meeting of the G-20, the BRIC countries demanded, and received, more voting power in global financial institutions like the IMF and World Bank (which they should, since they are increasingly funding them). And what is certainly the boldest and most telling strategic political initiative they have taken to date, all four BRIC countries have jointly declared that they do not support harsh sanctions against Iran and that they support Iran's right to develop nuclear power. What's that got to do with economic policy? Nothing! But it certainly does fly in the face of Team West's opinion of Iran, and that is why I think its important that you know that the BRIC is fast evolving into something much more than a simple economic group . . . . they are becoming a global entity on par with Team West. It's not official, it's not on paper, and it's not heavily coordinated yet, but for sure the BRIC is going to be a significant entity of the 21st century. Get hip to the BRIC!

BODACIOUS BRIC 2012 UPDATE: Exciting expansion has been enacted! The BRIC has just become the BRICS my friends! Say what? A new 'S' in the bric-house? That's right, the S is for South Africa which just joined the ranks of this increasing important global group. Now the gang includes the biggest economy of Africa, to join the biggest economy of South America, along with the 3 biggest economies of Asia.

At their last meeting, the members worked on a slew of trade issues, promised to invest heavily in each other's economies, and also made a public statement that the use of force "should be avoided" in Libya. What's that got to do with economics? Nada, which is why its important to note. This group, while still young, is already making unified political statements about world events . . . world events on which they share common cause, a common cause that is distinctly NOT the Team West view. Hmmmm . . . do I see the formation of a bi-polar world forming? Let's keep a close eye on this entity to find out.

WTO

Dudes In Club—157 total members

Dudes Observing the Club—Iran, Iraq, Sudan, Vietnam, Vatican City . . .

Dudes NOT In the Club—Palestine, Somalia, North Korea . . .

The World Trade Organization (WTO) is an international, multilateral organization that makes the rules for the global trading system and resolves disputes between its member states. The stated mission of the WTO is to increase trade by promoting lower trade barriers and providing a platform for the negotiation of trade. In principle, each member of the WTO is a privileged trading partner with every other member. This means that if one member gives another a special deal, he's got to give it to everyone else—like in elementary school if you were caught with candy.

Things that make the WTO sigh in delight are "open markets," "tariff reductions," and "long walks on the beach at sunset." The WTO is basically the application of capitalism on a global scale. The key idea is that competition creates efficiency and growth. *Any* country should be able to sell *anything* it can, *any*where it wants, at *any* price that *any*one will pay. The WTO can boast some successes in growing international trade, but these have also been accompanied by increased wealth disparity between rich and poor nations AND between the rich and poor within nations.

Formally established in 1995, the WTO is structured around about 30 different trade agreements, which have the status of international legal texts. Member countries must ratify all WTO agreements to join the club. Many of the agreements are highly criticized including the Agreement on Agriculture, which reduces tariffs hurting small farms in developing countries. One of the most famous anti-globalization protests occurred around the 1999 WTO meeting in Seattle that galvanized various groups like pro-labor, pro-environment, anti-fur, etc. under a single anti-WTO banner.

Fun Plaid Fact: The Kingdom of Tonga became the 150th member in 2005. The oldest animal ever recorded, a tortoise named Tu'i Malila, died in Tonga in 1965. Okay, this has nothing to do with the WTO, but turtles are cool.

IMF

Members: Everyone. Seriously. Okay, you got me! Everyone except North Korea, Cuba, Liechtenstein, Andorra, Monaco, Tuvalu and Nauru.

The primary responsibility of the International Monetary Fund (IMF) is to monitor the global financial system. The IMF works at stabilizing currency exchange rates. Doing this, they provide security to overseas investors and help promote international trade. The IMF's policies are also aimed at reducing the phenomenon of "boom and bust," where economies grow rapidly, then stagnate, then grow rapidly, then stagnate, then grow rapidly, et cetera. The main tool of the IMF is "financial assistance" (aka loans), which they provide to countries with "balance of payment problems" (aka big time debt). As a condition of the loans, the IMF mandates "structural adjustment programs." These programs are designed to turn a cash profit, allowing the borrowing country to repay its debt to the IMF. Here is a short glossary of "structural adjustment" terms and how they are interpreted by the locals:

IMF sez . . .	Locals sez it means . . .
Austerity	cutting social programs
User Fees	charging for stuff like education and health care and water
Resource Extraction	selling stuff out of the ground that rich countries want
Privatization	selling state owned stuff to rich companies (usually foreigner-owned)
Deregulation	removing domestic control over stuff
Trade liberalization	allowing foreigners to open sweatshops and exporting stuff made in sweatshops

Much like the WTO and World Bank, the IMF is often congratulated for growth in the global trade and production and simultaneously scorned for increasing the poverty gaps within countries and between countries.

THE WORLD BANK

Similar to the IMF, the mission of the World Bank (actually the World Bank Group) is to encourage and safeguard international investment. All the while, the World Bank attempts to help reduce poverty and spawn economic development. The World Bank works primarily with "developing countries" helping them develop in a Westerly fashion. Also, like the IMF, the World Bank loans are contingent on adopting "structural adjustments." While the IMF deals primarily with currency stabilization, the World Bank is primarily like a real bank, loaning countries money for very specific development projects like a hydropower plant or a disease-eradication program.

Unlike the IMF, which is headquartered in Switzerland, the World Bank Group is headquartered in Washington, D.C. and the US plays a very heavy hand in both its leadership and loaning activities. At least for now . . .

It should be noted that the World Bank is breaking new ground on the redefinition of the sovereignty issue that we covered in chapter 3. Due to government corruption in many states, particularly Africa, the World Bank is now putting further stipulations and oversight on all the loans it makes to countries. They are going in and making sure that the money they give a country to build an AIDS clinic doesn't end up getting used to buy weaponry for the state. The Plaid Avenger is proud as punch at such a bold move, but many states are hopping mad that this type of intense oversight violates their sovereignty—I'm with the World Bank on this one. Suck it up, sovereign states. If you want the jack, prove it's going to be used responsibly.

Watch for this issue to gain world attention soon. As of this writing, it's causing consternation in Chad as we speak . . .

NGOS

NGOs are Nongovernmental Organizations. These are basically every private organization that is not directly affiliated with a government, like Amnesty International or Greenpeace. We are talking about a growing number of highly influential international groups that are playing an ever important role in transnational politics. These groups transcend borders and unite common interests. NGOs are set up to represent a diverse array of special interests (environmental protection, human rights, et cetera). Here are a few examples of influential NGOs:

- Human Rights Watch—With a budget of ~$20 million a year, this NGO aims to document violations of international humanitarian law by sponsoring fact-finding research. HRW recently waged a successful campaign against the use of land-mines, which the U.S. government opposed.
- Freedom House—This NGO supports research for democracy promotion. Also, each year FH ranks countries on a scale from "Free" to "Not Free." Luckily, as of 2014, the United States is still "Free."
- Greenpeace—As the name suggests, this NGO hopes to achieve greenness using peaceful means. Greenpeace is also the only NGO to own a ship *(The Rainbow Warrior)* that the French government intentionally sunk. Funny story, actually; google it and find out. The greatest French military victory since the Napoleonic era.
- Amnesty International—This NGO is committed to protecting the human rights enshrined in the UN Universal Declaration of Human Rights.
- International Red Cross (and Red Crescent)—The sole function of the Red Cross is to protect the life and dignity of victims in armed conflict. The Red Cross is independent, neutral, and all that other crap. They help anyone and everyone.

We will discuss some of these NGOs in more detail in later chapters. Party on.

THE NUKE GROUP

Members: US, Russia, UK, France, China, India, Pakistan, Israel
Questionable Members: North Korea, Iran

Last, but certainly not least, is a most important gang of states on planet earth with this homogenous trait: they got nuclear bombs! Or perhaps maybe they do. Or perhaps maybe they are trying to get them. While not an "official" entity in the spirit of the other groups discussed in this chapter, I would be remiss without sticking this information in somewhere . . . . and what better place than a chapter on clubs, as this particular club has enough firepower to blow up all of the other clubs on the planet? The club with the biggest clubs! But it's much more important than that if you want to understand how the world works and how geopolitical power is actually wielded in real life in our day and age. What do I mean?

Well, who is in the club? Let's start with the original declared nuclear powers: US, Russia, UK, France, and China. Hey! Wait a minute! That's the exact same group that as the UN Permanent Security Council! How true, my quick-witted friends, and that is no coincidence! These 5 countries were the first to develop, test, and therefore prove that they possessed

THE NUKE CLUB

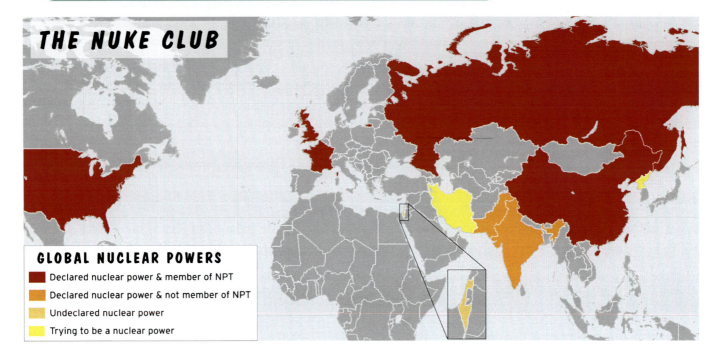

GLOBAL NUCLEAR POWERS
- Declared nuclear power & member of NPT
- Declared nuclear power & not member of NPT
- Undeclared nuclear power
- Trying to be a nuclear power

nuclear weapons. The fact that they admitted this to the world means that they have "declared" their status. Kind of like coming out of the nuclear closet. Because of their "first-ness" and openness, these nuke powers have the veto powers at the UN, as per their permanent status on the security council.

Soon after the development of nuclear weapons, most everyone agreed it would be a horrible idea for all countries on earth to have access to these weapons, so a movement to limit them emerged, culminating in the 1970 **Nuclear Non-Proliferation Treaty** (or **NPT**). This treaty has been signed by 189 countries, including the aforementioned big 5 declared nuke powers . . . only four countries are not signed up for it (more on that in a sec). The treaty has three basic pillars it strives to deal with:

1. non-proliferation, or non-spread, of nuclear weapons and/or nuclear weapon information;
2. disarmament, or getting rid of existing nuclear weapons; and
3. the right to peacefully use nuclear technology, which means all signers of the treaty are allowed to have nuclear energy, but not nuclear bombs.

As you can see, this treaty is mostly to ensure that nobody is making nuke weapons, but nuke power technology for energy production is allowed by the NPT, which makes enforcement of it tricky and a hot potato in current events. But before we get to that, what about the other possible nuke powers not yet named? That would be India, Pakistan, North Korea, and Israel. Ah! Yes! Those would be the exact four countries that have not signed the NPT (or dropped out of it in the case of North Korea). What a coincidence! Not! Here is the deal:

India developed and tested its nuclear weapons in 1974, and not to be outdone, Pakistan followed suit in the late 1990's. Why would these countries need nuclear weapons? Because they hate each other and have already fought three wars so far, with more to come. Once India became nuclear, Pakistan could not rest until it got the bomb as well. That's the way rivalries work. The tension between these two countries is so great that neither will give up their right to possess, and even create more, nuclear weapons, which is why both countries have refused to sign the NPT. But they have declared and proven that they have bombs, so they make the list of nuke powers, even though they cannot legally pursue nuclear energy industries since all that stuff is also regulated by the NPT.

Who is left? Israel, of course! With no reservations, everyone on the planet knows that Israel is also a nuclear power, but they have never (openly) tested, proven, or declared it. The US and many others never want them to declare it either, for fear it would spark a regional **arms race**. Israel has probably been a nuclear power since the 1960's, and it wants to have that nuclear edge mostly in order to ensure its survival, were it to ever be attacked by surrounding states again (see chapter 20). Because of this "secret" status, Israel has refused to sign the NPT, because to do so would mean it would have to open up for inspections and declare their stockpile . . . which, again, might cause a regional arms race.

Finally, there are those who might be trying to get into this nuclear club, but aren't quite there yet. North Korea originally signed the NPT but has subsequently quit, mostly because having the elusive illusion of possibly having nuclear material is the only bargaining chip they have left to play to get international attention as their state nears collapse. The koo-koo North Koreans exploded something underground a few years back and claimed it was a nuclear device, but no one is really quite sure what the heck they actually have. Including themselves. And I'm sure you have heard plenty about Iran recently too . . . they actually are a signatory of the NPT, which gives them the right to develop nuclear energy. Which they are, while claiming peaceful intent. But some of Iran's semi-crazy leaders have already made reference to themselves as a "nuclear power," which of course they are technically not. Yet. Maybe. Wowsers, this is confusing!

Why am I throwing you all this info on the Nuke Group? Well, unless you have been hiding out in an underground nuclear bunker since the 1950's, you know that the issue of nuclear energy/nuclear weapons has become an extremely hot topic in today's world. Like radioactive hot. Like 1.21 gigawatts hot. Crazy North Korea may be developing something which it then may use to blow up a neighbor. And there is great fear of terrorist organizations obtaining nuclear material and doing something nasty with it. But most of all, the world is currently at arms with itself over what to do with Iran: half the world thinks Iran is just developing nuclear power, the other half think Iran is trying to get nuclear weapons . . . it is possibly the most divisive issue of current times, and may result in war. That's why the UN permanent Security Council is debating these issues non-stop, why Team West is at odds with the BRICS, and why current US President Barack Obama held the first-ever "Nuclear Security Summit" in Washington DC in 2010, at which all these issues and more were debated. No state currently with nuclear weapons (and the lion's share of states that don't) wants to see more states go nuclear; these things are dangerous and deadly and could spell the end of humanity! Dudes! I've seen *The Road Warrior* and *The Matrix*! It's scary! At the same time, there are those states that want nuclear weapons. With no question,

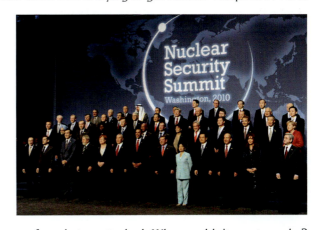

nukes are the absolute best deterrent that would prevent your country from being attacked. Who wouldn't want a nuke? I mean, let's be honest here: the main reason that the Cold War never turned into a hot war was because both sides had nuclear weapons; therefore, neither side could attack without suffering the same nuclear annihilation itself. Would the US have dropped atomic weapons on Japan in World War II if Japan was equally armed? Would the US administration be openly talking about invading/bombing Iran if Iran was already a nuclear power? Having a nuclear weapon is a game-changer. No wonder some countries may still want one.

This brief section was only to alert you to the nuclear status of our planet, not to fully explain and engage all the complicated topics surrounding these weapons of ultimate destruction. Hopefully, you now at least have a handle on the hotness and how it plays out in current events and the world regions. Regions? Oh yeah! That's what this book is about! Let's get to the regions now!

PART TWO
THE REGIONS

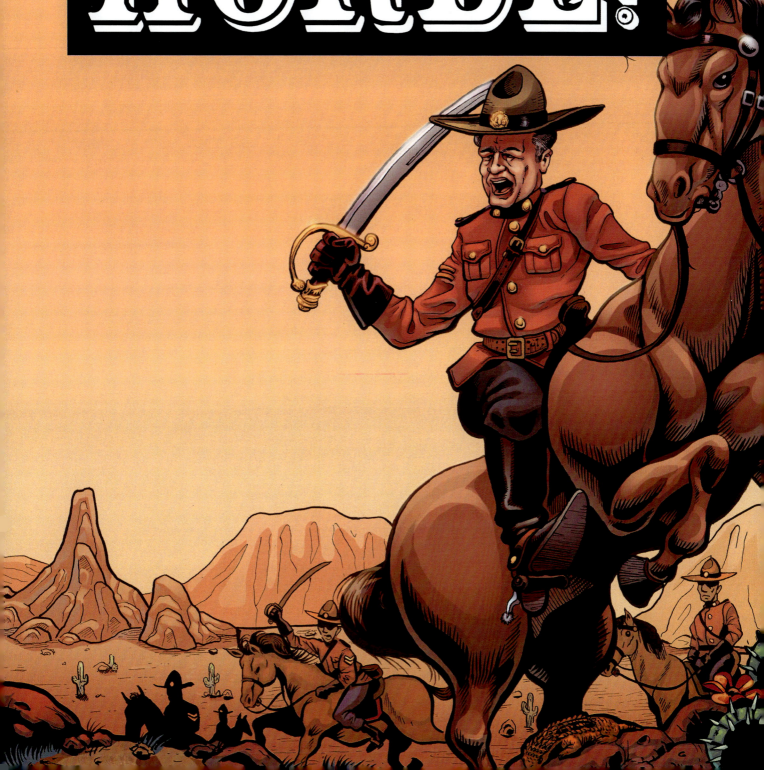

CHAPTER OUTLINE

1. Why Is This a Region?
2. The Greatest Region on Earth!
   - 2.1 + The Richest
     - 2.1.1 Physical Resources
     - 2.1.2 Physical Distance
     - 2.1.3 Evolution of an Economic Powerhouse
     - 2.1.4 Birthplace of Ideas; Technological Titan
     - 2.1.5 Big Region; Small Pop
   - 2.2 + The Strongest
     - 2.2.1 Military Powerhouse
     - 2.2.2 Projection of Power Abroad
     - 2.2.3 Multinational Corporations
   - 2.3. + The Free-est
     - 2.3.1 Old Man Democracy
     - 2.3.2 Focus on Individual Liberties
     - 2.3.3 Personally They Don't Give a Crap
     - 2.3.4 Platform for Success
     - 2.3.5 Core of Team West
3. The Worst Part of Being the Greatest
   - 3.1 — The Richest
     - 3.1.1 Unsportsmanlike Corporate Conduct
     - 3.1.2 Selective Self-Serving Self-Righteousness
   - 3.2 — The Strongest
     - 3.2.1 Doesn't Play Well with Others
     - 3.2.2 Powerful Power Projections
     - 3.2.3 Cultural Imperialism
   - 3.3 — The Free-est
     - 3.3.1 Free to Be Clueless
     - 3.3.2 Exporter of Freeness . . . by Force
     - 3.3.3 Hubris and Hypocrisy
     - 3.3.4 Freeness Envy
4. Uncle Sam Wrap-Up

North America

NOW that we've discussed all the preliminary stuff, we can get to the real meat and potatoes of this text: the regions. Let's start with the biggest meat and potato eaters: the North American region.

This region consists of two huge countries: the United States and their redheaded stepchild to the north, Canada. But wowsers, what an incredible impact on the rest of the world this region makes. Of course, I'm referring mostly to the powerhouse of the planet, the United States of America. For most of the following discussion, I'll be talking about the United States, but always keep in mind that their chilly Canadian cohorts are generally on board for all things North American, even US foreign policy. So is their population; 90% of Canadians live within 100 miles of the US/Canadian border. Heck, I'm not even sure why it's a separate country at all sometimes. I think the only real difference between these states is styles of bacon. But I digress.

Canadian Prime Minister Stephen Harper: "Don't forget about us, eh!"

WHY IS THIS A REGION?

Why is this a region at all? Think back to the 3 things that constitute a region. A region needs some space, of which North America has plenty. A region must also have some borders, which may be fuzzy, but this region's borders are actually very clear cut; it's everything north of the US-Mexican border. Also necessary for a region is homogeneity. It must have some traits that are roughly the same throughout the region, across the entire area.

This is one of the most homogenous regions on the planet based on a cornucopia of common characteristics. It has a high standard of living; it is one of the wealthiest regions in the world. If we head south of the border, we see that Mexico is distinctly different economically, which is one reason why it is not included in this region.

Another factor is language. There is, for the most part, a single language that dominates. Although there are many people who speak Spanish in the US—and of course there are also those wacky French Canadians—primarily both countries are English-speaking. Canada and the US also share historical and cultural backgrounds. Both countries were British colonies at one time. This cultural baggage, which includes religion and the aforementioned trait of language, also solidifies the homogeneity. The fact that the US and Canada are the oldest and most stable democracies is also important. Human rights, the belief in individual freedoms, economic activities, and similar governmental structures also make this a solid region.

THE GREATEST REGION ON EARTH!

Canadian lights not too far from the border.

Wow, that's a bold claim that the Plaid Avenger is making. Why would I suggest that the United States and Canada, combined into our North American region, would be the greatest on the planet? That does come with some caveats, of course. The greatest at many things, and simultaneously the not-so-greatest at others. Two opposing sides of a uniquely powerful coin here in the 21st century . . . heads or tails . . . call it in that air! Heads it is: We'll start with "the greatest."

+THE RICHEST

Why would I say that the United States and Canada is the greatest region on Earth? For starters: they're the richest. There's no getting around that. My plaid friends, I think you all accept this, as do most, that the United States is the richest country on the planet. We forget their Canadian cohorts to the north, though. The Canucks are also pretty well off in terms of per capita GDP, total GDP are a top 20 world economy, and of course both countries are at the core of the G-7, G-8, and G-20. Why, and in what respect, are they together two of the richest countries on the planet? Let's break this down.

PHYSICAL RESOURCES

One: physical resources. These two countries are the second and fourth largest countries on the planet in terms of size. Lots of land in which to move around and lots of space to grow. Space/land is a valuable commodity in and of itself for future potential growth of a country, and both these big boys have it. The US and Canada contain tons of natural resources too . . . and I mean everything across the board. These countries produce tremendous amounts of food, be it grain or grapes or chickens or corn or anything else. They have tremendous amounts of water resources. H_2O is an oft overlooked resource when people think about a place's richness, but hey, you've got to face it, friends—if you don't have water, you have nothing. The US and Canada have lots of food and lots of water . . . but also lots of the other natural resources. North America is virtually saturated with almost every type of resource possible: coal, oil, tobacco, lumber, copper, steel, gold, fertile croplands, and almost anything else. You use it, you want it—North America has it.

PHYSICAL DISTANCE

This North American region also has a strategic advantage in that it is far from other places. What's so special about that? Why would that make them rich? If for no other reason, you have to consider the fact that while the US and Canada have been involved in virtually every major world conflict of the last century, the fights have never occurred on their own soil. To my recollection, Pearl Harbor and the September 11, 2001 attacks are the only times that anyone for a century has even made it close to North American shores for a strike. While those were horrific events to be sure, they were pinpricks in comparison to the larger wars of which they were a component. Having two great oceans separating this region from the rest of the planet is a big security and strategic plus, indeed.

Specific example: After World War II, Europe was destroyed. China was decimated. Parts of Russia were blasted. Japan was completely leveled. The United States and Canada? Sitting pretty and virtually untouched. Besides Pearl Harbor, nothing happened on the soil of this region during those wartime eras.

Also, consider terrorism in the modern world: for those with malicious intent, it is very difficult to get to North America from other parts of the world. This is one of the reasons why the 9/11 attacks were a really big deal in the

North American region. People just couldn't believe it. Folks around the rest of the world are used to bombings, terrorist attacks, uprisings, but it's very unique in the North American region—it just doesn't happen. Terrorist attacks occur in Europe, Asia, the Middle East, and across Africa all the time, but not in North America. After 9/11, people in the United States were freaking out big time, because that type of thing just seems extraordinary to North Americas. . . .

Why do they happen in other places and not here? Distance! People that may be upset with the United States and Canada are very far away. North America is not an easy place to get to if you're a disgruntled Afghan. You can hate the US all you want, but you're not going to get there to do anything about it unless you are well-funded and organized, which rules out most of the people on the planet.

The US and Canada have chosen to get involved in world affairs when it suits them. Very few other places have this convenience. The result? Untouched for virtually all global wars and confrontations of the last 200 years, and even now in the 21st century, they have a wide safety buffer from the rest of the world's problems. Their distance is a key feature.

EVOLUTION OF AN ECONOMIC POWERHOUSE

The North American region has experienced 200 years of continuous growth. That's not something that any other region can brag about. Look through the rest of this blasted book. There is no other place on the planet that has essentially gotten richer decade after decade, century after century, like the US and Canada have for 200 years straight.

The formation of the United States and Canada, of course, goes back to the colonial era when the British, the Spaniards, and the French rolled across the Atlantic in boats and staked claims to the continent. From this nice little nest egg of an area, they proceeded to invest heavily into infrastructure and developing industries. It was a beautiful little place to get a start-up country going—a nice little fixer-upper.

The physical geography played a role in this too, namely the Appalachian Mountains. European settlers were all over the few hundred miles of land from the shores of the Atlantic to the mountains: that was the 13 original colonies. This became a perfect little incubator for the embryonic United States. It insulated the colonies away from Amerindians, who were on one side. The protection that the mountains provided allowed the colonists to gain control of the region and build up resources and population which, in turn, set up the right conditions for westward expansion.

The east coast womb.

This is where distance begins to tie in to the US history. As the colonies began to develop their own ideas about government, freedom, and self sufficiency, they realized that they didn't need the British overseeing them anymore. Being an ocean away from the colonial power afforded them the 'space' necessary to evolve and enact their ideas about independence.

During a little thing called the **American Revolution**, though the British had superior firepower and numbers, the distance was still too great to effectively fight a prolonged war. Distance helped win the war, and also kept foreign powers at bay while the fledgling country strengthened itself in the early years.

No other country in the history of the world has had such a large amount of growth continuously sustained for 200 years than the United States. This place has gone steadily upwards since its inception. Here's how:

From that point forward 200 years ago, the United States grew westward, as did Canada, adding more resources, more water, more fields to grow more food, more coal, more oil, more gold, expanding all the way to the west coast of the continent. The US and Canada had essentially 100 years of continuous physical and economic growth; gaining more stuff, more resources, more land. It was **manifest destiny** at its best, and mo' money, mo' money, mo' money. Running out of land or opportunity in Virginia? Then move to Tennessee, then Indiana, then Oregon! And did the economic expansion stopped when physical expansion maxed out? No way, dude! It just took a new direction. In the 1860s to early 1900s, the American Industrial Revolution began to kick off. Luckily, the Americans had witnessed a similar revolution in Britain almost a hundred years earlier, when the tea-sippers were the top dog.

"You all have little girly economies."

By the way, a Plaid Avenger note: if you broke off California from the rest of the continental US and made it its own sovereign state, it would have the 8th largest economy on the entire planet. Also, former Gov. Arnold Schwarzenegger himself would be the 18th largest landmass.

The Americans took all the best things from the European industrial revolution, and eliminated all the worst. While Europe was very destructive during theirs, the Americans were able to avoid a lot of the pitfalls, and go straight for the goods. The US shifted from an *agricultural* based economy to an *industrial* one. After the land and resource grabs, they exploded industrially.

Ahhh . . . the good ol' days of the manufacturing era.

In the 1960s and 1970s, there was another change. When other countries also began to industrialize, they could produce things cheaper than the US, due primarily to their lower labor costs. Things like automobile, textile, and steel production shifted to developing countries. Was this the end of American economic expansion? Are you kidding me? The US once again shifted gears and changed to a *service sector economy* with an emphasis on *technology*. You know: computers and what not. Nowadays, the next wave of transformation has the US as a leader of the *information age* . . . in which the economic focus is on manipulation and creation of computer programs and new medical breakthroughs and patenting DNA codes. Instead of making cars and textiles, the US now produces information as one of its key resources. This region is truly the first to undergo this technological transformation.

Long story short: 200 years of growth in various ways, either increasing land or resources, then increasing to an industrial capacity, and then increasing into the service sector, and now transforming the world as the leader of the technological and information age. Of course, you have the Great Depression in there, we don't want to forget that little tidbit; that was a decade blemish on a basically 200 year perfect record of economic growth. Even now, here at the outset of the 21st century, the North American region has the biggest total GDP on the planet, with no close second. If money talks, then this region has a lot to say.

BIRTHPLACE OF IDEAS; TECHNOLOGY TITAN

Why else is the North American region the greatest and richest region on Earth? It has do with what we just talked about: this is also a birthplace of ideas. The North American region is the place that came up with things like the telephone, the computer, and the Internet (thanks Al Gore!). This region has the freedom to do lots of things and grow industrially and technologically, and it comes up with all kinds of new crazy great stuff. This region has the highest levels of technology because it is always on the forefront of innovation. Japan makes cool stuff cooler, and

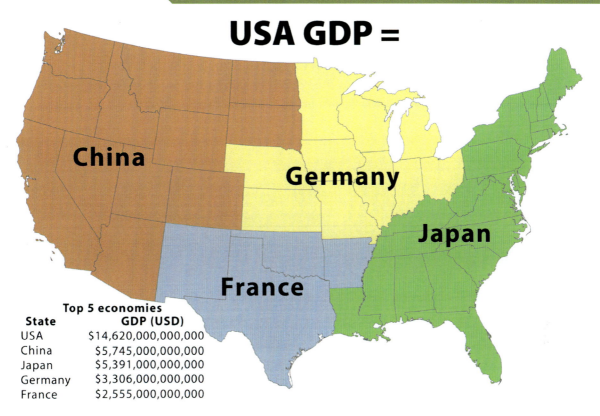

Top 5 economies	
State	GDP (USD)
USA	$14,620,000,000,000
China	$5,745,000,000,000
Japan	$5,391,000,000,000
Germany	$3,306,000,000,000
France	$2,555,000,000,000

China is growing fast, and India is becoming a software hub, but North America is still the top dog when it comes to the forefronts of science, engineering, and computer innovation. However, the competition is getting tougher. You students reading this book better get on your A-game and keep the innovations flowing . . . or they are going to flow right over to Asia!

Since World War II, the United States has been not only an industrial leader but on the forefront of science and technology in all capacities: the Internet, the computer, the telephone, the microwave, nuclear bombs. Put a man on the moon? You betcha! This region did it. That is one of the things that makes the US really rich. People come from around the world to invest here, go to school here, start businesses here, and they do all these things because this is the place to do it. Also, it has the highest levels of technology across the board in fields such as science, math, computers, military and nuclear capabilities, right on up to the upcoming space race. The US, because it is a technology leader, is still the only country that has made it to the moon. It will be joined soon by China, but that's for another chapter.

BIG REGION; SMALL POP

The North American region actually has a fairly small population given its size; this equates to a very high GDP per capita. Both of these countries are fully industrialized and developed, huge in terms of area, heavily urbanized, with a low population density overall. This may be argued by folks in the United States right this second who have problems with immigration: "We've got too many people here! They're takin' our jobs! Wah wah wah!" Whatevs.

The original—and equally unsuccessful—anti-immigration faction. Not pictured: Lou Dobbs.

There's around 310 million people in the United States, while Canada has only about 30 million; and both countries continue to grow population-wise, but pretty slowly and in a stable fashion . . . another big plus! About 340 million people total live in two of the biggest countries on Earth. There's a lot of space in this place and not really that many people in it, relatively speaking. There's tremendous room for growth. Even if growth does not occur, you're looking at tons of resources and a huge economy, both in the US and Canada, that's divided up amongst not that many folks on the global stage. If you're looking out at China, they've got a billion and a half people. India is working on 1.3 billion people; Sub-Saharan Africa has three-quarters of a billion, and even richy-rich Europe has over half a billion residents. The North American region? Ha! A fraction of all that, especially given the amount of space.

In conclusion: lots of space, lots of room, and lots of stuff per person makes the North American region fairly well off. The United States has the biggest GDP total on the planet. Canada is in the top twenty as well; both countries have some of the highest GDP's per capitas, and that's not likely to change anytime soon. Yes, China and India are growing fast, but neither will ever have the amount of richness per person that the United States and Canada enjoy right this second, if ever.

+THE STRONGEST

We just talked about why North America is the richest. Now let's talk about why it's the strongest.

MILITARY POWERHOUSE

The North Americans are also def the best and the strongest when it comes to military might. You can talk about whether you like the US or not, you can talk about whether you agree with its policies or not, but that's of no consequence to the Plaid Avenger. I'm just trying to explain

Team America on patrol.

why this is one of the richest regions on the globe, or the greatest region on the globe. Militarily speaking, you cannot dispute that the US has the strongest single military power on the planet. This is not by size, by the way. We all know size matters, but in this case, the US does not have the largest standing military, meaning troops on the ground. China holds the top slot with 2.5 million people in their military. The United States and Canada don't need to have the largest amount of people in the military because—technologically speaking, of course—we all know they are the best.

North America
CHAPTER SEVEN

The North American region has the most weapons per capita on the planet. We're not just talking about handguns. We're talking about everything from shotguns, right on up to intercontinental ballistic missiles, tanks, and warships. The United States has the most aircraft carriers on the planet and this is a very real projection of power. Militarily speaking, no country can compete with the United States, not even Russia, their old Cold War adversary. In terms of military spending, no one else is even in the US ballpark. Yearly military expenditures for the US now top 3/4 trillion dollars. Wow. That's twice what China spends, and almost half the world total. There is no contest when it comes to who's the strongest or most technologically advanced military on the planet: it's the North American region, particularly the United States.

PROJECTION OF POWER ABROAD

WOPR asks: Shall we play a game?

However, it's not just numbers and budgets. It's also about the ability for the Americans to project this power abroad. This is what makes them the strongest. Aircraft carriers are a great item to consider. With an aircraft carrier, you can push your power to all points on the globe, and the US projection of power to any point on the planet exceeds anything ever even previously imagined by former empires. Sure, the British had their fleet that did a pretty darn good job, and the Spaniards had their global Armada before that, but that was centuries ago. The United States has the technological capacity to annihilate so many more humans than the British did that no comparison can really be made. With a carrier, you can essentially "move" your country anywhere in the world on the water to set up an island to launch a strike. That is some serious global power. Fun fact: the US has 12 aircraft carriers—more than the rest of the planet combined!

The American region is the absolute best at moving troops, people, guns, and missiles anywhere on the planet. That is real ultimate power. One need look no further than current conflicts in which the American region is involved in: Afghanistan and Iraq, which are on the other side of the planet from their home turf.

Country	Military Expenditures 2013 (US$)
United States	$682,000,000,000
China	$166,000,000,000
Russia	$90,700,000,000
United Kingdom	$60,800,000,000
Japan	$59,300,000,000
France	$58,900,000,000
Saudi Arabia	$56,700,000,000
India	$46,100,000,000
Germany	$45,800,000,000
Italy	$34,000,000,000
Brazil	$33,100,000,000
South Korea	$31,700,000,000
World Total	$1,753,000,000,000

http://www.sipri.org/

If you start to look at American military stationed abroad, it's mind boggling. The US has active troops, dudes and dudettes with guns, in about fifty countries. That's astounding if you think about it. That you would have military people stationed all over the planet, even in countries where there is not an active conflict, is quite amazing. This region is certainly the most powerful when you consider the current active conflicts and military deployments, and consider that the United States is a natural leader of NATO (re-read chapter 6 if you forgot about NATO), and thus inherently involved in

The aircraft carrier: Carrying war straight to your door!

Maverick! Goose! Take to the skies!

all NATO missions as well. The Plaid Avenger argues that NATO is easily the most successful defensive organization of all time. I stand by that claim, and the United States is at the core of it.

This region also possesses the most intercontinental ballistic and nuclear missiles. As I suggested earlier, the US is the only country that has landed men on the moon. I won't say the US dominates space, but it has the strongest presence in space . . . for now. There is actually a new 'space race' on right now, which may see Asian powers surpass the US domination of space. Someday. Also, factor in the fact that the US is a big proponent of some sort of anti-missile defense shield, which will certainly, if it ever comes to fruition, make the United States even more powerful. Go learn about the Ronald Reagan era when he wanted to put lasers in space to shoot down other countries' missiles. Only a great power could even consider such a plan and then to put resources toward actually making it happen. I keep harping on space because that is the next frontier; the US is promising to build a moon base and perhaps a missile defense shield in space, and lots of other things in space as well. That just takes tremendous resources, and you've got to be great to pull off those kind of things.

By the way: I keep talking about the United States, but Canada is right beside the US in every single conflict in which it has been involved. All of them. Therefore, we can logically speak of foreign policy/military might as a singular North American venture.

MULTINATIONAL CORPORATIONS

Now let's shift to North American corporations in the world, both US and Canadian. These are some of the biggest, richest entities on the planet. I'm speaking of multinational corporations which operate globally. Every multinational corporation needs to have a home base somewhere, for many, this base is North America. Of the top 2000 largest corporations on the planet right now, over one-third call North America home (that is down from over half a decade ago). Exxon, Wal-Mart, General Motors: these are some of the richest entities on the planet, and with that wealth comes power. These folks have a lot of power to do the things they want to do in other parts of the world . . . and at home.

Consider an entity like Exxon. Sure, it's just a company, not a government, and it doesn't have political power like the US. Well . . . yes and no. Exxon makes like a quadrillion dollars a year; if it wants to look for oil in Namibia, it is going to get what it wants, regardless of Namibian opinion. Let's face it, the company makes ten million

2013 TOP SALES OF MULTINATIONAL COMPANIES

Company	Home Base	Sales (USD)
Wal-Mart Stores	USA	469.2 billion
Royal Dutch Shell	Netherlands	467.2 billion
ExxonMobil	USA	420.7 billion
Sinopec-China Petroleum	China	411.7 billion
BP	UK	370.9 billion
PetroChina	China	308.9 billion
Volkswagen Group	Germany	254 billion
Total	France	240.5 billion
Toyota Motor	Japan	224.5 billion
Chevron	USA	226.6 billion
Glencore Intl.	Switzerland	214.4 billion
Samsung Elec.	South Korea	187.8 billion
E.ON	Germany	174.2 billion
Phillips 66	USA	166.1 billion
Apple	USA	164.7 billion

From: http://www.forbes.com/global2000/list/ *value calculated May 2013 times more money than the country of Namibia; with that money comes tremendous weight to throw around. Whether through open economic pressure or illegal backroom bribery of officials, huge corporations can get their way.

Some of these North American companies are the biggest and the richest in the world, and many are getting richer and more powerful by the day. At this writing, Exxon just captured a world record by earning the highest profits in a single economic quarter ever—thank $100 a barrel for oil for that one! Folks are starting to openly debate whether or not multinational corporations are stronger than governments. The answer: of course! Uber-rich corporations are stronger and more powerful than small countries and weak governments. There's no doubt about that, and it's a situation that's likely to increase in the future. To restate: a lot of those companies are US or Canadian in origin. But let's shift to another topic, and the final subsection of why this region is the greatest.

+THE FREE-EST

OLD MAN DEMOCRACY

Both the United States and Canada are two of the oldest democracies on the planet. This is an entire region that prides itself in a somewhat egalitarian light; everybody is equal regardless of race, sex, creed, religion, or anything else, and everyone has an equal voice. That is one of the cornerstones of this entire region. They are the free-est. There are other countries around the world that are democracies, but the North American ones have been around the longest and have been the most successful for the longest stretch. In fact, these countries, mostly the US—sorry Canada, I have to poke a little fun at you—were so determined about democracy that they had a little revolution and kicked the Europeans out. They said: "Hey, Europeans, that's cool, we're glad you came here and set up shop for us, sent us some immigrants, set up some industries, but you guys can all go home now because you're not being fair enough to us."

Maybe you've heard of it: the American Revolution. 1776, yeah, baby! American-style full-on democracy was born in the US! Meanwhile, Canada invented hockey. Hahahahaha! Why am I making fun of the Canadians? They kissed some British monarchy butt for quite a bit longer, like another hundred or so years, before they threw off the yoke of the Commonwealth. But even during their Queen-kiss-up years, Canada was pretty much into the democracy thing too, kind a variant on the constitutional monarchy deal. To restate, North America is the home of two of the oldest, strongest, longest lasting democracies on the planet.

Got tea?

In fact, these guys have really set the trend for everyone else. You can look at Europe and say that they are also rich, developed democracies with a long track record. Yeah, that's true, dudes. But starting when? Was it before the American Revolution or after? That's right—it was after. The American experience was kind of the impetus for the French Revolution. The French Revolution then begat other revolutions across Europe, which eventually led to all of them becoming something closer to democracy. If you look at it as a chain of events, the Americans started things up. George Washington, Thomas Jefferson and my main man Ben Franklin totally rocked the hizzle with their democracy dizzle. Nice job, guys!

FOCUS ON INDIVIDUAL LIBERTIES

A focus on individual liberties is also a cornerstone of this region from its inception. This is something quite distinct from democracy itself. Democracy is a ruling system in which the people have a say in who's ruling them. That's cool. But on top of that, civil rights and individual liberties are extremely important to this region. Maybe this is confusing to you, but I just want to point this out: there are other democracies in the world, pseudo-democracies or real democracies, where they don't have this focus on individual liberties as much.

Countries like Malaysia or Uganda or Tunisia are totally democracies. They vote, they elect people, but there is nothing in their constitution that says that they believe every single person is exactly equal, and that the state is there to protect their individual rights. Look at Iran, which has a semi-democracy. People vote; in fact, their voter turn-out shames most US election participation. They do elect many of their leaders, but they definitely don't have the focus on individual liberties. The government still controls ultimately what people can read or say, and even the way they can dress. Perhaps making comparisons to Iran or Malaysia is too extreme, because they aren't as developed and rich like the US. Okay, how about Singapore or Russia? Both countries are rich and developed, but done so at the expense of individual liberties. They are tightly controlled democracies where too much individual expression may be detrimental to your business.

"We come for individual freedoms—and native babes."

Only in the North American region do they say first and foremost, "We have a democracy, but it's based on individuals having liberties." By the way, if you think about how the United States came to be, it's because people were fleeing from places that weren't giving them true liberty. Those Pilgrim peeps who went to Plymouth Rock were fleeing religious persecution back in Europe. They wanted more freedoms to individually do their own thing here in North America. That's how the thirteen original colonies started, and quite frankly, it's still going on today. People flock from around the world to head to the North American region because they know when they get there, they are free to live the way they want. This is not the case across the entire planet, even in established democracies.

I'm not suggesting all these liberties have been there since the beginning. Freedom of thought, religion, and speech were there early on. More recently, civil rights and liberties regarding race and sex were fought for and won by activists and concerned citizens. And the US not only sets the world standard for freedoms, but continues to be on the front lines of battles over civil liberties and rights: look at the fight for gay rights or the rights of an unborn child for examples of how passionate this region gets about individual liberty.

And part of the reason North Americans feel this way is that, quite frankly, they don't give a crap. Say what?

PERSONALLY THEY DON'T GIVE A CRAP

This region doesn't give a shake about you as a single individual. That sounds a little backwards. What do I mean exactly? We can make fun of North America for being a region of imperial power, of gun-loving nuts, and of isolationism. But if you get there—when you are actually in the hizzle—it's really freakin' cool. North Americans just generally don't give a crap who you are or where you are from on a personal basis. They are laid back. Do what you like! It's cool. Just don't ruin any of my stuff. This is a phenomenally great component of North American society.

If you look around the planet at the history of human society around the world, we have a pretty consistent record of kicking the living daylights out of each other. Why do we do this? It has a lot to do with intolerance of differences between people. Sometimes we kill each other over resources or land or whatever. However, conflict mostly arises between people of different religions, ethnicities, races, or nationalities—and sometimes it escalates to some pretty nasty business. Think of the atrocities of Nazi Germany or the Rwandan genocide or the implosion of Yugoslavia. The list goes on and on. People killing people who were not like themselves.

This is a common theme across the planet, except in North America. By no means are all Americans sitting around eating s'mores and singing "Kumbayah" together. Of course, there are people here who don't like other people, but this is at nearly the absolute minimum in the history of the world. Americans don't care where you're from, what color you are,

Britney Spears: a symbol of a tolerant America. We even give K-Fed a pass!

how smart or stupid you are, what god you pray to, or even what you do with your leisure time. Quite frankly, American tolerance toward their fellow man may be the best example the rest of the world should follow.

In real life in America, not caring equates to everyone being pretty much equal. Some people call it a meritocracy, meaning you only advance by working hard and doing good stuff—by earning your way. Your position in society is not, or isn't supposed to be, based on your religion or skin color; North America doesn't really have organized ethnic or religious clashes. Many people from around the world emigrate to this region to escape those very issues.

Let me elaborate on why I'm saying this is a positive thing. In most other parts of the planet—and this is today's world, not historically—people don't have the luxury of not giving a crap, meaning that there is serious ethnic, religious, and racial strife all around the world. If you are in the minority, practice a religion that's not fashionable, or are from the wrong ethnicity or tribe, you may not have equal rights at all in your country. Even if the country pretends you do, you may be discriminated against on a daily basis. You might be thrown out of the country or you could be caught up in ethnic genocide or civil war or religious persecution, which happens all the time across the planet.

That doesn't happen in North America because individuals are doing their own thing. Maybe it's because the countries' very foundations were as immigrant nations, but whatever the reason, they don't give a crap about the guy sitting next to them on the bus. They just don't, and that's a very powerful thing. I can't stress it enough: it's one of the reasons why folks from around the world say, "Wow. If I could just make it to North America, then I truly am free. Nobody cares that I'm from a Hmong ethnicity. Nobody cares that I'm a Zoroastrian. Nobody cares if I tattoo my face, dye my hair blue, and watch Jersey Shore. I can do what I want to when I get to those shores." By and large, that is true and that is one of its real benefits. It is one of the free-est places on the planet. Okay, maybe they should pass a law against Jersey Shore, but for now it is still protected behavior.

PLATFORM FOR SUCCESS

What this sets up, essentially, is that the North American region is a kind of platform for success. People know that once they make it to North America, all other factors are equal. You work hard, you pay your dues, you put your nose to the grindstone, then you can be successful. No, the streets aren't paved with gold in North America, as the old saying goes. They are paved with opportunity, because immigrants don't have to worry about things that they'd have to worry about in their home countries. The North American region is a real platform for success. Which reminds me to introduce you to a concept called **brain drain** (see inset box).

What's the Deal with Brain Drain?

Any person given a free plane ticket from their lesser developed country to any other destination in the world will most likely choose the North American region.

The type of people that actually make it here are smart, educated people with options. Also, wealthy people who want to become wealthier figure out ways to come to the North American region.

This is actually a problem, because the elites of other societies are leaving their native regions to emigrate to wealthy regions in order to become successful. There are all sorts of political, religious, and economic reasons to flee native lands and set up shop in North America. When the political problems arise, people leave. When people are afraid of losing their assets or afraid of religious persecution, they will go to a place that accepts them and allows them to continue growing. For a hundred years, the destination of choice has been the United States.

Brain Drain has been a fantastically successful concept in the development of North America. Whenever bad things happens around the globe, the US and Canada stand to gain.

Political crackdown in Iran? Economic meltdown in Thailand? Religious persecution in Sudan? North America gains in refugee and immigrant populations, usually of skilled, hardworking, and/or asset-laden peoples. Conversely, the country that loses the peeps is impacted quite negatively, thus the "drain" part of the term.

For example, after World War II, the Russians took half of Germany's rocket scientists and America got the other half: the foundations of both the US and Russian space programs. Brilliant inventors come here, and they use the US as a platform for success. There are other great platforms, but the US has been a very important one for the last 100 years.

This has a lot to do with immigration. People want to come here to express themselves. It has become a self-perpetuating cycle; the US is so rich and doing so well that people all over the globe want to come here with their ideas. People want to start businesses with the highest probability for success—and that is in the US. Success breeds success, and more people want to come. American success is a strong magnet in the world. Rich and poor alike have a strong attraction to the North American region for all of its opportunities. It's an extremely competitive place, but it does seem to work for the vast majority of its inhabitants. Poverty numbers are very low, compared to other regions; opportunities exist for even the most destitute. **2014 Update:** Wealth disparity is on the rise, even in the mighty North American region, and it is a major issue that is getting attention from leaders and protestors alike.

If you live in an impoverished society, one with no welfare program or unemployment benefits, you cannot take risks. New things come about by taking risks, and environments like that do not enable people to take risks. America will take care of you if you or your idea fails. You can afford to work hard, save money, start your own business. No wonder people think the streets are paved with gold—golden opportunities, am I right?

Another great thing about this region is its **hypermobility**. The size of the region allowed for the interstate system, developed by US President Dwight Eisenhower, whereas other countries that are smaller rely more heavily on public

We Like Ike! What's the Deal with the Interstate System?

The formal name of the United States interstate system is the "Dwight D. Eisenhower National System of Interstate and Defense Highways." The US interstate system was created by the Federal-Aid Highway Act of 1956, which, as the name suggests, was championed by Eisenhower. It was built for both civilian and military purposes. Some of you might be thinking, "Yeah! One in every five miles of road must be straight so that military aircraft can land and take off on them!" Well, maybe. The true military aspects of the interstate system are primarily to facilitate troop movement and to allow for the evacuation of major cities in the event of nuclear war.

The civilian aspects of the Interstate Highway System have helped shape American culture in more ways than we can possibly imagine. Most US interstates pass through the center of cities, which allows people to live outside the city and commute in for work, which has also played a huge role in the creation of suburbs and urban sprawl. The highway system also gives the federal government power over state governments. The US government can withhold interstate highway funds, which are huge amounts of money, from uncooperative state governments. The US government used this tactic to increase the national drinking age to 21 and to lower the blood alcohol level for intoxication to 0.08%. According to the Constitution, both of these issues should be decided by states. However, if they choose to disobey, they don't get their highway money.

Also, the system allows high speed transportation of consumer products. This makes the prices of everything, from bananas to concrete, cheaper. The result: the US is an automobile culture heavily reliant on fossil fuels for the movement of everything and for virtually all aspects of their lives. Americans are quite unique in this respect. It's also why they are the best stock car racers in the world. Who else has NASCAR? Who is more worried that the price of oil is reaching $150 a barrel?

Interstate Highways

transportation. People can go anywhere and do anything, anytime they want in North America, via a variety of transportation options. They even have four-wheel drive vehicles to take them places where roads are nonexistent.

Mobility allows people to take advantage of opportunity and expands individual choice. Any job, any opportunity, any time, any place. Not all folks in other countries have this convenience. There is an exactly proportional relationship between mobility and choice. The more mobile you are, the more choices you have; as a result, the US is more successful.

Living in the North American region furnishes infinite choices and provides opportunity to take risks; this is unprecedented anywhere else on the planet. If you have a great idea and you could have any choice of where to cast the dice to really make it work for you, it's a no-brainer for you to come to North America. It just makes sense. The odds are stacked in your favor. Not true in Europe for immigrants, not true in Asia or Africa as a whole—but def true in North America.

CORE OF TEAM WEST

To wrap up this free-est section, all of these factors put together are what make the North American region the true core of what I will refer to as Team West. This is a concept we'll come back to later in the book. North America, along with Europe and Australia, form a common block of ideology that sets them apart from other cultures in the world. You know what? Let's throw Japan in there as well. Even though they're way out in the east, they more closely follow the western tradition.

What are the identifiable traits of this team? As exemplified by North America, Team West has a basis in the western civilization tradition that values democracy in their governments, a focus on individual rights in their societies, and are strident free-market capitalists when it comes to their economies. This team consists of regions and states that are fully developed, largely rich, technologically superior, and focused on service sector and information age types of employment. Other attributes include rampant materialism, an obsession with pop culture, and unproportional power and leverage over the rest of the globe—but those are more negative attributes.

How appropriate, because it's time to get negative on the team leader right about now!

THE WORST PART OF BEING THE GREATEST

We're going to shift gears now and expose the underbelly of the greatest region. I've told you about how awesome the North American region is and why it's the greatest and the leader in terms of richness and power and freeness. Now let's take a look at why it's perhaps not so great. What's the worst part of being the greatest region? It's an easy schemata, because we're just going to follow the same outline we did before. We'll start with number one.

-THE RICHEST

Wait a minute! I thought I just said that being rich was great? Everybody thinks being rich is great, but the bad side of being the richest region on the planet is that US and Canadian policies, of course, favor their own peeps and companies.

UNSPORTSMANLIKE CORPORATE CONDUCT

In other words, they take care of their own. Why wouldn't they? Every country has its own interest as the number one priority . . . that is completely natural. US foreign policy is no exception: be it intervention into another country or manipulating the World Trade Organization or some sort of other pressures on other countries in order to help their own multinational corporations succeed. It happens. I'm not making fun of anyone, but I'm trying to get you to understand why other folks around the world may have discontent about American power. All states have self-interest, but being the richest most powerful region means you can achieve those self-interests better than anyone else can! The cards are stacked in your favor!

The United States and Canada have some of the biggest, richest multinational corporations in the world. Simultaneously, the US and Canada are two of the richest countries in the world. Therefore, it's almost a set of unprecedented power players that have really never occurred before—that the richest country can help out the richest multinational corporation.

This gives those corporations quite a bit of leverage and power in the world. Power to do what? Well, most free-marketers would say to do what business does: go out and acquire resources, produce products, and sell those products. That's true, but they also have a lot of power to screw with other people or governments, if they so choose. They have the power to ignore other countries' environmental regulations or to bend the rules to favor themselves as frequently as possible. There is no way that a local company in a less-developed country could possibly compete with a Wal-Mart or an Exxon; these big boys can pretty much take what they want, when they want it.

This does present a problem. It is a situation where there is a fairly lopsided trade balance around the world where multinational corporations have the power to take a lot more from poor countries and give a lot less back. It's just simply the way it is. It's not good. It's not bad. In my book, that's just the way it is. US and Canadian policy favors their corporations, which are already rich. This helps them perhaps take advantage of other countries. Also, the North American's global policy typically ignores the rest of the globe to maintain its own richness. Let me put in a disclaimer: every country does that. China certainly is going to try to favor Chinese policy. The French look out for France. But the North Americans are so powerful and so rich that, here in the dawn of the 21st century, their attitudes toward the globe are now looked upon with some animosity by others on the planet. And that is because they have . . .

SELECTIVE SELF-SERVING SELF-RIGHTEOUSNESS

Let me give you some examples, and there are many to choose from. The idea of free trade may be the most blaring example of North America not practicing what it preaches. The US and Canada are fervent supporters of this concept, which essentially equates to trade based on the unrestricted international exchange of goods. This means no tariffs (taxes) should be levied on other countries' goods that are coming into your country, and no helping out industries within your country to make their goods more competitive than imported goods. North America regularly touts, praises, and leads the charge for free trade to the rest of the planet. In particular, the US wants a free trade area for the entire Western Hemisphere (FTAA, see Chapter 3) and it pushes hard to beat down the countries of Latin America to support the idea. Also, the US is the unrivaled leader in bringing up lawsuits against other countries at the WTO for infractions of the world trade rules.

Your taxes already paid for it, so eat it, just eat it!

But get this—the US and Canada regularly cheat on free trade all the time! Both countries support agricultural subsidies for farmers, which essentially equates to paying big agri-businesses money every year in order to make them more profitable. Corporations can then charge less money for the food they produce, making it cheaper than food imports from Africa or Asia. Both countries also regularly slap tariffs on imported steel or textiles in order to kiss the butts of political lobby groups and voting constituencies at home, especially in election years.

Another example of this selective support on issues: US/Canadian policy on global warming. For around two decades, most of the other countries on the planet have been saying, "Hey! This warming is a global thing, part of a global commons, and we need to look after the globe by all working together to reduce carbon dioxide emissions." The US and Canada have basically been very frank by saying, "No, we're not doing a darn thing. We refuse to do anything because it's going to hurt our companies. It's going to hurt our richness. We don't want to change our consumption patterns. We don't want to change how much money we have, and therefore, we don't give a carbon crap about reducing CO_2 emissions. The rest of y'all can go do whatever you want. We're going to keep doing our own thing." As always, I am paraphrasing policy here, but that does pretty much cover American attitudes.

It's also important to point out that the North American region is the highest user of world resources per capita. People in the US and Canada use more oil, more food, more plastic, more everything per person than any other folks on the planet. Whatever! It's a free market economy and people can do whatever they want, right? But other folks on the planet, and there are quite a few of them, kind of look at this and say, "Dudes. You guys are really selfish. You use the most, but you don't want to help out with any global problems." Being the richest has come at some cost, mostly at a cost to the reputation of the region, which is increasingly not seen as a real world leader on world issues.

-THE STRONGEST

What's wrong with being the strongest? Somebody's got to be the strongest, right? When it comes to North America, and I'll mostly pick on the United States right here, there is a perceived or real threat of US imperialism by many folks across the planet. That is, as I suggested earlier, the US is the undisputed, strongest country on the planet; because of this, people think, "They scare me! They are unstoppable!" The US is so powerful, it appears that it could do anything it wanted. You know what? Quite frankly, that's true. If the US wants to bomb Uzbekistan tomorrow, it has the capacity to do it, and current events have shown that sometimes this does occur . . . e.g. Iraq, Afghanistan, Libya . . .

It is a very real consideration that people around the world say, "The US is so powerful, they cannot be checked by any other entity." Truth. Who would stop them? Russia? China? The UN? Give me a break! The UN stopping something? . . . hahahaha, that's a good one.

We need look no further than the current Iraq war. Most folks around the world said, "Hey! We think it's a bad idea." Most countries of the UN said, "No, we're not going along with that. We're not doing it." The US said, "Well, we're doing it anyway." Again, I'm not making fun of them, I'm not trashing the Iraq war or the Bush administration. I'm just saying, think about the perceived light of imperialism that most folks around the world now view the United States bathed in. It does cause more than a bit of consternation and concern for both enemies and friends of North America alike.

DOESN'T PLAY WELL WITH OTHERS

The current Iraq war is worthy of further consideration for a moment more. This story gets at a larger point . . .

There is a particular disdain of the United Nations by the US. Let me put it more bluntly: the US as a whole totally hates the UN. Why? Because the US is so powerful and resourceful on its own, that the only thing the UN does for it is to get in the way of US objectives. Does that make sense? The US has a certain opinion about things in the world, and it wants to act on its opinion to fulfill its own self-interests. Many in America would argue that indeed this is exactly the job of their government: to look out after their own self-interests, the rest of the world be damned. Since the US *can* do anything it wants, it *should* do anything it wants to benefit itself. Following this train of thought, what exactly is the point of asking the UN for permission, advice, or for any thing else?

You almost can't blame it either. The US did save Western Europe's butt from Hitler without asking permission from anybody. They saved the world from communist takeover as well during the Cold War. Other folks don't like this unchecked influence, even if it is supposed to be for good. This is something that people in the US just don't get. They don't get it because they see themselves as good: "We are the good guys! We help people! We helped the French and Brits in World War II! We saved the Koreans and Kuwaitis and Kurds! We have always helped to defeat bad guys around the planet!"

By and large, that is true. The US seems to be fighting the good fight, but that's not always the perception around the world, particularly in this day and age. Back in World War II, everybody understood that the Nazis were the bad guys, and recognized the US as fighting the good fight. In the current War on Terror, however, the enemies and objectives are not so well-defined. This unchecked ability of the United States to make judgment calls on all these issues bothers many people.

Another example involves nukes. Even though the Cold War is now over, and the US is busy fighting terrorism and not communism, the United States still maintains the **nuclear hit list option**. What is that? During the Cold War, all of the countries that had nuclear capabilities had lists of who they would blow up first. Number one on the US list was Russia, then maybe China because they were pinko commies too, then maybe France just for good measure, etc. All countries with nuclear capabilities had these lists during the Cold War.

US Nuclear Hit List still in play.

Recently, most countries have said, "Now that the Cold War is over, we'll get rid of the hit list and start to disarm our nuclear warheads. We're not going to point them at anybody." All the countries got together, particularly Russia, and said, "Hey, let's all do this! It'll be a good thing!" The United States said, in essence, "You guys are so cute! You should do that! But not us! We are going to hang on to our nuclear hit list, just in case."

At a time when many states want to ratchet down the nuclear issue, the US stands alone in its opinion. That has increasingly been the case for the last two decades. The US maintains its hit list, is not a full player in UN procedures, and openly refuses to sign treaties that the vast majority of countries in the world support. Things like the Law of the Sea Convention, which defines territorial rights of the ocean, or the Kyoto Protocol to reduce greenhouse gases, even legislation banning the production of land-mines. In all of these circumstances and many more, the US stands virtually alone in its non-participation. Oh, and if there is any other country to not play ball, it would be the Canadians. Especially on the global warming issue.

Is the Plaid Avenger trying to indoctrinate you into thinking the US is bad, or too powerful, or too pompous? Not at all. I'm trying to educate you on perhaps why the US has a bit of a bad rap on the world stage right now. Sometimes standing alone is a sign of strength; sometimes it is a sign of selfish stubbornness. You have to decide for yourself, as will the rest of the world.

POWERFUL POWER PROJECTIONS

The overwhelming strength of North America has also brought a sense of helplessness and outright fear to some parts of the globe. Specifically, the US has a basically open, identifiable, and (some folks would say) scary projection of real power as evidenced by the active wars in Iraq and Afghanistan. These active wars are possible, and proceed rapidly, because of the active US military presence around the globe. Whether for good or bad, there are North Americans with guns all over the planet.

More often than not, you see US soldiers more than you see any other country's soldiers. You can see UN soldiers, NATO soldiers, and EU soldiers sometimes, but those are groups, associations of countries, not single countries like the US. US soldiers are the only ones from a specific country that you can find all over the planet. This military presence is perceived as unchecked strategic military power. In a very real sense, you won't find Chinese soldiers in Iraq, or Afghanistan, or in the United States. Can you even conceive of having foreign soldiers on US soil? The thought is comical. Other countries accept that there are US troops around the world, on foreign soil in Europe, Asia, South America, just about everywhere. It is a reality elsewhere, but inconceivable in North America.

"Special delivery for . . . wait, who are we killing today?"

There are no other countries that have that type of real power evidenced around the entire planet, not just the active wars, but in deployment of troops. Factor in the largest nuclear arsenal on the planet, the most sophisticated and largest air force, and more aircraft carriers than the rest of the world combined, and you have the basis for other countries soiling themselves at the thought of US intervention. Sound fanciful? Ask Saddam Hussein of Iraq or Muammar Qaddafi of Libya how they feel about it. Well, Saddam and Muammar are very much dead, and so is Osama bin Laden . . . all thanks to US power projection. And don't even get me started on the drones! Now the US is the undisputed leader in unmanned death vehicles in the world . . . a powerful tool of death projection across the planet that is rising in popularity, and polarization!

CULTURAL IMPERIALISM

Finally, under the strongest category is something that you probably have never thought of before critically: **cultural imperialism**. With no doubt, North America is the most successful, if you can call it that, at this thing called cultural imperialism. Whether the US and Canada are true imperial powers is debatable. However, it isn't really up for debate that the culture of the US is the most successful thing being spread around the planet. What am I talking about here?

We just discussed power-driven imperialism, including an actual military presence, so what is this cultural imperialism thing? Imperialism usually means that people step in with guns and take over saying, "We are an imperial power; your stuff is now ours." Think about Darth Vader and the imperial storm troopers. They are taking over and ruling by force.

However, cultural imperialism is much more subtle. There are no guns, there is no iron-fisted dark lord, and there are no storm troopers. Cultural imperialism simply means that people begin adopting your culture. Think about pop culture. This is the one that most often springs to mind. People around the world from France to South Korea to Australia to South Africa like watching crappy American movies, listening to crappy American pop songs, and watching ridiculously crappy TV shows like *American Idol*. Think about the title: it's *American* Idol and it's watched and *idolized* by people all over the planet! How crazy is that?

Cultural imperialism is much more subtle, because nobody has a gun to anybody's head telling them to accept it. For some strange reason, people just like it. There have been millions of movies made in America that have been exported to every other country on the planet, many of which you'll never see because they suck so bad that nobody in this country will watch them—but people in other countries will, just because they're American-made. People are attracted to that successful vibrant American pop culture. You can go to Tibet and watch *Titanic*, you can go to Russia and listen to Run DMC (sorry, the Plaid Avenger is old school), or you can go to Burma and see an episode of *Baywatch*.

A lot of countries in today's world are passing laws to try to limit the amount of American pop culture that enters their countries. France is a good example, because every few years they attempt to ban the importation of American-made films. It never lasts long, but they try. Middle Eastern countries try to keep all that American pop music and porn out. Even China tries to tightly control Internet action so that none of those American democratic-human-rights-and-freedoms ideas can seep into their culture, which brings us to another point to consider. Pop culture is the main component of cultural imperialism that you know of, but here's one that is much more intriguing and important. . . .

Cultural imperialism from an *ideological* standpoint is much more important to acknowledge, especially considering how world events are going down right this second. I'm talking about the ideologies of capitalism and democracy being spread. As you know from current events, unless you have been living under a rock, the United States has an active military presence in Iraq and Afghanistan and perhaps will occupy some other places in the very near future. They don't necessarily import Britney Spears at gunpoint, but what is happening is that they are heavily influencing the societies to become like the US in terms of adopting democracy, individual liberties, and capitalist culture.

America's fifth column: Team Ocean.

The capitalist part is not that difficult, since every country makes money in some way or another on capitalism. However, some people in the world tend to have a problem with the democracy part. These are ideas Uncle Sam pushes across the planet quite openly. The US says, "Hey! We're going into Iraq because we want a democracy here. We're going to help them have a democracy. We're going to manipulate or push or try our best to get other countries to embrace capitalism because it benefits us and we think it benefits the world. We're going to try to get everyone to do it." Indeed, the US and Canada in most of their endeavors say, "Yes, and we believe that all people are equal and that we think individual rights and civil liberties should be the norm across the planet."

You're not gonna stand there and let Lady Liberty take it, are you? Of course not!

This is not something up for dispute. You can see this every day when the US government says, "Hey! We think China has horrific human rights abuses and we're going to complain about it at the UN." The US may complain about the Chinese treatment of the Tibetans and say that their human rights stink. That is essentially saying, "We believe that our system is right and yours is wrong," and that's something to consider.

Let the Plaid Avenger go on record as stating that I personally uphold the idea of democracy in the world and think human rights are the most basic necessity for every human being on Earth. I'm a bit biased since I'm from this region. I have this ideal myself. However, not everyone in the world does, and I'm willing to recognize that. I may not like it, but I at least recognize that another point of view exists.

The US planting seeds of democracy in the Middle East is of great consequence in today's world. It's the reason that your tax dollars are going to support troops who will continue to prop up governments and establish democracies in places that have no history or background in such cultural phenomena. Lots of people in the Middle East and other places in the world have no experience with democracy and don't necessarily want it. They do, however, feel as if the world power, i.e. the United States, may be pushing them toward it.

I don't think it's an exaggeration to describe it that way, and I think that's a fair assessment. It's up to you as American and world citizens to decide if that's kosher. However, I just want you to understand that democracy is a major part of your culture that you accept as right and good and proper. Other people in other places may not share that sentiment. Food for thought.

Look no further than the 2011 Arab Revolutions across the Middle East where grassroots movements are pushing for a change to western-style democracy too . . . and using US technologies of the Internet and Facebook to facilitate the transition! Fascinating! Think those Arab leaders being toppled from power are thanking the US for its cultural influence in the region? Me thinks not!

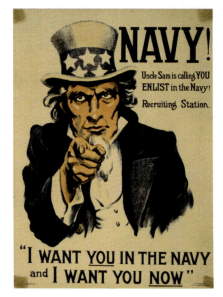

Now you know where the Village People got the idea for "In the Navy."

-THE FREE-EST

What could possibly be bad about being the free-est? The first thing I want to point out is the freedom to be clueless. North Americans as a whole (and we do have to pick on the Americans more than the Canadians in this respect) are generally speaking completely clueless about what's going on in the world.

FREE TO BE CLUELESS

Most Americans have no idea where Tibet even is on a map, much less what human rights abuses are happening there. We pointed out that peeps in this region are physically far away from other regions; therefore, they're not as heavily impacted by other regions, even in this global interconnected world. North Americans focus on their own thing. I won't call them isolationists, but they have a tendency to focus on themselves at the cost of simply just not caring about the rest of the world.

To sum this up: internationally, they don't give a crap.

It seems bizarre for the Plaid Avenger to say because this entire chapter so far has been spent explaining how the US is a central key player, deeply involved in the world's political and economic systems. But by and large, American citizens are utterly clueless about other countries. Many around the world would say that American politicians, whose job it is to care about foreign affairs, are about as clueless as those they represent. Well, I guess in that respect they are truly representin'. Representin' ignorance that is.

As the Plaid Avenger has traveled around the planet and talked to lots of people everywhere, a common theme reveals itself: many people perceive America as an unchecked power, and around the world people feel that America doesn't care about them. Perhaps they are too small or not enough like the United States, or they have no economic resources that the United States cares about, and so their perception is that the United States doesn't care about them. Perhaps they're right.

In this interconnected and globalized world where everyone knows everything all the time, citizens of the United States, by and large, know the least about what's going on in the world. If that's a radical statement to you, then stop surfing for shoes on Zappos and open your eyes.

If people in Sudan can get to the Internet, they know everything that's happening in the world and they pay attention to what's happening in global movements of ideas and people. Of course, they especially know the details of the relationship between the US and Sudan, and what the UN Security Council is doing about Sudan. If you ask anyone in the United States, they won't have an utter clue. Sudan? Security Council? Huh? Is *Celebrity Apprentice* on yet?

"Get your hoe ready!"???

That bothers a lot of people around the world. They say, "Wow, this is the richest group of people who have the most influence on the entire planet, and they don't give a crap because they don't even know what's going on. How could they not care enough to know, for instance, that this genocide is going on?" Isolation is a dual edged sword. We say the US is great because it has been isolated, but at the same time, that allows its people to be lazy. The general US population does not know what's going on, and that really burns people's bottoms around the planet simply because citizens of the United States have so much power individually. They could easily change some things if they wanted, but they don't because either they don't know and/or they don't care.

EXPORTER OF FREENESS . . . BY FORCE

As I suggested just above, this region is also a huge exporter of democracy and capitalism and individual civil liberties and rights or at least the concepts of them. That sounds like a pretty good deal, and the Plaid Avenger is all about individual liberties and justice, so I'm all for it. Let's get this game on! Mostly, the North American region exports these themes in its literature, ideas, technology, and pop culture. However, we can't overlook the fact that sometimes these good ideas—democracy, capitalism, and individual rights—are also exported by force if necessary. That can be a little problematic.

Sure, it's awesome that you want people to have a democracy, but perhaps not so awesome that you go there and kill them in order to make them into one. Current events are playing out right now to determine how successful forced democracy is going to work out in the Middle East, and it doesn't look too good so far for the forces of freedom. In terms of freedom, can it be forced upon a society? Can it be given, or can it only be earned? We shall see, unfortunately, at the expense of many lives.

North America is the free-est, with lofty and admirable goals for others, but being blinded by ambition has led to a big fat negative for North America. Which leads us to the next theme . . .

HUBRIS AND HYPOCRISY

For some of you reading this book, don't bother writing letters saying that the Plaid Avenger is some blatant tree-hugging bunny kissing liberal wannabe commie who's just making fun of the US. I'm not, okay? I'm trying to get you to understand what what's going on here!

It is problematic around the globe right this second that the United States and Canada say, "Hey! We're all about democracy. We're all about individuals. We're egalitarian. We think democracy is great." They do. I truly believe that. However, when you have things like the Abu Ghraib prison scandal in Iraq, as well as increasing civilian death counts in Afghanistan, drone strikes in Pakistan and Yemen, and then you have people being held in Guantanamo Bay without individual rights forever, you start to get a bad rap. The world, not the Plaid Avenger, is looking upon this and saying, "Wait a minute. You guys are talking this big game about equality and democracy, but you're not even doing it yourselves." Given current events, in the modern context in the 21st century, there's a bit of a problem with being the free-est when you're not living up to it.

FREENESS ENVY

Finally, there might be something going on that I like to call "freeness envy." Oh, man, am I good or what? Freeness Envy . . . ha! And that is something that some other cultures don't necessarily dig. What am I talking about here? Well, the North Americans are all about the freeness, man. Equality, democracy, freedom of speech, religion, choice, peace, love, dirty hippies, whatever. It's all about equal rights. Everybody's equal. Everybody's cool. Yeah, man, pass the greenery Snoop Dogg. . . . oops, I digress . . .

However, don't assume that the rest of the world holds these ideals as highly as the North Americans do. Let me give you some examples. The Saudi Arabian government and most of the Saudi Arabian population is not necessarily in favor of equal rights for women. The idea that women are completely equal in all aspects doesn't really play there. Let's go with something else like gay rights. You know, in North America, everybody's equal, but that doesn't play in Africa, man. In Sub-Saharan Africa, and parts of the Caribbean, gays are persecuted heavily; most folks in those societies would say, "No. We are not about those people being as free as we are." You can go around the world and look at different societies—and this is the people I'm talking about here, not just the governments—and lots of folks would say, "No, we're not about that type of freedom." China isn't really into freedom of the press. Countries in the Caribbean aren't really into gay rights. The Vatican isn't really into freedom of choice. The Middle East may not be really into sexual equality or freedom to draw cartoons.

Well, maybe not in the Middle East . . .

Freeness envy may be happening around the globe. The Plaid Avenger is all about individual liberties, so I am a big proponent of it. But when I go into other cultures, I don't assume that everybody around the entire planet wants democracy. Well, I think they should have it, but that doesn't mean they all want it. I think that all women should be equal, because in the Plaid Avenger's world, all women are equal in my eyes, but I don't assume that all cultures necessarily accept that, either. You have to keep this in context. Freeness Envy, huh? Great term.

UNCLE SAM WRAP-UP

Let's wrap this thing up. We've looked at the good side of the greatness of North America. We've looked at the negative side of the greatness of North America. Uncle Sam is really a bipolar fellow here lately. Sammy, my man, has a real Jekyll and Hyde complex going down.

Go get 'em Cap!

You know Captain America. . . . He's out there fighting the good fight, standing up for the impoverished, the people who don't have democracy or with no rights. Yes, the Cap'n does quite a bit; even though he's taken a bad rap in today's world, the United States and Canada continue to be the biggest foreign aid donors, the biggest funders of the UN, and also do a heck of a lot for the planet. Even though they're sometimes a bit heavy handed about it, they think they're doing it for good reasons. Who's to dispute that? No other country in the world is stepping up to be the leader for truth, justice, and the global way. You think China or Russia or even the EU is going to lead the way to global stability? Not likely.

There is of course, the perceived American super-villan that comes out every now and again. Sometimes this region does bad things abroad in the world, even when supposedly done for a good cause. However, there are other times that this region is quite openly selfish in terms of looking after its own interests. Since it's the most powerful region, it can do it in the most aggressive manner across the globe. Again, no judgement call here, that's just the way it is. The US and Canada are going to look out for their own corporate and economic interests. If that means telling people to kiss their gas on the global warming issues, then that's what they're going to do. And that's typically, what they've done.

Dude, you are scaring me.

The bigger issue to think about: we are in the midst of big changes in the world power structure that will most greatly affect the North American region more than any other. Why? Because the United States has been used to being the sole superpower for twenty or thirty years now. Ever since the Soviet Union went away, and the US won the Cold War, the North American region has been uncontested for power on the planet. It has the most political, military, and economic power, as I pointed out earlier.

But times are a-changing: China and India are on the rise, the EU has tightened up as a unit, Russia is back and bolder than ever, and other international players like Iran, Team Arab, and the Latin Leftists are all making regional impacts on the balance of power as well. The planet is morphing into a multi-polar world, a place with more than one superpower. This isn't up for debate, nor a future prediction—this is happening now. The world of the future is a place where the US is not the only primary actor making global decisions. The question then becomes, how is Uncle Sammy going to deal with this new world, this up-and-coming, changing world right now in the 21st century?

Will Sammy go lightly into this world? Will he see the changes that are coming and work with other big powers and other big countries to get the job done and still push his own agenda? Or is it going to be more of a rougher road, where the United States has a tough time giving up its top slot and is perhaps bound and determined to have its way at all costs? This could result in potential conflict, war, stonewalling economically or in other ways, or becoming isolationist and just putting up a big wall and looking inward to try to focus on itself only.

That is the big question. But this is a region of greatness and the US/Canadian team is not going to go away anytime soon, meaning it's going to maintain its powerful position as a major player in planetary affairs for some time to come. But will it be a bigger force for good or more of an internally-looking isolationist state? Only time will tell.

As the insightful Uncle Ben once told Peter Parker, "With great power comes great responsibility." Good advice for Spiderman, and probably for North America as well.

What next, Sammy?

The Regions
PART TWO

NORTH AMERICAN RUNDOWN & RESOURCES

View additional Plaid Avenger resources for this region at http://plaid.at/na

BIG PLUSES

- Biggest economy in the world
- Most powerful military in the world
- Leader of technological innovation in most fields
- Leader of democracy and human rights promotion worldwide
- One of the most solid infrastructures in the world
- Great educational system, decent social safety nets
- High standards of living, high degree of personal freedoms
- Multi-cultural, multi-ethnic, multi-religious region where everybody pretty much gets along
- Politically stable, solid rule of law

BIG PROBLEMS

- Overzealous focus on materialism has made region the biggest consumer of everything on the planet and a giant polluter
- Overzealous focus on materialism has made region's citizens fattest on planet and increasingly disillusioned
- Economic, political, and foreign policies typically focus solely on short-term solutions
- Two-party system has become entrenched, unresponsive, corrupt and grid-locked; citizen apathy is reaching all-time high
- Has a tendency towards over-doing it on the global stage, or alternatively, intense isolationism
- Chronic dependence on fossil fuels and illegal narcotics imported from other regions; you decide which one of those is worse

DEAD DUDES OF NOTE:

George Washington: Father of the US, first US President, dollar-bill guy, refused to be appointed King in favor of establishing the democracy, warned against two-party system.

John A Macdonald: Father of Canada, first Prime Minister, Canadian ten-dollar bill guy, helped forge the 2nd largest nation on the planet, thus ensuring it wouldn't be absorbed by the US.

Ronald Reagan: Commie-hater extraordinaire; claimed by some to have single-handedly won the entire Cold War. A demi-god to the conservative right.

PLAID CINEMA SELECTION:

Atanarjuat aka *Fast Runner* (2001) The first feature film to be written directed and featuring only actors using the language Inuktitut, used by the Canadian Inuit population. Excellent look at some of the indigenous people of Canada from their perspective rather than that of outsiders. And assuredly, it is the only film you can see a naked man running across icebergs and insane Arctic landscapes for over two hours.

Bon Cop, Bad Cop (2006) Archetypal buddy cop film which pairs two policemen from Quebec and Ontario who are nothing alike. Film shows great contrast of real cultural differences between these two provinces as well as examples of both Francophone and Anglophone humor. Second highest grossing Canadian film behind *Porky's*.

The Corporation (2003) Full-on documentary only for those serious about understanding how the business world works. Be forewarned: it does not paint a pretty pro-corporate picture, but is a worthwhile watch even for the future board members among you. While corporations are not an exclusive American phenomenon, this film pieces together their rise in the modern world, which has been extremely US-influenced and defined.

Roger & Me (1989) You've heard all the hype about the ultra-liberal Michael Moore, but so few have actually ever checked out his first, and easily best, docu-drama. Like him or hate him, this film is an excellent look at a by-gone era of American manufacturing culture, and will help you understand why the US car market crashed and burned, and also how the "Rust-Belt" formed in the now abounded post-industrial northeastern US.

Smoke Signals (1998) Atypical buddy/road-trip movie that features great insight into current Native American reservation culture, with fantastic diverse biome shots of western and northwestern US.

Super Size Me (2004) Documentary/comedy on eating patterns of Americans, and the real-life consequences when the nastiness is pushed too far. Features an attempt at an all-fast food diet!

LIVE LEADERS YOU SHOULD KNOW:

Barack Obama: US President—yeah, the head honcho of the world's sole superpower.

Stephen Harper: Canadian Prime Minister—huge US ally and head honcho of that other country just north of the US.

John Kerry: US Secretary of State—top US diplomat who has to deal with all that international relations stuff.

Chuck Hagel: US Secretary of Defence—the top dog in charge of the entire US military machine. Makes decisions on war and peace, and troop allocation and strategic focus for the mightiest state on the planter.

CHAPTER OUTLINE

1. World Maker, Shaker, and Breaker
2. Who Is in the Region . . . and Why?
3. Physically: Water, Water Everywhere...
4. Plaid Avenger's History of Western Europe
   4.1 The Beginning of the End: The 20th Century
5. The EU
   5.1. The Rise of the EU
   5.2. What's So Cool about the EU?
   5.3. Power Struggles & Power Structure of Europe
   5.4. Today's EU
6. Problems: Immigration and Culture Friction
   6.1. Culture Friction
   6.2. Immigration
7. New Faces, New Directions
8. Summary—Western Europe

Western Europe

WORLD MAKER, SHAKER, AND BREAKER

What the heck's that supposed to mean? Well just this: while the United States and the North American region in general may enjoy prominent status in today's world, it's Western Europe that really has shaped the current cultural, social, economic, and political world in which we live today. They've been at it for about 500 years longer than the US, and have had a tremendous impact worldwide in determining what's happening right now.

Let's face it—English is an international language not because of America, but because of the British, and their influence. Soccer is the world sport, not American football, for the same reasons. When we look at today's world, Western Europe may not be the world leader anymore, but it certainly was the maker and shaker. What about the breaker part then?

Well as you know, Western Europeans spent a lotta time in the last thousand years, and particularly the last century, beating the living crap out of each other. WWI, WWII. . . need I say more?! But today's world is very much different for Western Europe, as it is united as never before—making, and shaking, without breaking, in the 21st century. Let's get to it!

WHO IS IN THE REGION . . . AND WHY?

Everybody knows and understands that Western Europe is a region. It is the western side of the Eurasian landmass. But being a Plaid Avenger world region is not solely based on just the physical geography, so what is it that makes this a homogenous unit? We need to back up before we ask that question and ask who, what, and where is this region? What states? All the western European states? Which ones are those? All those cool ones that we take vacations to visit. Places like Norway, Sweden, Iceland, UK, Ireland, Germany, Belgium, Luxembourg, Switzerland, Austria, France, Spain, Portugal, Italy, Greece. Oh, wait, and Greece . . . Greece? But it's on the eastern side of Europe!

Look at the map here on the opposing page. All of those that are connected somehow are all Western Europe, but Greece is disconnected; it's over on the other side all by itself. Indeed, I think all of us would say, "Yes of course. Greece is definitely part of Western Europe." That gets at the heart of what it is to be Western Europe, of what it is to be in this region, and the homogeneous traits therein.

So what characteristics do these countries share that categorize them as a region? What could possibly be the same about all of these countries? Because, really, isn't it easier to point out the differences between France and Germany, or between the UK and Italy? Yeah . . . that's what makes the regional definition kind of tricky here.

What we have is a set of extremely distinct nation states. In fact, all of these countries are exceptionally different from one another. When we look back at the US and Canada, we said they share a common culture and language and

151

background. When we get over to Western Europe, we have Spain; with Spanish people who speak their own language and have their own culture, Spanish everything. Go next door and there's France, with French people who speak French; in Germany, there are German dudes and they speak German. All of these things bring to mind extremely distinct cultures. The Germans eat sausages; the French drink wine. The Germans attack, while the French surrender. Backgrounds and histories are all very different. On top of all that, Western Europe is a collection of states that vary in size: big states like France and Germany, and micro states like Luxembourg and Andorra.

However, there are a whole lot of homogeneous things about every state in this region, even though they have radical differences in backgrounds, histories, cultures, food, and drink.

But there is a bunch of stuff that is quite the same. Most of our culture here in the North American region is based on cultures from Western Europe, not Eastern Europe or Russia, but predominantly Western European backgrounds. What are the similarities?

Western civilization" is one. These are the places that created the big ideas on which our lives are based. I'm talking about the big things here: philosophies, legal systems, economic systems, medical practices, writing systems, and particularly religions. Christianity may have been born in the Middle East, but Western Europe became the cradle of Christianity and all its subsects. Europe expanded and grew the religion into a global movement.

As it did for so many other ideas. This is why Greece is thrown into the fray; it's the birthplace of all the Western philosophies. People like Socrates, Plato, and all those dudes from Greece that affected history in a major way. Ideas of democracy and western medicine even have their origins in Western Europe. All of the "-isms" that you learned in high school: political and economic systems like socialism, Marxism, communism, and capitalism were created or evolved radically in Western European countries. These countries have shaped the way we think about life and how we want to live it.

There are great cultural differences between these separate and distinct nation-states that make up the birthplace of western civilization, but *they are united in their ideologies*. Another uniting factor in this region is that it is a rich place. The quality of life is similar to North America, even exceeding that quality of life in many places. It is a very interconnected place and is very urban like the United States too. There are high levels of technology, high levels of consumption, and high GDP overall. Compared to the rest of the world, this region is rich! Considering the combination of quality of life and its ideological background as the birthplace of Western civilization, Western Europe is a distinct and homogenous region in and of itself. While many Eastern European states are increasingly 'catching up' with their western counterparts, and I soon may just refer to a single European region, I think here in 2014 there are still enough significant differences to talk about them as two distinct regions.

Jesus, Socrates, Marx, Descartes: bearded dudes of note in Western Civilization.

PHYSICALLY: WATER, WATER EVERYWHERE . . .

What can we say about this place physically? The Plaid Avenger doesn't want to spend too much time talking about the physical aspects of this region, but when it comes to Western Europe and its profound impact on the planet, we have to consider the physical geography for just a minute. This is a group of countries on the western end of the Eurasian continent. For those of you that heard Europe is a separate continent, that's *poppycock!* It's not a distinct continent in terms of geology or any other "-ology." It's just the western peninsula of the great Eurasian landmass.

It's a snobbish European thing to suggest that it ever was a stand-alone continent. They were making themselves distinct from the rest of the people on the Eurasian continent, perhaps putting themselves a notch or two above the rest, but we will get to that momentarily. What we have is a group of countries on the western edge of the Eurasian landmass that have several distinct things about them that have made it a region of major power players in today's world. They actually have not been around as long as Chinese society or Indian society, and not even Mesopotamia, for that matter; Middle Eastern and African civilizations have been around way longer than Europe. So how did the Europeans get into a position of dominance in the last 500 years?

In terms of physical geography, Western Europe is an interconnected place . . . look at the map. Water, water everywhere. Think of water's effect on trade and commerce. River systems, which go through every inch of Western Europe, interconnect economies. This makes trading very fluid, pun intended. Not only is Western Europe permeated by river systems, but water is all around it as well. We know Western Europe has peninsulas, but if you look at it, you can see that it is a peninsula itself. It is a peninsula of peninsulas. That is: if it's not an island like the United Kingdom or Ireland or Iceland, then it's a peninsula. Look at the Scandinavian Peninsula, the Iberian Peninsula, the Italian Peninsula. There is water surrounding all of them. You're never far from water in Western Europe.

What does this have to do with the Plaid Avenger History you need to know? It's this closeness and association with water that helped propel Europe into the limelight 500 years ago. Virtually all of the countries in this region were once major maritime powers, or at least maritime explorers. This makes Western Europeans some serious seagoing folk. We think about guys from Italy, Spain, Portugal, and Britain, even the Vikings of Scandinavia, going out and poking into the rest of the world. People did this in other parts of the world too, but the Western Europeans took it to the next level by taking over the entire globe with a passion and speed unrivaled in history. And they did it via naval power.

Another physical consideration about Western Europe is that while it's very far north—most of it is north of the US-Canadian border—it has a more moderate climate because of something called the **Gulf Stream**, which morphs into the **North Atlantic Drift**. This is a warm water current which forms in the tropical areas in the Gulf of Mexico, Caribbean Sea, and Atlantic Ocean. It actually sweeps up the Eastern Seaboard of the United States and flows very far north, next to Ireland and the United Kingdom, all the way to the top of the Scandinavian Peninsula around Sweden and Norway.

With water all around acting as a climate modifier, what we have is a place that is warmer in the winter and a little cooler in the summer than other places at equal latitudes. As we move into the continent

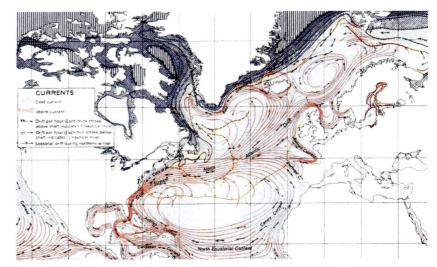

Gulf Stream/North Atlantic Drift: moderates even the far north areas of Europe.

towards Eastern Europe and Russia, we are going to see the places at the same latitudes get quite a bit colder. Western Europe is pretty moderate. What's so great about that? As we saw in America, a well-watered, moderate climate is conducive to human settlement and population growth. While a few thousand years ago nobody was hanging out in Western Europe, in the last thousand it has become increasingly populated, and has become one of the cores of population on the planet because, physically speaking, the situation is right. And also right for global domination. . . .

PLAID AVENGER'S HISTORY OF WESTERN EUROPE

We don't need to waste too much time talking about European history, as you have probably already had a thousand classes on it in during your scholastic career, but the Plaid Avenger can summarize the last couple thousand years for you very quickly. The big pluses: the agricultural revolution (they learn to produce a lot of food), the age of colonization (they learn to take over the world and get a lot of stuff) and the industrial revolution (they learn to invent machines to make a lot more stuff). Put it all together, and it's a rich region.

It should be noted for the record that the transformation of this region into the dominant world leader is really only a product of the last 500 years. Yes, I know the Greek and Roman Empires were really hip in their day a couple of millennia ago . . . but they were also very local . . . and then they crashed and burned, leaving Europe a provincial little playground until the "restoration" of the Renaissance. The region was NOT a global leader, and it was NOT a global force, prior to 1500AD. Other civilizations around the globe made Western Europe look like a backwater of buffoons. And it was.

But then those Europeans got savvy after their **Dark Ages**. They learned about sailing and navigation and shipbuilding from Muslim traders. They learned about the global trade network from Asian merchants. They learned about gunpowder from the Chinese. The Europeans took all this information and applied it in new and exciting ways which subsequently made them masters of the seas, masters of the global economy, and especially masters of military. China made fireworks with their gunpowder. Europeans made guns with it. You can figure out the rest from there.

If these guys were taking over the world by storm, then what were the negatives? In a word: competition. All these different ethnic groups, religious groups, and different nationalistic groups have spent a whole lot of time in the last couple centuries beating the living hell out of each other. You have probably heard of war after war after war that you had to memorize in high school; all of them occurred on European soil. The last couple of biggies were the World Wars of the 20th century, but there were hundreds of other confrontations before those.

Virtually all of those contests were based on competition between these European states for more power, more money and more influence on both the European and the world stage. The states of this region, as a whole, have spent a good deal of their time figuring out how to out-maneuver, out-flank, and generally beat up their nation-state neighbors. Why is that? How did it get to be this way? And how has it radically changed in the last 50 years? These are the important questions that you need to consider. The whole concept of a nation-state was formed in Western Europe. How did this concept form here if they have spent all this time fighting? Hmmm . . . perhaps is was precisely because all these groups were fighting with each other that the nation-state comcept evolved! See . . .

There are groups of people identifying themselves as distinct cultures, like the French, the Italians, the Swiss. Those terms mean something to us. It means something to them as well. The idea that you would have a distinct group of people and that you would outline a political area in which you reside is a Western European phenomenon, just like all the "-isms" and philosophies we talked about earlier. Unique, competitive cultures sitting side-by-side in the little chessboard of Europe. Yep. That's how conflict started.

I should also reiterate that there are people who begat people who begat people to make Western Europe one of the most populous regions on the planet, especially in the last 500 years. People are all over Europe. The coastlines and river systems are packed to the point that Europe as a whole is about half the size of the United States with about twice the population. We talked about the North American region having tons of space that fostered the evolution of the automobile,

Land and latitude comparison: US and Europe.

interstate system, suburbs, and individual transport systems; Europe is the reverse. You don't have all that space. You have double the population in half the space. We can see the physical manifestation of this with public transportation. People use trains and buses; not everybody owns vehicles there. It's quite a different society just from the standpoint of land and how little of it there is.

I said something about colonies a second ago, which has everything to do with everything. You already know from a previous Plaid chapter that the North American region is the number one region in terms of military, economy, wealth, and all that stuff. But that only came about in the last 100 years. Who used to hold those top slots? Western Europe did, and they had their day in the sun for a good 500 years. From Columbus right on down until about World War I, Western European countries had the tiger by the tail and controlled most of the world.

What does the Plaid Avenger mean by "controlled most of the world?" You mean like cultural imperialism from the United States? No. I mean *direct imperial control*. Because of the physical geography we talked about, Western Europe was full of maritime nations, and because of the certain situation at that time in their history, they started going out and exploring the world. Their technology increased and surpassed the technology available in other places on the planet. Thus, their exploration and exploitation potential increased.

These guys, at the exact right time in history, went out and bumped into the New World. They took over all the New World and colonized it. They said, "Hey, look! North America! That's ours! South America! We'll take that too! Divvy that up between Spain and Portugal! North America? We'll divvy that up between the French and the British!" That's not all. Throughout the last 500 years, a tiny handful of states from Western Europe controlled the rest of the planet.

As you can see from the graphic to the right, eight nations—UK, Germany, France, Spain, Portugal, Italy, Netherlands, and Belgium—controlled all the countries in pink. This is a massive territorial holding. Again, the Plaid Avenger is trying to get you to understand how it is that Western Europe has some of the richest countries in the world right now. Look at this map again. For 500 years, these guys siphoned the material wealth off the rest of the planet.

Let's think about a place like the Netherlands. There isn't anything there, my friends. It's flat. They grow tulips! How are they, of all countries, one of the richest in the world? You have to understand this much about history: it's because they controlled massive territorial holdings, many of which were exclusively economically exploited colonies. The Dutch just siphoned off wealth.

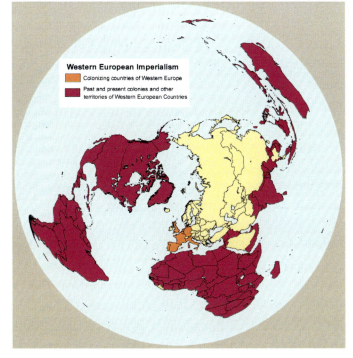
Colonial masters of disaster!

Think about the Spanish Armada, which controlled all of South America, Mexico, Central America, and the Caribbean. They brought back gold and silver bouillon . . . the booty! It was all there in the New World, my friends. What did the Spaniards do with it? Did they dig it up in Mexico and redistribute to the natives? Hell no! They took everything of value and brought it back to Western Europe. All of it. Meanwhile, the British were busy bringing back all the tobacco they could smoke up, as much cotton as they could weave into fabric, and as much rum as they could pull out of the Caribbean and disperse to their sailors.

All of this economic exploitation hugely benefitted Western European countries. This is not the case with Eastern Europe. You do not see Eastern European or Russian or Middle Eastern or Chinese colonies in the world. This taking over of the planet and exploiting it on a grand scale was a uniquely Western European phenomena and one that has been largely overlooked in textbooks, for whatever reason. All of the world's wealth went floating back to a small group of countries. That may sound pretty negative. Maybe it is. I think if I were somewhere in sub-Saharan Africa and had been a colonial holding for the last 500 years, which left me and my people poor while those European countries are rich as Midas, I might be a little bitter. Fortunately, the Plaid Avenger grew up in the United States, where we kicked those Brits out before they exploited us for too long. The United States is in a much different situation than many other ex-colonies in the world today precisely because of that fact. I do not believe that it is much of a coincidence that most of the poorest parts of the planet in today's world were the ones that suffered under the colonial legacy the longest . . . namely African ones.

But let's not beat up our European brothers anymore right now. Let's think about some of their other impacts on the world. What are the other things to consider when we look at the Western European region that had such a tremendous influence on the planet? What's the number 1 sport in India? Cricket. Brazil? Soccer. What language do they speak in Pakistan? What language do they speak in Chile? What religion do they follow in Mexico? What are the religious practices in the Philippines? What types of government do all the countries of the world follow? What are the major philosophies that most people in Africa ascribe to? These questions all have answers of Western European origin.

Virtually all the types of government across the globe, many modes of thought, major religions, and major languages were all spread throughout the world via the conquests of Western Europe. People in Brazil speak Portuguese because it used to be a colony of Portugal. A lot of people in India speak English because the British used to colonize those dudes. All sorts of little things, including dietary habits, holidays, and particularly the world's sports that people love for unknown reasons, have their origins in Western Europe.

And it's not just customs and habits, it's the people too: Why are significant portions of the populations of North America, South America, and Australia white? In addition to the movement of ideas and culture, you also have the mass movement of peoples. You have English and French and German and Italian and Irish and Scottish enclaves all over the planet. As a result of this movement, nearly all of European thought and culture is accepted as part of today's world culture all over the globe. You need to know the good and the bad. Why is Western Europe rich? It has something to do with them exploiting the rest of the world. Why can you communicate using English all over the world? Same reason.

If you are a pilot that flies between countries, you must speak English. It's an international standard. Why? It's not because America is so great, but because Western Europe, Britain in particular, has had so much influence on the planet over the last 500 years. America was just the heir to the throne of global power and influence that was created by the period of Western European colonial imperialism.

This colonial period is really the most important in European history, probably in world history. It led to the amalgamation of wealth that essentially made Western Europe the rulers of the world. We can debate whether the United States is an imperial power, but there's no debate about Western Europe. They were a hegemonic imperial power that controlled the entire known world and amassed incredible wealth from it. They don't have that position anymore, of course. The US has that top slot. What are some of the reasons for this? Well, the Europeans lost their colonial holdings and ran out of land. They could not continually expand as the United States has done over the last 200 years. They don't have any more resources because they have been using those resources for generations upon generations. Europe is like a geriatric version of the US. It ran out of its room to grow and is a young buck no longer.

THE BEGINNING OF THE END: THE 20th CENTURY

And that's enough history to set the stage. Western Europe is not number one today, although it is still very rich. It still has a lot of influence in the world, though what we are seeing in the 21st century is that European power is actually on the decline. How did it go from top banana to just another in the bunch? Europeans may not like to hear the Plaid Avenger say that, but it's true. They are slipping. They have a very unique solution on how to stop that slip, by the way, and we'll discuss that in the last part of this chapter. But back to the slip . . . wait a minute. Banana . . . slip. Am I good or what? But I digress . . .

As we already pointed out, they were on top of the world for quite a while, but the 20th century was unkind to not only Western Europe, but Europe as a whole. Just as America was exploding onto the world scene, Europe decided to beat the living hell out of itself for 50 years solid—and did a good job of it. These nation-states with their independent cultures and separate identities smashed themselves not once, but twice, in World Wars I and II. The Cold War settled in after that, and that didn't help matters at all. The same 100 years that Europe was destroying itself, it was losing its colonial holdings. They had already lost America long ago, but in the 19th and 20th centuries, they lost all the rest. Canada went away, South America went away, a lot of Africa went away, Australia went away. And the few colonies that they retained to the bitter end were giving the Europeans nothing but a headache too: India for the British, French Indochina for the French, the Middle East for everybody. These places broke out into independence wars, civil disobedience, and catastrophe in general. So little by little, as we approach the modern era, the Europeans lost these territories that, for a long time, gave them their wealth accumulation and serious competitive edge.

As the Plaid Avenger suggested already, America has continuously expanded economically because of its incredible amount of resources and territory. You have that with the Western European powers as well, but this reversed in the last 100 years. They lost all their territory. They lost the unfettered access to the resources of those places as well. This reversal of fortunes happened at the same time they battled each other in wars, destroying their entire infrastructure. Make no bones about it: World War II was the most destructive thing that could have happened to any region as a whole. There was total devastation across the entire continent. Factories, roads, and bridges were entirely wiped out. Again, this plays back into why America became #1 post-WW2, because none of that type of destruction happened in America.

Massive WWII destruction in Europe.

So, the first half of the 20th century was not kind to Europe. It lost colonies and they destroyed themselves to the point of collapse. At the end of this destruction, people woke up and realized they needed to do something different. They couldn't continue to beat each other up. Some very wise people figured out that individual Western Europe states couldn't compete on the world stage. These thinkers dreamt up a new way to get back into the game. What they thought up was something entirely new . . . and new rhymes with EU. . . .

THE EU

THE RISE OF THE EU

The EU is the salvation of Western Europe and the only real reason it is still a global player, period. What do I mean by that? Well, after the destruction of World War II, some smart dudes—incredibly, they were French—said, "We've got to stop killing each other. We need to economically integrate ourselves so that we are not competing with each other anymore." They thought that part of the problem was that the Germans hated the French and the French hated the British and the British hated everybody because they were in competition with each other. And they were right. The Western Europeans were once the masters of the universe, but those days were gone. To continue to compete with each other, just within the continent, was disastrous, as they already found out. So they said, "We should work together, we can all get a little bit richer if we all try and work together better. Let's start rebuilding from WWII by pooling our coal and steel industries."

That's how the EU started. Everybody needed coal and steel to rebuild stuff, and all of Western Europe had to be rebuilt. The smart guys who thought this up knew it would evolve into something else. They said, "We'll do this as a start, and it will tie us to each other so much that we won't be able to afford to attack each other. If we make this into a common industry, Germany won't be able to attack France, because it would be hurting its own economic needs." You can't beat up the people you're actively trading with because you will lose their trade. It was an interdependence that they formed in the coal and steel industries, but they wanted to make it something else. They wanted it to reach farther.

This is where we have the real rise of supranationalism in Europe following WWII. The EU grew and it said, "Well, let's not stop here; let's continue to make things more and more solid as every day passes so we can't compete anymore. We are so far behind now; we are so wiped out. America is totally whipping our butt, and we lost our colonies. How can we effectively compete on the world stage?" The answer was to expand the coal and steel thing into a free trade zone thing—a free trade block.

What does this have to do with world trade? Can Belgium compete with the United States' economy? No. Can Italy? No. How about Ireland? Not a chance—they are all too busy drinking Guinness. How about Germany, the number four economy

What's the Deal with . . . Coal and Steel?

In 1951, six European countries—France, Belgium, West Germany, Italy, the Netherlands, and Luxembourg—signed the Treaty of Paris establishing the European Coal and Steel Community (ECSC). The ECSC created a common market, free of trade barriers, for steel and coal. These two commodities were especially important, because both were key resources for industrialization and rebuilding after WWII. Trading coal and steel freely was the first move to quell European power rivalries by establishing this economic unity and interdependence. The ECSC is often credited with creating a community between former World War II enemies. In fact, the European Union can directly trace it roots to the ECSC. The ECSC member countries soon after established the European Economic Community, which was renamed the European Community; this became the first, and most important, "pillar" of the European Union in 1992.

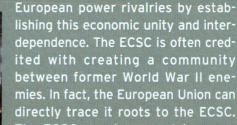

1952 ECSC: European Coal & Steel Community

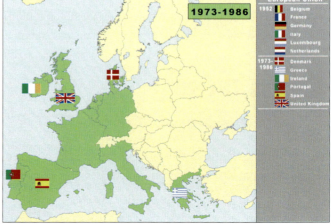

1957 EEC: European Economic Community, Expansion Phases

on the planet, can they compete? Nope. Bidding on a contract or trying to make some sort of international tie or trade tie with another country, the United States will win every time. So these countries got together and said, "Wait a minute! What if we all act under a common umbrella? Can all of our countries together as a unit effectively compete against the United States?" Yes, and they can compete with lots of other trade blocks around the world as well.

The EU evolved into a **trade block,** and, as you read about in chapter 6, trade blocks are all about decreasing tariffs and taxes between states to encourage trade. The French said, "Hey, Germany, we won't tax your sausages if you don't tax our wine!" They all agreed not to tax each other's stuff and therefore, people were able to afford to buy more of it. People bought more, people sold more. Mo' money. Once that got going and they got back on their feet during the last 50 years, the EU expanded into something that the world has never seen. That's why I am going to spend the rest of this chapter just talking about what's so cool about the EU.

WHAT'S SO COOL ABOUT THE EU?

Why is it of such great significance? Thanks to the EU, Europe is turning from a bunch of nation-states that competed with each other for a thousand years into the **United States of Europe.** What does that mean? The independent sovereign nation-states of Europe are becoming much more like substates of the United States than independent countries, in terms of free movement of peoples and elimination of borders. Borders are still there, but they don't really mean anything. If you walked in a straight line across Europe twenty years ago, you would get your passport checked twenty different times according to how many countries you crossed.

That policy is largely disappearing. In fact, the number one thing for you to remember about what's different from the EU and all other trade blocks, or even supranationalist organizations around the planet, is the *free movement of peoples.* Nowhere else on the planet do you have a coalition of countries in which the people in your country can move anywhere within all the countries of the club without having their passport checked. This free movement of people is a big, big deal. A 2012 note: This free movement of people is being seriously re-evaluated right now, especially for the most recent EU inductees, but it is still a critical and revolutionary idea within a trade block.

Compare this to NAFTA, the free trade union between the US, Canada, and Mexico. Do we have a free movement of people? No! You can go back and forth between Canada and the US and they will check your passport, but you can't just do anything you want. Can you move back and forth from Mexico to the United States? Oh, no way! The US has a huge wall that it is, in fact, trying to make bigger. The unique factor about the EU is free movement of people. Because of this fact, they have to have a common law system as well. They are building a common judicial system, and a common legislative system. Thus, the EU is becoming a United States of Europe.

1992 EU: European Union, Post-USSR Expansion Phases

Before I go any further, does everybody in Europe think this is the most awesome idea ever, with everybody doing shots of Jägermeister while extolling the great virtues of their fellow Europeans? Oh, no. Political leaders think a United States of Europe would be totally sweet, particularly leaders whose countries participated in the wars. Businesses and a lot of other people like the idea too. However, not everybody digs it, and the reason for the animosity lies in that cultural imperialism thing that we talked about in the last chapter.

What does that have to do with the EU? People in Italy are Italians and they have their Italian heritage. A lot of the French are fiercely defensive of French culture. Those Brits will defend the Queen and teatime with their lives. Because EU dudes are nation-states with independent cultures, there are lots of folks within them that see the EU as a threat to the survival of their culture. Sometimes you'll see a McDonalds restaurant being set on fire in protest of the EU. You can interpret any sort of anti-conglomeration or anti-homogenization attack on a multinational organization as a protest against the EU. The anti-EU opposition is losing the battle, but they are there. They will tell you, "This EU thing sucks! I don't want to be in the United States of Europe! I want to be Italian!" . . . or Croatian, or whatever nationality they are.

The EU is definitely continuing despite the small amount of dissent, but where's it going? Well, it's got a common defense system, which is a huge stride. Each country, for the most part, has its own little army, but the EU also has a common defense army. You can hear about the EU forces being sent into places like Yugoslavia, or EU forces being requested in Iraq. The idea of a unified army for these countries is a massive change in a region that has spent a thousand years beating itself up. They now have a common defense force, which pretty much eliminates the possibility of any future conflict. You can't fight wars with each other if you have the same army.

POWER STRUGGLES & POWER STRUCTURE OF EUROPE

The EU is growing because most member countries think that for their organization to compete better on the world stage, their economic numbers need to be higher. Those members think the EU should become bigger. The bigger the club, the more world power it has, and the more power they have as individual countries. That is the common perception in the EU, so they are expanding into Eastern Europe. This means places like Poland, the Czech Republic, and Latvia are now in the EU. Places as far east as Ukraine may be members of the EU soon. Bulgaria and Romania and Croatia were the most recent additions, and the rest of the Balkan Peninsula is trying to follow suit. This block is expanding eastward, unifying Europe more than it's ever been before.

This has set up some internal power struggles within the EU. There is something the Plaid Avenger calls **Europe's Continental Divide of Power.** These internal struggles for power within the EU have a lot to do with how the system is set up. It's a lot like the United States in that there is a legislature, a judiciary system, and something similar to a House of Representatives in which each nation-state has a say according to the size of its population. The EU also has something like a Senate, in which each nation-state has a single representative. We can obviously tell who has the power by looking at populations. Who's got the power? Big surprise: France and Germany. They're the big power players in population and economics within Europe, so they have much more say in what the EU does. A lot of smaller states within the EU say, "Hey wait a minute, we are not getting as much of a voice! This is unfair! We don't like this! I'm Liechtenstein! Hear me roar!"

> Here in the Plaid Avenger's book, we have been talking about Western Europe and Eastern Europe in separate chapters, but in another five or ten years there may be no difference; it may just be Europe. We will get to the remaining differences for the next chapter, but for now, we will leave it at that.

While the French and the Germans have battled each other throughout history, they are actually a team now. And what a team! It's the **Franco-German Alliance,** if you want to have some really cool terminology to throw around at dinner parties. These guys are also on the continent, so I call them **the continentals.** Germany is the number four economy on the planet, and France is number five. This makes them a huge power core of the EU. These two states, while they have historically agreed on

nothing, pretty much agree on everything nowadays. They are big pro-EU states quite frankly because they are power players in it. A lot of the EU's smaller states complain that if France and Germany don't like a proposal or idea, then it's not going to happen. There is definitely some truth in that. If France and Germany are against an idea, it can get stymied easily. This causes a true power divide between big states and small states.

The EU's number two power core is the UK. Perhaps you never thought of the UK this way, but it is kind of distinct from the rest of Europe. "Say what? Plaid Avenger, I thought you just said the UK was *part* of Western Europe?" It is physically; it's there off the coast of the Eurasian continent, and all of its history is European history. However, the British have, for quite some time, been slightly separate. Snobbish even. Tea-sippers, with the pinky in the air. Remember the old British blue-blooded aristocracy—the same ones who still think the Queen is the bomb. A bit of snobbery remains, and the British have seen themselves as distinct from the rest of Europe proper throughout history.

As I said before, the British were the predecessors to American power on the planet. They were on the world throne for a very long time, but not anymore. Here's a Plaid Avenger interpretation: the attitude of the British is that they are still number one. They would still very much like to be the singular world power. If you *can't* be the world power, what should you do? *Hang out* with the world power! If you're not the biggest kid on the block, *hang out* with the biggest kid on the block and make him your buddy. So the British actually have much more in common with, and are much more eager to hang out with the United States in world politics than they are with the Franco-German alliance on their own continent, in their own trade block.

Big states and small states argue over constitutional power structures and representation. The older EU states argue with the newest EU states over immigration policies. And the Franco-German axis may argue with the British over economic and foreign policy. But the times are a'changin' on this front as well, which brings us to . . .

TODAY'S EU

Western Europe's going through some fairly radical changes here in the dawn of the 21st century. The first that's already been alluded to, and that's the EU. Let's elaborate a bit more on the EU in today's world, because it really has become the face of Western Europe and Europe as a whole, led by Western Europe, though. And it could now be in some trouble here in 2014 and beyond . . . but let's start with the positive repercussions of their experiment in Union.

The EU, if taken as a singular entity, is the largest economy on the planet. It has the largest GDP. Yes, indeed, a Gross Domestic Product bigger than that of even the United States. Now again, that's putting all the member countries of the EU together into a single block, but that's of course, what they are. And although it perhaps started as trade, perhaps morphed a little bit into politics, it is something entirely new on the world landscape, and it's becoming more powerful every day.

What's so new? Well, the EU has been working hard to frame a constitution for itself, an endeavor which has not met with ultimate success—so far. But it's quite important to consider, if for nothing else, that when it does get passed eventually, and it will, it's going to dawn an entire new age for Europe. It really will lay the foundations of Europe being the United States of Europe, a different beast altogether than anything that has come before in continental Europe. And they're doing a whole lot of things to cement this idea in place and take it to the next level.

A constitution, and also a unified judicial system, which is becoming stronger every day. They have unified, singular environmental policies. They've already unified their monetary system. The borders between the original EU states are fairly solvent, meaning you can move around within them—free movement of people. We've already talked about that. With the introduction of lots of new states in Eastern Europe, from Eastern Europe, the free movement of people is changing a bit, but we'll get to that in just a second.

The thing I want to finish on, relating to the EU and its future in the world, is that it also has a common defense. This appears to be growing rapidly here very recently, as well. They want to have a defense structure—essentially an army—an EU army, that behaves and acts independently of the United States and even of NATO, of which most EU countries are a member.

To finally finish, the big point: foreign policy needs to be considered as well. Increasingly, and this is bizarre, the EU is more and more speaking with a single voice when it comes to foreign policy. That's important because here lately, the EU foreign policy line does not agree with, or contradicts, the US foreign policy line. This is, again, quite important to understand what's going on in the world. Meaning that the EU, a singular entity, puts out political statements about its attitude about things that are happening on the planet. It's not always completely unified, but the fact that they are doing it is what's important. Maybe a few examples are warranted here.

As President Robert Mugabe of Zimbabwe was destroying his own economy and harassing his own peoples, the EU stepped forward with a statement and said, "We do not condone this behavior. We are going to have sanctions against Zimbabwe." That "we" being the entire EU. We're seeing that increasingly the EU is acting as a singular entity to make statements about, say, Chinese human rights, or other issues that are occurring around the planet. This, combined with this singular EU national defense, are the most important points that are being developed rapidly here at the dawn of the 21st century, and are what's making the EU a real political, as well as economic, force in the world.

Why would they do this? Just like with the economic stuff, no singular European nation can compete with the US or increasingly can even compete with China, or Japan, or many other places in the world on their own. So they got together, and as a singular economic unit, they can compete quite well as one of the biggest players in their own right.

Now the same thing has happened with politics. They realize that, yes, while the UK has a big voice in the world, by itself it can't do as much, and certainly Belgium can't, and there's no way Poland can. But as a singular unit, politically their voice is much, much stronger. But they still don't agree on everything . . .

PROBLEMS: IMMIGRATION AND CULTURE FRICTION

Western Europe also has some big problems ahead of it. The main BIG issue that it's currently confronted with is: people. What? Why are people a problem? People are a double-edged sword in Western Europe because the populations of most Western European countries are stagnant, which means they're not growing, or actually declining—they're getting smaller. (Remember that demographic transition stuff from way back in chapter 2?) Therefore, to keep their economies going, moving forward and growing, you have to have people. You have to have people filling jobs—working on farms, working in restaurants, washing dishes, putting down the beds at the hotels. Western Europe, with its declining local populations, has had to rely on immigration from other regions in order to fill those jobs. It has to happen. That's a fact. But how is it happening?

We talked about distance being one of the United States' great physical attributes; it is far away from most other places in the world, and only borders one other distinctly different region. On the other side of the spectrum, Europe is very close to every place else. Western Europe can almost be considered the epicenter of every place nearby, in that it is infused with people from Eastern Europe, Russia, the Middle East, Africa, and pretty much anybody else that can very easily get to Europe. Europe, like the US, is extremely rich. The Middle East, and Africa, and Russia could be put in the poorer column. Maybe even the *extremely* poor column. This results in a great movement, a great migration wave, of people that are hitting Europe, and causing tremendous problems. Europe has generally welcomed them, but it is reaching a kind of critical breaking point now.

The French in particular have always had a sort of an open-door immigration policy with all of the citizens of its former colonies, particularly in Africa. "You were French citizens when you were a colony, so we are going to consider you French citizens if you want to come here." Well, that's all fine and dandy, except that the French state is now going broke!

A more lefty, socialist state which provides a lot of government benefits is starting to feel the economic strain as its population continues to swell with Arab and African immigrants. In addition, *collisions of culture* are starting to ferment.

CULTURE FRICTION

Cultural collision—what does that mean? That sounds a bit strong. Perhaps cultural friction is better. A lot of people are getting quite worried across Europe right now, that they're losing their Europe-ness. That perhaps the Belgians are losing their Belgian-ness, that the French are losing their French-ness. Why? Because the larger and larger numbers of immigrants from other places are bringing their cultures and languages and religions into the European homeland, and in more deeply integrated ways than ever in the past. Let's consider this for just a moment more.

A big debacle in worldwide news in September of 2005 was the **Danish cartoon of the prophet Mohammad** that originated in Western Europe. Why was *that* such a big deal? Because so many immigrants are of Middle Eastern Muslim and African Muslim background, both of which constitute growing percentages of the population in Western Europe. But cartoons are only the tip of the iceberg when contemplating the current European friction with Muslim culture.

Why would I pick on those folks in particular? Well, what these black African and Arab Middle Easterners that are of Muslim religion have brought to Europe is a whole new kind of layer of different culture into the European experience. There are mosques being built all over Europe. There are folks who dress differently being incorporated into Europe. There are folks with different ideas about, say, individual liberties and rights that are being incorporated all over Europe. Liberties like the value of freedom of speech to draw a cartoon of a religious figure. Ah! Get it now?

Result? An anti-immigration backlash has started to creep into European society. There has been a rise of more ultra-conservative rightist political factions across Europe—in places like Austria, Germany, and even France in particular. Those political parties are gaining popularity by saying, "We're losing our Austrian-ness, we're losing our German-ness. And we wanna kick out all the foreigners or at least limit them coming into our state to prevent this."

Burqa high fashion not hip in Holland.

Legislation has been passed in Switzerland and in Austria banning the construction of new mosques. In France, laws banning Muslim headscarves have been passed, and the French and Dutch are debating about banning the burqa altogether. 2011 update: France just officially banned the burqa, and other states are following suit. Speaking of the Dutch, a politician from the Netherlands now has 24-hour a day protection for life since he released an anti-Islamic film in 2008 mostly as an ultra-rightist political stunt, a stunt which resulted in Muslim countries around the world boycotting Dutch goods. Starting to see the problem here?

To make a long story short, Western Europe is torn right now. Its governments (being part of Team West, the core of Western Civilization) say, "Hey, we protect individual rights to do crazy stuff like offending Muslims by drawing a cartoon of the prophet Mohammed." However, they also have larger and larger Muslim constituencies, which is causing real conflict and clash in different parts of Europe who find offense in some of these things.

This cultural friction is not limited to the Muslims either. Let me give you another example, and we'll even stick with our Dutch wooden-shoe-wearing-tulip-growing friends. The Netherlands is also having problems with Catholic Christians from Poland! What? What is that all about? Well the Netherlands is . . . I won't say an atheist state, but it's not really a fervently religious group of folks. In fact, most of Western Europe is fairly blasé when it comes to attending church or being very religious, but the Poles sure are! Staunch Catholics, that bunch! As lots of Polish folks have migrated to western Europe seeking better economic conditions, their numbers are starting to tip the balance on societal views of everything from drug use to abortion rights.

That's a good topic to pick on. Catholic Poles are staunchly anti-abortion. Well, the Netherlands is known as being staunchly whatever-you-wanna-do! "Hey, we have a Red Light District—go have a hooker! It's all legal. Smoke some hemp! We don't care! You wanna have an abortion? Have three." Well, wait a minute. Now you have a big constituency of Catholic Poles in the Netherlands saying, "No, we don't agree with that." The Dutch government has to consider these things. So the Dutch may be losing their Dutch-ness to Catholic Poles now, as well as Muslims from North Africa. At least, that is the perception of some.

IMMIGRATION

One last point on the whole immigration and cultural friction issue that you should be aware of is that immigration is not equal across all of Western Europe, and that means immigration problems are not equal across all of Western Europe. I just wanted to point out this spatial feature of who's the most concerned about immigration within the greater EU. As might be evident, the closer a state is to, say, North Africa or the Middle East, the more concerned it is with immigration, because that's the most used and easiest traveled avenue to get into Europe.

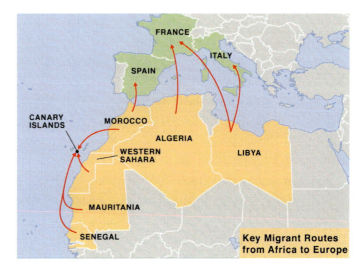

Meaning, if you want to migrate from North Africa to Western Europe, you go through the countries that are closest to you, namely Spain, Italy, and Southern France. As fate would have it, the countries that are most concerned with immigration, most worried about it, raise up the most fuss about it at the EU, are Spain, Italy, and France. Surprise! The further that European countries are from other world regions, the less likely they are to be complaining about any immigration problems, because the less likely they are to have any. Again, let's start with the evident. Norway, Sweden, Finland—these places are *far* away. They're also a lot colder. Who wants to go from North Africa to Finland? And Iceland? Don't even get me started! Like those guys would ever have an immigration problem. Even Leif Ericson bailed out of there.

You should be aware that there's also internal tribulations when the EU gets together and meets. Because states like France and Spain say, "Hey, we have a real immigration problem and we need to pass more stringent, strict laws to control this." Other places say, "Well, no, we don't really think it's that big an issue." It should be noted that the EU lacks a singular immigration policy for the block, which makes all of this a bigger debacle, as each state still does its own thing when it comes to this issue. But look for the EU to form a unified policy soon, and I'm willing to wager it's going to make getting into Europe a lot more difficult for potential immigrants.

Titanic 2011 Immigration Update: Holy Arab exodus, I was dead on the mark talking about the impending immigration crisis in Europe, which has now fully boiled over due to the Arab Revolution across the Middle East! In 2011, boatload after boatload of Tunisian, Egyptians and Libyans made their way, or tried to make their way, to Italian and French shores in an effort to escape the bloodshed and economic chaos of their home countries . . . and this sudden influx has caused open rifts within the EU.

Namely, Italy has been inundated with refugees, which they have started shipping to other parts of the continent . . . until France refused them! The Frenchies said "non!" No Tunisians coming into France! BAM! Immigration consternation exacerbation! Watch this story continue to unfold this year, and EU immigration policy to be radically impacted.

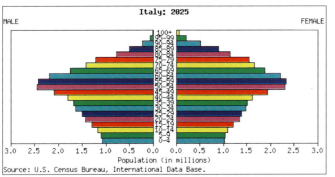

Bye-bye Italians! Hello immigrants!

Of course, the complicating factor here is that Europe is *dependent* on at least some immigration. European population dynamics, as we discussed in chapter 2, indicate that population is declining in Western Europe. In Italy, the population is declining because people aren't having enough babies. In Sweden, the population is going down perhaps due to too much movie watching.

Now lots of folks are saying, "Isn't that good? Less people means more stuff for the people there, right?" Not necessarily . . . who's going to work at the factories that prop up the country's GDP? Who's going to make money for the economy? Who's going to work in the service sector? Population is completely stable or declining in all of these countries in Western Europe, which means they actually need immigrants to come in and keep things moving forward economically. That's the rub. They cannot possibly stop immigration, and at the same time, it's causing tremendous conflicts both culturally and with the movement of jobs and people. *This is Western Europe's biggest problem.* Think I'm making it up? The conflict over the anti-Muslim film in the Netherlands, the rise of skinhead movements in Germany, full-on race riots targeting Africans in southern Italy, and even anti-Semitic crime in France have all been major headlines in the last years.

Holy double-down crazy 2011 update: Just before this book went to press in 2011, the EU moved to reverse decades of unfettered travel within the block when a majority of EU governments agreed the need to reinstate national passport controls amid fears of a flood of immigrants fleeing the upheaval in the Middle East.

Called it! This is a extremely significant political event! Europe takes a step back from a border-less world, and a big step to the conservative right! Wow! The economic recession that has been pummeling the continent will likely cause increased protectionism, more conservative ideology, and yet even tighter immigration policies in the near future. Yikes!

NEW FACES, NEW DIRECTIONS

Sammy needs you, baby!

To sum up and finish up our tour, we just need to talk about the power structure of what's happening in Western Europe right now as new folks have arrived—no, not the immigrants, but the fresh faces on the political scene. Leadership has rolled over all across Europe in the last few years, but let's just focus on the folks that make the biggest impact worldwide, and for the US in particular. Before we go any further, please, please, please remember this political fact about Western Europe: it is currently undergoing a significant shift to center-right all across the continent, especially in leadership. There are many reasons for this shift, such as economic recession, immigration issues, and cultural frictions; reasons which typically make people get all conservative and traditional, and vote for like-minded leaders. It could also be that all politics is cyclical, and its just time for the other team to have a go at it. Europe is definitely moving to right of center politically, and possibly socially.

There has also been a resurgence in extreme-right groups like skinheads in Germany, anti-immigration hate-groups in France, and borderline-fascist groups in Austria; many of these groups have been gaining support by playing up the immigration and cultural friction fears discussed in the previous sections. But those are just the extremes.

Whatever the logic, more conservative, center-right (and sometimes far-right) politicians are getting elected almost everywhere in the region. What I want you to know about for this section are the main conservative center-right folks that have been swept into power in that all-important **EU-3**. In UK, France, and Germany, leadership has flipped from left to right in the last few years . . . although in 2012 France just flipped back to the liberal left, which may start a trend for the future! Maybe. Let's look at these playas and how this shift is playing out.

First, the way it was: As we have previously discussed, the US and the UK are tight allies, and the UK has typically, in the last hundred years, gone along with all things the US desires, more so than they have with the folks in their own neighborhood, namely the rest of continental Europe. This staunchly close US-UK situation has been referred to for a century as the **Special Relationship**. You could see this highlighted at its best most recently as the US was ramping up for the current Iraq War, and came to the EU and said, "Hey, we're all buddies, we're all in NATO, hey EU countries, help us out. Support us for our Iraq invasion." The British, of course, said, "Absolutely! We're lap dogs of the US foreign policy, we'll do anything you want. Yes sir, yes ma'am, sure thing Uncle Sam."

New kid Cameron in charge of the UK, and quite possibly the sexiest prime minister since Margaret Thatcher.

However, the Franco-German alliance said, "No, absolutely not. We're not on board with that policy at all." Indeed, most of the rest of Western Europe went along with the Franco-German alliance on that. That's very typical of the way things have been for the last 10 to 20 years, maybe even more like fifty years. Yes, the Europeans *in general* are US allies and friends, but when it comes to global issues and foreign policy, the US has only been able to rely on the UK year in and year out. And it could generally count on the French to oppose it year in and year out. But this equation is changing; we can pretty much put that relationship on its head here in 2012. What do I mean?

UK first: The Brits just put conservative David Cameron into the Prime Minister position in May 2010, the first center-right (Tory party) guy to hold the post for nearly 14 years!

Of course, he is still a huge US ally, no getting around that, but Cameron will be much more reserved and will make the UK much more independent on the foreign policy front than the previous government. How do I know this? Well, Cameron is center-right while US President Obama is center-left, so they are ideologically not on the same page. And the Tory Party of UK will certainly support the war on terrorism, but historically it pulls Britain to a more independent route in the international sphere. Look for them to become more critical of US policies, but also more anti-EU and definitely anti-Euro given the financial debacle that Greece has caused the EU. They're still an ally, but not as staunch, and certainly will not be on board for everything the United States wants.

Let's shift to the continent: France and Germany—the biggest states, populations, and economies in the EU. Together they form a significant power center, and to restate, one that is typically not always in agreement with all things British, or American. What of our Franco-German friends? Strangely enough, starting in 2012, the alliance is under severe strain!

Current Chancellor of Germany Angela Merkel and former President of France Nicolas Sarkozy, are staunch conservatives center-right leaders that pretty much shared opinions and policies on virtually all things economic, social, and even on EU policy . . . but especially on how to deal with the current Europe-wide recession that has crushed the European economy, bankrupted Greece, put Italy and Spain on the ropes, and threatens to destroy the entire banking system of the continent. These two conservative titans formed an austerity plan that both France and Germany have been pushing others to follow: a plan that entails massive government spending cuts and belt-tightening, much to the chagrin of many poorer European citizens and states that are getting squeezed hard already . . . and there is more pain to come!

znomic growth which will 'save' them from the recession. In other words, the exact OPPOSITE approach of Germany's Angela Merkel, and virtually all other conservative governments and banking officials in Europe. So in 2012, the Franco-German alliance is under sever strain, and these two leaders are not getting along very well . . . which sucks for all of Europe as it sits on the brink of utter economic chaos! As if that wasn't bad enough, the Frenchie leader Holande has been embroiled in a scandalous love triangle, has botched most of his economic moves, and has plummeted in the polls here in 2014, adding to the sinking, stinky-French-cheese feeling in the state as a whole. And if they chaos culminates into catastrophe, the next victim could be the EU itself! But that will have to wait until the next edition of this book. Now back to Bavaria for the other major player of note. . . .

The new leftie in town: French President François Hollande

As for Angela Merkel, nobody is taking the **Teutonic** titan of a Chancellor for granted either. Merkel has had much success in the last eight years swinging the Germans back to the conservative side of the spectrum. Her predecessor Chancellor Gerhard Schroeder was much more liberal and much more anti-US. Germany's first woman leader has strengthened its economy, pulled in the reigns of immigration, and become a serious force in world affairs in her own right. When she talks, people listen. Merkel is more of a supporter of US policy, although not enough to get involved in any more 'wars on terror', as most Germans on the street are still vehemently opposed to both the US involvement in Iraq and in Afghanistan. But do remember this, my plaid friends: increasingly Germany has been invited to sit in on the workings of the UN Permanent Security Council. Even though it does not have an official vote, the German voice is becoming of greater significance on the world political stage by affecting UN policy decisions. Quite frankly, Germany is holding Europe and the EU together right now, almost single-handedly. They have the biggest and strongest economy, the most economic clout, and the most control over the European banking system . . . thus, Chancellor Merkel has unprecedented power to determine economic and fiscal policy for the entire EU, and she is now looked to as the leader and possible savior of not just Greece or the Spanish economy, but of the whole EU experiment as well! Germany holds the purse strings of Europe, and is demanding austerity policies as the solution to Europe's woes . . . but Frenchie Hollande isn't buying that program anymore, so we shall be watching closely to see this liberal vs. conservative policy battle play out in the EU, and the stakes could not be higher! The very survival of the EU experiment is at risk!

She's Merkel-icious!

So, big changes going on. New faces, new directions. These 3 leaders taken collectively carry a lot of weight in Europe, and in fact their countries together are often referred to as the *EU-3*. While Hollande is now leading a charge back to the liberal left in France (and currently failing at it), the vast majority of European states are still staunchly in the center-right column economically and socially, and that is a trend that is still growing . . . thus look for more conservative measures to pass in each of their countries, but also in the EU as a whole. I have only hit the big 3; there are also center-right leaders in Spain, Austria, Finland,and Switzerland. Not to belabor the point, but limiting immigration and "cultural preservation" legislation, like banning burqas, will almost certainly be percolating through the EU in the very near future. You heard it here first.

SUMMARY—WESTERN EUROPE

Increasingly, Western Europe and Eastern Europe are simply becoming Europe. However, we can still tease out enough stuff in today's world to make some finishing remarks about this Western Europe region. It is one of the richest regions in the world. It is one of the most politically powerful regions in the world. Along with the United States, it is the foundation stone of Team West: one of the most important economic, political, and even cultural forces on the planet. While the US certainly leads Team West in the world today, Western Europe is where Team West started, thus the term Western Europe . . . Team West: go figure!

Keep us in the game, coach!

It does have some new faces, some new attitudes, but the main big theme in today's world is the EU becoming somewhat of a United States of Europe. What that means for the future in terms of not just a Constitution, but defense and foreign policy, are important points to consider. Following that with these new faces in today's world, we're seeing a Western Europe that is being increasingly supportive of the United States, but still quite independent in its own right.

However, I must now be brutally honest with you, my plaid friends . . . this region has passed its prime, and its not likely to return to the glory days anytime soon. Yes, Western Europe is rich. Yes, Western Europe is a core component of the powerful and potent Team West. Yes, Western Europe is probably one of the most awesome places to party on the planet. BUT, Western Europe is no longer a center of innovation and creation; not for technology, not for business, and not even for demographics! They can't even crank out enough kids to keep up with replacement level! Which is, of course, why immigration is both a necessity and a problem for their region.

Western Europe is great, but mired in bureaucracy and tradition that simply does not facilitate it as a revolutionary center of activity anymore. Given its imperialistic phase and its centuries of conflict, this may not necessarily be a bad thing. Either way, these Europeans will continue to focus on EU evolvement to keep themselves in the global game as a serious player, knowing full well that its better to still be on the sidelines as the seasoned second-stringer than out of the ballpark altogether. At the core of the EU, the IMF, NATO, World Bank, UN, and Team West, this region has still got game, even if it gets winded easily.

2014 Final Update Note: With the economic recession still pounding Western Europe harder than ever, and with many countries on the brink of bank default/failure, the Europeans are facing the worst crisis of epic proportions since WW2. This battle between pro-EU and anti-EU attitudes (in combination with the crappy economic situation) played itself out in the 2014 EU elections! Radical far-right political parties in virtually every country made significant gains . . . meaning they won seats in the EU legislature. These far-right fringe folks are calling for immigration blocks, a return of powers from the EU to the sovereign states, and perhaps even pulling out of the EU altogether! Keep in mind, that the majority of seats held in the EU are still quite sane people, but the big gains of this fringe have caused every single leader in every single EU country to re-evaluate their policies to address this growing chorus of anti-EU peeps. It is kind of a big deal, because what we are talking about here is a full-on debate about the EU project itself, and a fight over the concept of the nation-state . . . remember, that is an idea that these Western European countries invented! And now some are fighting to return to the old-school definition of it!

Dark times ahead for Europe: Is it knight-knight time for the EU?

The fate of the Eurozone and the entire EU experiment are completely unpredictable at this point, which is why I won't predict anything. But follow close, and the next edition of this text will likely have to throw out this entire chapter and start anew. Let's hope the Europeans and the American economy survive the radical and imminent transition intact! Whatever happens, Europe will not be regaining any of its former glory anytime soon . . . and a more cynical forecast would say that the region is about to enter a new "Dark Ages." Let's hope that's not the case!

WESTERN EUROPE RUNDOWN & RESOURCES

View additional Plaid Avenger resources for this region at http://plaid.at/we

BIG PLUSES

- Biggest economy in the world
- The EU is the most highly organized and successful political organization of all time
- Interstate armed conflict is virtually impossible; very stable place
- The EU as a singular entity is the biggest economy on the planet
- Western Europe has some of the highest standards of living on the planet
- Multi-ethnic, diverse societies that generally get along with each other
- Fantastic regional rail transportation network which interconnects the region and runs extremely efficiently (except for Italy lol)

BIG PROBLEMS

- Rough EU roads ahead as the richer economies (Germany, France) have to continue to take care of the poorer economies (Greece, Portugal)
- Move to conservative center-right will certainly exacerbate anti-immigration friction that is starting to rear its head across the region
- Aging populations, over-extension of state benefits, and high costs of living will make economic growth extremely challenging in the future
- Western Europe will continue to lose its once overwhelmingly-predominate position as a major center of technological innovation, finance, and investment . . . mostly to Asia
- Cultural friction will continue to grow as folks feel they are losing their cultural identity to a monolithic EU and/or foreign immigration

DEAD DUDES OF NOTE:

Winston Churchill: The British Prime Minister guy that held the UK and Allied powers together during WWII. Great statesman, orator, historian, artist, and drinker by all accounts. Coined the phrase Iron Curtain and fostered the tight Special Relationship with the US

Adolf Hitler: Great public speaker and snappy dresser that tried to take over the world and kill everyone that wasn't white and German. His idiocy transformed Europe and became the impetus for forming the EU, the UN, and the UN convention against genocide.

Charles de Gaulle: National hero and dominant political leader of France during and after WWII, he was one of the few Frenchies who didn't surrender. Charismatic and proudly nationalistic, he pursued an independent path from both Europe and the US, which is why France was not a major payer in NATO, or great friends with the UK or US for decades.

Margaret Thatcher: Conservative Prime Minister of UK from 1975–90, was nicknamed the "Iron Lady" for her aggressive stance towards commies. She was the "Ronald Reagan of the UK" in that the two were identical in political and economic ideology. Oh, and she's not quite dead yet.

PLAID CINEMA SELECTION:

(Look, I know there are ten million awesome classic films from Europe that are probably way better than this list. I'm just giving you a handful of more modern picks that will intrigue the younger generations a bit more. Frankly, I usually can't stand anything labeled as a "classic" of European cinema.)

GoodBye, Lenin! (2003) Fantastic drama-comedy that takes place in Germany as the Iron Curtain falls, and the soviet economy/culture of East Berlin is replaced by western materialism/consumerism. A crowd pleaser.

Trainspotting (1996) Scottish cult heroine film, made Ewan McGregor famous pre-Obi Wan Kenobi. Great look at blue collar life in UK and drug culture. "Toilet scene" is classic insanity you won't forget.

Pan's Labyrinth (2006) Bizarre whacked-out insane fantasy film set in Franco's fascist Spain in the 1940's. Gives some insight into Spain's fascist period, and will cause hours of sleeplessness.

Gomorra (2008) A contemporary mob drama set in Naples that exposes Italy's criminal underbelly by telling five stories of individuals who think they can make their own compact with Camorra, the area's Mafia. Oh, and the Camorra actually exist in real life.

Amélie (2001) Wildly popular, clever, unconventional, light-hearted comedy from France. Nothing too serious, but a pleasant look at modern French life, and will make you not hate the French so much.

Run Lola Run (1998) Awesome action/adventure/time warp film that perhaps has no great geographic utility, but is a great high energy MTV-style flick that I use to introduce hesitant students to foreign film. They love it, despite the subtitles.

Volver (2006) Director Pedro Almodóvar is in love with the entire country of Spain, including its women, and it shows in this comedy of errors involving murder and family secrets. If you don't find the gorgeous Spanish scenery compelling—and why not?—then the gorgeous live-action Spanish scenery that is Penélope Cruz will keep you entertained.

Ocean's Twelve (2004) Okay, it's just a guilty pleasure, but I love watching this heist film which jumps across Western Europe. No great learning material here, although it does feature Interpol and a variety of excellent landscapes across the continent. And most people despise the "trick ending," which makes me like it even more.

LIVE LEADERS YOU SHOULD KNOW:

François Hollande: center-left President of France, 5th largest economy, EU power player, is failing badly at getting France's financial house in order; also failing at covert love trysts.

Angela Merkel: center-right Chancellor of Germany, 4th largest economy, EU power player, routinely voted the most powerful woman on the planet.

David Cameron: newly-elected, center-right Prime Minister of UK, 6th largest economy. Huge ally of the US, and all that will entail. Probably likes fish n'chips, but too soon for me to call it.

CHAPTER OUTLINE

1. The Bookended Region
2. The Physical Middle Ground
   2.1. Climate
   2.2. Land Situation
   2.3. Culture Club Sandwiched
3. Ideological Middle Ground
   3.1. Historically
      3.1.1. Team West vs. Russia vs. the Ottomans
      3.1.2. World War I
      3.1.3. World War II
   3.2. The Cold War
      3.2.1. Soviets Take Over
      3.2.2. Marshall Rejected
      3.2.3. NATO vs. the Warsaw Pact
4. The Thawing
   4.1. Flight of Fancy
   4.2. Re-alignment While Russia is Weak
5. Re-invigorated Russia Causing New Consternations
   5.1. Issue 1: Ukrainian Yearning: The Orange Revolution
   5.2. Issue 2 Russian Petro Power
   5.3. Issue 3: Nyet! To Nuke Shield
   5.4. Issue 4: Yugo-slob-ian Mess: Kosovo Chaos
6. Conclusion: The Transition is Almost Finished!?

Eastern Europe

THE BOOKENDED REGION

We just wrapped up Western Europe. We now know of its extremely rich and multifaceted world influence. And we are aware of how it destroyed itself in the 20th century. Let's move on to Eastern Europe. It has slightly different physical geography, slightly different cultural geography, and it's a place that has been radically different from Western Europe in the past. But things are changing . . .

Eastern Europe is the *bookended* region, as the Plaid Avenger refers to it, and bookended in a variety of ways. The bookend reference means there is something in the middle being held up, propped up, or pinched between two bigger sides. In this respect, physically, Eastern Europe is between the giant Russia to its east, and those Western European states to its west. (Western Europe—the region we just covered.) Ideologically, it's also in the pinch in the middle. Eastern Europe has been a buffer zone between these two same giants—Russian culture to the East, Western European ideas to its west. Because of this, it has essentially been the battleground between these two teams, and therefore a fuse to the powderkeg of big conflicts. Where did the major transgressions of the 20th century start? World War I, World War II, the Cold War? Yep . . . all got launched in Eastern Europe.

This region had been marked for a very long time by **devolution**, or shattering apart; big political entities breaking down into smaller units. This region is also distinct because it has been a **buffer zone** and a battleground of ideologies throughout the 20th century. It was a buffer between Russia and Western Europe, and as such, was a battleground for the Cold War. Commies in Russia thought one way, dude-ocracies in Western Europe thought another way, and everyone in Eastern Europe was caught in the middle. The book getting squished by the bookends.

On top of that, we're going to see that there are a lot of historical influences that have permeated Eastern Europe proper, making it extremely diverse in every aspect you can imagine: linguistically, ideologically, religiously, ethnically, culturally . . . It's all here. This diversity is one of the reasons Eastern Europe has historically yanked itself in lots of different directions and shattered apart. That's why it's a region, and just one of the many reasons why it's distinct from surrounding regions. Russia is Russia, Western Europe is Western Europe, and Eastern Europe is something in-between, for now.

But that was then and this is now. If you want a key word, a single word that keeps coming up in the discussion of Eastern Europe, the Plaid Avenger has one: **transition**. This is a region in transition. Of course, every place on the planet is changing and moving around, but this is an entire region in which just about all facets of life are on the shift: with an obvious place they came from, and with an obvious place they're going to. All the states in this part of the world are going through this process of transition. What sort of transition, Plaid man? A transition from what to what? We'll talk about that in more detail as we go along.

# THE PHYSICAL MIDDLE GROUND

When we think of Eastern Europe as I just suggested, we think of that region that's sandwiched between two much bigger and more powerful other world regions. But if we just look at it physically, just physically for a minute, it's also kind of a buffer zone in a very natural sense, in a variety of different ways.

CLIMATE

The temperature and precipitation patterns of Eastern Europe are more **continental** in character than areas to its west. Being further and further away from the Atlantic Ocean, and particularly its most moderating Gulf Stream effect, makes these states more prone to increased temperature disparity: that is, it can get much colder in the winters and perhaps even more hotter in the summers. As we progress further into the continent and away from large bodies of water, this continentality effect becomes even more pronounced. We'll see this played out to the extreme when we get into Russia, deep in the continent's interior, where it's way colder still. Nothing is quite like Russia, where the only thing that's not frozen is the vodka. Even the Plaid Avenger's beard froze up in that place multiple times on secret subversive missions. When we think of the inverse, we think about the coastlines of Western Europe. We think of a more moderated climate. It's not too bad there; it rarely freezes, even in places as far north as Great Britain or parts of Norway.

Eastern Europe is in between, in that it's not quite as bad, not quite as extreme as Russia but not quite as moderated as the West. As you progress from Western Europe inward, into the continent, you get more continentality—meaning less moderation, more temperature extremes during the year, and certainly cooler, if not downright colder, in the wintertime. Climatically, they're in a zone of transition, as well, from the West to Russia. But don't let me mislead you: this place does have some nice climates, and in fact some areas are exceptionally rich in natural resources and soils. In fact, Eastern Europe actually produces a lot of food. Ukraine has classically been one of the breadbaskets of all of Europe, and it continues to be. There is a lot going on here physically, but it's just not quite as pleasant, not quite as moderated as its Western European counterpart.

LAND SITUATION

Another big physical feature to consider with Eastern Europe is that big sections of these countries are landlocked. When we think of Western Europe, we think of maritime powers—all of them have sea access, all of them have coastlines, and, therefore, they all have big navies and armadas, and they're all big traders and were all big colonizers. Not so much so for the Eastern Europeans, if at all. Yes, there is some coastline along the Black Sea for some countries like Bulgaria and Romania. Yes, some of them have Mediterranean Sea access like Albania and Croatia. And yes, some have Baltic Sea frontage like Poland and Estonia. But none of these states in what we're considering Eastern Europe were ever big maritime powers, and they're still not. Unlike their Western European counterparts, none of these states were big colonial forces in the world. They didn't have the advantages we talked about in Western Europe of sapping off the resources and riches of the planet by controlling vast areas outside of Europe proper. Those Eastern European empires and states were never major maritime powers, nor colonizers, nor absorbers of wealth from other points abroad. And that sets them quite apart from their Western European counterparts, even up to this day.

CULTURE CLUB SANDWICHED

The last big physical thing to consider is that they were physically in the middle of some very big powers, that have very different cultures. What do I mean by this? Well, Eastern Europeans have their own culture, obviously: Polish folk have their Polish culture, Ukrainians have their Ukrainian culture, etc, etc. But all these folks in all the countries in this region are sandwiched between entities that have *bigger* histories, *bigger* cultures, and are *bigger* powers. By bigger,

Eastern Europe
CHAPTER NINE

Order up! Who wanted the Turkey, Polish sausage with Russian dressing on rye?

don't misinterpret, I'm not talking about "bigger is better." In some cases that's true, but I'm just suggesting here that they're *bigger* in terms of having more of an impact within their regions, but also beyond their regions as well. A main one to consider is Mother Russia: a very distinct culture, language, religion, and ideology that by its very size and strength has dominated areas close to its Moscow core. And what's close to the Moscow core? That would be all the Eastern European countries.

But Russia is not the only big power heavily influencing this regions. Team West and its cultures influenced the region, as has North Africa. You also have the former Ottoman Turk Empire down south. The Ottoman Empire is long since gone but Turkey took its place, and so there's a Turkish culture that abuts them. An important part of that Turkish culture is the fact that they are Muslim, and the Ottomans brought Islam into the region in general. That's important to note, by the way, because perhaps unlike any other world region or other part of the world, you have a variety of world religions that come together in one place, albeit, not always on friendly terms. You do have Islam which did penetrate into Christian Europe via Eastern Europe. But even before you get to that, you have to think about the divisions of Christianity. Of course, there's Old School Christianity that got divided into Eastern Orthodox; hey, that's in Eastern Europe. That then got divided into Catholicism; hey, that's in Eastern Europe, too. And then Catholicism was further branched into Protestantism, and that's in Eastern Europe as well.

A quick summary here: Eastern Europe in the middle of major world cultures—Russian versus Western versus, say, Arab/Islamic. Also, it's the middle ground of major world religions—Christianity, Judaism, Islam, and all the divisions of Christianity itself, as well. These divisions all coming together—different ethnicities, different people, different religions, different cultures, different histories—has served to play out within Eastern Europe, more often than not, as a battlefield of all these differences. This leads us to the concept of Eastern Europe as, not just a battleground, but a **shatter belt** . . . a zone of breaking down, breaking apart bigger entities to smaller and smaller ones. Perhaps I'm getting ahead of myself. Before we get to this idea of a shatter belt and a breaking down, a.k.a. **devolution** (another great word), let's back up the history boat for just a second and take these things one at a time as they proceeded throughout history.

IDEOLOGICAL MIDDLE GROUND

As pointed out above, Eastern Europe is in the middle of lots of different cultures, different religions, and different ethnicities who have battled it out across the plains of Eastern Europe over the centuries. I'm not going to bore you with all the details; I'll just set the stage so you understand the modern era, how some of these outside influences came to cohabitate within this region over time, and why perhaps it's still causing some conflicts today.

HISTORICALLY
TEAM WEST VS. RUSSIA VS. THE OTTOMANS

Historically speaking, and I'm only going back a few hundred years, Eastern Europe was kind of a battleground of big empires. We have some of the Team Western players like the Austrian empire, the Prussian empire (which evolved into Germany), the Russians, and the Ottoman Empire. Four big entities which virtually controlled all of what we consider now Eastern Europe. Just so you know the Russians and the Ottomans fought it out for

1815: Four main players.

long periods of time vying for control of these territories. The Russians and the Austrians did the same thing, as did the Prussians and the Russians.

These empires have radically different cultures as well, in things like language, ethnicity, economies, politics, and religions. Differences which sow the seeds of conflict for generations. Consider only the religious differences for a moment more. The Germans and Austrians were mostly Protestants and Catholics; the Russians were staunchly Christian Orthodox; the Ottomans were Islamic. They are all vying for cultural and political influence in this region. Are you starting to get a sense of the confluence of conflicting ideas in this area? Empires trying to expand, fighting each other, in this fringe zone we're going to call Eastern Europe, as we get a little further along.

Now that's the background set-up. We need to get into the modern era, and in the modern era there are some major devolutions that occur. Evolution has the connotation of growth, of building into something bigger and more complex. **Devolution** is just the opposite: a term that simply means breaking down—devolving into smaller, simpler pieces. Devolution in a political sense involves a big empire or a big country breaking down into smaller countries; that's a real big theme for Eastern Europe historically and perhaps even into today's world.

WORLD WAR I

The starting phase of devolution in the modern era was with the Ottoman Empire. The Ottoman Empire, which was a Turkish-Islamic empire, introduced Islam into southeastern Europe. Places like Bosnia, Albania, and Kosovo are still predominately Muslim today as a result of the cultural influences that the Ottomans brought in. You have to remember, the Ottomans were actually knocking on the door of Austria for a very long time in a bid to expand their empire into Europe, but they were weakened considerably and were on the brink of collapse by the time the 20th century rolled around. Let's fast forward: this declining empire most unwisely allied themselves with the Germans during the lead up to World War I (you can read more about that in the chapter on Turkey). But the Germans lost that war, which means their Turkish allies were also losers, which resulted in the carving up of the Ottoman territory. By 1915, there was no such thing as the Ottoman Empire. It's subdivided, as you see in the map into a variety of new states already—places like Romania, Yugoslavia, and Bulgaria.

1915: Goodbye, Ottoman Empire!

The Austria-Hungarian Empire, which kind of started World War I—or at least the assassination of their leader Franz Ferdinand triggered it—they lost the war as well, and thus their Empire became the next shatter zone. Ottomans shattered first, then the Austria-Hungarian Empire shattered next, which created several more countries—individual entities which declared independence.

We also have to point out that Russia was unwittingly pulled into World War I, and it got the crap kicked out of it by the Germans. World War I was just so bizarre! All of the major, and minor, powers in Europe had a complex web of military alliances with each other that—once the war started—obligated everyone to jump into the fray to protect their buddies. Pretty much everyone declared war on somebody within days of the Austro-Hungarian assassination spark. Thus, the Russians got sucked into a land war to help their Serb allies, just at a time when dissent and revolution were internally brewing back at home too. The results of which were that Russia, under the command of the inept Tsar Nicholas, sucked so bad on the battlefield that they lost big chunks of

1919: Goodbye Austro-Hungarians!

their western fringe to the Germans . . . and of course this did not sit well with already-aggravated Ruskies back home. And that was when our main Commie friend, Vladimir Lenin came to power in Russia in 1917, he essentially said, "Hey, we want out! We're out of World War I. We surrender. Germany can have all the territory that we have ceded thus far. They can have it. Take it! We're done!" This was actually a very popular policy back home in Russia, which was on its way to becoming the USSR. We will pick up the importance of this WW1 Russian territorial loss in a couple of paragraphs from now . . .

Even after the Russian withdrawal, Germany didn't really win the war either, and therefore, they lost that recently-gained Russian territory, as well as some of their own. The result of which was a bunch of new countries that popped up around 1920—places like Estonia, Latvia, Lithuania, Poland, even parts of Ukraine. They all declared independence. They were in this middle zone, again, this Eastern European middle zone between these major battling powers. A whole bunch of new countries popped up then, but they ain't gonna last . . .

Goodbye, German Empire!

WORLD WAR II

Because, of course, Russia then became the Soviet Union under Lenin's tutelage and, as the USSR grew in power, it wanted its Eastern European territories back. That brings us up to World War II, because the Germans were still over there hopping mad under Hitler and they wanted their lost territories and prestige back as well. Under "der Fuehrer," they decided to have a re-conquest of Eastern Europe and, what the heck, they'll take over Western Europe too, just for good measure. To ensure they could pull this off, Hitler got together with Stalin—what a fun party that must have been—and together these two signed what is called the **Pact of Non-Aggression**. Basically, Hitler said, "Uhh, okay, I'm gonna take over the world, but hey Stalin, you seem cool enough to me. Yeah, so we won't attack you as long as you don't get in the way of us wiping out Western Europe. And we know you want some of these Eastern European territories back, so you can have those and we'll take everything else." Stalin, in all his wisdom, said, "Word; that sounds cool to me. Game on!"

However, about halfway through the war, Hitler reneged and decided to attack the Soviet Union, pulling them into the war. Why would Hitler have done that? Oh . . . that's right: because he was an insane megalomaniac. You know the end of the story: Since Hitler attacked the USSR, the Soviet Union sided up with the US and Western Europe to beat the Nazis. During this Nazi smack-down, the Soviet Union swept in from the East, the US and allies swept in from the West, and the Nazi smack-down finished up with everyone high-five-ing right square in the middle of Eastern Europe.

Amazingly, if you look at the line where the Allies met, it's right in the middle of what we call Europe today. The troops met and high-fived each other when they finished killing all the Germans, or at least the completely crazy ones who continued to fight, then that was it. World War II was over. Peace! Peace out!

Well, kind of. It was great, for all of five minutes, before it became a face-off, again, but with new players . . .

THE COLD WAR

After the success of the allied powers with the Soviet Union at the end of World War II, you essentially have what happens for

As Borat would say: "Aaah-High-Five" in Europe.

the next 60 years—this ideological face-off. You've got the Soviets controlling Eastern Europe, where they swept in and cleaned out the Nazis, and the West who swept in from the West and cleaned out the rest of the Nazis. Although they were playing for the same side during World War II, where they met became the new face-off of major powers. This is more familiar ground we're getting into—the modern era. You, of course, know that this is the Commie world squaring off against Team West: the freedom-loving democratic capitalists in Western Europe. But how did this go down? How did this happen since they were all allies during the War?

SOVIETS TAKE OVER

Well, as I suggested, we had the Soviets, who were buddies of Team West at the time and helped wipe out the German threat. When it was over the Soviets said, "Well, you know what, you guys over in Western Europe are kind of crazy. We keep getting invaded by you. This Hitler guy was just the most recent one; the German Kaiser Wilhelm before that, and even Napoleon did it before him! You Western Europeans are nuts!"

A PLAID AVENGER TIP ON WHAT NOT TO DO: Never invade Russia. No one has ever successfully invaded Russia. Everyone who invades Russia loses. Always. Period. Napoleon. Yep. Hitler. Yep. They sucked at it. If megalomaniacs can't pull it off, who can?

The Soviets said, "Hey, you people over in Western Europe keep invading us, so we're going to stay here in Eastern Europe, for a couple of different reasons." One: they wanted to reclaim a lot of these territories they lost in World War I. That is Estonia, Latvia, Lithuania, parts of Poland and Ukraine were pulled back into Mother Russia—now the Soviet Union. Two: Russia very openly said, "We're going to stay in Eastern Europe to create a buffer zone so that there are no further intrusions from the West." Now the way this turned into essentially a Soviet takeover to make this Soviet buffer zone, but it was done in such a way that it wasn't as imperialistic-looking as it truly was.

Here's how they did it. Just as the Americans, French and British hung around Western Europe to help with reconstruction, the Soviets claimed they were following the same playbook by chilling out in Eastern Europe to mop up and clean up. The Soviet official line was, "Okay, we're here helping out. We'll stay in Poland. We'll stay in Estonia. We're going to stay here in Hungary. We're going to help clean things up and help rebuild just like you guys are going to do in the West. And ya know what? We'll even help them run elections. This'll be great!" Lo and behold, every Soviet-overseen election that occurred in Eastern Europe resulted in a landslide victory for Communist candidates. What a surprise! Go figure. The Communist party just went through the roof in popularity!

Now was any of this real? I don't know, perhaps a little. I wasn't there personally. I was busy deep undercover protecting the Champagne stocks in the underground vaults of France. In the east, the Russians really were liberators of many of these places during the war, so perhaps there was some sympathy, some empathy, and some popularity of communism at the time, but certainly not as much as would have swept a tide of elections across all of these countries. Basically what I'm saying is, this was all farce. Soviets held up these elections and said, "Well, they all elected Soviet leaders, they all elected Communist leaders, so they're just under our umbrella now. We're just here helping out. Isn't that great?" It was, indeed, a Soviet takeover to create this Soviet buffer zone.

People in the Western European realm, and the US as well, were exceptionally unhappy about these developments. Maybe you younger generations today might think, "Why didn't they just go in and get the Commies then?" You have to remember that they were the allies during World War II; they were on our team, and we could not have won the war without them. And World War II had just finished. Nobody wanted to fight a new war. Nobody wanted to then declare war on the USSR and have to do all that fighting all over again.

So this Soviet 'takeover' of Eastern Europe happened as Team West was busy rebuilding the west—rebuilding and restructuring: laying the foundations for the EU to rebuild Western Europe. It happened when the eastern side was being rebuilt and occupied by the Soviet Union. Where these two teams met during the war, of course, became the division between these two forces . . . and is where something called the Iron Curtain then fell. See map box below . . .

When all this action was going down, all of those countries in Eastern Europe fell into one of several different categories of which I want you to be familiar. First, some of this territory of Eastern Europe was simply absorbed back into the Soviet Union and became part of other entities and simply just went away. Parts of Poland were worked back into the Lithuania SSR and the Ukrainian SSR. So **absorption** was one option. But what is an SSR?

Ah! That's the second option: some of these briefly independent states became **republics** of the USSR. See, USSR stands for the Union of Soviet Socialist *Republics*. Kind of like states of the United States of America, like Wisconsin is a political component of the USA. Some of these entities in Eastern Europe actually went from being an independent sovereign state, to becoming a republic of the USSR. I'm thinking specifically of Moldova, Estonia, Latvia, and Lithuania. They ceased to be sovereign states, and became a part of the USSR.

What's the Deal with . . . the "Iron Curtain"?

In 1946, British Prime Minister Winston Churchill delivered his "Sinews of Peace" address in Fulton, Missouri. The most famous excerpt:

> From Stettin in the Baltic to Trieste in the Adriatic an "iron curtain" has descended across the Continent. Behind that line lie all the capitals of the ancient states of Central and Eastern Europe. Warsaw, Berlin, Prague, Vienna, Budapest, Belgrade, Bucharest and Sofia; all these famous cities and the populations around them lie in what I must call the Soviet sphere, and all are subject, in one form or another, not only to Soviet influence but to a very high and in some cases increasing measure of control from Moscow.

This speech introduced the term "iron curtain" to refer to the border between democratic and communist (soviet controlled) states. Because of this—and because most Americans have no clue what a "sinew" is—Churchill's address is commonly called the "Iron Curtain Speech."

The "Iron Curtain Speech" was received extremely well by President Harry Truman, but much of the American public was skeptical. Throughout the speech Churchill's tone was very aggressive towards the Soviet Union. Many Americans and Europeans felt that this was unnecessary and that peaceful coexistence could be achieved. The United States had recently considered the USSR an ally. In fact, Stalin, whom the American press had dubbed "Uncle Joe" to boost his popularity during WWII, was probably the most pissed about the speech, feeling he was betrayed by his allies. The "Iron Curtain Speech," besides coining an important Cold War term, set the tone for the next 50 years of US-Russian relations—which is ironic, considering it was given by a British dude.

Iron Curtain. But which side was Iron Maiden on?

The Regions
PART TWO

So long sovereignty, hello SSR!

Soviet territory regained, and soviet satellites acquired after WW II.

The third and final possibility, and perhaps the most important option, was that some of these sovereign states actually retained their sovereign state status but became **Soviet satellites.** Mainly, I'm thinking of Poland, Romania, Bulgaria, Hungary, Czechoslovakia, and East Germany. These were countries. They were sovereign states. They had a seat at the UN. However, they didn't really have control over their own countries, and everybody knew it. Everybody knew the Soviets were pulling the strings of the Polish government, of the Romanian government, of the Czech government. *Everybody* knew it. They did have seats at the UN, they were supposedly sovereign states, but the Soviet Union truly controlled them, because the USSR had their patsy commie officials running the show in the governments of these places. Does that make sense?

That's the scenario as it was for about fifty years during the Cold War. The Soviets either controlled directly or indirectly (due to their massive influence) every place that is now called Eastern Europe. Team West was on the other side of the curtain: the democracies, the free market capitalist economies that were supported by the US. Those are your two teams during the Cold War. Eastern Europe was close enough to see all the economic growth and political freedoms stuff going on in the democratic countries, all while they were getting paid visits by the KGB to make sure they still loved being Commies. Now do you see how Eastern Europe is a battleground in the middle of this most recent ideological game? Stuck dead in the middle of the commie vs. capitalism showdown!

MARSHALL REJECTED

The other term I want you to think about as well, or at least understand and know, is that the Soviet satellite states did not accept the **Marshall Plan:** a US-sponsored program of aid, loans, and material support to rebuild Europe. Just after WW2, the United States, in its infinite wisdom, said, "You guys are screwed over there! Your whole region has been leveled!" Some smart folks in the United States government said, "We should help them out." In particular, US Secretary of State George Marshall said, "Look, we gotta help these dudes out. We need to get them back on their feet, because if we don't, their economies will get worse, collapse and then turn into complete chaos, and if we don't help Western Europe out, the Soviets—who we are already worried about—are right next door. The Soviets will sweep all the way through if we don't do something!" Probably a fair statement. That Marshall was a smart cookie.

More on the M-Plan: this aid package was offered to all of Europe. The US went to every single one of these countries and said, "Here, we'll give you a ton of money to help you out with industrial capacity and infrastructure to get you back on your feet economically." It was even offered to the Soviet Union. The countries in yellow text on the map accepted the Marshall Plan and took the aid, the sweet cash. Lo and behold, these are the richest countries in Europe right now. The countries labeled in white refused the Marshall Plan, and those are the not as rich countries of Europe right now. While we certainly can't pin everything in the modern era on a singular aid package from the US, it certainly had its impacts back in the day. And it reinforced the division between east and west, as the teams seemed to be now fully set.

If you look at this map of who accepted the Marshall Plan and who didn't, you'll see our same Iron Curtain division between Eastern and Western Europe again demonstrated perfectly. We know that one reason why Eastern Europe is poorer is because the Soviet Union eventually lost the Cold War, mostly because their economy sucked so bad. The second reason is they were stymied out of the gate because they were influenced by Russia to decline the Marshall Plan.

We've already talked about what a Soviet satellite was, and the Soviet influence in Eastern Europe. Make no bones about it; Poland would have probably loved the Marshall Plan. The citizens of the Czech Republic would have loved the Marshall Plan, but they were under Soviet influence, and they were talked into declining it. Maybe there was stricter coercion than just talk going on. Who knows? That's why Eastern Europe is, generally speaking, not quite as developed and rich as Western Europe even today, but they are trying to catch up quickly.

NATO VS. THE WARSAW PACT

Back to the story. Once those Soviet Union and Soviet puppet states did not accept the Marshall Plan, the writing is really on the wall at this point. The lines are drawn. The Iron Curtain has fallen, the rift is exposed, and this is most evident by this nice Cold War relic map shown below of the formation of NATO versus the Warsaw Pact. **NATO** was formed by the US and all of those Western European states who were looking over at the USSR and Eastern Europe saying, "Oh, we feel threatened by them. They might invade us. They might come and kill us. Therefore, we're going to form up NATO, which says if any of you Soviet-type people attack any Western European state, the US is going to come to their aid—in fact, all the NATO countries will come to their aid." That's why NATO was formed, on one side of that Iron Curtain.

This is a sweet Cold War relic!

The USSR, not to be outdone, said, "Oh yeah? You guys have your own NATO club? Fine! We'll start our own club. We're calling it the Warsaw Pact." The **Warsaw Pact** was essentially an anti-NATO device based on the same premise that an attack on one constituted an attack on all. Of course, everyone knows it's bunk, since the participating countries were simply puppets of the USSR anyway. But the Soviets said, "Oh, no, no, no. Everybody's free around here. So we asked Poland if they wanted to join, and they said yes. We asked Romania, and they said yes too." The goofball Soviets even went out of their way to name it the Warsaw Pact to try and demonstrate that it was the Poles who had thought it up. Yeah, right.

What you had was an entrenchment of ideas—NATO on one side, Warsaw Pact on the other. Free western democracies on one side, the Communist Commies on the other. Why am I talking about this in detail? Because that's what Eastern Europe has been through for the last seventy years. Now you know the end of the story, though. It won't last for too much longer as we approach the modern era . . .

THE THAWING

What's happening today? What we've had since around 1988 is that the Soviet Union began to **devolve**. There's that word again! The Soviet Union fully collapsed in 1990. They finally figured out, "We can't do it anymore. We give up." During this entire Cold War, the Soviets kept insisting that the Eastern European states were voluntarily part of their sphere of influence, and specifically told the states themselves, "If you guys don't want to be part of the Soviet Union, just have a vote and we'll let you out." Basically, that was a bluff. Occasionally, the peoples of some of these countries would take them up on it, and have street demonstrations and stuff like that. Every time that happened, the Soviet Union sent in the tanks and shut it all down. Everyone knew the Soviets were lying. They'd say, "No, really, you guys are sovereign states. Really!" Wink wink, nudge nudge. Not really.

As 1989 approached, when the Soviet Union started to collapse, this notion crept back up again. You may have heard of this **Mikhail Gorbachev** guy. He was floating around saying, "The Soviet Union's in trouble for lots of different reasons. However, if you guys over in Poland want self-determination, maybe we'll *think* about letting you guys go again. If you really want self-determination, go ahead and have yourselves a vote." This caused an explosion. Once a little bit of the leash was let out, everybody ran. What you had was an instantaneous devolution, where Eastern Europe pulled away as rapidly as possible from the Soviet Union. You see here in this independence dates map is that the USSR, a single political entity, had turned into fifteen different countries virtually overnight.

Free at last!

Czechoslovakia, Poland, Hungary and lots of other places said, "Yeah! The Soviet Union is going to let us out! Good, we vote to be out, we're out! We're truly sovereign again, we're free!" Places like Estonia, Latvia, and Lithuania said, "We want out too!" Romania, Bulgaria, Ukraine, "We're out!" Everyone wanted out. But it didn't stop there! Even after all these states are out, places like Czechoslovakia said, "Uhh, we're already out, and we want to devolve further into the Czech Republic and Slovakia for lots of different reasons." (See **What's the Deal with . . . the Velvet Revolution?** box on page 185.) There is another, separate wave of devolution in what was Yugoslavia, which all occurs at roughly the same time, but for different reasons, but we will get to that later.

FLIGHT OF FANCY

This flight from Soviet influence didn't end with declarations of independence. Oh no! That was just the beginning of their run for the border! Let's take a closer look at three states in particular that set the trend for what was to happen next: Poland, Czechoslovakia, and Hungary. These three states crystallize all of the stuff we've been talking about. During the Soviet occupation and the era of Soviet influence, every time the Soviets bluffed about possible independence, people in these three countries took to the streets to challenge it. As you can see from the map, the biggest street protests and riots in the last 45 years of the Cold War era took place in Poland, the Czech Republic, and Hungary. These countries were never entirely happy with being under

Hotspots of Uprising

Soviet influence. In fact, after World War II, they initially were like, "Yay! We're free! We can be just like Western Europe now!" It's hard to be free when the Soviets set up a puppet government for you.

Now, guess which three countries pushed to get out immediately after the devolution process began in the early 1990's? Guess which three countries wanted in NATO immediately? Guess which three countries petitioned to be in the EU immediately? That's right, kids! It's the same three countries: Poland, Czech Republic, and Hungary. As soon as it was possible, they immediately voted themselves out of Soviet influence. They were the first out of the blocks. But that wasn't enough for them. The peoples within these countries had been so unhappy being under the Soviet yoke for over 50 years that they wanted to ensure that it didn't happen again. All three countries immediately petitioned to join NATO.

We talked about NATO in chapter 6, so you know about the impacts of being a NATO member. These three Eastern European states wanted to become NATO members immediately to ensure no further Russian influence. I say again, *ensuring no further Russian influence.* These guys did not want to be anywhere near the Soviets; they wanted to be a part of Western Europe as fast as they could run to it! You know that NATO Article 5 says, "Hey, anybody that's in our club gets attacked, then we take that as an act of war against all of us." Poland, Czech Republic, and Hungary said, "Sweet! We're in the NATO club! Russia can't touch us. We're like the UK, France . . . we might as well be Canada! Russia can't do anything to us!" That was exactly the case. All these countries also immediately petitioned to get into the EU. Eastern Europe, being under Soviet sway, was just as broke as the Soviets. They had not done well during the Cold War. They started with a blank slate in the early '90s—broke, ideologically bankrupt, embracing the west, embracing NATO, wanting out of Soviet influence, and particularly wanting into the EU as quickly as possible for the sake of their economies.

RE-ALIGNMENT WHILE RUSSIA IS WEAK

As you probably already picked up from some of the details in this chapter, we are in an era of transition for this Eastern Europe region. And now it becomes quite obvious what they are transitioning from and to—from that Soviet era of occupation and control, they are mostly realigning and transitioning to become adopted into the capitalist democracies of the west. This happened at a brisk pace after 1991 when the Soviet Union officially voted itself out of existence, and the entity broke up from one huge power into fifteen sovereign states, as already pointed out.

We also already pointed out, many of the states, Czech Republic, Hungary, and Poland, were quick to embrace the West; Estonia, Latvia, and Lithuania were right on their heels, by the way. Because, as you now have learned in this chapter, they used to be independent sovereign states in between World War I and the end of World War II, but then were reabsorbed by the Soviets. Those guys were always chafing under Soviet rule, so Estonia, Latvia, and Lithuania were the second round of states that jumped ship into the arms of the West. Many others have since followed. All of this realignment and transitioning of these countries of Eastern Europe was occurring right after the Soviet crash . . . quite frankly,

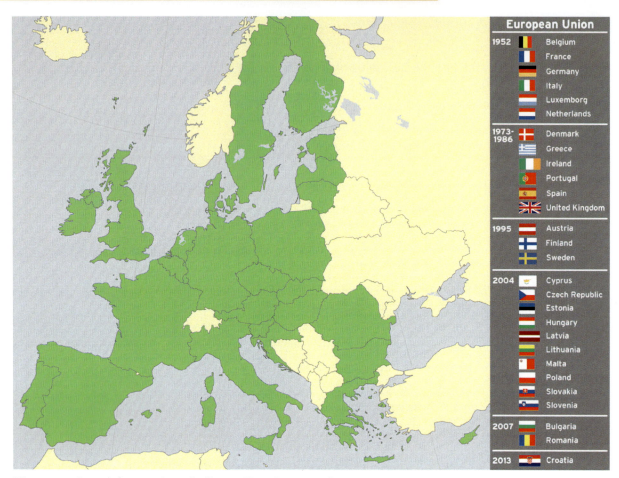

EU creep into Russia's former sphere of influence. Those Euro-creeps!

when Russia (and Russia became a new country, as well, at this time) was excessively weak. I mean, they just lost the Cold War, and they mostly lost the Cold War because they were freaking broke. You'll read more about that in the next chapter. Their economy was in shambles, their power structure was shattered, and their government was in chaos. It was precisely in this period of Russian weakness that so many of these Eastern European countries just *ran* to the west.

This transition, of course, happened in a couple of distinct ways by some distinct entities we've talked about many, many, many times already in this great text. Number one was the EU—the European Union. Most, if not all, of these countries *immediately* applied for EU entry status. Many of them were soon granted it. As you can see by the maps to the right, there has been a progressive wave of Eastern European countries entering the EU since the very beginning of their "freedom" from Soviet domination.

As already suggested, Hungary, Poland, and the Czech Republic were the first three that jumped in. They were followed by a whole host of countries that jumped in by 2004, and the fun's not over yet. Romania and Bulgaria entered in 2007, and there are still multiple potential candidates. Most of the countries that constituted the prior Yugoslavia have asked for entry. It's quite important to note that Ukraine, a huge country and a former part of Russia historically, has applied multiple times and debates within the country are determining just how hard and fast they should push for EU entry. We'll come back to Ukraine in a bit.

Perhaps the most telling tale to tell about the push for the EU in Eastern Europe is Czechoslovakia, a country that used to be one, that's now two—another shattering within Eastern Europe—simply to get into the European Union. That sounds bizarre—you've got to bust up your country just to join a supranationalist organization? Indeed, it is a bit bizarre, and you should know why, when, and where that happened. It was called the **Velvet Revolution**.

That brings us to the other avenue for the Team West love embrace by these newly independent Eastern European countries in the 1990s, and that was NATO. No surprises here. In fact, you can essentially look at the story told by those maps of EU entry and see that the NATO entry tells the same tale. As already suggested, Czech Republic, Hungary, and Poland were quick to escape the Soviets and jump under the NATO security blanket. Estonia, Latvia, and Lithuania right on their heels—just like with the EU. Many of the other countries who joined the EU are also now NATO members.

This has been miffing Russia a bit as they have watched the continued eastward expansion of these western clubs to their Russian borders. And that, my friends, is worthy of an entire new section. . . .

RE-INVIGORATED RUSSIA CAUSING NEW CONSTERNATIONS

What's all that about? Well, this eastward expansion of western institutions, like EU and NATO, is now being slowed, stalled, or stopped, depending upon your point of view. What am I talking about? Hey, I'm talking about Russia, man. These guys are back. As I already pointed out, all of these Eastern European countries jumped the Soviet ship and headed for the west when Russia was weak—right after the Soviet Union crashed, when Russia was down and out, when they were poor, when they were politically bankrupt. But that time has passed. They're back and they're flexing their muscles in more ways than one. And by that, I am thinking specifically of

What's the Deal with . . . the Velvet Revolution?

What's up with Czechoslovakia? Why did it split into two, the Czech Republic and Slovakia? Were there two different ethnic groups that wanted their own self-determination and their own countries? Not really. While there are ethnic Slovaks and ethnic Czechs, neither group had much of an idea that a partition was even occurring. Most couldn't have cared less. There was no animosity between these ethnic groups. So what's the deal? Why did they do it if there wasn't a problem? Why did they split?

They split because the western side of Czechoslovakia, where the Czech Republic is now, was much more like the West. It bordered Germany; it had the industrialized sector, and was richer, with a higher GDP. Slovakia, the eastern side of the state, was much more Russian/Soviet influenced. It was poorer and more agricultural. Folks in the Czech Republic, as the Soviet Union was collapsing, said, "Hey, we want to get into the EU. Help us out, Plaid Avenger! What should we do?"

I said, "Well, let's look at this strategically. To get into the EU, your economy has to be decent and it has to be stable. As a whole, your economy is neither. But if you were to lop off the poor suckers on the eastern side of your state, your GDP per capita would go up! All your averages would go way up!" Indeed, that's exactly what happened. People in what is now the Czech Republic said, "Hey, we'd be better off on our own without Slovakia dragging us down!" Czechoslovakia underwent a transition called **The Velvet Revolution** in 1993. This revolution was like velvet, nice and smooth. There were no shots fired. From the stroke of a pen, one country became two.

Where did it go?

Vladimir Putin. Have you seen this dude topless? Watch out, the man is a menace! But seriously . . . okay, seriously, he is ripped . . . Russia as a great power is back on the world stage, and is no longer allowing encroachment into their arena of influence. We can look at some current events to underscore this Russian resurgence.

ISSUE 1: UKRAINE YEARNING: THE ORANGE REVOLUTION

Like the Velvet in Czechoslovakia, the Orange Revolution in Ukraine was defined by the east/west differences of folks within the state, although unlike the Velvet, it did not end with the permanent division of the state into two new states. Yet. While the Velvet Revolution occurred over two decades ago, the Orange one just happened in 2004–2005. Russia has exerted influence and/or control over Ukraine off and on throughout most of its history. Russian influence is very strong in areas physically closer to it, like eastern Ukraine with whom it shares a border. Back in 2004, Ukraine had a big move towards true democracy. The scenario included two dudes. The first was Victor Yushchenko: the pro-democracy, pro-EU, pro-NATO candidate. A real poster child for the west. The EU supported him, and the United States thought he was awesome. They loved this dude!

His opponent was Victor Yanukovych: an old-schooler, very conservative, more Russian influenced, and in fact, he's the candidate that Vladimir Putin from Russia came over and campaigned for. To try to help lock up the election before it even was held, former elements of the KGB even unsuccessfully poisoned Yushchenko! Talk about a street fight!

How hilarious is this? I can almost hear the boxing announcer: "In the red, white and blue trunks, fighting for Team West, hailing from western Ukraine, it's Victor Yush! And his opponent, in the red trunks, representing the red Russians, from eastern Ukraine, its Victor Yanu!" Hahahaha dudes, could you make this stuff up? Victor vs. Victor—I wonder who will be the victor?

Why's the Plaid Avenger bringing up this election in Ukraine of all places? Because it exemplifies what's still happening in Eastern Europe, which is this battle between the West and Russia; it's a battle that's not so much for outright control as it is for *influence* within this region. Russia still has serious economic and security interests in this area, and still likes to think of it as within Russia's sphere of influence. When this election went down, the pro-Russian candidate won, and everyone in the world said it was a fraudulent election. There were massive street protests, and this ultimately turned into the 2004/05 **Orange Revolution**. So much heat got put on the Ukrainian government, they threw out the election results, re-ran it, and then the pro-western Yushchenko won. We can see this as part of an ongoing battle for influence in Ukraine, which is representative of the broader battle for influence in the region as whole.

The Russian candidate was downed because the pro-western candidate won—downed, but not out. In the Post-Orange Revolution Ukraine, there are still a lot of pro-Russian people. There's a pro-Russian political party, and in March of 2006, the same party gained enough seats to win back control of the Congress. The Plaid Avenger knows that those in the US think democracy's great, that the good guys won, and that's that. Not so! This is an ongoing battle for

Bush 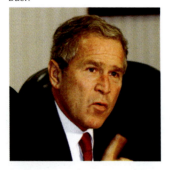 Yushchenko  Yanukovych  Putin

Bush supported Victor Y. while Victor Y. was backed by Putin. Y ask Y?

control. It's not over! Most other countries have gone the way of the west, but it's definitely not over yet for the Ukrainians.

And the country is about evenly split between the western pro-West and the eastern pro-Russia, as you can clearly see from the results of the 2006 election cycle in the map to the right. Could the divisions in this country be any geographically clearer?

Because of the pro-Russian political party gaining the majority of seats in their Congress, they got to choose the Prime Minister position . . . which promptly went to Yanukovych! (The President is voted in by direct election, Prime Minister appointed by

majority of Congress.) So after the 2006 election, you had this bizarre situation where President Yushchenko was pro-West, and Prime Minister Yanukovych was pro-East! Talk about a country with a split personality!

This internal division EXACTLY symbolized the fight for influence in Eastern Europe between Team West and Russia. Yushchenko continued to push for EU and NATO entry; Yanukovych actually announced that no way in hell his country would join NATO. The US sent aid to Yuschchenko and his allies; the Russians sent aid to Yanukovych and his party. The Russians and pro-west Ukrainians even had several economic battles over Russian supplies of oil and natural gas to the country.

Meanwhile, the entire country's economy has tanked and they are more reliant on outside aid than ever to keep themselves afloat, which means this pitched battle for influence has gotten even more important. Are you Yanuk-ed out yet? I hope not because the story gets crazier as we play it forward to the present, as the truth is always stranger than fiction. Dig this . . .

The Ukrainians went back to the presidential polls in 2010, and take a wild stab who won. Victor Yanukovych, of course! Seriously? Yep, seriously, and apparently legitimately this time. So is the Orange Revolution dead? Umm . . . kind of, I guess. I mean, Ukraine is still a democracy, and they did have a free and fair election, but unfortunately for those revolutionaries, the same pro-Russian guy they had the revolution against is now the guy who won and is in power.

The first order of business for Yanukovych was to solidly state there would be no NATO in Ukraine's future, which coincided with Russia giving a huge price break to Ukraine on oil/gas contracts and promising them a bunch of foreign aid as well. Isn't it funny how coincidences like that happen? Yanukovych also immediately extended leases on critical Russian naval bases located on the Crimean Peninsula, a move which infuriated pro-Western politicians who retaliated by throwing eggs at the Speaker of the House when the bill was passed. No. Really. Google it.

In particular, there is a serious fight brewing over the future of Ukraine's southernmost province otherwise known as the Crimean Peninsula, but we will save that story for world hotspots in chapter 25. By all means, flip to it now if you can't wait to find out more! **2012 Update:** tensions within Ukrainian continue to simmer, as

Second time's the charm for now-President Yanukovych

European leaders are currently boycotting the Euro 2012 football finals held in Ukraine, in protest against Yanukovych's jailing of former Prime Minister Yulia Tymoshenko. Also, a massive fist-fight broke out in their Parliment over a law put forward by Yanukovych to recognize Russian an official language of their state. I told you this fight was far from over!

Ummmmmmm . . . BOOM! Called It!

2014 Insane on the Brain, Ukrainian Unraveling Update! So glad I pointed out the Ukrainian rift for all these years to all the plaid students who used this text! Because that prediction was dead on the mark . . . literally. Unless you have been comatose since your bobsledding accident in the 2014 Winter Olympics, you have at least heard that Ukraine melted down politically once more. Massive street protests culminated in the overthrow of President Viktor Yanukovych, which prompted the Crimean Peninsula to declare independence and ask for absorption into Russia! Which then happened! The Ruskies have had tens of thousands of troops massed on the Russian/Ukrainian border for months, and now there

Ukraine aflame!!!

are similar "join Russia" protests across eastern Ukraine that have turned bloody and violent. Will Russia invade and convert other parts of the state into Russian territory? Who knows? It is all such convoluted chaos right now, that anything could happen! Team West and NATO are furious, the Ruskies are indignant and flexing their muscles further, and some are predicting that this is the start of a new Cold War!

I think that may be a bit of an overstatement, but this is certainly a titanic regional game-changing event. So much so that I put it on the cover of this book, and will go into the situation in much greater detail in a new chapter 25 entitled: "The Cover Story." Flip to it now if you can't stand the suspense and want to know more ASAP!

ISSUE 2: RUSSIAN PETRO POWER

By this, I mean that Russia possesses vast amounts of natural gas and oil, and they are increasingly using this commodity as a political pressure point, or an outright political weapon of choice! For now, know this: Russia provides something on the order of about one-third of all European demands for energy. That's a lot, dudes. By Europe, I mean Eastern and Western Europe depend on Russia for about one-third of its energy needs. What's that got to do with current events? What's that got to do with a reinvigorated Russia? Just this: they have petro power now. To reassert their strength and influence in Eastern Europe, they are playing the fuel card. Meaning, when those Eastern European states get a little too uppity, when they do things Russia doesn't like—for example, if the Ukraine says they want to join NATO—Russia says, "Ho, ho, ho . . . hold on there comrades. You get your oil from us. You make us angry—and the price of your heating fuel might double overnight. You make us more angry—and you get no oil at all. You dig that? It gets cold there in the winter too, don't it? How do you like them apples?"

Does this sound like fiction? It shouldn't, my friends; it's already been occurring. Russia has raised prices at various points in the last couple of years to essentially punish states that are doing stuff that they don't want them to do. They did it to Ukraine and Belarus in 1994 and again in 2006 when they doubled the prices to their Belarusian brothers. They completely dried up

Caption: Russia keeps laying the pipe.

shipments to Latvia in 2004–06 to pressure the Latvians into a port deal. Most recently, the Russians shut down a section of pipeline that supplied a Lithuanian refinery under the guise that the infrastructure was just too old and needed to be replaced. I'm sure that was totally unrelated to the fact that Lithuania was threatening to veto an EU-Russian economic pact. Total coincidence, I'm sure. Oh, and if you beleive that, then you will also believe that Russia tripling the price of oil to the pro-West government of Ukraine in 2014, and demanding full payment of all outstanding bills, is also a huge coincidence. But of course you don't believe that, because you now know how the rascally Ruskies operate!

Even though the price of oil has dropped drastically since its historic highs of $150/barrel back in 2008, Russia has made trillions over the last decade, with more rubles to come . . . but it's not just about that. Yes, they get rich from it, but more importantly, it has given them political power due to the economic leverage that controlling that commodity brings. Russia is like the crack dealer to Eastern Europe in particular: they've got the stuff that those Europeans need. If you anger the dealer, you might not get your energy fix. That's not a situation the Eastern Europeans are happy about. The Russian influence is back. That's not all that Russia is doing to flex its muscles in this region.

ISSUE 3: NYET! TO NUKE SHIELD

Another thing that's extremely topical—and we haven't seen the end of this story yet, either—is the proposed missile defense shield system that is being pushed hard by the United States to be implemented specifically in the Eastern European countries that are NATO members. Specifically right this second, we are talking about the Czech Republic and Poland. This is specifically incensing the Russians.

Maybe I should back up—what is this *missile defense shield* nonsense about? This is a concept the United States has been toying with for 60 odd years. It has never really come to fruition. But the idea is, you set up a bunch of missiles and a radar system which can detect if any missiles are coming into Europe. Then, you launch your missile to blow up the incoming missile before they land. Again, it's never worked; out of perhaps ten million tests maybe they've done it once successfully, but that's not the point of this rant right this second.

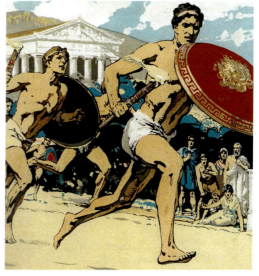

Early version of European Missile Defense Shield.

It's the fact that these new NATO members in Eastern Europe have said, "Uhh, okay, yeah, we'll do it since we still support the US." At a NATO summit which occurred in February of 2008, all the NATO countries—all of them—agreed to go forward with the US plan for the missile defense shield. And just to kind of wrap this up, Russia is seriously *aggravated* about it. They have been pounding their fists on the table, saying, "Nyet, this is not going down. This is seriously threatening us and we are going to use economic leverage and political leverage to intimidate the Eastern European countries that are going along with this."

What do they mean by that? Well, they've already made the fuel threat. When the Ukraine said they wanted to join NATO, Russia said, "Yeah, that's fine. You join NATO and we will re-target nuclear missiles at you." This is something that Russia has also promised to do to any of the states that jump into the missile defense shield program. This is serious stuff, man. Again, this story is still ongoing. The United States says, "Hey, look Russia. Come on, dudes. The Cold War's over. We're not enemies anymore. This is mostly a defense system against . . . Iran, ooh, Iran. Yeah. Iran's going to send a missile somewhere, so this is about that. Or other terrorists might bomb our NATO allies."

But Russia says (and you've got to empathize with them a little bit here), "Uh, yeah right. Come on. NATO's been encroaching to Russian borders for the last twenty years. Now you're putting up this big missile defense system. It's an obvious attempt to neutralize or marginalize Russian power in this region and in the world."

The Plaid Avenger's take on this mess is that the United States is probably telling the truth, but Russia sees it in a very different light . . . and, again, I always try to empathize. Not sympathize, not agree with, but empathize. The Russians do have a long history of being screwed with by folks over in Western Europe, from Napoleon, to Hitler, right on up through the 1980 US hockey team's miracle victory over the Soviets at the Winter Olympics. So in no way, shape, or form, or any time soon, are they going to be okay with an encroaching military technology that is set up on their borders. And they're really ticked off about it. Vlad "the man"

The Russians are still riled up about that game.

Putin has been saying, "No, we're going to do everything we can in our power to make sure that does not happen, including veiled threats about missiles and open threats about energy issues." As always, sucks to be in the middle of the mess, but Eastern Europe seems to have a historical niche for it. **2012 Update!!!** At the big NATO summit in 2012, the NATO and the US officially announced that the first phase of the shield network in now up and operating! Two more phases in the future will add more radar stations and missile interceptor launch sites! Russia no like! Yikes! Are we entering a new Cold War phase for Eastern Europe? Let's watch and find out! **2014 Update!!!** Given the new tensions between Russia and the US over Ukraine, look for NATO to increase exercises and troops deployment to Eastern Europe, and look for the US to invest billions more into the missile defense system . . . even if the system don't work, it will infuriate the Russians, so money well spent either way.

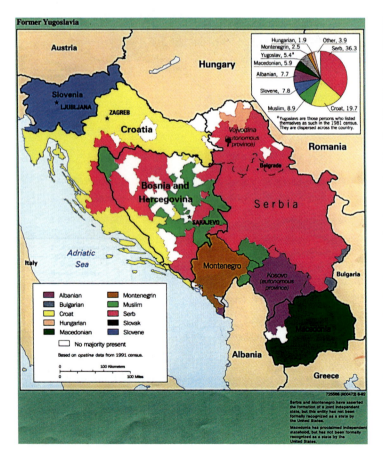

ISSUE 4: YUGO-SLOB-IAN MESS: KOSOVO CHAOS

Finally, for the current events underlying what's happening in Eastern Europe with this reinvigorated Russia, comes the latest chapter in the disintegration of what was Yugoslavia. I've intentionally kept the mess out of the chapter up until this point because it's a debacle that muddies the Eastern European waters a little too much to tackle it up front. But now that you understand the rest of the region, I am confident that you can now figure out this confounding coalition of convoluted crap with the greatest of ease. Well, we at least have to give it the old college try, since events here are once more crystallizing the fight between the West and the East. Let's do it.

The Plaid Avenger said earlier that Yugoslavia was different than the Soviet Union. Let's revisit them so you'll understand what's happening in today's former-Yugoslavia. First off, they were never part of the Soviet umbrella. They were commies, with a commie-run government after WW2, but not Soviet. It was a communist state under the tutelage of **Marshall Joseph Tito**. "Marshall" is really just a nicer sounding title than "oppressive dictator extraordinaire." The Plaid Avenger suggested earlier, as we were talking about the historical background of this region, that perhaps no other singular country has more different ethnicities and religions and cultures as did the former Yugoslavia. Emphasis on *did*.

They had Slovenes there, Croats, Bosnians, Herzegovenians, Serbians, Montenegrins; I don't even know what half these terms mean! On top of that, you have Christian Serbs, Muslim Serbs, also Christian Bosnians, a group that encompasses Orthodox and Catholic Bosnians, Muslim Bosnians . . . It's confusing! It was a multi-ethnic, multi-religious, multi-media mess.

Tito double vision: Josip or Jackson?

Why has there only been serious conflict and devolution there in the past twenty years? It's all because of Joseph Tito; not the Tito of the Jackson family, the other Tito, the dictator. Tito was a strong-armed dictator, like Stalin and lots of other folks in the communist realm. When ethnic or religious tension reared its ugly head in what was Yugoslavia, he sent in the army and crushed any uprising or disturbance with the iron boot. Through force, Tito held together this state full of all these different ethnicities and religions. Tito was the only reason it didn't devolve years ago. However, he died in 1980. Since Yugoslavia was a military state, it was able to perpetuate itself for another decade, but eventually imploded from the stress of diversity.

What's the Deal with Slobodan?

We all know this guy! He was arrested for war crimes, and died in The Hague before he even got through his trial. What did Slobodan do that was so important that the Plaid Avenger has to tell you about it? We know from Chapter 3 that the ultimate test of sovereignty is that you can kill citizens in your own country with no international repercussions. The government can do anything it wants to in its country if they are a sovereign state; it's their right.

"I'm dead, and I'm still pissed off."

So what's the deal with Slobodan? He's another strong-armed guy like his predecessor pal Tito. Except when he came to power, his state was disintegrating. He helped perpetuate the conflict that led to the breakdown of Yugoslavia. During that period, he essentially allowed genocide to occur. He was an Orthodox Serb, which was the majority ethnic and religious group. He allowed the Serbian people to start picking on and beating the crap out of the ethnic Albanian-Muslim minorities in the Kosovo region, which were perhaps petitioning for independence. He not only allowed violence; he promoted it.

This started to spiral out of control in the early 1990s to the point that people in the outside world—particularly Billy-boy Clinton from the United States and lots of folks from the UN—began debating the limits of sovereignty. The rest you know from our talk on sovereignty back in chapter 3. After the US/NATO intervention, Slobodan was eventually arrested for war crimes and died while on trial in 2006. Oddly enough, when his body was brought back to Yugoslavia, lots of people were cheering him. He's considered a war criminal by most of the world, yet lots of Serbs have him held up as a hero. That's typically a bad sign. We'll talk more about that later.

Look at the time frame and do the math. Tito died in 1980; the state held on for about ten years. That brings us to about 1990, the same time that all the other parts of Eastern Europe were devolving, splitting, splintering, fracturing, shattering into separate countries because of the implosion of the USSR. It all hit the fan in Yugoslavia as well. Without the strong-armed dictator Tito there to hold the different groups together by force, the whole country collapsed on ethnic lines, followed by wars fraught with ethnic discrimination, vicious bloodshed, and human rights violations. Long story short, Eastern Europe in the last 20 years saw the USSR devolve from one entity to fifteen sovereign states, Czechoslovakia devolve from one country to two, and Yugoslavia devolve from one country to five in the 1990's. In 2006, Montenegro became #6. And the fat lady has not sung yet, my friends, which brings us up to current events. . . .

Kosovo still causing consternation

As you can see, the Yugoslavians have had kind of their own tale that's a bit separate from the USSR, but of course related, and that brings us full circle to today's world. And the shattering may not be over yet! Slippery #7 may be on its way, but this time it won't be without a fight. Kosovo may be the next to go. You by now know the story of Slobodan, genocide in Kosovo, and the US/NATO invasion of Serbia to stop it. The end of the tale goes like this: In February of 2008, Kosovo declared independence. Immediately, a bunch of Western European states and the US recognized their independence, which, of course, *infuriated* both Serbia and Russia. Russia is not very happy about this. NOTE: Not all Western European states recognized Kosovo, and therefore, the EU as a singular entity did not recognize it either. The big boys like the UK and France did, but many other minor European powers did not, for reasons we shall get to in a minute.

We have this situation that, again, crystallizes this new power struggle within Eastern Europe that's related to the old power struggle. Russian influence versus Western influence. The Russians, their historic ally Serbia (that is, what's left of Yugoslavia), and other entities around the world said, "You can't recognize Kosovo. You guys were promising all along you wouldn't." Because, of course, the United States and NATO intervened in Kosovo, kicked out Slobodan, and protected the Kosovars. But they always claimed that they were merely preventing genocide, and not carving out a new state. Russia argued, "Hey, all along when you guys did that intervention thing, you said that you weren't setting up a new state, that you weren't going to let them have independence, that you were just going to stop the civil war, and basically you're liars."

Russia is not alone on this issue either. China, as well as many European countries, have refused to support Kosovar independence because they think it sets a bad precedent. If there's one small, little group of people that are pissed off at a country and you're going to allow them to declare independence, then there's going to be a whole lot more shattering going on, and not just in Eastern Europe. You're setting a precedent for other folks to do it around the world. Russia don't want the Chechans declaring independence; China don't want Tibetans declaring independence either. It's interesting to note that places even in Europe like Spain did not support Kosovo independence because they said, "Hey look, we have a small group of radicals who want an independent Basque country, so no way. There's no way we're going to support an independent Kosovo, because then the Basque people will say, 'We're going to be independent too.'" You see how complicated this issue has become.

Back to the point: this is all about Russian influence here. The Russians are supporting their old Serb allies, saying, "No, this is nonsense. We ain't recognizing Kosovo and nobody else should either." And the West is saying, "Oh, but, you know, they want to be a democracy, and peace-loving and all that stuff. We are going to support 'em.'" Yep. Eastern Europe right back in the middle again. I guess old habits die hard in the end.

The point of this last section is that Russia is back. They are re-flexing their muscles. They are reasserting influence, not control, but influence over their old Eastern European sphere of influence, and the West is still pushing in as well. **2014 UPDATE**—Ok, I guess we can now report that the Russians are actually also reasserting real control, since they officially re-absorbed the Crimean Peninsula of Ukraine back into the Russian motherland! And perhaps they are going to "re-absorb" more parts of Ukraine, as the state teeters on the brink of civil war! Maybe the Ruskies will take back Moldova too! Who knows? Honestly, not even the Russians know quite yet what they are going to do, and all of us will just have to watch as events unfold. But Eastern European states are once again back in the middle ground battle-zone between competing powers . . . that much we can say for sure. Same as it ever was.

CONCLUSION: THE TRANSITION IS ALMOST FINISHED!?

A new era, a new time, and it seems like the Eastern European transition is almost done. Most of these states have joined the western block institutions, with perhaps just a few more to go. Most countries are in the EU. Most are in NATO. They are Europe now. Most are part of Team West. Most. Some may be leaning back towards Mother Russia. Some.

But Eastern Europe has historically been in a vice and perhaps it may be ready to explode again. This region does have a strange history of being under the influence of these greater powers to its east and its west, which is why I started the chapter by calling it "bookended." Somehow, Eastern Europe is the one that sparks all the trouble between the sides. Seriously, think about it. Go back to World War I: It was started in what is now Yugoslavia, when Archduke Franz Ferdinand (it's not just a band) was assassinated in Sarajevo by a young Bosnian Serb from the Serbian radical group named the **Black Hand**. World War II started when Hitler invaded Poland. Then the Cold War battle lines were drawn in Eastern Europe, with most of the missiles either deployed on it, or pointed at it.

Eastern Europe today . . . at least for now.

Why list all these transgressions again? To stress a not-so-obvious point: all major conflicts of the last century were sparked in this bookended region. Hmmm . . . that certainly is food for thought, isn't it? Major players seem to get sucked into confrontation over this swath of land between Russia and Western Europe. Sucked in, and then life really sucks for all involved.

The disintegration of both Ukraine and Yugoslavia also started here in Eastern Europe—go figure, because they are located there—and it's not done yet. That's why I bring up this Kosovo situation, which is once again pitting an east versus west, a Russia versus Team West. Both the Ukrainian and Kosovo situations are promising to polarize these sides unlike really anything else that's going on here at the dawn of the 21st century. I know what you're thinking: "Hahahahaha what a load of bull, like a major war is going to start over some insignificant little hole in the wall like Kosovo, or Crimea, or **Transnistria**?" Yeah, you're probably right. My bad. How stupid am I being? I mean, the odds of that happening are about as likely as a global war that killed millions being started over the assassination of an unknown Austrian Archduke while motor-cading through Sarajevo. Ummm . . . oops. Bad example.

The question is, when will these people quit? How many more subdivisions can occur? How much more shattering before it's over? Quite frankly, the answer is perhaps never, because it's outside forces which seem to promote, antagonize, and continue to push in this battleground buffer zone that we call Eastern Europe. As alluded to earlier, and elaborated much more on in chapter 25, Ukraine is now the country to watch as the next chapter of Eastern European devolution, and it promises to be the most exciting, action-packed episode yet! And never, ever discount the possibility of Bosnia or Serbia blowing back up again; tensions continue to simmer under the lid of the former Yugoslavia. But that's all for now. We keep talking about Russia being involved as one of the players in this battleground of ideologies in Eastern Europe, so perhaps we should now turn our attention to the Bear. Oh Vlad . . . are you out there . . .

EASTERN EUROPE RUNDOWN & RESOURCES

View additional Plaid Avenger resources for this region at http://plaid.at/ee

BIG PLUSES

→ Due to lower wages and overhead, Eastern Europe is attracting lots of foreign investment and jobs from Western Europe
→ Eastern Europe produces a lot of agricultural products and is becoming a manufacturing hub for Western Europe
→ Incorporation into the EU promises to help raise standards of living and the economy for most Eastern European states to eventually reach Western European standards
→ Incorporation into NATO promises to ensure political and military stability for its Eastern European members

BIG PROBLEMS

→ Many states of the region have a long way to go to achieve western-style standards of living
→ Possibility of ethnic/religious/nationalist conflict rearing its head again is highly likely, particularly in the Balkans
→ Non-NATO states in the region (Ukraine, Belarus) and even some NATO members (Poland, the Baltic states) will continue to be torn between their western allies and having to suck up to Russia
→ Many Eastern European states are heavily reliant on energy supplies from Russia
→ Ukraine. New Cold War warming up? 'Nuf said for now.

DEAD DUDES OF NOTE:

Archduke Franz Ferdinand: Leader of Austria-Hungarian Empire who was assassinated by a radical Serbian nationalist in 1914; the Empire then declared war on Serbia, which triggered all of Europe to declare war against each other, thus World War I.

Marshall Josip Tito: The communist strong-armed dictator that held together Yugoslavia for decades, despite the wildly diverse ethnic/religious mix of the state. And when he died, it all came unraveled. He was Serbian and an ally of the Russians, but never a part of the USSR.

Slobodan Milošević: Former Serb President of Yugoslavia, this is the dude whose encouragement of Serbs to persecute Muslim Albanians in Kosovo resulted in the US/NATO bombing of his country into submission. He died in jail during his war crimes trial at the Hague. Still is looked upon as a nationalist hero by some Serbs.

Eastern Europe
CHAPTER NINE 195

 PLAID CINEMA SELECTION:

Everything is Illuminated (2005) A freaky Jewish-American man (played by hobbit Frodo Baggins aka Elijah Wood) road trips to find the woman who saved his grandfather from Nazis during WWII in a Ukrainian village. Bizarre and intriguing, and great landscapes shot on location in Ukraine and Czech Republic.

No Man's Land (2001) Set in war-torn Bosnia-Herzogovina in 1993, a Serb and a Croat are caught in a catch-22 situation in a trench between opposing armies' with a guy laying on a live land mine. Also features: ineffective UN, physical scenery of Slovenia, and realistic rendition of how confusing this war is to outsiders and insiders alike.

Before the Rain (1994) Time twisting tale in 3 parts that shows the internal political turbulence of Macedonia as it pulled away from war-torn Yugoslavia and became independent. Shot on location in Macedonia, builds on the futility of the cyclical nature of violence endemic in this region, pitting families against each other, and their neighbors. After you watch it, retrace the timeline, and also figure out who actually killed who.

4 Months, 3 Weeks and 2 Days (2007) Set in 1987, on of the last years of the communist/dictatorship Ceausescu era, in Bucharest, Romania, this film documents the struggles of two adolescent girls, as one goes through an illegal abortion. At times, mildly disturbing, the power of cinema is evident throughout the entire film.

I Served the King of England (2006) Filmmakers from both the Czech Republic and Slovakia joined to create this film depicting Czechoslovakia during the 1940s. Nice historical sweep of the area from pre-war to German occupation to soviet occupation , and an excellent look at a variety of landscapes in Eastern Europe and Germany.

Katyn (2007) War torn Poland during WWII and the events leading up to and eventually culminating in the Katyn Massacre, where the soviets murdered 15,000 Polish POW officers and citizens. Includes actual German and Soviet newsreels from the time. This is as topical as it gets: did you hear about the Polish President dying in a plane crash in April 2010? He was heading to a Katyn memorial service at the time. Freaky!

Force 10 from Navarone (1978) Awesomely cheesy, action WWII film set in Yugoslavia and other parts of Eastern Europe. Shows little-known Nazi action in the Balkan Peninsula and actually filmed in parts of Yugoslavia and Montenegro. Stars a young Harrison Ford, as he shot it at the same time Star Wars was being made. Sorry, it's a plaid guilty pleasure.

LIVE LEADERS YOU SHOULD KNOW:

Viktor Yanukovych: His fraudulent election was the cause of Orange Revolution and, amazingly enough, was also the cause of the second uprising/revolution in Ukraine in 2014. His pro-Russian, anti-Western leanings brought him to power, and were the reason for him being thrown from power. Talk about a double-edged sword.

Viktor Yushchenko: previous pro-West president of Ukraine that surfed to power on the Orange Revolution wave. Tried unsuccessfully to incorporate his country into EU and NATO, but political stagnation and inefficiency got him tossed out of office. Oh, and he's the dude that got poisoned by ex-KGB during his run at the presidency.

Yulia Tymoshenko: International political hottie extraordinaire and previous Ukrainian Prime minister. Has her own pro-Yulia party, and is adept at playing both sides of the pro-West and pro-Russia sides of the game to her advantage. You will see her rise again in Ukrainian politics, but from the sidelines, not as a major player.

Petro Poroshenko: the billionaire businessman and "Chocolate King" of Ukraine who was just elected President in 2014. Is likely pro-Western, but will have his hands full just keeping the country in one piece . . . that will melt in your hands, not in your hands!

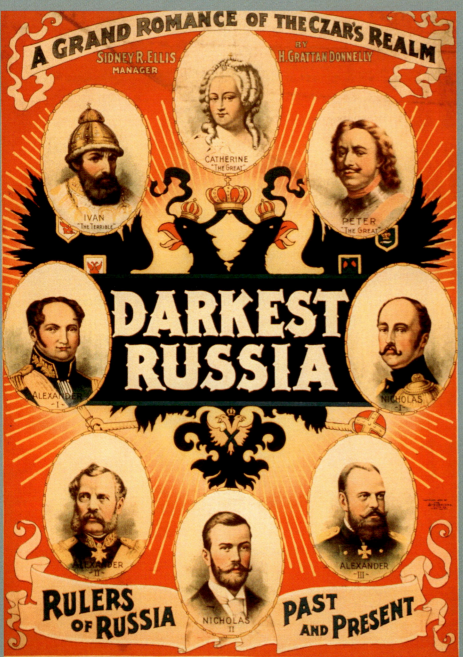

CHAPTER OUTLINE

1. The Bear is Back
2. The Hair of the Bear
3. From Cub to Grizzly
   - 3.1. Historic Growth
   - 3.2. Serf's Up, Dudes!
4. The Bear Takes a Beating
   - 4.1. Godzilla Attacks
   - 4.2. World War I
   - 4.3. That's Revolting: Commies Take Command
5. The Bear Battles Back
   - 5.1. Stylin' with Stalin
   - 5.2. The Bear Enters World War II
   - 5.3. Is It Getting Chilly in Here? The Cold War
   - 5.4. Commie Econ 101
6. Catastrophic Commie Implosion
   - 6.1. Ruble Rupture
   - 6.2. Afghan Body Slam
   - 6.3. The Great Communicator Says, "I Hate Commies"
   - 6.4. Holy Glasnost, This is Driving Me Mad! Pass the Salt, Perestroika
   - 6.5. So Long to the Soviet: The End
7. Radical Russian Transition
   - 7.1. Economy Takes a Dump
   - 7.2. Oligarchs Over-do It
   - 7.3. Purgin Population
   - 7.4. Environment Endangered
   - 7.5. Stolen Sphere of Influence: The Realignment
8. Resurgent Russia: The Bad Boys are Back!
   - 8.1. Prez to Prime Back to Prez: Putin Power!
   - 8.2. Petro Power!
   - 8.3. Global Warming? No Sweat!
   - 8.4. Geopolitical Jump Start
   - 8.5. Don't Like Putin? Crimea River!
9. Ghost of Stalin Returns

Russia

THE BEAR IS BACK

Russia is the largest country on the planet. They were the Cold War adversary of the US; you know, the bad guys. We refer to Russia as the Bear, and this wild woolly bear seems to change focus and direction every semester that passes, just as a wild bear hunts in the woods. I'm scared! Not really, but it is a region that is in transition, much like Eastern Europe; in this regard, it is changing every day. However, unlike Eastern Europe which has a very distinct direction of change, Russia is what the Plaid Avenger calls a fence-straddler—that is, it is playing the field in terms of with whom it does business, with whom it has a political alliance, and with whom it will throw in its future.

Time to bear all!

Russia has been a distinct culture, a world power player, a part of the Soviet Union, and a major shaper of world history and events of the 20th century. It has experienced tremendous political and economic upheavals and can almost be considered behind the times here in the 21st century . . . but hang on, because the Putin-inspired takeover of the Crimean Peninsula here in 2014 proves that Russia is back on course for a possible huge power grab! How did this region go from a global power to a globally broken basket-case? More importantly for our understanding of today's world, how is it successfully getting back into the game? All of these things and more, we will explore as we tell the story of the Bear.

One big bear. US/Russia size comparison.

HAIR OF THE BEAR

We always start our regional tour with a breakdown of what's happening in the physical world. When we think of Russia, several words typically come to mind: big, cold, and vodka. There's some truth in this. Russia is a cold place, a big place, and those Russians do love their vodka. But kids, just say "No" to the vodka . . . unless you are in Russia, of course, and then you say, "Nyet" . . . although apparently few of them do.

Russia is the largest state on the planet, twice as big as Canada, the second largest. Does size matter? Do I even need to ask? Of course it does! Size matters in most aspects of life. This huge country crosses eleven time zones, spanning almost half of the globe. When the sun is setting on one side of Russia, it is rising on the other side! Just think of all the problems associated with infrastructure and communications in a state this big. Think of all the problems associated with just trying to keep all of your people within your country aware of what's going on at any given second, much less having to move things around in it, like military equipment.

Don't even try to think about having to defend its vast borders. Your head will explode. Russia has a top slot in terms of how many different countries it borders, which I believe is now fourteen in all. But it's not all bad. This massive territory contains loads of stuff—what stuff? All kinds of stuff: oil and gold, coal and trees, water and uranium and lots and lots of land. What do lots of people do with lots of land? They typically can grow lots of food, but that's not always the case in Russia because of its second physical feature—it's cold.

Maybe that's why the bear has such a thick coat. Virtually all of Russia lies north of the latitude of the US-Canadian border. This high latitude equates to the cooler climates found on our planet; indeed, some of Russia lies north of the Arctic Circle, which means most of its northern coast remains frozen year round. To compound matters, Russia lies at the heart of the Eurasian continent; because of this fact, it has perhaps the greatest extremes of **continentality** expressed by its extreme temperature ranges, both season to season and also day to day. There are some parts of Russia in which the temperature within a 24-hour period may change 100 degrees: that is, it could be 60 degrees Fahrenheit at 3:00 in the afternoon and 12 hours later it might be −40 degrees Fahrenheit. That's extreme. Maybe this tough climate has something to do with Russian attitudes and their dour outlook on life in general. A tough place with a tough history which brings us to our last physical descriptor: vodka.

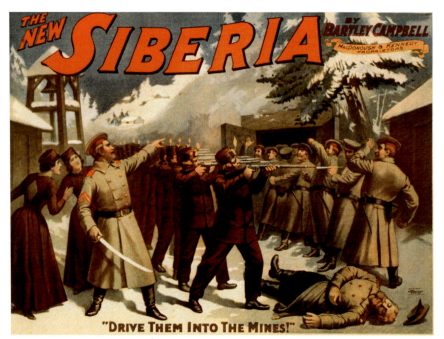

Siberia! The Spring Break destination of the Soviets!

Russia is the greatest consumer of vodka on the planet. Both in terms of total quantity and per capita consumption, no one can touch the Russians when it comes to drinking vodka; alcoholism rates are high, and this mind-numbing stuff continues to impact society and health in a variety of sobering ways. Perhaps it's the bleak and challenging climate that makes the Russian life so hard and vodka consumption a necessity to deal with the challenge. Perhaps this is why vodka is such an integral part of Russian history. Did someone say Russian history?

FROM CUB TO GRIZZLY

How did the Russian state get to be the largest country on the planet? How did it get so much stuff? Where did these guys come from? What does it mean to be Russian? The "original Russians" were actually Swedish Vikings who moved into the area around modern day Moscow to Kiev, probably around 1000 to 1200 C.E. Thus, Russians look European and share many of their cultural traits.

HISTORIC GROWTH

Looking at the maps across the bottom of the page, we can see that Russia, in 1300, was more like a kingdom than an empire; indeed, it was not a huge territory. It

From the land of Volvo, we come to conquer Kiev.

was a small enclave of folks that called themselves ethnically Russian but were politically subservient to the real power brokers of that era: the Mongols. **The Golden Horde** was a political subunit of the Mongol Empire that controlled parts of Russia and Eastern Europe at the time. It was not until 1480, under the leadership of Ivan the 3rd, a.k.a. **Ivan the Great,** that Russia stood up to the Mongols, threw off the yoke of Mongol oppression, and began its growth into the land juggernaut we know today.

Ivan united his people, kicked some Mongol butt, and expanded the empire. His son, Ivan the 4th, a.k.a. **Ivan the Terrible,** continued this trend by feeding the Bear and expanding the empire further. Ivan the Terrible earned his name by having an incredibly nasty temper, eventually murdering his son and heir apparent with an iron rod. Nice guy. Good family man.

Soon after the Ivans created this empire called Russia, an imperial family line was put into place that lasted uninterrupted up until the 20th century. They were the Romanovs, to whom you've probably heard references before. I'm not going to go into great detail on all of them, but just to put a few into perspective, let's list some of the more famous names. **Peter the Great** popped up around 1700 and was known for many things, notably creating and building the town of St. Petersburg. Hmmm . . . I wonder where he got the name?

Why is this significant? Because it shows what Peter was all about, and that was embracing Europe. Even back then, Russia lagged significantly behind its European counterparts in terms of industrialization, technology, military, and economy. Peter was all about catching the Bear up. St. Petersburg was often called "a window to the West" because the city

Russia in 1300   Russia in 1462   Russia in 1584

embraced Western technology and architecture and there was a real sense that it was opening Russia to interaction with the rest of Europe. Here's another example of how Russia is tied historically to the West: the term "Czar" in Russia was taken from the Roman Empire's "Caesar." In addition, Moscow was often referred to as "the third Rome" throughout history, as it viewed itself as the protector of true Christianity, in its distinctive Eastern Orthodox tradition. (Rome #1 was Rome; after the Roman Empire collapsed, then Rome #2 was Constantinople; after the Byzantine Empire crashed, then Rome #3 was Moscow). Russia has embraced and associated itself with the West in many ways over the years, although in most cases, it lagged behind.

Peter expanded the empire in all directions. This brings us to an interesting component of the Russian Empire's growth: Why expand? Many historians have speculated that there has been an inherent drive to expand the state in an effort to gain coastline. All major European nations with world dominance during this era had a lot of coastline and were maritime powers. Because of Russia's position on the continent, it is conceivable that most of its growth occurred in part to reach the coast in order to become a world power as well. This is speculative to be sure, but it does make some common sense.

Russian ambassador dealing with Napoleon.

One resource that's certainly driven Russian continental expansion was **fur.** Given the climate of this part of the world and the way people dressed, it certainly is the case that the trading of fur—that is, stripping the exterior of live animals and making coats out of it—was the main economic engine behind the continued growth of the land empire. Cold climate = animals with lots of fur = animals we want to kill for their fur = fur coats worth lots of money = more land = more furry animals to continue driving the economy. Speaking of continued land growth, we come to another familiar name in history, **Catherine the Great.** She radically expanded the empire across the continent, was a familiar face in European politics, and helped propel the Russian state into serious power player status on the continent during the 1760s and 1770s. Catherine continued to modernize in the Western European style, and her rule re-vitalized Russia, which grew stronger than ever and became recognized as one of the great powers of the continent for the first time ever.

The last face to consider during our old school Russian tour is that of **Napoleon.** Wait a minute! He's not Russian! True, but he did invade Russia in 1812 in one of the many great blunders in history. Napoleon was doing pretty well conquering Europe until he invaded Russia. Here's a little Plaid Avenger tip from me to you: don't invade Russia. Don't ever invade Russia. No one has ever successfully invaded Russia. As Napoleon—and later, Adolf Hitler—found out, it's easy to get *into* Russia, but it's impossible to get *out*. As the French forces advanced to Moscow and eventually took over the city, they did so in the middle of a horrifically cold Russian winter, and because of their dwindling supplies, were forced to retreat. They were attacked continuously on their way out. Bad call, Napoleon. You silly short dead dude! Russian Trix are for kids!

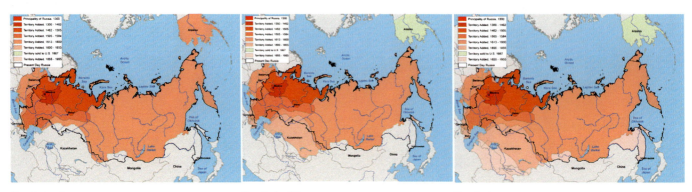

Russia in 1800　　　　　　　　　　　Russia in 1867　　　　　　　　　　　Russia in 1955

Ivan the Great: Mangled the Mongolians.

Ivan the Terrible: Skewered his son.

Peter the Great: Wanted to be Western.

Catherine the Great: made Russia into a European power playa'.

I bring this up to reiterate a common theme in Russian history: Russia always seems to come out stronger at the end of extreme turmoil. After Napoleon's invasion, it comes out sitting pretty as the world's largest territorial empire. We will see this theme again after World War II.

SERF'S UP, DUDES!

I've painted a pretty picture with lots of faces and names that you've heard before, but don't let me suggest that life and times in Russian history were good. Mostly they really sucked, for the lower classes in particular. During the imperial reign I've described thus far, life was fine for the royal court, but life as a commoner was brutal. We have a sort of a feudal system in Russia for most of its history. Serfdom in this country really turns into something more equivalent to full-on slavery. What we're talking about here is a typical feudal structure where there is a lord who owns the land and under him, the mass of people in the country are workers tied to that land. As such, they have no rights to hold landed notes, no human rights, and are basically slaves of the landholder. In combination with the fantastic climate of Russia, one can see how living here for most folks was not a fun time. Chronic food shortages and mass starvations were common occurrences as particularly brutal winters, bad crop harvests, and repressive taxation systems kept the peasants in a perpetual state of misery.

Why talk about the plight of Russian peasantry? Because the dissatisfaction among a vast majority is soon going to culminate in a revolution; a revolution the likes of which the world has never seen. It wasn't like the aristocracy didn't see it coming, either.

In an attempt to placate the masses, Tsar Alexander II passed the sweeping Emancipation Reform of 1861, which was supposed to end this miserable peasant situation. Say what? Emancipation didn't occur until 1861? That's late in the game! Consider: that was the same year that the US started their Civil War in order to emancipate slaves! Unfortunately for Russia, this proclamation on paper didn't amount to much in real life, and the crappy peasant existence continued. By the turn of the century, freed slaves in the US had more rights than supposedly freed peasants in Russia, not to mention that the vast majority of Europe as a whole had long since abolished both slavery and feudalism.

As we progressed toward the year 1900, many Russian folks were still essentially slaves of the land. This was a time when the rest of Europe was industrializing and getting more connected. Europe had political revolutions, which created states that emphasized equality for individuals, even the lowest classes. People in Russia knew what was going on in the rest of Europe. They heard about the French Revolution and Britain's change to a constitutional monarchy. If you look at a political map of Europe's changes over time, you'll see that things started in the West, progressed eastward, and these changes took a long time to make their way to Russia. Indeed, economic and political revolution reached there last, but when it did come, it came big.

As changes were enacted in Europe, as common folk in Europe gained more and more rights and perhaps even more and more wealth, Russia was stagnant. Russia was falling behind yet again. Dissatisfaction was also on the rise, and things in the 20th century made it quite a bumpy ride for the Russian Bear, particularly for its royal line.

Dimitri! Where's the party, dude? Looks like the fun never stopped for the Russian peasantry!

THE BEAR TAKES A BEATING

The 20th century, taken as a whole, was not kind to Russia. It started the century on a downward slide. As Russia fell farther and farther behind the times and as popular dissent increased, the imperial government did the worst thing possible: it lost a war. One of the things that kept peasants in line was the concept of a strong central government, even though it may not be popular or even good. Citizens wanted a government to protect them from foreign powers, invasion or destruction from invaders. Even though the monarchy was not popular, at least they maintained a strong military presence to guard their citizens and territory. When they failed to do that, full failure of the state was not far behind, and Japan provided the first kink in the armor of the **Romanov** line.

GODZILLA ATTACKS

In 1905, the Japanese declared war on Russia. The Japanese, having risen in power for the last fifty years up to that point, began encroaching on Russian lands in the east. This came to a head when the Japanese took over part of mainland Asia claimed by Russia. **Tsar Nicholas II** deemed it necessary to go to war to reclaim this land and to put the Japanese in their place. Easier said than done. The Russians sent their entire fleet from Europe to take on the Japanese in the Sea of Japan. After this extensive voyage, the Russian fleet arrived to be beaten down by the Japanese fleet in a matter of minutes. It was the most one-sided naval battle in history. The entire Russian fleet was obliterated. Back home in Moscow, popular dissent turned into popular hatred after this stunning defeat. The **Russo-Japanese War** was costly and unpopular and served to really get people thinking about replacing the monarchy with a whole new system altogether. But the fun had only just begun!

Back home in Russia, the peasants and workers alike had about enough. Later in 1905, a general strike was enacted empire-wide to protest the slow pace of reform and general discontent with the aristocracy. The system was broken, and the people knew it. This protest was met with an iron fist by the government, and things turned nasty, fast. The 1905 Russian Revolution is best remembered for the legendary Bloody Sunday massacre; cross-toting, hymn singing protesters were slaughtered by government troops as they marched to the Tsar's Winter Palace. Brutal! The Romanovs had restored order, but not for much longer.

WORLD WAR I

The Russo-Japanese War may have been damaging and unpopular, but at least it was far away. However, the next phase of fun happened closer to home, when Archduke Franz Ferdinand of Austria was assassinated in what later became Yugoslavia. This was the spark that ignited World War I and everybody declared war on each other. Russia had diplomatic ties with Serbia, who was pulled into the war immediately, so the Ruskies had to jump in as well. As we pointed out, this came on the heels of a loss to the Japanese on the other side of the Russian empire. From the onset, World War I was extremely unpopular because people at home were saying, "Hey, you already lost to the Japanese! Life here is sucking! Things are going down hill fast and now we are in another war? Nobody even knows what we are in it for! Serbia? Serbia who?"

Nicholas II rides to the front lines of WWI: "The Monk made me do it!"

World War I was fought on Russia's front doorstep; for three long years, there was a catastrophic death toll on the Russian side. The Germans made huge gains into Russian territory and snapped up large parts of the front. Meanwhile, back at the bear cave, popular dissent was growing wildly, fueled in part by the shenanigans of yet another famous Russian: **Rasputin**. "The Mad Monk" as he was referred to by many Russians, was a shaman/con-man who worked himself and his magic into the inner circles of aristocratic power, including being a direct advisor to the royal family themselves. In point of fact, Tsar Nicholas II was strongly advised by Rasputin to personally lead the charge on the front lines of WWI, even though everybody knew good old Nick was not up for the challenge. Chaos then ensued both on the war front, but more importantly, back home as well. (check out inset box on Rasputin, next page).

Archduke Franz Ferdinand

My death started WWI. Sorry!

Tsar Nicholas II

My death made the Revolution irreversible. Sorry!

Vladimir Lenin

My death launched Stalin into power. Sorry!

The Mad Monk, Rasputin

I'm still not dead. Someone get me the hell out of this coffin!

I don't need to get too much more into World War I history after this, because the Russians didn't have a lot to do with it. About halfway through the war, internal dissent within Russia reached an all time high. The Bear reeked of revolt.

THAT'S REVOLTING! COMMIES TAKE COMMAND

The revolt occurred in February of 1917 and Tsar Nicholas II abdicated, meaning he quit before he got fired. When the Tsar, who had been out fighting in the battlefield during World War I, returned to Russia, he discovered his people were in open revolt. He abdicated, and put his brother on the throne. Faster than you can say, "I hereby resign from the throne," his brother abdicated as well. A temporary government was set up, but in terms of who is really going to take power, nobody could tell.

"Let's redistribute some wealth, people!"

On October 25, 1917, this culminated in an event that people all over the world know, **the Bolshevik or Communist revolution,** led by our good friend, **Vladimir Lenin**. Communism was not something that everybody in Russia were just jumping up and down about . . . it is likely that most people had never even heard of it. Karl Marx and Friedrich Engels wrote about the concept in Germany and Austria; they weren't Russians. Lenin was a revolutionary even in his youth, and came in contact with a lot of these ideals during his college years. His older brother, who was executed because of his socialist activism, also influenced him. Lenin became a lawyer, but was eventually exiled to Siberia because of his radical revolutionary activities.

In Siberia, he wrote and published a lot of socialist literature, and became a prominent figure in the revolutionary movement. He eventually fled to Finland, and later Switzerland. While there, Lenin made appearances and speeches to other socialist groups in Europe. When the open revolt in Russia started to happen, Vladimir and other revolutionaries boarded a train and headed

What's the Deal with Rasputin?

The biography of Grigori Rasputin, a.k.a. the Mad Monk, is often fortified with folklore, which is fine by the Plaid Avenger because the folklore that surrounds Rasputin is hilarious. What is clear is that Rasputin practiced some sort of Christian-like religion and gained favor with Tsar Nicholas II by helping to medically treat his son through prayer. The Russian Orthodox Church didn't like Rasputin—mainly because churches never like competing ideology, but also because Rasputin loved sinning. Much of this sinning involved prostitutes.

Big City Russian Pimpin'.

During World War I, Rasputin advised Tsar Nicholas II to seize command of the Russian military. This turned out poorly for two reasons: (1) Tsar Nicholas II wasn't a good army commander and (2) while Tsar was away, Rasputin gained considerable control of the Russian government and helped screw up the Russian economy. Needless to say, a lot of people were not happy with him. In December of 1916, a group set out to assassinate the Mad Monk. First, they attempted to poison him. The would-be assassins loaded two bottles of wine with poison, which Rasputin drank in their entirety. The assassins waited and waited, but Rasputin continued to display lively behavior. In a panic, they shot him point-blank in the back. When they came back later to deal with the body, Rasputin jumped up, briefly strangled his attempted killer, and then took off running. The group of assassins gave chase, shot Rasputin AGAIN—this time in the head with a large caliber bullet, and then beat him with both blunt and sharp objects. Finally, they wrapped his body in a carpet and threw it off a bridge into the Neva River, but, the river was frozen over, so Rasputin's body just smashed into the layer of ice. The assassins climbed down to the frozen river and broke the ice under Rasputin so his body would sink into the water. They eventually succeeded and Rasputin disappeared into the freezing depths. Three days later, authorities found Rasputin's body and performed an autopsy. The autopsy revealed that Rasputin had died from drowning and, in fact, his arms were frozen in a position that suggested he died while trying to claw his way through the ice and out of the river.

Me-oww! That cat was a freaky-freak. And his lives ran out. Maybe . . .

back into Russia after a long absence from their homeland. Once Lenin returned, he became a prominent figure in the Bolshevik party and leader of this "Soviet Revolution."

One of his ideas that gained popular support was not necessarily that communism was the greatest thing ever, but instead, "We need to get the heck out of World War I!" He received popular support for his Soviet ideas by default, because everyone pretty much agreed with his other political stances that monarchy, peasantry, and Russian life in general sucked, and change was necessary. The power structure was completely unfair. What also gained popularity was the promise to get Russia out of the war in exchange for the support of his cause. Long story short, the Communist revolution became an internal power struggle, and the Bolsheviks came out on top. "**Bolshevik**" means "majority," but in reality, the movement was anything but a majority. The Bolsheviks had many political rivals in the struggle to control Russia. The commies were actually a very small group of people who enacted this revolution and took over the whole nation.

True to their word, as soon as the Bolsheviks took over the government at the end of 1917, they immediately bailed out of World War I. They agreed to let the Germans have any invaded territory and signed a peace treaty. As you can see from this map, this resulted in huge territorial losses. The Russians lost territories that later became Estonia, Latvia, Lithuania, Moldova, and large parts of Poland. I am telling you this specifically because it is going to become Russian territory again after World War II. The Ruskies never truly intended to give away those lands permanently. In their minds, it was always a temporary fix.

Now as I just suggested, not everybody in Russia immediately embraced this communism gig. In fact, there were many holdouts. As you might expect, there were conservative people in the aristocracy and the military who thought that the monarchy, the old established way, should return and things should revert back to the way they were.

As soon as the Bolsheviks took power, one of the first things Lenin did was put the entire royal family under house arrest. Shortly thereafter, a civil war broke out; from 1918 to about 1920, there was open fighting throughout the country. The **Russian Civil War** was fought between the new party in charge, the Communists, and the old conservative holdouts and much of the military. The parties who fought the Russian Civil War referred to it as "the Reds versus the Whites." Obviously, the Reds were the communists and the Whites, the loyalists. The Red Russians versus the White Russians!

Again, our story here is that the 20th century was not very kind to Russia. It had a disastrous World War I, and then an internal revolution which turned into a civil war. The civil war is eventually won by the Reds. BTW: once the civil war broke out, Lenin ordered the assassination of the entire royal

Check out the Russian losses in WWI.

family. Why did Lenin do this? I thought he was a nice commie. The reason Lenin did this was because he believed that in order to succeed, Communist Russia had to sever all ties with the past: "You people are fighting for a monarchy? You want to restore the imperial royal line? Well, I will fix that! They can't be restored to the throne if they're all dead!"

This made the statement that no matter who won the war, there would be no return to monarchy because there were no more monarchs. The Romanov line ended with the assassination of Nicholas II, his wife, and five children including Anastasia; rumors suggesting Anastasia escaped execution circulated for decades (see inset box on right). The civil war was finished by 1920, and the Communists had power over the government and the country. Unfortunately, fate was still not smiling on Mother Russia, as the country saw back to back famines in 1921–23 as the result of horrific winter weather—like the weather is even good in the good years? However, by the mid-1920's, the worst seemed to be over and it was time to get that commie transition on!

What's the Deal with Anastasia?

Anastasia was born the Grand Duchess of Russia in 1901. When the Bolsheviks took power in Russia, Anastasia's entire family was executed because of their links to the Romanov dynasty. However, legend is that Anastasia and her brother Alexei might have survived the execution. This legend is supported by the fact that Anastasia and Alexei were not buried in the family grave. Several women came forward in the 20th Century claiming to be Anastasia, but guess what: she's dead. Regardless of the intrigue and the crappy animated kid's movie, The Plaid Avenger is certain that Anastasia died of lead poisoning with the rest of her family. Lead poisoning induced by bullets. Lots of bullets.

Got Dead? Yep.

THE BEAR BATTLES BACK

The next event of great significance happened in 1924, when Lenin died. For vehement anticommunists, that was a day of celebration; for Russians, it was a day of mourning, because Lenin was the founder of the party, a rallying post, and a popular leader of the communist movement in Russia. He had the grand designs about where society was going, with an ideal of equality where everyone shared the wealth, and the whole utopian society thing. Why was his death titanic? Well, because after he died, who would succeed him? The answer was **Joseph Stalin.**

STYLIN' WITH STALIN

From 1924 to 1953, Joseph Stalin, one of the biggest psychos history has ever known, was in power of what was now called the Union of Soviet Socialist Republics (USSR), the post–civil war title for Russia.

Stalin's ascension to power was problematic for several reasons. For starters: he was crazy. After he gained power, he was psychotic and became more psychotic as every year of his reign passed. He consolidated all power to the center under himself, basically as a dictator, and that's what he was. He set up the infamous secret police force, the **KGB**, who sent out spies amongst the people, and conducted assassinations of all political rivals, their families, their cats, their dogs, and their neighbors. Anyone who spoke ill of Stalin ended up in a grave with a tombstone over his head. No, I take that back. They ended up in a mass grave with dirt over their heads. He was a nasty guy in a tough place in an extremely gut-kicking century for Russian history. But our story is not over yet, kids—the fun is still not done!

Before I go any further, I should say there is always a bright side to every individual. Smokin' Joe Stalin's silver lining was that part of the commie plan was to consolidate agricultural lands and speed industrialization. The Reds wanted to catch the country up with the rest of the modern world economically, technologically, and militarily. As much as I hate to admit it, that is exactly what occurred during the Stalin era.

Essentially Stalin oversaw a "crash course" of modernization, industrialization, and collectivization. These hugely ambitious goals could not have been achieved just by planning, though; the Russian people themselves have to be given a large share of the credit to have pulled this off. Perhaps Stalin's biggest contribution to these gains was not just organization and planning, but he somehow instilled a die-hard sense of uber-patriotic nationalism in the people that made for explosive societal gains. Specifically, the Russian people were convinced to work harder, work longer, make more out of less, consume less, and totally work hard for the country, not for themselves. And they did!

Of course, Stalin used all sorts of coercion and open force to achieve these aims when necessary. And again, he was nuts. But if we are going to credit Stalin with anything other than intense insanity, we can credit him with the Soviet infrastructure moving forward at breakneck speed, and they indeed caught up in a matter of a few decades. They created the atomic bomb shortly after the US did, and even beat the US into space with the launch of the **Sputnik** satellite. Fifty years earlier, they were all beet farmers. That is some fast progress!

THE BEAR ENTERS WORLD WAR II

By World War II, the USSR was starting to be a major world force. Before the war began in 1939, Joseph Stalin and Adolf Hitler met and signed a nonaggression pact. The meeting went down like this, brought to you Plaid Avenger style: Germany said, "We are going to take over the world, but here's the deal: we won't attack you as long as you don't attack us." Smokin' Joe Stalin, in all of his wisdom, said, "Okay, go ahead and take over Western Europe and the rest of the world. That sounds good to us. They were always kind of bothersome anyway. Also, we won't attack you as long as you don't attack us. Deal!" The war officially kicked off in 1941, when Germany attacked everybody. Hitler later made the fantastically idiotic mistake, after taking over most of Europe, of reneging on the nonaggression pact. In other words, he attacked the USSR anyway.

As discussed before about Napoleon, one of the greatest historical blunders for anybody is to invade

Joseph Stalin: Scariest Psycho of the 20th Century
Unfortunately, the award for "Scariest Psycho" is highly competitive. There's Hitler, Pol Pot, Mussolini, Idi Amin, Pinochet, Bob Barker, and many more. But the Plaid Avenger is fairly certain that Joe Stalin is the nastiest of them all. Stalin was one of the Bolshevik leaders who brought communism to Russia in 1918. When Vladimir Lenin, who was the original leader of the Bolsheviks, unexpectedly died in 1924, Stalin slowly assumed power. In 1936, Stalin initiated **The Great Purge** which lasted for two years. During this time, "dissenters" were shipped off to Gulag labor camps and often executed. Most "dissenters" were actually just normal folks who had been wrongly accused by other normal folks who were being tortured at a Gulag labor camp. As you can see, this was a self-perpetuating cycle. If everyone had to sell out eight friends to stop getting tortured, and each friend had to sell out eight friends, pretty soon you would have a ton of political "dissenters." It's like an incredibly violent email pyramid scam. Anyway, The Great Purge resulted in the death of perhaps 10 to 20 million Russians.

While The Great Purge was probably Stalin's sentinel work of psycho-sis, it was far from his last. Stalin organized a giant farm collectivization which left millions homeless and millions more hungry. He also continued purging dissenters until he died in 1953. Historians estimate over 45 million Russians died directly from Stalin's actions (this figure does not include the estimated 20 million Russians that died during WWII). Norman Bates got nothing on Stalin.

Russian soldiers line up for their daily vodka ration—of three liters.

Russia. No one's ever done it successfully, and Hitler was one in a long line of idiots who tried. After he attacked the USSR, the USSR was then obliged to defend itself and was pulled into World War II. This is of great importance: the USSR was the real winner of the war in Europe. Once the Germans declare war on the United States, who joined the rest of the Allies, it became the Germans versus the world. The Germans were really in a pinch as they were attacked on all flanks, the Allies on one side and the Russians on the other. While I am certainly not going to devalue the role of the Allies in the west, Russia really took out a lot of Germans and caused them to divert resources and men to the Russian front, which is the reason why World War II was won by the good guys.

Had the Russo-German nonaggression pact been upheld by Germany, it would be hard to tell what the map of Europe would look like today. It certainly wouldn't look like it does now. And the Russian death toll was astronomical. There were almost 9 million Russian military deaths, and at least 20 million civilian casualties—29 million people total! Take 29 and multiply it by a thousand, then take that and multiply it by another thousand! The Plaid Avenger's not trying to insult your intelligence. I just want you to take a second and think about how many folks died in this thing. Just on the Russian side!

This was some of the most brutal fighting on the entire continent. The Russian front was bloody, nasty, and deadly, and when all was said and done, the Russians beat the crap out of Germany. It was part of the main reason the Germans had to surrender in the end. I really want to stress the Russian losses. 29 million killed. We think about just the US's role in World War II (which was great by the way), but the US suffered maybe half a million to Russia's nearly 30 million deaths! As a result of WWII, Russia experienced an epic population loss and made a major impact on the European theater of war. The war ended in 1945, the end of which set up the scenario for the next fifty years.

IS IT GETTING CHILLY IN HERE? THE COLD WAR

At the conclusion of the war, the Allies came in from the west and the Russians were mopping up in the east and they met each other in the middle of Europe. They all did high fives and then they split Germany in half. Hitler was dead in the bunker, and there was a line where the Allies met after the war. The Allies were the United States, Britain, France, and the USSR. That's right! Smokin' Joe Stalin was on our team! Where the two forces met, as you see on this map, is halfway through Europe. That line quickly became known as **The Iron Curtain.**

What does this mean? Well, the Russians occupied Eastern Europe; after the war was over and everyone finished celebrating, the Soviets said, "Maybe we will just stay here for a little while. We'll make sure everything has settled down. We'll help rebuild this side of the continent." The United States, under the **Marshall Plan,** was building up Western Europe. Both parties occupied Germany to make sure it wouldn't start up trouble again—thus we had an East Germany and a West Germany, which reflected events happening in Europe as a whole.

In their effort to do this, the Soviets were pretty sinister. Under Soviet tutelage, "elections" were held all over, in places like Poland, Czechoslovakia, Hungary, Yugoslavia, and parts of Austria. We all know the outcome: lo and behold, the Communist party won resounding victories in every single place they held a vote! Everyone in the West knew this was a farce, but nobody wanted to start another war by calling out

*Austria remained occupied by Allied powers until 1955, at which time it became independent upon condition of neutrality.

The metallic drapes were drawn.

the Russians publicly about this scam. Remember, they were allies at the time, and they helped defeat the Germans together. The United States just wanted to get the heck out of there. They were not about to start a new war with Russia. The Western governments hesitantly went along with these newly "converted" communist states.

This set up a scenario where puppet governments replaced the previous governments. There's a term for this you should already know called **soviet satellites.** Some examples were sovereign states like Poland, Czech Republic, and Hungary that actually had seats at the UN—but everybody knew that the Soviets had the real control. These were puppet governments, to give the illusion of being expressive governments of their people. The situation simply evolved into Soviet occupation and control at this point. One of the reasons Western Europe and the United States allowed this to happen is that the Soviets very adeptly pointed out that they were staying in these Eastern European nations to make them a buffer zone because countries in Western Europe historically kept attacking them. That was true (e.g., Napoleon's France, Hitler's Germany).

These Eastern European states behind the curtain, that ended up being Soviet satellites, were actually parts of the territory that the Soviets had lost at the end of WWI, so the Soviets regained that loss. I like to point this out because it plays into what is happening in today's world. Whole countries that were sovereign states for a while between World War I and World War II (like Estonia, Latvia, Lithuania, Belarus, and the Ukraine), were totally reabsorbed by the Soviet Empire. These places declared independence after World War I, and then suddenly found themselves no longer sovereign states but soviet republics or sub-states of the Soviet Union. That's why the map of Eastern Europe changed so rapidly. Places came and went as sovereign states were reabsorbed.

COMMIE ECON 101

The first half of the 20th century was fairly repressive, brutal, chaotic, and completely violent for Russia, but things stabilized for them internally during the Cold War. We have already set the stage in Europe for the East versus West ideological battle for control of Europe, which is going to turn into a global phenomenon that has shaped virtually every aspect of every other region that we talk about in this book. What's the deal with the USSR as full-fledged commies after World War II?

As I have suggested previously, the Soviet Union experienced massive growth during Stalin's regime. He died shortly after World War II, but a lot of the industrialization which was radically successful under him continued on. Many of the programs, while oppressive and brutal, made the state a stronger world power. Indeed, it was the rise of the USSR which created the bipolar world that defined the Cold War. Stalin did a lot to get them up in the big leagues, and then he checked out. He brought about massive industrialization, particularly in the weapons sector, which continued after his death.

What happened under the Soviet experiment post–World War II? What did they do? What did it look like there? What did they make? What did they produce? How would that be part of their eventual undoing? During the Soviet era one of the primary goals, even under Lenin, was to catch up industrially. They did this by centralizing everything. That's what communism is known for. The state runs everything, all aspects of politics—of course that's easy, it's what all governments do—but also all aspects of the economy—and that's typically not what the governments do. That is the communist way: full political and economical control of the entire country.

This is called **central economic planning,** and it entails the government's approval of where every 7-Eleven is located, where every ounce of grain is grown, where railroad tracks are laid down, where coal will be mined, where whole cities will be built to support something like an automotive industry. Every single aspect of life that we take for granted in a capitalist system was controlled in the Soviet sphere. This was done very early in the Soviet Empire to accomplish specific goals, one of which was called **forced collectivization.** Russia had been a peasant society, land based, rural, farmers digging around in the dirt, for hundreds of years. It couldn't do that in the 20th century if it was going to catch up and become a world power; it needed to get people off the land and into the cities. Why the cities? To work in the big factories that were industrializing and creating stuff.

Goal number one was forced collectivization. Pool all the land together, because it now belonged to the state: "You used to have rights to it and a deed on it, Dimitri, and

Tanks for the memories, commies!

maybe you used to grow cabbage and beets on it, but those days are gone now, comrade! You've got two options: go to a city or get in a collective, government regulated, growing commune." The state controlled all the land and agricultural production, because the state had one huge tractor to do the work of 1,000 men, and it had pesticides and fertilizers, which made huge monoculture crops. This new system produced tons more food. Whereas 1,000 dudes had to farm a piece of land before, now just ten can get the job done. 990 dudes headed to the city to accomplish the next goal: **rapid industrialization.**

To achieve rapid industrialization, the Soviet government needed to get everybody in and around the city into big factories. What were the factories going to produce? All of the things the West has that the Soviets needed to catch up on. Things like tanks, petrochemicals, big guns, rifles, maybe some big fur coats every now and again because it's cold there, aircraft carriers, missiles, bulldozers, heavy machinery, etc. The question you need to ask yourself at the same time is: what were they not making? The big difference between the communist expression and the capitalist expression in the 20th century comes down to this question. The answer is that the Soviets didn't make the items that normal people buy. Instead, they made huge stuff that only countries used. Like I told you earlier, the Soviet system stressed more work and *less consumption* by the individual, so that the state can become stronger.

You have to remember, the Soviet way was not focused on individual citizens or individual rights. The Soviet government didn't care about personal expression or fashion statements or if you liked building model airplanes. For them, the Soviet Union was an awesome state and an awesome idea and its citizens should be ardent nationalists and do everything for their state. By and large, people were pretty cool with that; at least most of them were, because to not be cool with that meant the KGB would run you down in the middle of the night and shoot you. People accepted it. Lots of them even liked it.

What wasn't produced in the Soviet economy? Consumer goods like cool clothes, sunglasses, lawn chairs, microwave ovens, refrigerators, independent-use vehicles. Anything that you'd go to a mall to buy today did not exist in the Soviet world. Knick-knacks did not serve the greater goal of the government, which was to catch up with the capitalists. That's just the way it was.

As much as the Plaid Avenger likes to make fun of knick-knacks and other crap you don't need, it played a role in why the Soviet Union unraveled—but that's for the next section. They did indeed catch up and became a world power under this system. One of the other things the Soviets did with the big things like tractors and bulldozers and weapons was to export them abroad. These are items that the Soviet Union is still known for. Russia is, to this day, a huge manufacturer and exporter of arms. Example: the Russian made AK-47 is easily the most popular and most widely distributed rifle on the planet.

The AK-47; Russian export extraordinaire.

Russia also exported a lot of this stuff at cut rates to other countries around the world. Why would you export a bunch of missiles to Cuba? That's right, for the Cuban Missile Crisis! You also want to send around machinery and petrochemicals and similar items that you produce to make money and recoup costs, but more importantly, to promote your influence in the world. That is what the Cold War was all about: coaxing other countries to join your side by providing them with things they really need, building bridges, selling them weapons and chemicals, and maybe even lending money. Anything to get people on your side. The United States and the Soviet Union both did this all over the place.

Only in a few places does this battle of ideology turn hot and people start shooting at each other. Two places of note where this occurred were in Korea, resulting in the Korean War and in Vietnam, resulting in the Vietnam War. We might even go as far to say as this also happened in Central America for all the Central American wars, during which both these two giants funneled in weapons so that the locals could fight it out between their opposing ideologies. The commies versus the capitalists in all these places was really what the wars were all about, and the two giants funded their respective sides.

CATASTROPHIC COMMIE IMPLOSION

How did the Cold War end for the Soviets? Why did I suggest that knick-knacks on the shelf may have been part of the winning strategy of the United States, when all is said and done?

RUBLE RUPTURE

The Soviet Union, from the 1960s through the 1980s, simply overextended itself. The United States and Western Europe's economies were based on producing a little bit of everything: tanks, aircraft, and petro-chemicals, but also consumer goods like cars, washing machines, toys, and Slap-Chops.

When you have stuff that individual citizens can buy and sell, you don't have to solely rely on big ticket items to fuel the economy. How many bulldozers can you sell in one season? I mean, The US system ended up championing in the end, because people buy consumer goods all the time. People like to buy refrigerators and new cars and blow dryers and pet rocks; but the US also made and sold bulldozers and missiles too. Long story short; US/Team West got richer, Soviets stagnated.

Hurry! Buy now! These things are flying off the shelves!

Russia's economy stank because it was based on flawed principles and was focused solely on items that eventually made it unsustainable. But there were other reasons these guys were going broke. Namely, the USSR liked to give lots of money and support to their commie allies worldwide. During this expansion of Soviet influence across the planet, they really started to overextend themselves. They were giving stuff to Angola and the Congo in Africa, buying sugar from Cuba that they didn't even need, just so Cuba would be their ally, and lending money to places in Southeast Asia. By the 1980s, they were going broke while their economy was also stumbling.

Another ruble-draining effort was being stupid enough to get involved in a war in Afghanistan. Geez! Who would be dumb enough to get bogged down in an unwinnable war in Afghanistan? Oh, ummm, sorry US and NATO, I forgot about current events for a second. You guys should have really learned more from the Soviet experience, which was an . . .

AFGHAN BODY SLAM

Let's go into more detail on this mess, because it does play into current events more than most want to admit. Ever since the USSR came into existence, it crept further and further into control of Central Asia. eventually absorbing all of those -stan countries and making them into Soviet republics. All except one: Afghanistan. The USSR stayed very cozy with the leadership of the country, though, and gave them lots of foreign aid to ensure that they stayed under the commie sphere of influence.

However, there were other forces within Afghanistan that didn't like the Soviets and, for that matter, their own leaders. A group of Muslim fighters we'll call the **mujahideen** decided to wage a war to overthrow the Afghan government. The government feared a greater coup was at hand, so it invited the USSR to invade them to help out. Sounds good so far, huh? Yeah, right. This was a huge freakin' mistake for the Soviets.

In 1979, the Soviets invaded Afghanistan, and started a decade-long war which will serve to demoralize and humiliate the USSR. Remember, this was during the Cold War, so the US CIA—under orders from the government—funneled tons of weapons and training to the mujahideen to keep the Soviets pinned down. It worked like a charm. In fact, it worked too well! After the mujahideen eventually repelled the Soviets, they then proceeded to have a civil war, and the winners of that civil war became the Taliban. Crap. Any of this starting to ring a bell yet? The Taliban are buddies with and shelter al-Qaeda, and after 9/11, the US declared war on both groups. Now the US finds itself fighting against forces it helped arm and train back in the 1970s. Oops.

But that is a tale for another time; back to our soviet story. The Soviet/Afghan campaign of 1979–89 was a devastating war for Russia, comparable to the Vietnam War for America. The active conflict in Afghanistan started to siphon away resources at a rapid rate. At the end of ten years of fighting, many Russian lives were lost, many Russian rubles were spent, and all for nothing; they were forced to walk away from the whole mess with their tail between their legs. Check out an awesome flick which shows how this went down: *Charlie Wilson's War* starring Tom Hanks. As a bonus, it has male rear nudity—of Hanks, himself! Actually, ew.

THE GREAT COMMUNICATOR SAYS: "I HATE COMMIES"

Once the 1980s rolled around, a new component is introduced: the Reagan Factor. Ronald Reagan was the most hilarious US president ever, in the Plaid Avenger's opinion, and was certainly one of the reasons for the demise of the USSR. He is often credited as being the entire reason, which is preposterous, but his administration did a lot to accelerate the processes in play regarding Russia's economic decline. The drive for military buildup during the Cold War was all fine and dandy when the Soviet Union was expanding and growing industrially and economically, but this started to take its toll on them in the stagnant 1970s and 1980s. When the Americans developed a new type of missile, so the Russians also developed a similar one in order to stay competitive. Then the Americans built a new type of tank, so the Russians built one as well. It was a "keeping up with the Joneses" sort of situation. You have to be as cool as your neighbors by having the same stuff, the newest and coolest stuff. That had been happening since the 1950s. **The Space Race** was a classic example of that competitiveness. Then in 1980, Ronald Reagan was elected president of the United States, and hilarity ensued.

"I hate commies."

Reagan hated commies. If you learn one thing about Reagan, it's that Reagan hated commies. He hated commies when he was a Hollywood actor and ratted out a bunch of other actors as communists during the McCarthy hearings. He hated commies when he was the governor of California, and he really hated commies when he became the President of the United States. He hated them so much that he was willing to send money and arms to anybody on the planet under the guise that they were fighting commies. In conclusion: Ronald Reagan hated commies. Have I made that clear yet? When he came in power in 1980, he had to deal with domestic issues because the US economy sucked. One of the primary things that he and his administration did very early on was accelerate military spending. This was a very clever move because it did a few things at once: It helped the American economy by creating jobs building more bombs, and also, Reagan knew that the Soviets were trying to keep up militarily, so he was making them spend more money as well. Money they didn't have.

This spending craze happened during the entire decade of the 1980s, just as internal dissent became more prevalent within the Soviet Union. Rioting broke out in places like Czechoslovakia, Poland, and Hungary, and as the economy continued to worsen in the Soviet Union, people began to starve. The US media showed scenes of people in long bread lines in the Soviet Union. These guys weren't just broke; they were going hungry at the same time they were spending millions, if not billions, on weaponry to keep up with the US. It was a crafty move that paid off huge dividends for the US. When the final Soviet leader came to power, Communist Party Secretary General **Mikhail Gorbachev**, he inherited a state that was broken and riddled with holes. Gorbachev knew his administration was screwed. The comrades continued to lie to themselves and used the KGB to scare everyone so they wouldn't utter it out loud, but the people at the top knew that the party was over. The Communist Party, that is.

20TH CENTURY COMMIE COUNTDOWN

Lenin: 20th century premier commie and snappy dresser.

Stalin: 20th century premier psycho with a serious 'stache.

Krushchev: Placed missiles in Cuba. Nice job, laughing boy.

Brezhnev: Patented the Unibrow, kin to Herman Munster.

Andropov: He "dropped ovv" after only 16 months in office.

Chernenko: Not to be outdone, he croaked after only 13 months.

Gorbachev: "Oh crap, this place is falling apart."

HOLY GLASNOST, THIS IS DRIVING ME MAD! PASS THE SALT, PERESTROIKA

What Gorbachev did was enact three things. Two of them are words you should know. One is **glasnost,** which means "openness." The second is **perestroika,** which means "restructuring." The third thing he did was try and limit military funding. Glasnost meant Gorbachev was tired of the secrecy of the Soviet government. He didn't want to lie to people any more, and he wanted to stop the KGB from terrorizing people. He wanted citizens to be more open with the government so it could improve. Places in Eastern Europe such as Poland, who wanted their own votes and no longer wanted to be a part of the Soviet Union, were let out. Under perestroika, Gorbachev knew they had to restructure the economy and reel in military spending. They also needed to cut off subsidies to countries they could no longer afford to prop up. This all leads to number three: not being able to spend any more money on the military. Or at least not as much.

This third enactment led to the **SALT,** first in the early 1970s and then again late in the decade. The **Strategic Arms Limitation Talks** were about curbing weapons production—not stopping weapons production altogether, not getting rid of weapons—just slowing down the speed at which they were being made. What you have to understand about the Cold War is that, if humans survive for another 1000 years, it will be looked on with hilarity and humor; the whole reason that we haven't killed each other yet is because there are so many bombs on the planet between the Soviets and the USA. There was a principle that basically sustained our life on earth, known as **MAD. MAD** stood for **Mutually Assured Destruction,** which essentially meant if anybody lobs a bomb, then the other side will throw a bomb, in which case both sides will throw all their bombs and everyone will die. Who is going to do that? The insane logic of MAD is what stopped us from attacking each other, but it made us continue to make more bombs. Both sides already had enough bombs to annihilate the other side, but they just kept making more. The US would say, "We have 1000 bombs that can each destroy five countries at once!" Then the Soviet Union would build 1001. That's where you get into these astronomical numbers of bombs, a bomb for every darn person on the planet. Why? I can't really answer that, because it makes no sense. But I digress. I get a little agitated thinking about MAD; how fitting.

Back to our story: this equated to Gorbachev realizing that they had to stop doing this. During the SALT talks, they agreed, "Let's not build this type or class of bomb anymore, or build half as many as you were going to and we will build half as many. Also, how about we eliminate this type of submarine, and you guys eliminate that type of submarine." When these talks started, there was some capitulation, but for the really big thing, Gorbachev would say, "Let's not build these big intercontinental ballistic missiles," but Reagan (because he hated commies so much) built more of those missiles because he knew the Soviets were going broke. Indeed, not only did he *not* agree to weapons elimination, but accelerated production and built more. In the same year, Reagan appeared in front of the US Congress during the State of the Union address and said that the USSR was an "evil empire" and that the USA must do everything in their power to combat evil. He was really throwing all the cards down on the table—what a huge bluff in the global game of poker.

Here is the bluff that won the game: Somebody made mention to Reagan of how cool it would be if the US put missiles in space; thus when the Soviets shot nuclear weapons at anyone, the US could shoot their bombs out of the sky with these space missiles. This missile system evolved further to become a space laser to shoot out bombs and was called **SDI,** the Strategic Defense Initiative, given the nickname **Star Wars.**

When this idea came out it was merely that: an idea. Then some people started throwing around some funds for this idea, which was most likely sketched on a cocktail napkin by a science fiction writer. Somehow Reagan got his hands on this cocktail napkin and started to circulate it around. Anybody heard about this Star Wars thing? It sounds pretty good. When news of this reached Gorbachev in the Soviet Union, the comrades said, "Oh, crap! They are going to have an orbiting missile defense system! In space! We are going to have to spend millions and billions of research dollars to figure out how to get one of these too and we are already broke. We can't do it!"

SO LONG TO THE SOVIET: THE END

Gorbachev went to Reagan and said, "We will stop making these bombs, guns, and tanks, just don't do this Star Wars thing!" Reagan, in all of his wisdom, said, "Sorry, we can't; it is already built. We are too far along and can't stop now." This was a complete line of bull. There was nothing in space. Nothing was even tested. This huge bluff paid off because Gorbachev decided to throw up his hands and said, "Well, that's it then; we can't keep up. If we can't have a missile defense, that means you guys win. You could nuke us, so we quit. MAD is over and so are we!" This was when the USSR really fell down, around 1988 1989.

Several things collide here. The Soviet economy was in trouble, they had overextended themselves with their propaganda around the world and with Soviet aid in other countries. They had a war in Afghanistan with active fighting for 10 years, from 1979 to 1989, which proved to be disastrous. It took a huge toll in not only millions of dollars of equipment, but

"We're not MAD anymore; we're broke!"

also the death of 25,000 Russian soldiers. When all was said and done, they had not done anything there for 10 years. They failed to control Afghanistan, so they had to walk out of it. Glasnost and Perestroika are starting to be interpreted literally by Eastern Europeans and the Soviet people themselves, who were now calling for restructuring and/or independence. In 1989, the Soviet Union had to throw in the towel: "Poland, you want out? Go ahead. Estonia, Latvia, Lithuania, you want out too? I guess you guys are out as well. Central Asian republics, we're done with you too." It all disintegrated in very short order, and all those countries declared independence.

Fifteen new sovereign states emerged from the ashes of the USSR. The strings of the Soviet satellites' puppet governments were cut. The map was redrawn in one fell swoop. In 1990, they adopted economic and democratic reforms into what is left of the USSR, which became the United Federation of Russia. In 1991, Boris Yeltzin was elected president of Russia. He recognized the independence of all the countries that had declared it. In that same year, the newly formed Congress voted for the official and permanent dissolution of the USSR. It was no more. From 1991 forward, it was called Russia.

RADICAL RUSSIAN TRANSITION

By the 1990s, the commie threat was gone and the USSR was dismembered, so everything in Russia should be all champagne and caviar, right? Unfortunately, everything still sucked for Russia. It has gotten a lot better in the last few years, but we are going to carry it forward from 1991, when all this becomes official in today's world. That first decade of post-Soviet independence for the Ruskies sucked as bad as the decade before it. The pain of a radical transition had to be suffered through as they approached the 21st century. What kind of transition, and what kind of pain?

ECONOMY TAKES A DUMP

As we pointed out during the final decades of the Soviet Union, their economy was in bad shape, and changing their name doesn't change the facts. Now it's the "Russian" economy that sucked. Their industries were still in Cold War mindset and only produced big stuff like tanks and missiles that didn't have much use in today's world. You could still sell such items, but not nearly enough to rebuild an economy. They had tremendous problems with shifting their entire industrial sector to more capitalist-centered stuff, normal consumer goods. Capitalism was still a new concept for them, and they were still breaking in their capitalist cowboy boots. The transition from commie to capitalist was full of pitfalls and road bumps and full-on collisions, which made for an extremely rocky economic road to recovery.

On top of that, Russia lost its international status. They used to be "the other world power" but in the 1990s nobody would give them the time of day, much less a bank loan. This has changed in the last few years, but right after 1991, no one was willing to help Russia. Russia used to be a somebody, but now it was a nobody. It's also important to note that the USSR

The Bear gets skinned.

went from a singular sovereign entity to fifteen separate ones. It lost tremendous amounts of territory. Those other fourteen countries that weren't Russia were plots of land it no longer owned and there was the agriculture produced on that land, and mineral and energy resources under it, and the people who live on it were a workforce. Those are the basic foundations of economies. This territorial/resource loss was a tremendous blow to the Russian economy, an economy that was already hurting.

On top of this, you have to think about the Soviet era, during which the Soviets used a lot of resources from these countries. For example, most of the food production for the Soviet Union came from the Ukraine and Kazakhstan, which became separate countries. A lot of oil and natural gas came from Central Asia, and not only was Russia no longer profiting from these resources, it now had to buy those resources with cash money . . . and they used to own the stuff! It was a double-edged sword with both edges toward Russia. They were getting sliced and diced. Finally, most of the nuclear and weapons stockpiles were in what was Ukraine and Belarus, and there were a lot of expensive complications involved in destroying and/or relocating those weapons.

The second problem with the economy was the influence of organized crime: the Russian Mafia. Crime is everywhere, so organized crime is everywhere as well . . . but it is really strong in Russia. In fact, if you have ever seen adventure movies or international crime dramas, there is always a Russian mafia somewhere. They have always had a presence, even back in the days of communism when they created the Russian black market, which moved untaxed alcohol, weapons, and hardcore drugs. Indeed, they are still doing a tremendous job trafficking drugs and weapons internationally. They're also trafficking people. Yes, I did say people. A lot of the Russian mafia deals with the movement of women and children for sexual exploitation purposes. It's a fairly nasty business, but I guess that's what mafias do.

During the confusion and transformation of the Russian economy in the 1990's, these illegal criminal elements had a complete field day. The Soviet system was fairly corrupt internally to begin with, and that was perpetuated under free market capitalism where there are not a lot of rules. In addition, the government was broke and couldn't pay federal employees, such as the military and police. In such circumstances, corruption becomes endemic and easy to do at all levels. People do what they have to do to stay alive. The influence of organized crime is a major function of what is happening, even in today's Russia. Vladimir Putin himself came to power on a platform of being tough on crime, and in fact, nobody would be elected who is not.

This powerful criminal element in Russia not only stymies local business, but has negatively influenced international investment as well. But the open and outright blue-collar criminals were not alone in the 1990s. A new dimension of white-collar crime arose to give the underworld a run for their money (ha! Pun intended!): **the Oligarchs**.

OLIGARCHS OVER-DO IT

The **oligarchs** were white-collar criminals who, during the transition period of communism to democracy and capitalism in the 1990s, worked for the government or had insider ties with the government and bought whole industries and businesses under the table before they would go to auction. In communism, everything is owned by the state—all the oil, land, timber, energy production, everything. In capitalism, individuals own everything and the state owns virtually nothing. When a government goes from communism to capitalism, it starts selling everything. Ideally, this process would allow any individual the opportunity to buy former state industries at fair market prices. However, in Russia, this did not happen; most purchases were made by government insiders at rock bottom prices.

Here's an example: Yukos was Russia's oil company, a government owned oil company that was going to go privatize. If you knew some government officials when it was going up for sale and could get the price, and you knew people who worked at a bank, here is what you would do. You find out the day before the sale occurs and go to your friend at the bank and say, "Lend me half a billion dollars," with the promise that you will personally give him 100 million bucks as a bonus after repaying the loan. He smiles and you take the check for 500 million bucks from the bank over to the natural resources department to your buddy who is overseeing the sale of the oil company. You hand him the check for 500 million; he stamps it "sold" and

Top Five Russian Oligarchs			
Who?	What did he steal from the people?	How much? (USD)	Where is he now?
Roman Abramovich	Oil (Sibneft)	$14.7 Billion	In England, owns big-time soccer team Chelsea FC. Also owns four giant yachts and is building a fifth.
Vladimir Lisin	Aluminum and Steel	$7 Billion	Most likely sleeping in a pile of hundred dollar bills.
Viktor Vekselberg	Oil (Tyumen)	$6.1 Billion	Buying Faberge Eggs. Seriously, he digs them.
Oleg Deripaska	Aluminum (RUSAL)	$5.8 Billion	Hanging out with good friend Vladimir Putin.
Mikhail Fridman	Conglomeration of Valuable Things (Alfa Group)	$5.8 Billion	Lost much of his wealth in Russian tort suit—for stealing from the people, probably not enough evidence for criminal case.

hands you the deed to the oil company. You and your conspirators walk out together the next day as owners of this oil company, and sell it for 2 or 3 billion dollars, its true value, and then you go back and settle up your loan for 500 million with your banking friend and you split the rest. Congratulations! You have joined the ranks of the oligarchs! This was a really seedy big business tactic in the wild west of capitalism where there are no rules. These guys became ultra-millionaires and billionaires overnight.

What is the big deal with this? What's the problem? The Russian people got screwed, that's what. You have state owned resources whose sale should have contributed to the economic growth of an entire country, which instead turned into a billion dollars in a Swiss bank account under one man's name overnight. It was a legal transaction, apparently, but also a massive loss to the government.

In his rise to power, Vlad "the Man" Putin brought some of these crooks to justice—including Yukos head Mikhail Khodorkovsky, formerly the second richest man in Russia—although his motivation for doing so is questionable. It was likely a move designed to consolidate power more than a move to achieve justice.

Another platform in Vladimir Putin's campaign was, "I'm going after those Oligarchs! Going after crime and those chumps that robbed the Russian people!" That is one of the reasons he's such a popular leader. He is seen as a strong anticrime, pro-government force, and he's backed it up because the owner of Yukos is now sitting in jail. As a result, Putin helped Russia stabilize itself a little more. But maybe I am "Put-in" the cart before the horse in this story. . . .

PURGIN POPULATION

Another issue that is extremely problematic for Russia is the population itself. What's happening to the people in Russia? Russia's population is one of the classic examples, if not the classic example, of a population in decline: negative fertility rates and dropping birth rates. The population total is declining, with only about 150 million people in Russia; that number keeps getting smaller every year, which doesn't do much for Russia's economy. You need working people to keep things moving. A lot of things are going on that can account for Russia's demographic decline. It is hard to pinpoint a single factor, but nevertheless, the population is shrinking. Shrinkage is just the start of problems.

If we looked at some of the social indicators for what's happening in Russia, you would swear that you were looking at an African nation. The life expectancy for males is around 47 years, a little more than half that of the United States. You might guess this life expectancy for sub-Saharan Africa or Central Asia, but you typically would not think of Russia. Several things may be contributing to Russia's decline. One is *lack of health care*. Because of the collapse of the economy and the corruption associated with it, health care has become a huge issue. Access to good health care is almost nonexistent, but again, this may be changing. People aren't as healthy as they should be and don't have access to certain operations or preventive care. Drinking an average of 30 liters of vodka a year probably isn't helping matters either. Other unhealthy attributes include . . .

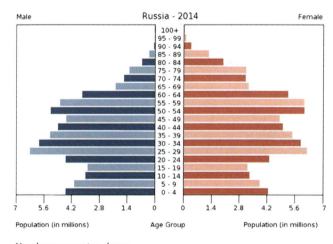

Numbers are going down.

ENVIRONMENT ENDANGERED

In its rapid industrialization, forced collectivization, and striving to catch up with the West to be a global power phase, the Soviet system completely ignored the environment. There was no limit to the amount of toxic spilling and dumping, or atomic weapons testing. Anything the Soviets could do to get ahead was done with the thought that once they won, they'd go back and clean everything up. Oops, they lost, and it's all still sitting there. Parts of the Kara Sea glow green sometimes from all of the accumulated toxic waste dumped into the river systems. Also, be sure to check out the Aral Sea as soon as you can, because it is disappearing due to misuse and pollution during the Soviet era. There are no less than fifty sites in Russia with pollution of catastrophic proportions. Don't forget to include all of the old nuclear weapons silos that are sitting around, deteriorating. There is impending environmental disaster on a large scale here, just based on past pollutions and degrading weapons. Russia has dealt with this huge problem during the last twenty years, with some international help from the United States and several others.

STOLEN SPHERE OF INFLUENCE: THE REALIGNMENT

The last thing you should be aware of in Russia right now is that a lot of its ex-territories and ex-states in its sphere of influence have now disappeared under radical realignment—much to the chagrin of Russia, because it still sees itself as a world player. What am I talking about? Eastern Europe is now desperately trying to become Western Europe by realigning with the West. Russia is losing its sphere of influence all over the place, though it's desperately trying to hold on. It is still actively courting Central Asia politically because there is a lot of oil and natural gas there. They are also courting China and want to keep good strategic ties there. It is really losing influence over Eastern Europe, and what's happening now only rubs it in their face.

That NATO expansion we talked about in previous chapters is still troubling the Russians. Something quite radical, that would have been unthinkable a decade ago, has happened: places like Poland, Hungary, and the Czech Republic joined NATO very quickly after they declared independence in 1991, mostly to ensure no further Russian influence. The next wave of folks was 2004 when Estonia, Latvia, Lithuania, Romania, and Bulgaria, places that were once firmly in Soviet control, joined NATO. Russia now finds that its former territories, which it sometimes harshly subjugated, are sovereign political entities that want nothing to do with it. They are NATO members and could theoretically have NATO weaponry pointed at Russia. This is a big loss of status and influence for Russia. Think about this in an abstract context. The Baltic States go from being owned by Russia, to ten years later being sovereign states with weapons pointed at Russia. That's a fairly big change. But the scales are starting to tip back to the Russian side. . . .

NATO creeps ever closer to the Ruskies.

RESURGENT RUSSIA: THE BAD BOYS ARE BACK!

Watch out! Things continue to change fairly rapidly for Russia, and it is the understatement of the century to say that things are looking up. Yes, I've talked about how crappy its economy has been. Yes, I've told you all about its people problems, its environmental problems, its crime problems, its international status problems. But what a difference one man can make, and the Russian man of the century is, with no doubt, Vladimir Putin. Putin, along with petroleum, has brought the Russians from the brink of the abyss back to world power status in less than a decade. There are a few other factors at play here as well that are serving to bring the Russian region back to a starring role on the world stage. Let's wrap up this chapter looking at this incredible reversal of Russian fortune.

"I can snap your neck with my bare hand. Enjoy your dinner."

PREZ TO PRIME BACK TO PREZ: PUTIN POWER!

This guy is unstoppable! So rarely in life can you truly credit a single individual with changing the course of history but, for better or for worse, that is an apt description for our main man Vlad. It's no wonder that Time magazine voted him Man of the Year for 2007—he really has made that big of a difference in his country, and in the world. Vladimir Putin is also easily the most bodacious beast of a leader on the planet: as a former KGB agent and judo blackbelt, he could handily whip the butt of any elected official on this side of the Milky Way. And the people love him! Putin held 60 to 80% approval ratings his entire eight years in office, and stepped down as President with closer to 90% love from the Russians. Stalin would have killed for that kind of popular support—oh, wait a minute, he did kill to get that kind of support. But I digress. Why all the love?

Putin is only the second president Russia has had. He was the hand-picked successor to Boris Yeltsin, a fairly popular leader in his own right. In his eight year run from 2000-2008, Putin oversaw the stabilization of the economic transition process that had thrown Russia into chaos for its first decade. He was tough on the oligarchs, and tough on crime, which helped stimulate international investment. He also took a fairly pro-active government role in helping Russian businesses, especially those businesses dealing with petroleum and natural gas. More on that in a minute. GDP grew sixfold, and propelled Russia from the 22nd largest economy up to the number ten slot. The economy grew 6–8% on average every year he was in office. Investment grew, industry grew, agricultural output grew, construction grew, salaries grew; pretty much every economic indicator you could look at has gone up during his tenure.

President? Prime Minister? It's all Putin to me!

Unlike most world leaders, Putin was very savvy with this cash flow too. He paid off all Russian debts. Imagine that: Russian National Debt = 0. Dang. That's legit. Putin also stashed billions, if not trillions, in a Russian "rainy day fund" that is set aside for any future hard times. How refreshing! Most leaders usually stash that extra cash in their personal Swiss bank accounts. But not Putin. No wonder Russians love him!

However, the love is not just based on economics. Vladimir Putin re-instilled a great sense of nationalism in his citizens. After the demise of the USSR, Russia was a second rate power with even less prestige, at the mercy of international business and banking and stronger world powers like the US, the EU, and NATO. Russia pretty much just had to go with the flow, even when events were inherently against their own national interest, like the growth of NATO, for example. Putin brought them back politically to a position of strength. He played hardball in international affairs, and re-invigorated a Russian national pride that has long laid dormant.

Back off, NATO! Putin is protectin' his 'hood!

Of course, this has come at a cost: Putin achieved a lot of this by consolidating power around his position, controlling a lot of state industries, cracking down on freedom of the press and free speech, and manipulating power structures of the government. In fact, he stepped down from the presidency in May 2008, and stepped immediately into the Prime Minister position the same day, maintaining a lot of command and control of the system simultaneously. That crafty Russian fox! He is increasingly reviled and even hated by Team West because people see him as leaning back towards totalitarianism, but also because he increasingly clashes with western foreign policy on the international stage. **2014 Update:** After a little constitutional "correction" which changed the term length of office from 4 to 6 years, Vladimir Putin was once again elected President in 2012 and assumed the top office. He is in the Russian hizzle until 2018, and possibly to 2024 if re-elected again. Another Putin decade looms large. . . .

But hold the phone! I keep talking about Putin, and have completely dissed the other guy who held the top slot in the "in-between Putin" years. Let's remedy that right now! Dmitry Medvedev was the hand-picked successor to Putin, and was President from 2008 to 2012 when he basically stepped down by refusing to even run for a second term, allowing Putin to walk back into the position. He pretty much followed and even strengthened virtually all of Putin's policies, and was therefore considered by many in the west as a mere Putin puppet. There could be some truth to that. However, he did have the popular support of the Russian population, and why on earth would he stray too far off of the successful path that Putin had paved? Answer: he didn't. What he did do in

My main man Medvedev.

Medvedev and Putin: the Russian Dynamic Duo

office was to start a massive military makeover which seeks to revamp and remodel the Russian armed services into a state-of-the-art ultra-modern military that will certainly be causing consternation for the US and Team West in the future.

Dig this: there is already speculation that the Russian constitution will be amended to allow Putin to run for president again, in essence, scrapping their term limits. Given the rabid popularity of both men, I think their policies are here to stay for some time. Or perhaps forever. **2012 Update:** Ummm . . . yep. That happened. And Medvedev is now the Prime Minister. A perfect position swap occurred.

In conclusion, Putin power is not to be underestimated. Perhaps 12 more years as President, and if not, he can hold the Prime Minister position indefinitely either way, so he will be around for some time to come. The Russians love him for making them strong, and making them rich and making them proud again. Let's look at some specifics of how he pulled this off and the implications for the future.

PETRO POWER!

Putin is awesome. On that point we are clear. However, we do have to at least partially, if not fully, credit his great success in turning the Bear around on this one single commodity: petroleum. Dudes! Russia has made total bank on oil and natural gas in the last decade. To understand the importance of oil for Russia, one need only consider this: when the USSR crashed in 1991, the price of a barrel of oil was about $10. In 2008, the price of a barrel of oil approached $150. The price may have dropped a bit since, but oil is still the preferred energy source of choice for the entire planet. My friends, you should know this: Russia has a ton of oil! Look at the map! You do the math!

Increasingly, Russia has also reeled in all control of the petro industries to the state. They **privatized** a lot of those industries back in the 1990s, but they have been busy **nationalizing** a lot of them back since 2000. Remember those terms

Sometimes having a lot of gas is a very good thing: Russia may become the center of a natural gas OPEC-like cartel!

from Chapter 4? Russia sure does. It now has controlling interest in virtually all the oil and natural gas businesses in the country, which even more of the profits swing back directly to the state.

To reiterate a few points from this chapter and the last: oil = power for Russia. Economic and political and international power, that is. Not only have they paid off their foreign debt with oil money, they have re-invested that oil money back into their economy, and also set up their rainy day fund with oil dollars. Since the Russians supply one third of European energy demand, this gives them all sorts of economic and political leverage over their Eurasian neighbors. Mess with Putin, and you might not have heating oil next winter. But the Europeans aren't the only ones who need oil. Look eastward and you see Japan and China both vying for petro resources. Russia is really sitting pretty right now. Energy master of the continent!

GLOBAL WARMING? NO SWEAT!

I can't get out of this section without referencing the global warming situation. While the rest of the planet may be wringing their hands in a collective tizzy about rising temperatures, melting polar ice caps, and rising sea levels, let me assure you that Russia is not sweating the situation at all. Ha! Not sweating the warming—am I good or what?

Seriously though, think of the strategic benefits that are being bestowed upon Russia as the thermometer continues to creep upward every year. Russia has forever been a land empire due to its lack of accessible and navigable coastlines. Additionally, almost all of its river systems empty into the ice-locked Arctic Ocean, making them essentially useless for transportation and exporting commodities. But just wait! As the permanent ice cap covering the North Pole disappears, Russia will become more open to the world like never before in recorded human history!

"Comrades, the North Pole is ours now. Bye-bye, Santa!"

You may not be paying attention to any of this, but the Russians sure are. In preparations for its ice-free northern coastlines of the future, Russia is staking a claim to the entire Arctic sea east of the North Pole. Seriously, I'm not making this up. The race for the Arctic has begun! Russia stands to be the biggest beneficiary as well. Not only will it open up their territory for greater sea and land access, and greater export power, but it is widely believed that there are massive oil reserves in the Arctic basin, reserves which will become accessible once the ice is gone. Russia is all about the global warming! Let's get this party started! No, actually let's end it with. . . .

GEOPOLITICAL JUMP START

You got your Putin, and you got your petroleum, and you add to that a huge dose of nationalistic pride. Bake for twenty minutes, and you end up with an extremely resurgent and resilient Russian cake on the world political table. These guys are playa's once again. Their huge economy, their huge oil reserves, and their huge potential for the future is fast becoming the envy of the world. They can afford to play the fence when suitors come calling. What do I mean by that?

Russia has been invited to become a strategic partner state of the EU— not a full-fledged member, mind you, but a partner. Europe realizes that the Russian economy and Russian energy is such an integral part of their own lives, that to not have Russia at the table for major decisions would be folly. Russia has a real impact on some EU policy. The same can be said of NATO. While Russia is not a member, the group realizes that almost all major decision-making should involve the Russians since they play such an increasingly important role in Eurasian affairs. Russia is typically invited to major NATO summits now. Why doesn't Russia just join the EU and NATO fully?

Because the Russians are forging economic and strategic political ties to their east as well, mostly with China. They are at a historical east/west pivot point right now; they are straddling the fence about which relationships to make or break. I think they're being extremely savvy and are going to avoid taking sides in anything. Could Russia join the EU? It's already a strategic partner of the EU. I bet it will be invited to join as a full-fledged member, but I also bet it will decline.

Why? It is also strategic partners with China, the other huge economy on the other side of the continent. Russia will not be stymied economically by joining a club that can possibly limit their economic options. The Bear is also still a major player in Central Asia, an area with tons of natural gas and oil that has to be moved out of Central Asia to the rest of the world that wants it. That oil and natural gas usually moves out through Russian territory, supplying most of the fuel for Eastern and Western Europe, in addition to increasingly supplying fuel for Japan, China and India.

Beyond the geopolitical ramifications of energy and economics, Russia is back in full action militarily speaking! Big time! You do know that, in August 2008, Russia invaded the Georgian regions of South Ossetia and Abkhazia, right? It currently still occupies these areas, and has gone as far as to recognize their declared independence, which is infuriating the US and Team West as a whole.

You will have to turn to chapter 25 to get all the details of this conflict and its future ramifications, but I just want you to know this for now: Russia is back! The Russian–Georgian War did not change the balance of power in this region, it simply was an announcement that the shift in the balance of power had already occurred!

Russia is now openly and powerfully reasserting its influence in its own backyard, and that is a big deal. Russia now feels that it has regained a position of strength to not only stand up to what it sees as threatening Team West expansion to its borders, but to stop that advance with force if necessary. With guns! This open, bold, and even proud use of force by the Russians has changed the whole attitude of the US, NATO, and even the EU when it comes to political maneuvers near the Russian border. The bear has lashed out!

At the risk of redundant repetition, what supranationalist organizations are the Russians all about if they don't really want to play with the EU and NATO? Well, remember the BRIC? They dig that one, and it should be noted that BRIC is specifically not a "Western" institution. Of even greater significance is the SCO. Flip back to chapter 6 or ahead to the Central Asia chapter to get the full run-down on this group, but just let me tease you for now by telling you this much: the SCO is going to be a bizarre cross between an Asian version of NATO and a Russian version of OPEC, and Russia has every intention of being the leader of this grand experiment. Stalin would be proud.

DON'T LIKE PUTIN? CRIMEA RIVER!

Holy wowsers huge 2014 update on resurgent Russia! Unless you have been hiding under Vladimir Putin's pectoral muscles, you have heard about Russia invading, occupying, and now completely absorbing the Crimean Peninsula, in what was formerly Ukraine! Full details of this Putin Peninsula pinch can be found in Chapter 25: The Cover Story, but I just had to at least give it a shout out here. This is a huge deal. A re-defining sovereignty in the modern world deal. A re-defining of Russia's place in the world deal. And a possible start to an expansionist era of Russia that sees them take back territories that contain ethnically Russian peoples. These peeps are partying like it's 1799, because no one has seen such old-school style empire building for almost a century.

And in that light, let me introduce you to a new organization to be used to expand the Ruskies' reach: The Eurasian Union. While originally an idea posed by Kazak President Nursultan Nazarbayev, the Eurasian Union, is without a doubt the wet dream of Russian President Vladimir Putin, who now openly seeks to reassert a resurgent Russian influence and outright power into areas it lost during the collapse of the Soviet Union in 1991. It is being proposed as a economic/political trade block alternative to the EU . . . and one that has Russia at the center. Belarus and Kazakhstan are already in; Armenia wants in; other states are being pressured hard to join, or possibly face the wrath of Russia. More details on this will be released in other regions, as well as the aforementioned Cover Story chapter.

Crimean crisis just the start of the show?

Yeah. That should do it. Problem solved.

But know this for now: the Crimea craziness is a gargantuan gambit by Putin to expand the power, influence, and control of Russia to other states . . . and so far, so good, for the victorious Vladimir and his legion of fans . . . which includes the vast majority of Russian peeps who support him totally. As in totalitarian. Which is where it looks like this is going. Yikes!

GHOST OF STALIN RETURNS

Which is a good jumping off point. I guess any mention of Joseph Stalin is a good point to get the heck out of Dodge. I want to leave you with this: the memory of Smokin' Joe Stalin is actually being softened in today's Russia, and that is a very telling sign of what's happening in the society. Some folks in Russia are looking back with pride at what most of us consider one of the worst dictators in history. Why? This vibrant and growing economy, this resurgent world role, and this overall restored sense of Russian greatness has not been felt since the Stalin era, and quite frankly, the Russians are quite proud to be Russian again.

Add in trillions of petro dollars, increasing empire due to global warming, and a renewed sense of global political power, and you got yourself a region that will be shaping world events of the future. Growl! The Bear is back!

Team West taught the Russians too well about that capitalism stuff!

The Regions
PART TWO

RUSSIAN RUNDOWN & RESOURCES

View additional Plaid Avenger resources for this region at http://plaid.at/ru

BIG PLUSES

- Biggest state by land area, one that is extremely rich in virtually all natural resources
- Specifically, a huge oil and natural gas producer: energy resources critical to world economy
- Virtually no national debt
- Regained sense of national pride and political world leadership
- Has veto power at the UN Permanent Security Council
- Has as many nuclear bombs as the US, if not more, as well as a serious military, second only to the US.
- Is a founding member of some of the most promising future international coalitions like BRIC and SCO
- Is still considered quite important to the EU and NATO too, enough to get invited to the meetings.
- Global warming? No problem for Russia! Will increase usable land area and resource base

BIG PROBLEMS

- Gi-normous size problematic for infrastructure, defense, and cultural cohesiveness.
- Economy and social structures, like health care, still not fully recovered from Soviet era crash
- Male longevity rates are lower than most African countries; alcoholism rates among the highest in the world
- Population overall is shrinking.
- Organized crime, rampant corruption, and tax evasion have seriously stymied international investment and hinder internal development
- Economy still heavily reliant on exporting natural resources, mostly energy.
- Has some of the worst environmental disaster areas on the planet
- Anti-immigrant, anti-foreigner, and flat out racism are significant issues in Russia

DEAD DUDES OF NOTE:

Tsar Nicholas II: Last of the royal Romanov line, and last monarch of Russia, who was assassinated along with his whole family in 1918. His piss poor rule transformed Russia into an economic and military disaster which helped fuel the revolution which left the commies in charge.

Rasputin: The un-kill-able "Mad Monk" who recommended that Tsar Nicholas get Russia involved in World War I. He didn't instigate the royal family's demise, but he sure as hell accelerated it. May still be alive somewhere in hell.

Vladimir Lenin: "Father of the USSR" Passionate organizer, orator, and propagandist who led the Russian Revolution of 1917, in which he implemented the first ever communist experiment at the state scale. Then he died.

Joseph Stalin: The semi-psychotic who took over control of the USSR after Lenin's death. Formed the KGB, purged out all political adversaries, and may have been responsible for the deaths of 30 million Russians. But, he also oversaw the industrialization and expansion of the USSR into a world power, and helped kill the Nazis in WWII. So it's a mixed bag.

Nikita Khrushchev: Leader of the USSR at what was perhaps the height of the Cold War. Was the bonehead that decided to put Soviet missiles in Cuba pointed at Florida, which brought the world to the brink of nuclear war aka the Cuban Missile Crisis of 1962.

PLAID CINEMA SELECTION:

Prisoner of the Mountains (1996) Set in the Caucus Mountains with incredible scenery, this quiet "war film" is set during the First Chechen War . . . while the war itself was still happening! Themes to watch for: cultural differences in the region and the piss-poor state of the Russian military in the early 90's. Still topical, as tensions with Chechnya are still part of current events.

Tale in the Darkness (2009) A Russian independent film, which strives to explore the life of a female police officer in Far East Russia. This drama reaches a sort of "Men are from Mars, women are from Venus" conclusion.

Burnt by the Sun (1994) Set in USSR circa 1936, this film shows the effects of Stalin's insane political purges of his own peoples, even those loyal to him. A Soviet war hero on summer retreat at his dacha with his family becomes the target of KGB investigation and elimination.

Siberiade (1979) A film about the small village of Yelan hidden in the backwoods of Siberia. This epic, four part film shows the evolution of the small village until at the end of the film, it is no longer remote, as oil has been found in the village. Show realistic evolution of Russian culture as well as providing an early reflection of the processes of globalization.

Newsmakers (2009) A crime drama set in Moscow whose plot involves a savvy female detective setting up a real-life reality TV show as a ruse to flush out a criminal gang that got the better of the cops in a live shoot-out.

Oligarkh aka *Tycoon* (2002) Not a great film, but does chronicle the conversion of soviet command economy to full-on unrestrained capitalism that occurred as the USSR imploded. Greed, corruption, and cronyism via a personal storyline.

Brat aka *Brother* (1997) Hardcore bleak and gritty realistic gangster film in St. Petersburg that epitomizes the way it works at the local level in Russia. No big money or flash here, just desperate people who do desperate things. Spawned a whole culture of glorifying young gangsters in films, often called "keelers," much like gangsta' rap did in the US.

Nochnoy dozor aka *Night Watch* (2004) Okay this one is just for fun, and to throw a monkey-wrench into the film mix. This is a Russian vampire/wizard/good vs. evil/horror film that is now one of the highest grossing films in their history. It's *The Matrix* of Moscow.

LIVE LEADERS YOU SHOULD KNOW:

Mikhail Gorbachev: Oversaw the collapse of the USSR, implemented the glasnost and perestroika policies, and helped bring the Cold War to a peaceful end. Is a hero to the West and won the Nobel Peace Prize, but looked upon almost as a traitor in Russia.

Vladimir Putin: Current President of Russia, having previously served as such from 2000–2008, got Russia's mo-jo back, got them rich, and got them powerful again on the world stage. Look for him to be in Russian politics indefinitely.

Dmitry Medvedev: Current Prime Minister of Russia, the Putin right-hand man. Many think he is merely a Putin puppet, but has so far shown himself to be an adept and strong leader in his own right who is continuing the successful Putin policy legacy.

Sergey Lavrov: Current Russian Foreign Minister, which is the equivalent of the US Secretary of State, the head diplomat of the country. This dude is wickedly smart, savvy, and has been behind the scenes making sure Russia regains its power status on the world stage.

CHAPTER OUTLINE

1. G'Day, Mates!
2. Let's Go for a Walkabout
3. America, Junior
   - 3.1 Background
   - 3.2 Societal Structures
4. Awesome Ally
5. A Word on Their Weird Way to Wealth
6. Pacific Shift
   - 6.1 Economically
   - 6.2 Politically
   - 6.3 The Peeps
7. No Worries
8. A Sinister Show and Tell

Australia and New Zealand

G'DAY, MATES!

We're heading south from Japan to our friends in the Australia and New Zealand region. When the Plaid Avenger is traveling around the world and can't make it back home to America, I just stop off in Australia, or as I like to call it, the **Mini-America of the southern hemisphere**. If you ever want to fire up people from Australia, just pass that along. It infuriates them for some reason. They tell the Plaid Avenger that they're distinctly Australian and unique in their own way. Yeah, right! You dudes and dudettes are exactly the same as us: albeit an European and American 21st-century cultural-amalgamation-sensation south of the Equator!

The Plaid Avenger is always straight shooting, so I am not going to lie to you; this region is not one of tremendous significance on the world stage. But like Japan, it does play its part to effect current events and regional activities. Its primary role right now is as a platform of European culture and US foreign policy in the southern hemisphere. Even that is changing quickly of late as the mates from "down under" are shifting their political and economic focus to be more in tune with their Asian 'hood. But I am getting ahead of myself. Let's first focus our attention on the physical traits of the region.

LET'S GO FOR A WALKABOUT

Physically, Australia and New Zealand are two island countries, even though Australia is classified as a continent. If you look at it, it's really just a big island. They are two islands of extremes. In Australia, the vast majority of the interior is desert and steppe. It's very similar to the American Midwest. There's a bunch of cattle ranching going on; it's

Area comparison.

Lights out in the middle!

Deserted desert interior in Australia

the outback, after all, but there aren't too many people there. In fact, a massive percentage of the interior of Australia is so dry, it has promoted a primarily coastal settlement pattern. Everybody's hanging out on the coast and the vast majority of Australia's population is located on these coastal margins, particularly the southeastern coastal margin.

As you can see from the lights at night, virtually everybody is on the east coast of Australia. Before we go any further, let me begin pointing out the parallels between Australia and America. Here is one outlined for you on the map: population primarily in coastal areas, with a high concentration on the eastern seaboard. In New Zealand, we have the same pattern, but for different reasons. New Zealand, much like Japan, is a mountainous country. In fact, Japan and New Zealand are almost identical. They are both island nations, made of several different islands, and both are on the borders of major continental plates; both are volcanic in origin, so the interior of the country is very mountainous. The terrain makes it a no-brainer for most people to live on the coast, especially those little hobbits which seem to be over-running the country here lately. Gandalf, help us!

New Zealand: mountainous center spine

Climatically speaking, these two countries are opposites. New Zealand is cooler and wetter, with a climate more like the Pacific Northwest section of the US, or even like the UK. Australia has some Mediterranean style climates on the southern coastlines, and even a little tropic savanna-type areas in the north, but the interior is largely steppe and desert; a dry area with limited rainfall, few trees, and scrub and short grass vegetation. What are those climates good for? Cattle and sheep production. There is a lot of grazing action going on in Australia. Big exports of wool, lamb, and beef.

One last physical note: what Australia lacks climatically, it more than makes up for in physical resources. They have tons of coal, iron, copper, opal, zinc, and uranium. Put that together with the agricultural commodities, and you have a serious export base to work with. Think about that for a second; what types of countries mainly export primary products? Hold that thought, we'll be back to it soon enough.

AMERICA, JUNIOR

Why does the Plaid Avenger refer to this region as the mini-America of the south? Where do many people from America who like to travel abroad want to go? Australia! Why? Because it's just like home! People want to see the same stuff, eat the same stuff, and speak the same language as in the US, because they are more comfortable in that setting. It's far enough away that you think you're actually being adventurous! There's actually something to the idea of Australia just being a transplanted southern piece of America or Europe, but just "down under." Down under the equator, that is.

Australia is quite unique in the southern hemisphere of this planet for a couple of reasons. For one, it's the only region in the southern hemisphere that is habitated primarily by white, English-speaking, European descent-type people. It's also the only region south of the equator that is totally rich and developed. It has standards of living and material wealth on par with that of Western Europe, Japan, and the US, and no other region south of the equator can say that, yet. The standard of living thing is another reason why Australia is the Mini-America of the south. But oh, there's so much more.

BACKGROUND

Why is Australia so white? Because it was colonized by the pasty British white peoples, of course! Both the US and Australia were originally British **convict colonies.** In the UK back in the day (in the 1600's and 1700's), one of the subsidiary purposes of Britain's colonies was to get rid of British criminals. Britain was perhaps slightly overpopulated, and laws were very strict. The historical anecdote that explains this fairly well is the establishment of the **baker's dozen.** The baker's dozen is 13 instead of 12. Why? There was actually a law that stated if a baker shorted you a donut, he could be put in jail. So the baker's dozen was born. Throw in an extra one, because who the hell wants to go to jail over a donut?

This was a pretty legally strict society where lots of people got tossed into jail for sometimes menial offenses. Among the options given to convicts were the gallows or a boat ride to a colony. Guess which one people chose? You know there is a 'criminal' element to America's background, and the same goes for Australia. Here's the funny part: the British used to ship their convicts to their American colony, so when did they start shipping them to Australia? Right around the 1780s. Why is that? In 1776, America had a revolution, and we kicked those British tea-sipping, prisoner-exporters out, eliminating the US as their felon-absorbing resource. The British, who were floating around the world, figured out that they had claimed a huge chunk of land down in the southern hemisphere. Look at that, a place to send convicts! Australia was established in 1788 as a convict colony, in part because the British couldn't send them to America anymore.

SOCIETAL STRUCTURE

How else is Australia like America? Let me count the ways. If we look at virtually any facet of life in this part of the world, we can look at America and see that it's pretty much the same. Let's start listing them off, shall we? Australia is a highly **urbanized** society. There are roughly identical urbanization rates between Australia and the US. This point is of significance because everybody has the opposite impression about Australia. Everybody thinks they're all about the outback, the Crocodile Hunter, and Crocodile Dundee. There are all these wild and crazy guys down there! However, if you ask any Australian how much time they spend in the outback, "You've got to be kidding me, mate," is a likely response.

Peeps are largely coastal urbanites.

Why is that? Quite simply, the outback sucks. It's crazy that anybody would want to go to the outback. It has all kinds of dangerous creatures in it, spiders that will jump onto your face, the top ten poisonous snakes in the world, and so on. Nobody wants to go out in "the bush." It is a classic mythology of Australia. It sounds cool, makes them seem all brave and manly, but nobody hangs out in the interior of Australia. Most people live in cities and suburbs, which you are all probably familiar with. They are all content to stay out of the outback, and have the nice little picket fence around their manicured suburban lawns.

And this relates to the standard of living. This is a very rich place. Per capita, it is on par with the US and Western Europe and any other rich place. Standards of living, levels of technology, material wealth: this region is staunchly in the 'fully developed' category. People live there just like they live in the US, and have all of the same creature comforts. This reiterates why nobody is out in the wild, because rich people go and see the wild when they're on vacation, and then they get the heck out of there because the wild sucks.

One of the reasons why they have a high standard of living: there are not a whole lot of people living in Australia. Australia and New Zealand populations are extremely low, only about 28 million folks across this entire region . . . 23 mil in Aussie-land, and less than 5 mil in NZ. New York City, L.A. and Tokyo each have bigger populations than the entire continent of Australia! Look at the population pyramid! As stable as stable gets. Only through immigration will the population of the region increase, much like the US. But there's more!

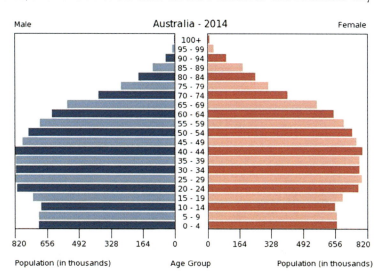

A stable yet small population.

Australia also has similar dietary habits, which ties back in with standards of living. They are big meat consumers, just like in the US. The only big difference is that the Americans like to slay the cows and eat hamburgers, but the Australians are all about lamb. They love to silence the lambs. And then eat them . . .

They are also big beer and wine drinkers, like the US. In most places that were colonized by Western Europeans, the beer and wine tradition

Lambs! How cute.

And how delicious!

still exists. Australia is one of the booming wine regions now, soon to be the number one wine exporter on the planet.

Perhaps the Plaid Avenger is getting too shallow, talking about standards of living and beer and meat consumption. Let's get back on point. What other parallels are there?

This may just seem like a funny side note, but this may play a part in why the two nations are so similar today. Both countries have a criminal background, a criminal profile; remember, they started as convict colonies. How has that played into today's society? This is a stretch, but stay with me. What do people like to do in both of these societies? We've already pointed out the beer drinking thing: both are beer drinking societies, and both like to party. What else do they like to do while consuming alcoholic beverages? I don't know—watch brutal sports? Yes! The Americans have their football, Australians have rugby. And the Aussies are even more hardcore than the US: they take the pads off and beat the crap out of each other, while everyone who isn't playing drinks beer and watches.

On a more serious note, each country has a rugged, individualistic archetypal character. The Americans have the Marlboro man, a lone, rugged warrior out on the plains, wrangling cows and looking out for coyotes. That's part of the common symbology, the perception of what it is to be an American. He embodies individualistic pride. They've got the same stuff down in Australia, except they wrangle crocs and look out for dingoes. Do these types of characters represent the majority of either place? No, but these characters are popular symbols in this society. There really aren't these archetypal figures anywhere else in the world. It may be partially due to the fact that both places have large expanses of land with low population density. They have frontiers, and there has to be the rugged individual to explore those frontiers.

Here's another similarity between Australia and the US: the settling convicts exterminated nearly the entirety of their respective native populations. There is a history of repression of native peoples in both places. In the US, it

was the Native Americans, the Amerindians. In Australia they had the Aborigines; New Zealand have the Maori. All of those peoples suffered immensely in the onslaught of British colonization in exactly the same ways. And it was particularly bad in Australia.

In Tasmania, an island off of the south coast, there were some indigenous people called the Tasmanians who were openly hunted during a period of the settlement of Australia. The government essen-

American Cowboy.

Australian Cowboy.
See the difference?

tially said, "Hey, settlers, want some free land? Go down to Tasmania! If the natives give you any trouble, don't feel bad about killing them." It became a sport to go out and hunt the indigenous Tasmanians. This was done so efficiently that they killed all of them. Every. Last. One. That's the criminal background manifesting itself in one of the nastier ways in history.

Another historical consideration of why both societies evolved out this frontiersman mythology has to do with how both countries grew. Both started on the eastern seaboard of a large uncharted land mass, and proceeded to expand and conquer the continents in a continuous westward expansion. Interesting, isn't it? Australia even underwent a western "Gold Rush" at almost the exact same time as the famous Californian rush of the same name, but with one slight difference: theirs was more profitable!

Brutal sports, slaughter of indigenous populations, mostly white, cowboy image, and even the English language all play into the cultural baggage of the US and Australia. This is why the Plaid Avenger refers to it as the Mini-America of the south.

Put all these historical, physical, and cultural factors together and you are starting to get a sense of why the Plaid Avenger draws so many parallels between the US and Australians region. But you don't have to take my word for it! There is proof a'plenty that these two states have a tight relationship: let's just take a look at their foreign policies for a minute.

AWESOME ALLY

When it comes to Team West foreign policy, one could not find a better friend than those Aussie mates. They have been there year in and year out for their western allies, for every single international conflict and conflagration. We can be even more specific: first, Australia has always supported every endeavor of the old British motherland, and then later came on board for all things American. This bunch really sticks together.

The 'Roo Brigade will always be ready to serve freedom!

I'm not talking about supporting them on paper, or in a UN vote, or economically. I'm talking about Australians participating side by side with their English-speaking brothers-in-arms in World War I, World War II, the Korean War, the Vietnam War, the Cold War, the War on Terror, which has spawned the two newest Aussie supported wars: the campaign in Afghanistan and the war in Iraq. Every conflict, every time, they are there for the West. Check out one of Mel Gibson's first starring roles in a movie named *Gallipoli*, about Aussie troops fighting the Turks way back in WWI.

Being a small country with a small population, the numbers of Australian forces that have participated in these conflicts is not a huge number, but it's the thought that counts, especially when the thought is a bunch of dudes with submachine guns. But I digress. Point is, that they have regularly been looked to as a vote of support for western ideology worldwide; most currently, counting themselves as one of the "Coalition of the Willing" in the lead up to the Iraq War. They are the only folks south of the equator you can say that about.

So historically strong are the Australian/American ties that the Plaid Avenger counts them among the three most reliable, solid platforms of US foreign policy in the world. The UK, Japan, and Australia can be counted on to support US endeavors, almost with no questions asked. In the past, this essentially made these countries the American lapdogs in terms of foreign policy, but times do change.

While I stand by the description of Australia as a loyal ally of the US, modern times have forced them to be more pragmatic. Sometimes, being a loyal ally has to be pulled back due to popular opinion. Most Australians were opposed to the US-led invasion of Iraq, and the government at that time did take a popularity hit for its staunch participation. In addition, the Aussies and the Kiwis are having to adapt to a world which sees the rise of Asian powers, as is the rest of the world. But while this region remains entrenched as part of Team West, they have to start being much more sensitive to the feelings of their Asian trading partners . . . which is increasingly putting them between a US rock and a Chinese hard place. More on that later.

But one need look no further than **ANZUS** to prove the tight relationship between these Pacific partners. ANZUS—The Australia, New Zealand, United States Security Treaty—is a binding military alliance between the states signed after WW2 that is extremely similar to NATO Article 5, meaning an attack on any is considered an attack on all. It primarily focuses on the security in the Pacific, although the treaty in reality is related to conflicts worldwide.

ANZUS on the ready, sir!

Unlike NATO, the countries do not have a fully integrated defense structure, nor a dedicated active force waiting on the sidelines ready to go. However, this three-way defense pact is a commitment to defend and coordinate defense policy in the Pacific, and includes joint military exercises, standardizing equipment, and joint special forces training. In addition, the Aussies are host to several joint defense facilities, mainly ground stations for spy satellites and signals intelligence espionage for Southeast and East Asia. Oh China! The Aussies are watching you! Well, maybe its the Americans in Aussie-land that are watching you!

As an interesting side note, New Zealand was "uninvited" from ANZUS from 1984 to 2012, because back in the 80's they declared their country a "nuclear-free zone" and thus refused to let any US navy ships that were nuclear-powered or nuclear-armed come into their territorial waters. Of course that ticked off Uncle Sam mightily, and got the kiwis kicked out of the club. But the world has changed, and the US needs their Pacific allies more than ever, so in 2012 Barack Obama officially ended the ostracization, and the ANZUS crew is stronger than ever . . . and what timing! Why would I say that?

Because also in 2012, the US and Australia announced the FIRST EVER permanent US military base on Aussia soil. It was originally proposed as a small coastal station way up north in Darwin (Northern Territory) that would be home to a few dozen Marines . . . and within 6 months it was expanded to house closer to 2500 US military service personnel. I predict it will likely get even bigger in the future. I also have insider tips from some Marine friends of mine that there are covert bases already in NZ as well. Can you say "countering Chinese influence in the Pacific"? I knew you could! Interesting times my friends!

A WORD ON THEIR WEIRD WAY TO WEALTH

This is where things get a bit trickier, so the Plaid Avenger is going to have to sort a few things out for you. We've made it expressly clear that the US is the powerhouse economy of the planet, but China, at number four, is catching up. Japan is at the number two slot and Germany's at number three. Where's Australia? It's in fifteenth place. In terms of total GDP, how rich is this place? Not very. However, in levels of material wealth per person, they are totally awesome. How could this be? How could they have a standard of living identical to ours if they are not a huge exporter of manufactured goods or technology or other rich stuff? It is a strange circumstance, and perhaps a unique circumstance to Australia, that when we think of features that make it the most unique, it's not an exceptionally wealthy place as a total.

Australian number one export. Talk about a return on investment! Ha! Boomerang? Return? Get it?

What do they produce? What do they really do? What do you buy from there? Do they make computers? Cars? Linens? DVD players? Software? Video games? I don't think so. What have you ever bought that said, "Made in Australia"? Here's the quick answer: didgeridoos and boomerangs. That's not much of an export economy to put them among some of the wealthiest countries in the world. Well, that's not what has made them wealthy.

Australia is perhaps the only country in the fully developed world that has gotten rich from the export of *primary products*. And it is still a big part of what they do. Remember that primary products are things extracted from the earth like coal, oil, minerals, diamonds, uranium, wool, cattle, and meat. What is all this stuff worth? When it comes right down to it, not worth much. They are a bunch of unprocessed materials. How can the Aussies be rich if they are doing stuff that poor countries do? Well, for starters, there are only 23 million peeps in the entire country, and it's the size of

the US. They export so many goods because of the resource-rich land, and the wealth generated from that is spread between so few that they are rich overall. A pretty big GDP based on natural resources, divided by a small number of peeps, makes for a really high GDP per capita number.

But don't let the Plaid Avenger lead you too far astray. If you look at the numbers, over 60% of the workforce is in the service sector, but who are they serving? Pretty much just themselves. Seriously, no innuendo implied. They work in malls and mailrooms and breweries and bakeries and accounting and telemarketing centers. They produce computers and cars, but many of the manufacturing facilities are owned and operated by multinational companies (my favorite example: the Subaru Outback—a car named for Australia, made by a Japanese company), and the products are only built to be consumed in Australia. In other words, they make Apple computers there, because people there want Apple computers. They are not exported out of Australia. There are no cars or refrigerators exported from Australia. That's because they are too busy making serious bank on exports of primary commodities. Their internal economy has enough juice to keep them going and growing, but it is a matter of low population and lots of primary resource wealth that makes for such high GDP per capita. They are the only place on the planet that I know of that has gotten away with that. Bottom line: they may have 65% of the people in the service sector, but they make 65% of their total GDP on exports of primary products.

You'll often see information about sheep and lamb being a huge export to places like the Middle East, since they consume more lamb than they do things like beef and chicken. You'll also see information about the coal and oil that Australia has being exported to places like China and Japan, both of which are hungry for those energy resources. Australia also signed a uranium deal with China on April 4, 2006, to export raw uranium to be processed and used. No other "rich" country on the planet is exporting raw commodities at this scale. Everybody else processes things, because that's where the money is. It's fascinating that their primary source of income is from raw products. They are definitely an economic conundrum of the rich/fully developed world.

Throw him on the barbie, I dare you.

PACIFIC SHIFT

What is in Australia's future? To answer that we might ask ourselves what's changing, because while we've been saying that this is the mini-America of the south, things are definitely on the move.

ECONOMICALLY

As China and other Asian states increases in world power and wealth and are requiring more resources, Australia is reorienting its economic focus to nearby countries in Asia—instead of trading primarily with other white English-speaking countries like the US and Great Britain. In the past, these two countries were the primary trading partners with Australia. Seriously, what a pain it is to ship exports that far. It's a long commute for meetings and it's difficult to maintain trading relationships with their white, English-speaking allies. They're on the other side of the planet! Nothing, other than fine Australian wine can be shipped all the way across the world anymore and still turn a profit.

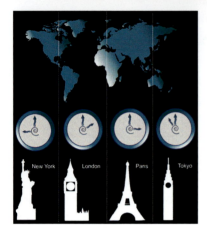
Aussies really on Tokyo time

Also, consider what impact longitude has on trade relationships. If you are at the same longitude, you are in the same time zone. Now, Australia is doing business in real time, during their business day, instead of having to deal with the massive time difference between it and other trading partners like the US and Europe. It's a tremendous complication to be awake when your trading partners are asleep.

They have reoriented their trade relationships to more local areas are neighboring regions like southeast Asia, China and Japan. "Why continue trading with the white people that look like us, when we can make lot more money trading with the Asian people that don't look like us?" Money talks. This is the way it is. Plus, the booming economies and large populations of Asian countries make for a much bigger demand on Aussie resources. Team West economies have been stagnant or slow growing, while China and ASEAN countries have been on fire with economic growth. And they are closer too! So there is much more money to be made right now supplying Asian demand, not propping up old trade ties on the other side of the planter.

In conclusion: Aussie economic future lies in Asia. Over the next few years, look for the portion of Australia exports of raw goods to Asian countries to increase, and dramatically. Raw material exports are not the only thing on the menu, my friends. Many Australian businesses, like so many others across the planet, are moving manufacturing facilities as well as research and development operations to Asian locations to take advantage of both cheap labor and the large local talent pool. I suppose the future of the continent may also be as a giant national park serving tourists from around the world serving shrimp on the barbie after you scuba on the Great Barrier Reef. And there is something to that: tourism is a big money maker, particularly since Australia and New Zealand are beautifully scenic areas, with the added bonus of being fully developed and politically stable . . . which means people love to come visit to live well, be safe, and buy great stuff.

Those same reasons are why many multinational companies (even Asian ones) are located their corporate headquarters in Australia/NZ; headquarters that run their global operations in Asia. Say what? Heck yeah: corporate heads want to do business in Asia to make their companies rich....but they want to live in a awesomely nice and clean and stable place like Australia while they do it! High end sectors like finance, banking, and research are taking hold in Oz as well, since a critical mass of highly educated, internationally-connected peeps has evolved there.

Even more so than America, Australia's future is tied closely with Asia. Asia is a booming region on the planet, a place where a lot of things are going on economically, and Australia is right there to help them along and make some profit at the same time. As we will see in the Mexico chapter, it is good to be next to a gigantic economic engine, and Australia's proximity to China, who will be the largest consumer of raw goods on the planet in the coming century, will enable Australia to turn huge profits. Former Prime Minister John Howard (in office 1996–2007) was quoted in the past about Australia refocusing their efforts and economy to better compliment China's rising power. He has called Australia "an anchor of stability" in this region. He also said, "When we think about the world, we inevitably think of a world where China will play a much larger role."

POLITICALLY

Let's stay with Former Prime Minister John Howard for just a minute more, so I can explain to you how Australia's role in the vicinity is changing politically as well. To do this, I must elaborate on the most hilarious "story of the sheriff" which ruffled many feathers. It goes a little something like this:

A decade ago, former US President George W. Bush *complimented* Former Australian Prime Minister Howard during a press release by referring to Australia's status as the "sheriff of Asia." What the heck was that supposed to mean? Most Asian countries interpreted this as "the white dudes in the area are in charge," and that the long arm of the US law was being stretched through Australia to keep order in the area. This seriously ticked off all of Australia's neighbors. Malaysia, which is a awesome state in its own right, nearly declared war over it. To paraphrase the Malaysian prime minister, "Think that all you want, but if you ever set foot on our soil we will declare war on you instantaneously, no matter what the US says about it."

Even John Howard was a little miffed. He was probably thinking, "Thanks for the compliment, Mr. Bush, but try not to ever say anything about me in public again." This was a problem especially since Australia is reorienting itself toward Asia. These are the guys with whom they are trying to buddy up! The last thing they need is negativity about their foreign policy ties to the US. They still want to be allied with the US, but they don't want to be throwing it in people's faces.

The Plaid Avenger suggested in an earlier chapter that Europeans are slightly apprehensive to support US foreign policy, as they have an increased risk of terrorist threats due to their proximity to the Middle East and Central Asia. Australia is in the same boat. They're closer to other regions that may be slightly hostile to the US foreign policy. Australia is right there beside Southeast Asia, parts of which are known hotspots for extremism and terrorism. There are some seriously extreme fundamentalist Muslims in this area; even my Muslim friends would concur. Terrorist cells are known to exist in lots of places in Southeast Asia (e.g., Indonesia, the Philippines, or Malaysia), and Aussies have been targeted by terrorist attacks in the past (look up 2002 Bali Bombing for an example).

This is why John Howard was quick to offer a modification of Bush's comment, because there is a real threat nearby. The US is far enough away to be safe from imminent threat, but it's not hard for terrorists to make it from Southeast Asia to Australia. Because Australia is seen as the face of American foreign policy in the area, it is very surprising that Australia has not seen any terrorist activity on their soil already. However, there have been several foiled terrorist plots in recent history and this situation is not likely to let up anytime soon. The Aussies remain ever vigilant.

Bush was quoted as saying that he didn't think of Australia as a deputy sheriff, "but as a full sheriff." In fact, Australia does supply soldiers in most UN activities in the countries surrounding them. In many cases, they are actually doing patrols and peacekeeping directly for the UN in places like the Solomon Islands, Indonesia, and other hotspots where the UN needs peacekeepers. The idea of them as sheriff does have some weight, and is going to cause them some problems in the future. Many countries in the 'hood remain perpetually pissed that the white man is on their soil at all, even as peacekeepers.

To end this rant, know this: this is changing fast. Another Former Prime Minister Kevin Rudd (who served after Howard) was a bit more liberal and conciliatory than his conservative predecessor, and he made moves to soften the Australian image in this part of the world. He decided to pull Aussie troops from Iraq, and was much more engaged with local Asian countries' leaders to head-off any friction that might arise due to Australian presence, as UN representatives or otherwise. Oh yeah, and he spoke fluent Chinese, and not just to order from a take-out menu either. Given Australia's changing focus, I assume it may be a common attribute for future leaders to be just as fluent. . . .

THE PEEPS

First off: there hardly ain't none of them! Say what? Yep. There are only about 23 million Aussies, and 5 million Kiwis (plus or minus a few Hobbits.) Altogether this region has less peeps than New York or Tokyo or Rio, but spread out over an area the size of the continental US! And it's not like the equation is going to change much in the near future either, as both countries have full-on stabilized, low pop growth rates. As in the US and Europe, the only way their pop gets any bigger is via immigration from other places, and (just like in US and Europe) this inflow of people is changing their ethnic and demographic outlook here in the 21st century . . . but how?

Because Australia is doing a lot of business with China, Japan, Indonesia, ASEAN, etc, they will become more like those countries culturally, as interaction with and immigration from Asian countries increases. This is changing very rapidly just in the modern era, because quite frankly it was not allowed to happen any earlier. How so, Plaid Avenger?

At the expense of aggravating my Aussie friends, I will have to tell you that a racist streak has run through the society since its inception—a bad habit that they probably inherited from the Brits. Perhaps racist is too harsh, but certainly they had a superiority complex when it came to other peoples in their neighborhood. The Australian treatment of the **Aboriginals** was bad from the get go, mostly treating them as third rate citizens, at best. There was also an official state policy from 1870 to 1970 which made it perfectly legal for the state to take Aboriginal children from their parents to re-educate and 'civilize' them in white families. These folks are now referred to as the **Stolen Generation**.

Aborigines: Not held in high regard.

I guess that is better than what the Aussies did to the Tasmanians, which was to kill them all in an open hunting season. On top of that, Australia had a white-only immigration policy in place for most of its history. What? Yeah, I'm afraid it's true. If you were of European or American descent, then you had an open door to the country; but that same door was slammed shut for Asians or Africans of any stripe. Pretty nasty business.

What is this madness? No wonder Rudd apologized.

To be fair to our friends "down under," they have made great strides in the last few decades to make amends. Much has been done to alleviate the impoverished plight of many Aboriginal communities, and even more has been done to overcome the negative attitude and stereotypes of the group. In fact, Australia picked an Aboriginal woman to carry the flag into the introductory ceremonies for the 2000 Olympics. That brings me back to what former Prime Minister Kevin Rudd did his first month in office: in February 2008, he made an official government apology to the Aborigines for all past reprehensible deeds of the Australian government, specifically citing the Stolen Generation. This was big news, and perhaps a critical turning point for the society.

Back to the story: Since 1976, when their historically strict immigration laws became more relaxed, the country's Asian population has increased. Surprise, surprise. More people that are close by, from regions adjacent to Australia, are coming there because it is a rich place where there is more opportunity to succeed than there may be in their home countries. Again, it's America, Jr.! All of the poorer people nearby want to get there so they can set up shop. Australia may not be full-on encouraging it, but at least they are allowing it. They are changing direction, changing focus, and becoming more Asian. When you visit Sydney now, you can bump into a very vibrant and growing Chinatown for the first time in its history. These changes are occurring nationwide. As you may remember from the international organizations chapter, ASEAN is now a rallying entity for inter-regional action in this part of the world, and Australia is a part of the ASEAN +3 dialogue. They are also a new member of the EAS: that East Asia Summit that is a open trade/politics/planning talk shop that everyone in the Asian 'hood is on . . . and now so are Australia and New Zealand, despite their lack of Asian-ness.

Who else have we talked about that is becoming more Asian due to increasing immigration from Asian states? That's right: America, Sr.!

Australia and New Zealand
CHAPTER ELEVEN

NO WORRIES

This is a region that plays a dual role as a US foreign policy anchor and as an economic player with China. They have a lot of natural resources and stable population growth, that is being bolstered by Asian immigration too. There is still the terrorist threat, however; we'll just have to see how they balance their security against their economic interest.

Australia would like to be a power broker between China and the US. This is promising; they have far fewer complications to worry about when dealing with China, as opposed to Japan, which has loads of historical emotional baggage. Japan may be a little more abrasive than Australia when dealing with Asian relations in general, and this gets the Aussies ahead.

Australia is going to have a leg up dealing with China and all the other Asian economic giants, because of proximity as well as the fact that they don't carry a lot of cultural baggage. What do I mean by that? They haven't dissed. They haven't invaded anyone. They never colonized anyone. They are pretty antiseptic all the way around. That is a big plus in today's world, particularly for any state wanting to get in on the action in Asia, which is, of course, everyone. And it sure don't hurt that they have an absolute ton of resources and services that those growing Asian economies will be snapping up indefinitely. Dudes! The koalas and the kiwis are sitting pretty down there right now! Down under is the place to be! Down under Asia, that is.

Uncle Sam's little brother down south is still a staunch ally of the US . . . and the awesome ANZUS pact makes them secure, all while US troop presence is increasing across the region. Luckily, they remain just distant enough to dodge a lot of the negative press associated with such a role. Of course, the Aussies are distancing themselves slightly from US foreign policy of the last decade . . . but dang, who isn't? Australia is a pretty chill place all the way around: politically, economically, socially. That's why we like to go vacation there, because Australia is a laid back sort of place. Throw a shrimp on the barbie, crack open a Foster's, and enjoy the prosperous future, America Junior.

A SINISTER SHOW AND TELL

Here's a great game that all the kids love to play! It's called "Quickest Kill." Known for it's exotic and often lethal wildlife, the Australia/New Zealand region is hot to a whole slew of the world's deadliest animals. Of the following creatures listed below, which one do you think could take out the kid sitting next to you in geography class the fastest? And which one do you think is responsible for the most deaths? Have a round table debate in your class, and you get bonus points for letting one or more of these creatures loose while defending your choice. It's the Aussie version of 'Hunger Games'! Good luck!

Salt Water Croc

Eastern Brown Snake

Stonefish

Red-backed Spider

Death Adder

Great White Shark

Funnel-Web Spider

Inland Taipan

Blue-ringed Octopus

Tiger Snake

Box Jellyfish

Gollum

AUSTRALIA RUNDOWN & RESOURCES

View additional Plaid Avenger resources for this region at http://plaid.at/aus

BIG PLUSES

- Koala bears and kangaroos and hobbits. Who doesn't love them? Ok, besides Sauron.
- Small population that is about evenly balanced with resource/industrial base
- Location, location, location! In the neighborhood of the hottest, fastest growing Asian economies, to which Australia sells tons of goods
- 13th largest economy in Australia; very high standards of living across region
- Resource/agricultural product rich
- Stable democratic governments
- No real enemies on the planet; no international conflicts with anyone

BIG PROBLEMS

- Crocodiles, the Sydney funnel-web spider, 9 of the top 10 most deadliest snakes in the world. Crikey!
- National legacy of racism: still has friction with its Aboriginal groups, and immigration is becoming a hot button issue much like it is in US
- Economy not very diversified; heavily dependent on natural resource exports
- By mere association with Team West, combined with its proximity to SE Asia, Australia is a high-risk target for international terrorism

LIVE LEADERS YOU SHOULD KNOW:

John Howard: Popular former Prime Minister of Australia from 1996–2007. Kind of the "Ronald Reagan of Australia": Center-right conservative, pro-business, pro-US, and presided over a period of strong economic growth and prosperity. Strongly supported US in Iraq and Afghanistan. Mostly lost in 2007 simply because voters were bored.

Kevin Rudd: Prime Minister of Australia from 2007–10, and the polar opposite of Howard. Center-left liberal who was more focused on establishing stronger ties with Asia, and possibly not following US foreign policy so adamantly. Speaks Mandarin Chinese fluently, supports Kyoto Protocol, made official apology to Aboriginals, and pulled troops out of Iraq.

Tony Aboott: Current Prime Minister since 2013, center-right conservative, thus swinging the power pendulum back to the other side. Is more "business friendly" and no fan of Kyoto Protocol nor a carbon tax, is anti-immigration, and re-started a program to appoint Australian knights and dames. Seriously.

PLAID CINEMA SELECTION:

Australia (2008) Australian cowboy version of *Gone With the Wind*. At nearly three hours in length, this epic is based on real life events that occurred in Northern Australia during World War II. Shows, at length, much of the northern territory of Australia during wartime, including several aspects of Aboriginal life, and the national legacy of racism to boot.

"Crocodile" Dundee (1986) Probably the most well known Australian film of all time. Has two versions, an Australian version and an international version. The Australian version features more regional slang and extended scenes. Despite its comedic aspect, the film shows a lot of great examples of the outback, including both scenery and wildlife.

Matariki (2010) Complex film tells the plot through five interweaving stories, all in the days leading up to Matariki, the Maori New Year. The film shows a wonderful view of the landscape in South Auckland, New Zealand. Funded completely by the New Zealand Film Commission.

The Piano (1993) Dramatic film about a mute pianist and her daughter living during the mid-19th century in New Zealand. This wonderful film covers many aspects of language, as three languages are spoken in the film if you include sign language. Great scenery as the purples and greens of New Zealand capture the eye and don't let go.

Rabbit-Proof Fence (2002) Closely based on real events, a real fence, real people, and real national racist policies of the time. The story of three girls who are forcibly taken from their home and put in a camp because it was believed that the Aboriginals were a danger to themselves and should be bred out of existence. Shows struggles of Aboriginals in western Australia during the 1930s.

Romper Stomper (1992) Drama about a group of bored Neo-Nazi skinheads clashing with Vietnamese immigrants in a Melbourne, Australia suburb. Inspired by actual events, this film stars a young Russell Crowe in his pre-Gladiator days. The violent closing scenes take place within the natural beauty of Victoria's Twelve Apostles rock outcroppings (of which there are not actually twelve).

Walkabout (1971) Artsy-fartsy piece with little dialogue and loads of symbolism, this film was extremely controversial when released due to its overt sexual themes and nude scenes with a minor. But it is just awesome at showing the physical beauty and bizarreness of Australia, Aboriginal culture, and the disconnect between the "modern" human life and the "uncivilized" human experience. Not for those who need explanation and closure in films.

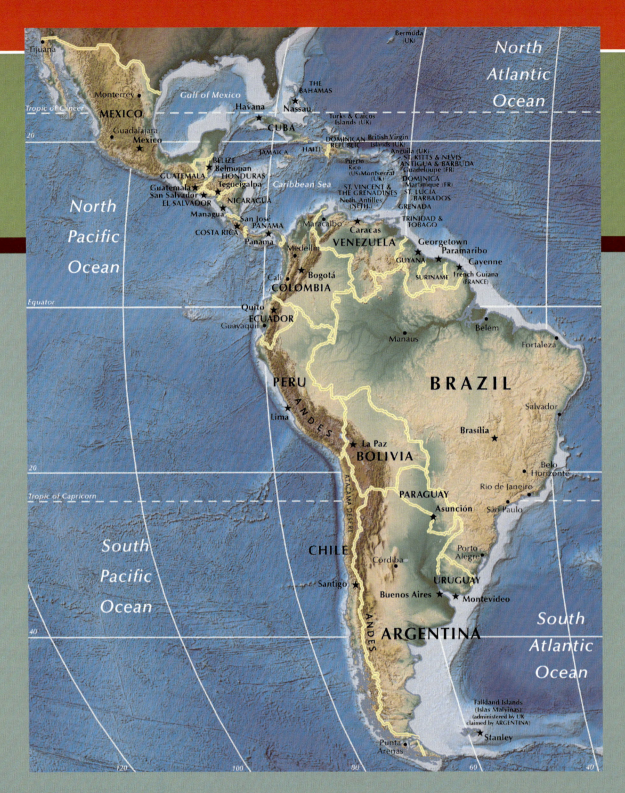

CHAPTER OUTLINE

1. A Single Region?
2. What Is Latin America?
3. Latin Locations
   - 3.1 South America
   - 3.2 Middle America
     - 3.2.1 Mexico
     - 3.2.2 The Caribbean
     - 3.2.3 Central America
4. What Is Latin about Latin America?
   - 4.1 Common Culture
   - 4.2 Urbanization
   - 4.3 Wealth Disparity/Landlessness
   - 4.4 In-"Doctrine"-ation: A History of US Involvement
     - 4.4.1 Cold War Effects
     - 4.4.2 Drugs
   - 4.5 Leftward Leaning
5. Losing the Latins: US Undone
   - 5.1 New Kids in the Block
   - 5.2 Don't Get "Left Out" of Latin America!
     - 5.2.1 How Far Left Are These Leaders?

Latin America

A SINGLE REGION?

Latin America is a region with a question mark after it. The Plaid Avenger has never really considered it a region in the past, because as you know, creating a "region" involves identifying some sort of homogeneous singular trait that you can apply to the geographic space in question. I've said for years this place is too big. You can't apply singular homogeneous traits across all of Latin America because it encompasses everything from the south of the US-Mexican border all the way to Tierra del Fuego, the tip of South America, which is almost in the Antarctic. It's just too darned big, and too darned complex! A single same-ness that applies to everything from the Rio Grande to Rio de Janeiro, or the Atacama to the Andes? Not hardly. Except maybe the term 'Latin America' itself . . . and BTW, where did that come from? A: . . .

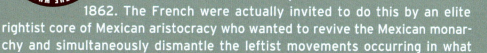

What's the Deal with . . . the Latins in Mexico?

What happened was this freaky-freak French king Napoleon III (not Napoleon the short, dead dude we all know, but one of his later kin) sent over this dude named Maximilian (actually, an Austrian) to sit on the Mexican throne in a feeble effort to reestablish France's presence in the New World in 1862. The French were actually invited to do this by an elite rightist core of Mexican aristocracy who wanted to revive the Mexican monarchy and simultaneously dismantle the leftist movements occurring in what was independent, sovereign Mexico at the time. So this French dude Maximilian was in charge, and when he was out scouting around he said, "Hmmm. . . . We're French, we're not even Spanish. What rallying point can we possibly use to get the locals to think that we should be in charge here?"

Maximilian being executed.

What our brilliant French brethren came up with was that the Spanish, Portuguese, and the French languages are all linguistically linked. They are all part of the Romance, or Latin-derived languages. In a fit of what must have been desperation at the time, Napoleon III told ol' Maxi to say, "Look, I may be just the French guy here in Mexico, but we are all brothers under the Latin language, so we're all family here in *Latin America*." Again, a totally bogus, politically made-up term, but somehow it stuck. The Mexicans deposed Maximilian's derriere fairly quickly, but the term stayed—in fact, kicking out the French is what the Cinco de Mayo holiday is all about; it's not Mexican Independence Day! That is a different holiday altogether! May 5 is all about forcing out the French! Which is always a good time for all.

After thinking about the French fool Maximilian's antics for a while, the Plaid Avenger has realized that, indeed, there are a lot of traits that can be recognized across the whole of Latin America. We're going to look at some of those traits in this introduction pre-chapter to the more unique subregions of Latin America.

WHAT IS LATIN AMERICA?

So . . . this "Latin America" is a term that everybody recognizes, everybody gets, you know where it is, but it's based on a word that is completely and utterly meaningless: Latin. Do all of these people speak Latin south of our border? Heck no. Latin is a dead language. Nobody speaks that Caesar-ized stuff anymore. In fact, there are really only two predominate languages spoken in the region: Spanish and Portuguese. That, and a smattering of small states that speak English or French in the Caribbean.

How did we get this term Latin America: are they all of Latin or Greek ancestry? Obviously not. As with many things on the planet, we can blame the French. In that pretty little piece of propaganda, the French called for a Latin brotherhood based on all their languages (French, Portuguese, Spanish) being of Latin roots. Pretty shaky foundation for a regional identity, but there it is.

Geographically, the term means everything south of the US/Mexican border. That's common knowledge across the planet. Mexico, which we teased out for obvious reasons earlier, is not part of the US/Canadian region. There are too many differences, including its Latin-based language, levels of development, poverty, and lots of other issues which distinguish Mexico from the United States. So even though it is a NAFTA member and southwestern US is increasingly becoming part of a "greater Tex-Mex" region, for now Mexico still shares more commonalities with states south of that border. . . . Before we get to those similarities, let's identify frequently referenced regions in this part of the planet.

LATIN LOCATIONS

There are a few terms that the Plaid Avenger wants you to know before we get into these subsequent chapters. These definitions will help us understand a lot of terminology used on the global stage. We already talked about Latin America encompassing every single country south of the US/Mexican border, in the entire western hemisphere. Now let's break down some more specific regions within Latin America.

SOUTH AMERICA

The first one is easy enough. South America is both a continent and a region. The South American continent is that other major chunk of land in the western hemisphere. It starts with Colombia and then heads east to Venezuela, Guyana, Suriname, French Guyana, and then turns down south to Brazil. South of Colombia is Ecuador, Peru, Chile, Bolivia, Paraguay, Uruguay, and Argentina. It is important to note that most all of the countries of South America are fairly good sized; Brazil itself is a monster country, being the fifth largest in the world. This makes South American states quite territorially, physically, and economically distinct from the slew of much smaller micro-states to their immediate north. Food for thought, and I'm not talking about salsa either.

 +  +  =

MIDDLE AMERICA

The term **Middle America** is everything between the southern border of the United States and the South American continent. It's a fairly generic definition that usually only gets play in high school and college level textbooks anymore, but I suppose it doesn't hurt to know the reference when you see it pop up. For this magnificent treatise of learning, I will further break this area down to more manageable and meaningful subregions, described below. Study the Middle America map equation above to be cartographically clever.

MEXICO

The first subdivision is Mexico itself, solo. Mexico is a country, a state in its own right, but it's also radically different from all the states around it, including the US, and it's also quite different from the Central American and Caribbean states. Mexico is its own subregion that we're going to define in the next chapter. In respect to size, resources, economy, population and level of development, Mexico stands apart from all its neighbors in Middle America: it is a giant of population, economy, and resources when compared to the rest of the Middle America 'hood. And its shared border with the USA make it quite distinct from all the rest of the Latin American states as well . . . as does it's NAFTA membership. Combine that huge economic interaction with the US with the huge cultural interaction with the US, and you have a sub-region that really straddles two different worlds.

THE CARIBBEAN

The Caribbean is a group of island states comprised of the Greater Antilles and the Lesser Antilles. The Caribbean, when we think about it, calls to mind a distinct culture in terms of . . . everything. Cuisine, language, stuff they drink, how they party—it's all different. Caribbean means something to us, and it means something that's different than Mexico. We all understand that, right? We go to a Caribbean restaurant or a Mexican restaurant, but we never really see the two put together. (Note to self: that might be a good idea. Instead of Tex-Mex cuisine, how about Car-Mex cuisine—or is that a lip balm?) The island nations in the Caribbean Sea, south of the United States, are a distinct subdivision.

CENTRAL AMERICA

The last sub-region of Middle America is **Central America.** This is the one that causes the most confusion for younger students of the world. It is everything between Mexico and South America, noninclusive. Mexico and South America are the bookends. There are seven distinct countries in what is widely accepted as Central America: Belize, Guatemala, El Salvador, Honduras, Nicaragua, Costa

Rica, and Panama. You may hear reference to Central American civil wars or Central American gangs; this group of countries is the origin for that descriptor. Yeah, good times.

We've got a bunch of Americas here, and Central America is quite distinct in that it has little in common with Mexico, the Caribbean, or even South America. It has a lot going on, particularly in terms of the violence that we will talk about in much more detail when we get to the Central America chapter. It's a distinct place; a bunch of small states that bridge both North and South America, but they are all quite unique, even from each other, in all many aspects.

South America plus the three regions of Middle America—Mexico, Central America, and the Caribbean—that's Latin America all the way around. Now that we know where it is and where the definition comes from, let's talk a little bit more about what Latin America *is*. What homogeneous traits can we use to define this vast region?

WHAT IS LATIN ABOUT LATIN AMERICA?

COMMON CULTURE

Portugal got the short end of the continental stick . . .

First, we can point out some distinct elements so we don't have to keep repeating ourselves in subsequent chapters. Number one is culture. There is kind of a common culture south of the US/Mexican border, be it in the Caribbean, Central America, Chile, Argentina, or Brazil; there are some things that do remain the same. One of the kind-of-the-same things that we already pointed out is language. While Latin America is a bizarre term in and of itself, Latin Americans do primarily speak Spanish, and the only other really big language is Portuguese.

How did this come about? Easy enough. It came about because of colonial endeavors in this region that date as far back as 1492 when Columbus sailed the ocean blue, came over here and bumped into the Caribbean . . . and he was sailing under the Spanish flag. After his "great discovery," the big naval powers at the time, Spain and Portugal, started floating over here in fairly short order as well. (Great Britain didn't come along until later. It wasn't as big of a naval power as the Spanish at the time, so it was a latecomer. It therefore had to head north for colonial expansion which is why it gets the leftovers—North America.)

Let's get back to our story here. Why do we have these two main languages, Spanish and Portuguese? Columbus came over in 1492. Two years later, a fairly important event occurred which I want you to understand and know about: **The Treaty of Tordesillas.** The Treaty of Tordesillas occurred in 1494 when these European countries were bumping into the New World, colonizing, taking over, and staking claim to pieces of it. Of course, there was friction between the countries for hundreds of years at home anyway; now they were just taking the fight abroad. Much of the friction was between Portugal and Spain, two of the main colonizing powers in this part of the world. Who was going to own what? Are we going to fight over it? The scramble for stuff was fast turning into a full-scale fracas. Both these countries, being predominantly Catholic—which is another common cultural tie we'll see more about in just a second—would listen to the papa, the **Pope,** the main man in the Vatican. And therefore to alleviate

Pope responsible for Tordesillas . . . and Catholicism in Latin America.

conflict, the Pope said, "Hey guys, come on now, we're all civilized colonial imperial masters here. Let's all get on the same page, get around the same table here, let's work together! We don't need to fight! We're going to settle this fair and square. Papa is going to just draw a line on the map and everything on one side we'll give to the Spanish and everything on the other side we'll give to the Portuguese. Now you guys be good!" The line happened to be 45 degrees western longitude. Check out the map on the previous page. And the caption.

As you can see from the map, the Portuguese look like they got shafted on this deal. They only got the tip of what is now known as Brazil. Why is this? Did the Pope just not like the Portuguese? Well, maybe a little. But you also have to keep in mind, this was during early exploration in 1494, only a few years after Columbus got there. They didn't even know what was there yet. They were just bumping around the coastline; with no comprehension about the actual size of the continents . . . neither North nor South America, quite frankly. What they thought was a good deal was based on known circumstances at the time, which really wasn't much. As we all now know, this is a pretty big place. South America is the fourth largest continent on the planet. As exploration continued and the true scope of the land's magnitude unfolded, the Portuguese did pick up what is now modern-day Brazil. Its boundaries naturally fell back to the Andes—a nice, easily defined natural border. Anyway, the Treaty of Tordesillas is the cornerstone of why the Spaniards ended up controlling so much of the New World—basically, all the rest of it outside Brazil.

Spanish Territory in North and Central America

And it all started with Mexico. We think of today's Mexico as that place "south of the border," but Mexico in its days as part of the Spanish Empire included all of western North America, as well. It was everything that's now California up to Washington State, to Utah, to New Mexico, to Texas. Spanish territory also included Mexico, all of Central America, most of the Caribbean, Florida, and all the way down the western seaboard of South America. Check it out on the map to the left. That is why today these territories are Spanish-speaking. I guess in today's world the Spanish-speaking territories might even include California, Florida, New Mexico, and Arizona, but that's a separate issue in immigration that we'll get to later.

This all means that those old colonial ties formed this common culture that's still in place today. It's a common culture primarily based on language, but also on one other thing I mentioned earlier: Catholicism. Two primarily Catholic countries colonized virtually all of Latin America. You can still see the deep, deep-seated Catholicism throughout Latin America today. There are no countries in Latin America that are *not* Catholic. When the Plaid Avenger travels down there, he can see some freaky-freaky stuff that doesn't look like Catholicism. You can see some rites and rituals down there that could make the Pope soil his robes, no doubt. You'd say, "That's not Catholicism! What is this voodoo hoo-ha? What are people doing with voodoo dolls and holding up bloody chickens saying Hail Marys?" Then there's this crazy stuff that's going on down in Brazil; they have these big parties that don't look like traditional Catholicism: the "Carnival." But what you have is indeed the basis of Catholicism mixed in within indigenous culture, local culture, and imported African culture.

Latins love the Savior.

So a couple of very strong cultural characteristics, language and Catholicism, do serve as a starting place for some homogeneity of "Latin American-ness." But there are others . . .

URBANIZATION

Urbanization is a primary feature that is consistent across every place in Latin America, and I do mean *every place*. I've never even thought about this until recently, but this region is one of the most urbanized on the planet. Typically, when we think of urbanization, we think it means that most people don't live in the countryside; most people live in cities . . . and we typically associate this with fully developed countries like the US, Canada, Japan, and Western Europe. That's where you *typically* have people who are all jammed in the cities, and hardly anyone out in the country. For some reasons that we will get into in a minute, Latin America is more urbanized than many fully developed places. This means almost everyone in these countries is jammed into something called an urban area, typically a very big city.

On average, upwards of 80–85 percent, sometimes upwards of 90 percent, of the population of a Latin American country is located in just a few major cities. This is highlighted best by Mexico City, which will probably soon be the world's most populated city with over 25 million inhabitants—a full one-fourth of Mexico's total population.

Latins packed into the cities.

Why do people go to the city? It is suggested that in the developed world people go to the city for all the reasons we already talked about back in chapter 2. That's where jobs are. Jobs are concentrated in urban areas. People want to go to urban areas because there's health care, doctors, clean water, sewer systems, electricity, movie theaters, good restaurants. The reason everybody wants to move to a big city or urban area is because good stuff is there. The standard of living is higher and that's where your jobs are.

Is that true of Latin America? Not all the time. It is a kind of conundrum in Latin America. In most urbanized places in the Latin world, all of the **pull factors** that we just mentioned—the good things that pull people to the city—are simply not available for the masses that come. There is the *perception* that all these great things are in the city and the *perception* that all these jobs are available, but it is simply not true for a lot of folks who end up going to the city.

Now those are the pull factors, but there are also some **push factors**, or the not-so-good things that push people from rural areas to the city. One of the main push factors, a major theme across Latin America that we'll discuss at length, is **landlessness.** Because most people do not have access to land, or resources on the land, they are pushed away from it. Owning no land in title or having no serious claim to the land is just another reason to go to the city. So there are a lot of pull and push factors that make Latin America one of the most urbanized places on the planet . . . a trend that is growing.

One last note: An interesting phenomenon in Latin American cities that most Americans don't get is that they are set up in a kind of "economically reversed" scenario from the US urban model. Say what? In America, what's found deep in the inner city? In fact, what is the connotation of the term "inner city"? I'll tell you what it connotes: slums, projects, poverty, ghettos. That's not where people want to be. As a result, most people who have money don't live in the inner city in America. They've got money, so what do they do? They move *away* from the city and into the "burbs," which we talked about back in the North America chapter.

Vertical growth of slums or favelas around Rio.

In Latin America, the situation is just the reverse. The city center is still the prime real estate, so the rich people concentrate themselves and their businesses in the true city center. Where do all these impoverished masses go that I have been suggesting flood into the cities? They make a ring around it. They get as close to the city as they can, usually in ramshackle, shanty-like town dwellings they put together out of corrugated-cardboard and any other thing they can pull out of a landfill, and build them in undesirable, unused parts of the urban fringe like mountain sides. These shantytowns get very big and grow into almost permanent fixtures in rings around the cities. Whole shantytowns are a phenomenon that's very easy to spot in any major Latin American city. Just drive straight into or out of the city and notice how the poverty line fluctuates one way or the other. It's a distinct characteristic that has something to do with urbanization. It also has something to do with . . .

WEALTH DISPARITY/LANDLESSNESS

Perhaps there is no other region that we will talk about in this book or that you can go visit on the planet that has wealth disparity as extreme as Latin America. What is **wealth disparity?** Disparity is the difference between highest and the lowest, the difference between the greatest and the least. In terms of wealth, no place in the world is like Latin America in that so few people have so much of the wealth. I'm just going to guess-timate some numbers here. These are Plaid Avenger Figures that vary from country to country, but on average, the extreme amounts of wealth are held by the upper 5 percent of the population. The richest 5 percent typically own something like 80 percent of all the stuff. That's all the land, all the factories, all the businesses, everything. Maybe you think that's not bad—perhaps that's the way it is in the US as well. Not really. Because the other part of the equation is that 95 percent of people have got to split up that other 20% of the stuff. Of course, there is always a significant, or at least partial, middle class; some people have got to own some stuff, but there's always a significant majority of people in these countries that own nothing. No title to their land, no title to their house, no other economic means except their labor to sell. That is a kind of common feature across Latin America from Mexico down to the tip of Tierra del Fuego, and is particularly nasty in Brazil and lots of other places where people kill each other over land.

Times haven't changed much economically.

What's the Deal with Landlessness in Brazil?

Unofficial stats in Brazil refer to 1.6 percent of the landowners control roughly half (46.8 percent) of the land on which crops could be grown. Just 3 percent of the population owns two-thirds of all arable lands. The Brazilian constitution requires that land serve a social function. [Article 5, Section XXIII.] As such, the constitution requires the Brazilian government "expropriate for the purpose of agrarian reform, rural property that is not performing its social function." [Article 184.]

This is a big deal for everybody. It concerns politicians, business people, and the landless poor. In Brazil, they have a law on the books that basically says, "If you can successfully squat on a piece of land, cultivate it, and make it produce something for one year, then you have a legal stake to it. You can take it! It's yours! Here's the deed in your name!" You may say, "Hey, that sounds like a pretty good policy," and maybe it is.

However, the scenario develops a lot of squatter settlements: large groups of people who are squatting on owned land that is typically owned by some rich businessperson or some rich urban dweller who is not out there in the countryside. If they find out that people are squatting on their land, they send in henchmen to go clear them out. When the landless poor fight back or try to continue their stay on the land to finish out the year so they can have legal claim to it, the situation can turn violent.

This situation has also led to the formation of the Landless Workers' Movement, or in Portuguese, Movimento dos Trabalhadores Rurais Sem Terra (MST). This is the largest social movement in Latin America with an estimated 1.5 million landless members organized in 23 out of 27 states. And they can get violent as well.

This is still an issue that is alive today in Brazil and all across Latin America where hired gunmen are going and literally cleaning out villages and killing everybody on site. Because it is private property, the owners, ranchers, and other types of folks can just say "This is legally mine and these people wouldn't leave, so I killed them." This is a very hot issue. In her first months in office President Dilma Rouseff pledged millions to resettle landless folks and encourage farm production in rural areas.

Dilma sez: "Land reform is necessary to build a country with justice, food security and peace in rural areas."

This brings us to the issue of **landlessness**. Because of this lopsided scenario of so few people owning so much, including the land, the vast majority of people can't stake a claim to anything. In such societies where people don't have anything, their options are very limited. Mostly they go to cities, as already suggested. They can also try to work on someone else's land without the landowner's consent. This is a very unstable situation because the owner can show up at any time and kick them off. This is a particularly resonate issue in Brazil where landlessness has turned into an occupational hazard (see box on left).

This problem of wealth disparity and landlessness is a common theme across Latin America, and was a primary motivation of the independence movements across the region as well (these movements in Latin America began in the 1820s–30s). This dude named **Simón Bolívar** headed up many of these egalitarian independence movements, and is viewed historically as the George Washington of Latin America. Wealth disparity/economic equality was one of his central themes to rally folks to fight. But the issue wasn't resolved at state inception, and it has plagued Latin America ever since. Just one example for now: The Mexican Revolution in 1910 was fought over land: so many people got so frustrated about landlessness, that they had a revolution to remedy it. One of the core parts of their new constitution included equal rights for people and access to land. All politicians of any stripe have had to deal with this issue historically, and still do today.

The George Washington of America: Simón Bolívar.

Pancho Villa and his crew fought in the Mexican revolution for land reform. But even 100 years later, Mexican President Enrique Peña Nieto had to include land reform in his political platform. If you're going to run for office at all in Mexico, no matter what political party you are from, you have

Pancho, Peña, Rouseff, Castro and Hugo: All leaders for land reform?

to address the land issue. The main political party in Mexico is called the PRI. It's a land reform party—go figure. It was founded to redistribute land and work out ways to give people access to land. We already referred to Dilma in Brazil (see previous page) dealing with land reform, and she has also had to deal with massive citizen protest in 2013–14 that are demanding better government services and opportunities for the masses. Then there are peeps like that late Hugo Chavez in Venezuela who was all about equal economic rights in a country with huge wealth disparity, and started his socialist "Bolivarian Revolution" program in order to level the playing field. And don't forget historic figures like Fidel Castro, who led the Cuban revolution to basically reclaim land and businesses from the rich and redistribute them to the poor in an old-school communist-style revolution. This issue of wealth disparity and landlessness is a prevalent theme whether you are in Brazil, Mexico, Cuba, Nicargua, or Chile.

IN-"DOCTRINE"-ATION: A HISTORY OF US INVOLVEMENT

The Plaid Avenger has talked to many folks from Mexico all the way down to Argentina, and can tell you with no reservation that people respect the United States. Nobody hates any specific person in the United States, but taken as a whole, Latin America's historical relationship with the US in today's world is largely seen as negative. That may seem like a bold statement, and certainly there are those that still support US policies, but I can tell you who those people are. They are the rich people in Latin America. If life is good, you've got no reason to have qualms with the United States. Unfortunately, as we've already pointed out, that's not the majority by any stretch. Most people see the United States with a bit of an imperial taint, or in a bit of a **hegemonic** light. Certainly, given the US's involvement in virtually every country in Latin America, it's not hard to see why they have kind of a bad taste in their mouth when it comes to historical intervention by the US.

To what is the Plaid Avenger referring? You've got to know this, because it still applies in today's world. The number one thing you've got to remember from the US's history of influence is **The Monroe Doctrine.** It's this antiquated, 200-year-old statement that was made in 1823 by President James Monroe. It was a foreign policy statement that said in essence *Disclaimer: this is a Plaid Avenger Interpretation:* "If any European power messes in any place in this hemisphere, the US will consider it an act of aggression against the United States." In essence, if Spain were to go try to retake Mexico or Chile, if the Portuguese were to try to retake Brazil, if the British try to take back Jamaica—the US would consider it an attack on US soil. Heck, it doesn't even have to be a full-on takeover; any intervention at all would be considered an act of aggression. "If you mess with anyone down there, we will consider it as you screwing with us." It's extremely similar to NATO article 5 in saying, "If anybody here gets messed with, it's an attack on all of us."

"Don't mess in our hemisphere, bitches!"

Now why on earth would the US say that? It seems kind of silly. I mean, in 1823, what sort of position is James Monroe in? The US was a new country that had only been around about 30 or 40 years. It had only expanded *slightly*

Uncle Sam ready to whip some imperialistic Eurotrash back in the day.

over the 13 original colonies, and they were certainly not a world power. They did a great job shooting the British from behind trees, but other than that, they weren't capable of fighting anybody. They could take care of their soil, but weren't up for fighting anybody else on foreign soil. This was largely a toothless threat. Maybe you are thinking, "Why is the Plaid Avenger telling us that this is important?" Here's why: This statement became a cornerstone that remains relevant in US/Latin American policy TO THIS DAY.

It didn't mean anything at the time when Monroe said it, but it has come to mean *everything*. Why did Monroe make it at that particular time in 1823? Mexico declared independence in 1820. The Central Americas seceded and most of the South American countries were declaring independence at or around this time. It was seen largely as a supportive gesture. The US was basically thinking, "Yes, our Latin brothers, kick all Spanish and other colonial powers out. We just did it in America so we will encourage everyone else to do it. We're the good guys and we're helping the other good guys, so it's all good!" Again, it was a show of support more than a credible threat to the Europeans: the US could not really take on the Spanish or the British in a foreign land war at that time. Forget about it. No contest.

The Monroe Doctrine led to a bunch of other things, such as the **Roosevelt Corollary.** The Roosevelt Corollary was issued in 1904, about a hundred years later, and at that point, the US was quite a bit more powerful than it was during Monroe's tenure. The US was also under a very powerful president at the time, President "Rough Rider" Teddy Roosevelt. What was Teddy known for? What was one of his most popular sayings during that time? "Speak softly and carry a big stick." Indeed, that saying can be applied directly to what became known as the Roosevelt Corollary, which was the foreign policy towards Latin America at the time. Teddy said, "I like the Monroe Doctrine's policy that if anyone messes around in our backyard we'll consider it an act of aggression against us. That's good, but let's take it a step further. If there is any flagrant wrongdoing by a Latin American state *ITSELF*, then the US has the right to intervene."

In other words, if any Latin American countries south of the US border attack each other, then the US gave itself the right to intervene. More than that, if they just screw up internally, the US was giving itself the right to intervene as well. This had serious repercussions for what sovereignty meant at the time. Of course, I can't go back in time to hear their exact thoughts, but there is no doubt that it was not held in high esteem by Latin American states that were considered sovereign then.

In other words, you had the United States saying, "Sure, you guys are sovereign, as long as we agree with your sovereignty. Otherwise, we give ourselves the right to intervene." This became kind of a big deal because Teddy was carrying that big stick, and he was not afraid to smack people, or entire Latin American countries, down with it. Under Roosevelt's corollary, relations deteriorated slightly between these regions. However, a bright spot in

"Speak softly, and carry a big stick. Just in case a piñata party breaks out."

US/Latin American relations under the Good Neighbor Policy was just around the corner . . . maybe.

The **Good Neighbor Policy** was a popular name for foreign policy at the time of the next President Roosevelt—Franklin D., that is—in the 1930s. In a marked departure from the heavy-handed foreign policies up to this point, FDR said, "You know, we're good guys, we're your buddies. We don't need to come down there and beat you with a big stick. My fifth cousin Teddy was a funny guy, but we don't really need to be that heavy-handed. We'll throw out that Roosevelt Corollary and we'll just be here to help if any leader needs us."

FDR sez: "Sup. We gonna chill over here. If y'all need us, holla."

That sounded pretty good, and it was certainly an improvement over the Roosevelt Corollary. But under the Good Neighbor Policy, there were multiple scenarios where US troops were sent down at the request of "leaders" that sometimes could also be referred to as, oh, I don't know, let's call them *military dictators*, who just happened to be supporting US foreign and economic policies at the time. Even though it sounded better, there were still slight implications that perhaps things were not completely on the up and up. That brings us to the last part of the US's history of involvement.

COLD WAR EFFECTS

After WWII, there came the War of Coldness. The Cold War has already been referred to several times in this book; you may be thinking, "Ah I'm tired of freakin' history; I don't need to know any of this stuff," but you can't understand the world unless you understand the historical and political movements of at least the last hundred years. Nothing has affected the world more than the Cold War and its politics. Even Latin America was affected.

We might think of Latin America and say, "What? There was no hot war down there, much less a cold war! There are no Commies down there; there's no Cold War frictions in them parts!" Not so! Latin America was actually quite radically impacted by the Cold War because of US anti-communist policies that were applied across the planet. That's the reason the US got involved in Vietnam, Korea, and dang near everything else that was active at the time. The US even supported leaders with questionable character, just as long as they didn't associate with the Soviets. Supporting a brutal dictator who was suppressing his own peoples in Latin America? Sure! No problem, as long as he ain't a commie!

When we think of the Cold War and Latin America, the first thing that pops into the American mind is Cuba and Fidel: that flagrant flaming Commie that the US still hates to this day. There have been lots of repercussions between the US and Cuba (i.e. why Cuba's pretty impoverished today), but all of the other Latin American countries were impacted as well. Some of them had much more violence with a much greater death toll than Cuba ever did.

What I'm talking about is a renewed distrust of the US as a result of its Cold War activities. The American government was so rabidly anti-communist that any movement towards the political left by any Latin American country was viewed by the US as a hostile act. And so it became ingrained in US foreign policy for the last 50–60 years that it was absolutely intolerable for anybody to be left-leaning.

If you think back to our chapter on global politics and governments, not every single system on the left is Commie—but all forms of socialism were viewed as being a slippery slope that would eventually lead to the Soviets marching into Arizona. The US government believed that any form of socialism, however mild, would lead to communism or would lead to an opening for the USSR to make inroads. It really was battled at all cost. No cost was too high; no moral too low to violate in order to ensure that Latin America stayed firmly in the US's backyard of influence.

Sole Western Hemisphere Commie.

Let's get into some specifics. . . .

What did the US do in this all-out barrage to stop communism in Latin America? Be forewarned: This is going to hurt for the uninitiated. It's a little hard for many proud Americans to hear, but the US did some pretty nasty things, quite frankly. While they typically champion democracy on the planet, at the time of the Cold War, the USSR was seen as such a threat that the US said, "Well, we're all about democracy, and it would be great if we had democracies there, but we can't allow anybody to go near the left. So it would be better to support someone on the extreme right as opposed to anybody that might be even the slightest bit Commie."

What this equated to was US support for people who might be considered brutal dictators at worst, and elitist dudes of questionable ethics and character at best. During the Reagan years in the 1980s, the threat of Soviet infiltration by arms sales to places like Nicaragua was interpreted as an immediate hostile threat to the US. In response, support for dictators was sometimes pitched to the US Congress as basically, "We're about to get freakin' *invaded* by the Commies. They're going to get into Central America and they're going to sweep through Mexico and then they'll be knocking down Texas's door!"

In hindsight, this seems a bit preposterous. To be fair to the Reaganites and their ilk, we do have to consider that at the time, the Soviets were as aggressive as the US was, had as many nukes as the US did, and had previously tried to hide missiles in Cuba. So the commie-infiltration precedent was present. There was a very real fear of global domination by the Soviets.

You can listen to speeches by Henry Kissinger and the like that say, "You young people just don't understand that we had to do these horrible things because if we didn't, you'd all be wearing red right now and we would all be slaves of an oppressive giant Soviet Empire." The Plaid Avenger is not here to speak on whether that's true or not, because I'd be wearing plaid no matter if it were commie plaid or otherwise. But what this equated to in the Reagan era was not only supporting extreme dictatorships, but also hatching plots to overthrow—and sometimes assassinate—democratically elected leaders. This also equated to supporting extremist rightist factions and rebel groups. Right wing death squads in Nicaragua comes to mind, also found in Guatemala and El Salvador too. The US supported *anybody* as long as they weren't left-leaning and weren't socialists and didn't support any of those other ideologies, especially communism.

A lot of these groups ended up slaughtering thousands, and tens of thousands, of their own people. Many just ended up as bands of guerillas running around the countryside causing mayhem to the elected governments. The end result of all these anti-communist policies in Latin America, particularly Central America, was civil war. These excessively destructive civil wars were supported in part by movements of US funds or arms, or funds for arms. One of the more famous ones is the **Iran/Contra scandal**, during the Reagan era, when guns were floated into Nicaragua in support of anti-leftist movements to overthrow the democratically elected leftist regime, which we'll discuss more in the Central America chapter.

All these things together, in terms of US intervention or involvement in Latin American affairs, bring up a term that's often used for Latin America: **the US's backyard.** You'll see this term used even in modern political science magazines and international news. It really summarizes the way the US has felt about Latin America, which is, "It's not really our house, but it's our backyard. We're not really cleaning it up or taking care of it *unless* someone starts coming around and messing around in it." The US doesn't want anybody messing around in its backyard; that's why it's been heavy-handed at times throughout history.

2014 Update: This era may be coming to a close, as the USA has recently renounced the Monroe Doctrine altogether for the first time ever, and is increasingly losing influence within the region as a whole as more and more states turn to other powers like China and India, or become big powers themselves, like Brazil and Mexico. More on this later.

Drugs: the current "injection" of US influence into the region.

DRUGS

Oh yeah, I almost forgot about drugs! That is the hot new thing with US intervention in Latin America. The Cold War is over. There is not really any Good Neighbor Policy or Roosevelt Corollary going on. No foreign power is invading—that we know of—and the US is not going to do anything about it if they invade each other. The current and active deal with US intervention in Latin America is all centered on **drugs.** What the Plaid Avenger already knows from personal travels is that Latin America produces the bulk of the world's cocaine . . . and the United States *consumes* the bulk of the world's cocaine. Talk about a most horrific symbiotic relationship.

This creates a situation where the US government, armed with an anti-drug policy named "The War on Drugs," facilitates or makes it an imperative for us to intervene in other countries to stop drug production all over the world. The Plaid Avenger won't get into a big debate about the pure insanity of such an endeavor. I'll leave it to you students of the world to figure out if it's a good method to stop drug use or not, but certainly it is the US policy: "We don't really care so much that people are hooked on drugs up here; we just want to make sure they don't produce them down there." That will somehow solve the problem? Yeah, good luck with that one!.

This brings up one particular aspect of US foreign policy today called **Plan Colombia** (read box to the right).

What is the Deal with Plan Colombia?

Plan Colombia is a program supported by the United States to eradicate coca production in Colombia. It may sound good, but Plan Colombia has become extremely controversial for several reasons. For one, although the coca plant is used to manufacture cocaine, it has also been used by indigenous peoples in the area for thousands of years for health reasons. Many of these people depend on coca to make a living. Furthermore, some of the methods that the United States uses to eradicate coca, such as aerial fumigation and the application of deadly fungi, pose severe health problems for people exposed to it.

Plan Colombia is also controversial because Colombia was undergoing a civil war at the time. Many people claim that the goal of Plan Colombia wasn't really to stop drugs, but to help the Colombian government fight the Marxist rebel group FARC, which gains much of its funding through the drug trade. When Plan Colombia was first introduced by the president of Colombia in 1998, its main focus was to make peace with the rebels and revitalize the economy of Colombia. However, policymakers from the United States revised it, and the focus became more about military aid to fight the rebels and the elimination of drug trafficking. Human rights organizations are indignant at Plan Colombia because they see it as a way of strengthening right-wing paramilitary groups in Colombia that are committing atrocities against peasants who are speaking out for equal rights and economic reform.

It's your tax dollars, so you should know: the US government has spent close to six billion dollars on Plan Colombia since the year 2000. In 2006, it was reported that coca production actually increased in the last three years. Hmmmmm . . . I'm no mathematician, but something don't add up here. . . .

Fun Plaid Fact: After Plan Colombia was revised by the Americans, the first formal draft was written in English, and a version in Spanish wasn't created until months after the English copy was available. In related news, many Colombians have accused Colombian pop star Shakira of being a language sellout for releasing an album in English.

US direct intervention right now is mostly focused on Colombia, Ecuador, Peru, and Bolivia: the big drug-producing and exporting countries. Plan Colombia, in particular, has equated to around 6 billion US tax dollars in an effort to stop Colombia from producing drugs. Money well spent! (Did you read the inset box yet?) Mexico is the current hot spot for huge drug related violence, and an all-out drug war between the Mexican government and the powerful drug cartelts . . . but thus far, the US has not gotten involved too much, and for the first time ever, maybe they really should! This Mexican drug cartel war is radically affecting the US, and spilling over into the states in very real, and very dangerous, ways. Mexico is seeking active US involvement in their drug war; Colombia has worked with the US for years with drug wars and drug policy . . . but other countries like Bolivia, Venezuela, and Ecuador are not so keen on US policy. However some others, like Bolivia, are increasingly not. That brings us to a related topic . . .

LEFTWARD LEANING

This is the most fun, exciting, new, and current part of "What's Latin about Latin America." Through a combination of virtually all the above reasons that Latin America is Latin, this notion is the one that pulls it all together. As we've already cited, particularly during the Cold War era, the US was very troubled by and directly intervened in leftist or left-leaning countries in Latin America. God forbid they embrace some sort of socialism, and certainly not communism! Nonetheless, some people went left anyway. Castro springs to mind. Cuba has been communist and certainly in the "lefty" column for this entire time.

By and large, he has been alone in the hemisphere until very recently. What we've seen in the last decade—perhaps because of the wealth disparity or landlessness or poverty in Latin America—is a general bad taste in Latino mouths about the US's history of intervention. This has really culminated in a lot of countries heading back towards the left column. One that springs to mind is Venezuela in South America. A rabidly left country (some might even say it's already communist), Venezuela boasts a new brand of socialism that strives for social equality and redistribution of wealth to a limited degree through social programs, formerly under the tutelage of their self-avowed socialist President Hugo Chavez. Although Hugo is now hu-gone (he died in 2013), the socialist movement he spawned is very much alive. President Evo Morales of Bolivia has recently joined the ranks of hard-core leftist, and has been busy nationalizing industries and moving his country in a fully socialist direction. Ecuadorian President Rafeal Correa is pretty far on the left side of the tracks now too.

Current US President Barack Obama has been an overwhelmingly popular figure across all of Latin America, so the standard anti-US sniping from Castro and Chavez is now not in vogue. Obama has been actively trying to reach out to restore diplomatic street cred in Latin America, and has spoken openly about thawing relations with Cuba . . . and even shook hands with Chavez at an OAS meeting back in April 2009! Change may be coming, and these historical animosities may be softening!

It's not just the bold and brash loud-mouths in Latin America who are embracing the left. Brazil's Dilma Rousseff is a left-leaning president as well. Argentina has been led by a left-leaning government for years. Ecuador, Nicaragua, Haiti, and Peru have headed that way as well. As you can see from the map on the following page, the future of Latin America does seem to be in the left-leaning categories. Let's explore why that is.

Why is the left progressing and gaining popularity? Many people in the world are starting to look at Latin America as a singular entity—one of the reasons I decided to do this chapter—that perhaps may become a new axis of power on the planet. What am I talking about? Well, as a group of disparate countries that didn't have a lot of common economic or political goals, now they do. As they have this leftward move, we can look at this entire region as representing a more common, singular ideology. There is no other region like that on the planet at this second. We can look at most of the planet which has progressively over the last 50–100 years been going toward something that's more on the right, more strictly capitalist, democratic systems. While certainly these are all democracies down there, they are going more left in terms of social and cultural issues, becoming much more openly liberal. In other words, the overwhelming focus in Latin America is to remedy the very wealth disparity that we talked about earlier.

Why is this happening here? Doesn't everyone want social justice and equality for people across the planet? Well yeah, lots of people do. But as I already suggested, this is the place on the planet that has the greatest wealth disparity. (The Middle East is a close second, and is partly the reason they are undergoing the revolutionary activity of the Arab Spring.) The landless, impoverished masses make this a perfect lab setting for this kind of experiment to evolve. Why is it here? Why is it right now? You have to understand that when you have any state, country, or place where most people are incredibly poor, you are asking for a revolution. When most people have no stake in the land, no claims—it's all fine as long as the minority, who has the power and wealth, can keep them down. When it becomes too lopsided, it becomes tougher and tougher for the elite to keep a lid on it, and things will eventually boil over.

Societies like this are always on the brink of revolution (see Mexican Revolution, Communist Revolution, Bolivarian Revolution, and the very much current 2011 Arab Revolutions!), and Latin America is leaning back to that point today. It is because of this inequality that people are voting for the left, voting for parties whose *primary goal* is to alleviate wealth disparity. They want to make things more equal. They are striving to improve infrastructure like roads and schools as part of their primary goal. I'm not saying that this isn't a goal of the other parties, but this is the *primary goal* of leftist parties.

The primary leftist agenda involves things like human rights, investment in education and healthcare, and equal access to land for the impoverished masses. That is the main unspoken priority, and that is why the leftist agenda is so popular. In democratic countries, where nobody has jack to their name, the leftist candidates are extremely appealing because they are telling the people, "Hey, we are trying to make this better for you or more equal for you." Thus, it should not be a radical surprise that there is a big movement towards the left across the region that has the greatest wealth disparity on the planet. That's why people are voting for the leftist candidates.

Why are they not voting anymore for the rightist candidates? It's got a lot to do with the US's historic involvement and where we are in today's world. These are all established democracies, and in the 21st century, it is increasingly hard for a military dictatorship or for a government supported by an foreign entity like the US, to hold power because issues are getting clearer and fewer people are being influenced to vote against their interests. The blatant corruption is getting easier to identify, so it's very difficult for extreme right-wingers to hold power anymore.

Just look at all that leaning!

2014 Leftist Latin Update: the trend described above still holds true generally speaking, but with a subtle shift: the center-right and right-wing political powers of Latin America continue to lose power, mostly because the left-leaning governments/parties are becoming much more moderate, moving to be just center-left. Anti-capitalist, anti-US extremism still exists in places like Venezuela, Argentina, Ecuador, and Bolivia, but is fast falling out of fashion for the region as a whole. The most successful countries currently are the ones on the moderate center-left path. Despite this change, and the fact that the majority of Latin American governments are much more moderate leftist without an extreme agenda, the US still really despises the far-left folks like Castro of Cuba and Morales of Bolivia, and they really, really hated Chavez of Venezuela. . . .

What's the Deal with the US Hatred of Venezuela?

Why did the US despise Hugo Chavez so much, and still hate the Venezuelan government? Venezuela has the means to produce over 3 billion barrels of oil per day, 60 percent of which is bought by the United States. Using this revenue, Venezuela has started to pick up some serious military hardware in recent years. Former President Hugo Chavez worked hard to secure arms deals with countries such as Brazil, China, Russia, and Spain. Take these newly acquired MiG jets, attack helicopters, AK-47s and Scud missiles, put them into the hands of two million well-trained Venezuelans and you've got yourself a bit of a hemispheric headache. While Venezuela may not have this strength right now, these are the plans set in motion by Chavez, convinced of a coming invasion by the United States.

Hugo on the US Hate List.

Why in the world did Chavez believe that the big bad US is going to march into little Venezuela? Maybe it was the name-calling by former Secretary of State Condoleezza Rice when she accused Venezuela of being a "sidekick" to Iran. Perhaps Chavez was offended when former Secretary of Defense Donald Rumsfeld compared him to Hitler. Or maybe Chavez took it personally when evangelist Pat Robertson called for his assassination on national television. In any case, Chavez certainly became suspicious of his neighbors to the north after the US refused to denounce an unconstitutional, and extremely undemocratic, 2002 coup which would overthrow his democratically elected self, even though it only lasted a few days. Virtually all countries denounced the coup within hours, but the US stayed mysteriously quiet. Oops. Probably a bad call on the US's part.

The US continues to criticize the policies of democratically elected Chavez as being "undemocratic," and in heated response he at times has vowed to cut every drop of oil exports and to mount an all-out guerilla war should the US step foot in Venezuela. And, given the former Bush's administration's doctrine of preemptive war, a simple cry of "terrorist!" could drive hundreds of thousands of US troops to South America. Sound crazy? Yeah, I guess. But that's probably what people in Afghanistan and Iraq thought as well.

Hang on! Don't be misled by the Avenger's rap on this dude; I'm not promoting the pronouncements of this proud peacock. He was certainly leftist, certainly socialist, and certainly legally democratically elected, but that doesn't mean he did a particularly good job. While billions were made from oil revenues in his tenure as president, and perhaps millions were pulled out of poverty, Venezuela is far from a socialist utopia . . . or even a functioning society! Crime is rampant, infrastructure is crumbling, and the economy is largely mismanaged at an epic scale. The country has been rocked in 2014 with mass protests, dozens killed, and an increasingly authoritarian government clamping down hard in order to hold the country together. Hugo himself died in 2013, and many of us are wondering if his socialist dream may be slowly fading away as well. . . .

LOSING THE LATINS: US UNDONE

Why the US is *really, really* worried all about this: The US is troubled by this leftist lean because it is largely seen across the planet like this: "The US has screwed up their foreign policy so bad that they have lost control and influence in their own backyard." This may be an extreme statement, but it is a fair statement, nonetheless. Part of the reason they have done that, and part of the reason rightist regimes have lost power, is that they have been perhaps a little too heavy-handed over time. Most of the US involvement and incursions into the region were for reasons previously mentioned, such as anticommunist intervention, but even through the Cold War and to the present day, another reason for US involvement is to protect US economic interests. This is seen as extremely problematic for locals, who are usually on the losing side of what benefits the US economically.

In situations when the US has invaded places like Nicaragua or Belize, or has helped assassinate a democratically elected leader in Chile, it was because of this fear that in lefty/commie countries, a redistribution of land and resources was going to occur—you remember: **nationalization.** That was unacceptable to the US, largely because there were US corporations down there yelling, "Hey, that land/resources you poor people are taking is US property!" This was argued during the Cold War era, about Chile, in fact. A company said, "Hey! US government! You can't let commies take over Chile. They will nationalize our company (which means the commies will take it over and make the profit), and this is US property." A lot of US involvement has been due to protecting these US corporate interests. We'll examine this more in future chapters. Suffice it to say for now, the US's pro-capitalism, pro-free markets, pro-US corporations attitude is hugely distrusted by many Latin Americans . . . and as the region becomes more independent and wealthy, they are pivoting away from US policies and US leadership because there are . . .

NEW KIDS IN THE BLOCK . . .

The perception of US involvement as self-serving, coupled with massive wealth disparity, in part explains why much of Latin America has gone to the left. A lot of leftist candidates, particularly Chavez, Castro, and Evo Morales in Bolivia are saying, "We're not even pretending to do the neo-liberal capitalist policies. To be a free market with free and open trade works for the United States, and it looks good on paper, but it isn't working for us."

A lot of these leaders are saying, "We're not anti-US, we're just anti-free trade." The current president of Bolivia says, "We've done it. We've tried to do free trade, and we're still poor as squat! We won't do it anymore! We're not going to give priority to American corporations, and we're not going to give tax breaks to American anything!" Why is that? Because there's some new kids in town that many countries may give incentives to: China and India and Japan just to name a few. These countries not only are grabbing up tons of natural resources, but are expanding their exports into Latin America as well. Lots of investment flowing in to start new businesses and partnerships with the Latins from all points abroad has been the theme. That's another reason America fears a loss of influence in Latin America.

To be honest, you can't really blame the Latins for taking advantage of the international interest in their region. Specifically, the Chinese are courting countries around the world, making sweet trade deals with them, in order to feed the Chinese economy's ever-increasing hunger for natural resources. Chinese foreign trade/foreign aid deals are even sweeter because they come with no strings attached, unlike deals from the US. On top of that—and this is critical—in the last decade, the Chinese and Indian and even many African leaders have personally visited virtually every single Latin state, and multiple times, on multiple visits, in multiple years. Former US President Bush only managed to head south of the border twice in eight years. Obama has been twice, and one time his Secret Service agents got busted with Colombian hookers. Starting to get the picture here? It gets worse: Russia has shown a renewed interest in floating more military ships into the area and strengthening ties with old and new allies. Iran is even in this game, having opened dozens of cultural centers and working on economic pacts across the region. Meanwhile, the USA does not even have a diplomat in 10 Latin American countries due to confirmations being grid-locked in Congress. 'Nuf said.

And we must also point out that Latin America as a whole is on the upswing, meaning there is a lot more "local" demand for goods and services as the middle class grows, and many of those goods and services are being provided by local companies themselves. Add to the growing powerhouses of Brazil ad Mexico, which are both top 20 world economies and natural leaders within the region . . . and the picture of a much diminished US role starts to take shape.

Now I have spent a lot of time explaining the viewpoint of the Latin Lefties, but I don't want to exclude the ideas of the other side of the political/economic spectrum. About people on the political right: I don't want to suggest that they only want to make money and they don't give a damn about people; that's not the case. Even these people on the opposite side of the spectrum (real anti-socialists) would argue, "No, we want to make these countries richer, too. We want their citizens to have more stuff and not be poor, but we don't think social programs are the way to do it. We think the way to make people richer in Brazil and Colombia and Mexico is to have free trade." Free trade is the typical conservative approach to alleviating poverty. I don't want to deify anyone that is socialist because there are people on the other side who also want good things. They just don't think leftist methods will work: "You can't just give them a welfare check! That's not going to solve anything! Then nobody will be rich! What we need is free trade." Thus . . .

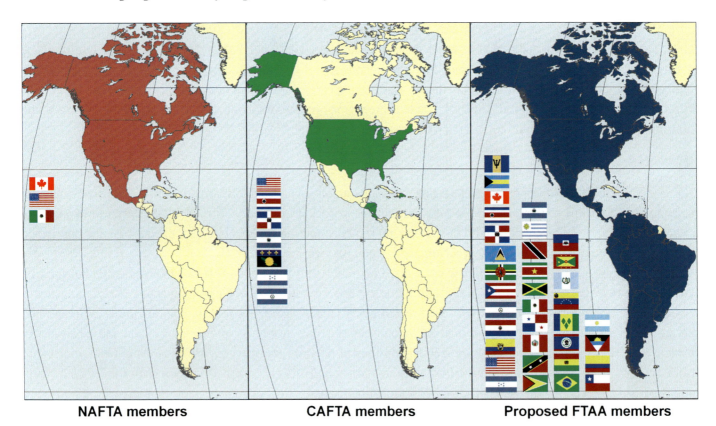

NAFTA members **CAFTA members** **Proposed FTAA members**

The **Free Trade Area of the Americas** (FTAA) already is and will be a hot issue for this hemisphere over the next decade. It's going to be a rallying point for anti-globalization as well as globalization powers. There are going to be big revolts over it; there are going to be heavy stones thrown over it. It's already a big, big deal that's just going to get bigger as the adversaries of capitalism (and/or the US) use it as fodder for their fire.

I bring this up because free-traders say, "Oh, we want Brazilians to be happy, but the way to accomplish that is a free trade union." **NAFTA** is a free-trade union between Canada, Mexico, and the United States. **CAFTA** is an ever-growing free trade area between the US and a handful of Caribbean and Central American countries with the inevitable goal of being the FTAA. The **FTAA** is a proposed free-trade area of every single country in the Americas. The United States, of course having an edge in all of this, is a big fan and proponent of the FTAA. It thinks the FTAA will make it richer, for one, but it also thinks it will help it to reestablish influence in the Latin American region as a leader of the FTAA. Anti-US, anti-globalization forces and leftist politicians in Latin America say, "No. We've been playing that game for a hundred years and we're still poor. We don't like it. We don't buy it."

We shall see how the battle for free trade pans out in the coming decades.

Chapter closer: These pervasive themes are not only historical, but they play into today's Latin America. Now let's take a look into some of Latin America's subregions to provide more specific details, so you can understand how each one works into today's and tomorrow's world.

DON'T GET LEFT OUT OF LATIN AMERICA!

HOW FAR LEFT ARE THESE LEADERS?

The Latin American leaders below are arranged in order of increasing dedication to full-on liberal socialist policy; the further to the left, the more fully the incorporation of socialist ideology into their political and economic policies. But can you name all these peeps and the countries they lead? Hint: US President Obama is thrown in as a marker of just barley left-of-center, and the dude to his right is actually center-right, conservative.

_____ _____ _____ _____ _____ _____ _____ _____ _____
_____ _____ _____ _____ _____ _____ _____ _____ _____

Leaders: Rousseff, Obama, Castro, Correa, Santos, Chavez, Ortega, Kirchner, Morales
Countries: US, Bolivia, Brazil, Nicaragua, Colombia, Argentina, Cuba, Venezuela, Ecuador

LATIN AMERICA RUNDOWN & RESOURCES

View additional Plaid Avenger resources for this region at http://plaid.at/latin

BIG PLUSES

→ Sizable chunk of real estate on planet earth with a boat load of resources
→ Has never invaded or infuriated any other country or region
→ Not a target of international terrorism at all. Who else can brag about that?
→ Becoming a serious place of interest and investment for China and other rising powers

BIG PROBLEMS

→ Biggest wealth disparity on the planet
→ Political instability chronic in some areas, possible just about anywhere; Venezuela is in trouble right now
→ History of outside political and economic domination has left many residents with an inferiority complex
→ Heavily dependent on exports of natural resources and basic manufactures
→ Environmental degradation becoming rampant in exchange for economic growth

DEAD DUDES OF NOTE:

Simón Bolívar: The '"George Washington of South America": hero, visionary, revolutionary and liberator . . . he led Bolivia, Colombia, Ecuador, Panama, Peru and Venezuela to independence and instilled democracy as the foundations of all Latin American ideology.

James Monroe: 5th President of the US and important for this chapter for his **Monroe Doctrine** which became the cornerstone for US foreign policy in the entire hemisphere, right on up to the present. The Doctrine pretty much sez: any foreign power which messes with Latin America, will also be messing with the US.

Theodore Roosevelt: 26th President of US, and "Rough Rider" that helped invade Cuba in his spare time prior to becoming a politician. His **Roosevelt Corollary** was an amendment to the Monroe Doctrine which asserted the right of the US to even intervene in the internal affairs of Latin American states to "stabilize" them if necessary.

Franklin Delano Roosevelt: 32nd President of the US and creator of **Good Neighbor Policy** which sought to soften the apparent US hegemony over Latin America by renouncing the US right to intervene unilaterally.

LIVE LEADERS YOU SHOULD KNOW:

Nicolás Maduro: Current President of a crumbling Venezuela. A former bus driver, then Foreign Minister and then Vice President under Hugo Chavez, this dude is not up for the challenge of taking over for his boss. Civil war imminent.

Evo Morales: President of Bolivia, first indigenous dude to become so. Staunch member of the leftist/Chavez team, has nationalized lots of industries in his country, and also used to be a coca farmer!

Rafael Correa: President of Ecuador, highly educated economist and linguist who is also pushing hard for socialist reform and even an overhaul of how his country deals with international financial institutions too. Also on the Bolivarian Revolution train.

Dilma Rousseff: President of Brazil, the largest Latin American state by size, population, and economy too which is 8th biggest in world. First woman leader of the South American juggernaut, and at a time when Brazil is gaining a serious international political power position; is a BRIC state that is increasingly speaking with an independent mind on many foreign policy issues, including Iran, who they support. Dilma is definitely center-left, but not really on-board for the extremes advocated by Chavez, et al.

Cristina Kirchner: First female President of Argentina, a top 30 world economy, and, along with Chile, one of the most fully developed states in South America. Has attempted socialist reform in her country, and is a strong ally of leftist/Chavez team, although she maintains good relations with US and Team West.

Juan Manuel Santos: center-right President of Colombia. Distinct in the region for being an open, 100% committed, ally of the US and no fan whatsoever of leftist policies of his neighbors. Gets billions form US to fight drugs and is following in the footsteps of his center-right predecessor Alvaro Uribe, whose economic and social policies he is continuing to advance.

Fidel Castro: The un-killable king of communism in the Western Hemisphere, leader of the Cuban Revolution of 1959, provoker of the Cuban Missile Crisis of 1962, grand poobah of Cuba from 1959 to 2008, and sole reason for the 50 year old US embargo against Cuba. He is revered in leftists circles as a demi-god, and his death (coming soon!) will transform the US/Cuban relationship overnight.

Raul Castro: Current President of Cuba, much quieter older brother of Fidel who is continuing to carry on the wanna-be communist legacy. But, many analyst assume that Raul is already making slow moves to open up the island's economy and politics in preparations for his brother's death, at which time Cuba will change dramatically. Maybe.

Daniel Ortega: Current President of Nicaragua, a post he first held back in 1985–90 as the leader of the leftist Sandinista movement which overthrew an US-backed dictator (Somoza). Carried out controversial land reform and wealth redistribution (that is, communism), which brought the wrath of Uncle Sam against him. That is why the Reagan administration illegally funded and armed the US-backed Contras to take him out. Like Fidel Castro, the US still hates Ortega after all these years.

LIVE LEADERS YOU SHOULD KNOW:

Enrique Peña Nieto: Current President of Mexico, center-left, liberal who is re-vamping the Mexican economy and society in surprisingly fiscally conservative ways (privatization, breaking teacher unions) and who may shift Cartel War tactics to minimize violence against citizens.

Carlos Slim: Mexican business magnate, investor, and philanthropist. From 2010 to 2013 was richest man in the world. Pretty much dominates telecommunications marker in Latin America.

Conclusion

So here we are at the end. Hopefully everything about the "Western world" is clear by now, right? Nope. We've barely scratched the surface. But that was the point of this adventure—not to know everything about these incredibly large and diverse regions, but to become more proficient with concepts, ideas, and theories used to better understand places, patterns and processes. This wasn't about memorizing countries, capitals, mountains, rivers, and so on—a common misconception of what geography is about. My goal for the term was to get you curious about our incredibly complicated world, and although we were only able to look at roughly half of it, you know at this point that it's impossible to draw lines around parts and treat them as if they have no connection to the rest.

Regional Geography—the classification system we used this term—is both a useful way to divide up the world in order to learn about it, and an increasingly outdated way of looking at issues like population, politics, economics, etc. You've learned that the forces of globalization are leading to more interconnection and interdependence, and that these forces are not slowing down anytime soon. Regional Geography helps us understand the parts, but it can fall short of showing us how the parts fit together.

For this reason, we spent the first part of the term looking at broad topics—so we could gain a sense of some of the ways the world is changing "globally" before looking at specific places. These topics helped us understand how to recognize patterns, how to analyze processes. Our examination of specific places—our western regions—was laughably brief. Is it possible to learn everything about Europe or North America in a week? Of course not. Not only that, but are these places all equally "Western?" How do we reconcile the East/West split in Europe? What about Russia's schizophrenic foreign policy behavior? Where does Latin America fit? It was colonized by Europe, but it generally took a different direction than the U.S. and Canada. Even the experts who study and write about this stuff can't agree.

263

Plaid Avenger's World
CONCLUSION

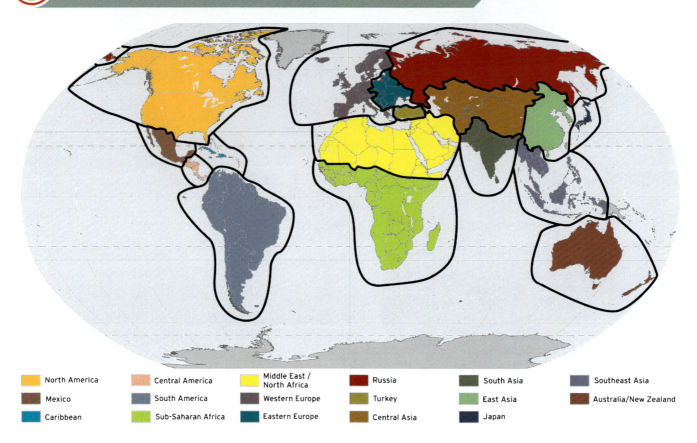

North America	Central America	Middle East / North Africa	Russia	South Asia	Southeast Asia
Mexico	South America	Western Europe	Turkey	East Asia	Australia/New Zealand
Caribbean	Sub-Saharan Africa	Eastern Europe	Central Asia	Japan	

At a philosophical level, this lack of a cohesive system for dividing up the world should encourage you to see the subjectivity inherent in labels like "the West." The critical thinking I've been talking about all term should help you recognize that this problem (where do places fit in this West/non-West binary?) is actually very common in all sorts of ways, in academia and in life more generally. And that's where perspective becomes important. An implicit goal of this class was to provide you a broad overview of some of the world in order that you could make up your own mind about these debates. As I said in the beginning, we weren't trying to fully understand a topic in this class, the way you might understand how a chemical reaction works or the ways to analyze and describe a financial system. Rather, we were adding material, complexity even, to our mental maps. These categories of "West" and "non-West" may be helpful as an organizing principle (someone in the Oregon Legislature decided that this should be a category in the baccalaureate core), but now that we're finished you can discard these categories—you're now free to create your own.

There's obviously still much to learn. Thinking back to the beginning of the term and our old/young woman graphic, there's still quite a bit we all don't see. But I hope I've given you some useful tools you can use to develop your own mental maps. I also hope I've given you a sense of the range of issues that can be examined using geography as a lens. I'm not concerned that you all change your major, but I want you to see the "geographic perspective" as a useful tool of observation and analysis for whatever you happen to be majoring in, and for much more beyond your college career. Some claim that geography will make you smarter, or more successful, and so on, and I might agree, but I also think it's a necessary exercise at a very basic level: you live on this planet . . . you might as well learn about it while you're here, right?

See both sides of the systems now?

Plaid Avenger's World
CONCLUSION

So whatever you do from now on, I hope you remember some of the basic lessons from this course, that it's a big, beautiful, terrible, complicated world we're living in, and that this world is changing, and it always will. I hope you remember that there's often more than meets the eye, and that learning is a never-ending process. While you may need to specialize to be an accountant or a nuclear engineer, you become a much more interesting and intelligent person if you learn about other topics, places, and people. You might seem smaller or less significant now that you have a better sense of the vastness and diversity of our planet, but on the contrary, you're very important. You're you—the only one. And you're already playing a very large role. You're connected to people and places, through your communication, your politics, your consumption. In the end it comes down to how you choose to act in it. Now that you know more about the geography of our planet, it's difficult to un-know.

My advice? Don't seek to simplify, to order, or to categorize unnecessarily between "self" and "other," "us" and "them," "here" or "there." Try to embrace the diversity, complexity, and even confusion.

It's a plaid world after all . . .

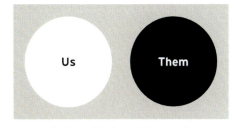

Just say "no" to a black and white world.

Image Credits

INTRODUCTION

Page ix: map courtesy of Katie Pritchard; **Page x: top:** map courtesy of Katie Pritchard; **bottom:** courtesy of Katie Pritchard; **Page xii: top:** courtesy of Katie Pritchard; **Page xiii:** both images © Shutterstock, Inc.

CHAPTER 1

Page 4: top: © 2010 JupiterImages Corporation; **bottom:** map courtesy of Katie Pritchard; **Page 5: top and middle:** © Shutterstock, Inc.; **bottom:** courtesy of Katie Pritchard; **Page 6:** courtesy of Katie Pritchard; **Page 7: top:** © brave rabbit, 2010. Used under license from Shutterstock, Inc.; **bottom:** © 2010 JupiterImages Corporation; **Page 8:** © 2007 JupiterImages Corporation; **Page 13: a–f.:** © Shutterstock, Inc.

CHAPTER 2

Page 14: © 2010 JupiterImages Corporation; **Page 17, fig. 2.2:** map source: US Dept. of Agriculture; **Page 19: bottom:** © Shutterstock, Inc.; **Page 20: top:** © Shutterstock, Inc.; **Page 21: right 5 images:** © Shutterstock, Inc.; **Page 22: bottom 3 images:** © Shutterstock, Inc.; **Page 25: top right and left images:** © Shutterstock, Inc.; **Page 29:** Image © Tom Wang, 2012. Shutterstock, Inc.; **Page 30:** © Shutterstock, Inc.; **Page 31, fig. 2.14:** courtesy of Katie Pritchard

CHAPTER 3

Page 34, fig. 3.1: courtesy of Katie Pritchard; **Page 38: top:** official White House portrait; **bottom:** photo by SSgt. Lance Cheung, U.S. Air Force, from Defense Visual Information Center; **Page 40:** © 2003 by Damon Clark. Used with permission; **Page 41: left:** © 2007 JupiterImages Corporation; **center:** © 2007 JupiterImages Corporation; **right:** © 2007 JupiterImages Corporation; **Page 42: fig. 3.2:** map source: *The World Factbook*; **fig. 3.3:** map source: *The CIA World Factbook*; **Page 43: top:** White House photo by Pete Souza; **bottom:** Government of Argentina; **Page 44:** map source: *The CIA World Factbook*; **Page 45: top:** map source: University of Texas Libraries; **bottom:** maps courtesy of courtesy of the University of Texas Libraries, Perry-Castaneda Library Map Collection; **Page 46: bottom left:** New York City Police Department; **bottom left center:** photo by Joseph Randall Blanchard (ca. 1898), from Library of Congress; **bottom center:** Swiss Federal Council of the year 2007 from The Federal Authorities of the Swiss Confederation; **bottom right center:** official White House portrait; **bottom right:** Dept. of Defense photo by Erin A. Kirk-Cuomo; **Page 47: top:** New York City Police Dept.; **bottom left center:** Saudi Information Office; **Bottom center:** Dept. of Defense; **bottom right center:** Dept. of Defense photo; **bottom right:** National Archives & Records Administration photo; **Page 48: left:** Image © Neftali, 2012. Shutterstock, Inc.; **middle:** Image © Hung Chung Chih, 2012. Shutterstock, Inc.; **right:** © Hulton-Deutsch Collection/CORBIS; **Page 49: left:** photo by Joseph Randall Blanchard (ca. 1898), from Library of Congress; **right:** official White House portrait; **Page 50:** Image © Atlaspix, 2012. Shutterstock, Inc.; **Page 51: top left:** photo by AIC William M. Firaneck, U.S. Air Force, from Defense Visual Information Center; **top right:** Government of Argentina; **bottom left:** Image © Neftali, 2012. Shutterstock, Inc.; **bottom right:** U.S. Air Force photo by Tech. Sgt. Craig Clapper; **Page 52: left:** Image © tristan tan, 2012. Shutterstock, Inc.; **right:** Dept. of Defense photo by Helene C. Stikkel; **Page 53: top:** caricature by Edmund S. Valtman, from Library of Congress; **bottom:** Image © Patrick Poendl, 2012. Shutterstock, Inc.; **Page 54: left:** photo from Iraqi Freedom II CD Collection by Joint Combat Camera composed of Army, Navy, Marine, and Air Force photographers; **right:** Dept. of Defense photo; **Page 55: left:** National Archives & Records Administration photo; **right:** National Archives & Records Administration; **fig. 3.4:** courtesy of Katie Pritchard; **Page 58: top left:** Bundesregierung/Laurence Chaperon; **top left center:** Dept. of Defense photo by Erin A. Kirk-Cuomo; **top right center:** U.S. Navy photo by Mass Communication Specialist 2nd Class Jesse B. Awalt; **top right:** © European Community, 2008; **middle left:** Turkish Embassy; **middle left center:** official White House photo; **middle right center:** © Saurabh Das/AP/Corbis; **middle right:** Saudi Information Office; **bottom left:** photo by Roberto Stuckert Filho/PR, courtesy of Secretaria de Imprensa, Brasil; **bottom left center:** Elza Fiúza/ABr;

Credits

IMAGE CREDITS

bottom right center: Dept. of Defense photo by D. Myles Cullen; **bottom right:** © European Community, 2011; **Page 59: top left:** © Yao Dawei/Xinhua Press/Corbis; **top left center:** Government of Argentina; **top right center:** Tânia Rêgo/ABr; **top right:** Dept. of Defense photo by Cpl. Mark Doran, Australian Defense Force; **middle left:** © DENIS BALIBOUSE/Reuters/Corbis; **middle left center:** © NATO; **middle right center:** © European Community, 2009; **middle right:** Dept. of Defense photo by Erin A. Kirk-Cuomo; **bottom left:** © European Union, 2011; **bottom left center:** official White House photo by Pete Souza; **bottom right center:** Dept. of Defense photo; **bottom right:** © NATO

CHAPTER 4

Page 60: images © 2007 JupiterImages Corporation; **bottom left:** Image © v.s.anandhakrishna, 2012. Shutterstock, Inc.; **bottom right:** Image © Diego Cervo, 2012. Shutterstock, Inc.; **Page 61: left:** photo by unknown (ca. 1920), from Library of Congress; **left center:** Elza Fiúza/ABr; **right center:** © European Community, 2011; **right:** stipple engraving by MacKenzie (ca. 1805), from Library of Congress; **Page 62:** photo by unknown (ca. 1920), from Library of Congress; **Page 63:** stipple engraving by MacKenzie (ca. 1805), from Library of Congress; **Page 64: left:** photo by unknown (ca. 1920), from Library of Congress; **left center:** photo by Warren K. Leffler, from Library of Congress; **center:** Government of Argentina; **right center:** White House photo by David Bohrer; **right:** Dept. of Defense photo by Erin A. Kirk-Cuomo; **Page 65: left:** photo from Official Russian Presidential Press and Information Office; **center:** © European Community, 2011; **right center:** official White House portrait; **right:** stipple engraving by MacKenzie (ca. 1805), from Library of Congress; **Page 66:** photo by Jack Delano (ca. 1940), from Library of Congress; **Page 67: top:** © Shutterstock, Inc.; **bottom 3 images:** © Shutterstock, Inc.; **Page 69:** © 2007 JupiterImages Corporation; **Page 70: top left:** © 2007 JupiterImages Corporation; **top right:** © 2007 JupiterImages Corporation; **middle right:** © 2007 JupiterImages Corporation; **bottom left:** © 2007 JupiterImages Corporation; **bottom right:** © 2007 JupiterImages Corporation; **Page 71: top right:** © 2007 JupiterImages Corporation; **middle left:** © 2007 JupiterImages Corporation; **bottom right:** © 2007 JupiterImages Corporation; **Page 72: top:** © 2007 JupiterImages Corporation; **Page 73:** National Archives & Records Administration photo; **Page 75:** map courtesy of Katie Pritchard; **Page 76:** map courtesy of Katie Pritchard; **Page 77:** © 2009 JupiterImages Corporation; **Page 78:** map courtesy of Katie Pritchard; **Page 79:** From *The Silent War* by John Ames Mitchell, Illustrations by William Balfour Ker (New York: Life Publishing Co, 1906). Courtesy of Library of Congress.

CHAPTER 5

Page 80: Dept. of Defense photos; **Page 82: right:** Courtesy of Library of Congress; **left:** © 2009 JupiterImages Corporation; **Page 83: top:** Photo by Walter P. Miller (1929), Courtesy of Library of Congress; **bottom:** Courtesy of Library of Congress; **Page 84:** © Shutterstock, Inc.; **Page 85:** © 2009 JupiterImages Corporation; **Page 86:** © 2009 JupiterImages Corporation; **Page 87:** © 2009 JupiterImages Corporation; **Page 89:** © 2007 JupiterImages Corporation; **Page 90:** all photos © 2007 JupiterImages Corporation; **Page 91:** © 2009 JupiterImages Corporation; **Page 92:** © Shutterstock, Inc.; **Page 93: fig. 5.1:** courtesy of Katie Pritchard; **Page 94:** map courtesy of Katie Pritchard; **Pages 96 & 97:** NASA/Goddard Space Flight Center Scientific Visualization Studio

CHAPTER 6

Page 100: top left: © 2007 JupiterImages Corporation; **top right:** Frank and Frances Carpenter Collection, from Library of Congress; **middle:** © Royalty-free/CORBIS; **bottom left:** © NATO; bottom right: Copyright © African Union, 2003. All rights reserved. Used by permission; **Page 101:** © 2007 JupiterImages Corporation; **Page 102:** map courtesy of Katie Pritchard, flags from *The World Factbook*; **Page 103: top:** map courtesy of Katie Pritchard; **bottom:** map courtesy of Katie Pritchard; **Page 104:** map courtesy of Katie Pritchard; **Page 105:** map courtesy of Katie Pritchard; **Page 106:** maps courtesy of Katie Pritchard; **Page 107: middle:** OECD logo used by permission; **bottom:** © 2007 JupiterImages Corporation; **Page 108: top:** © NATO; **bottom:** © Royalty-free/CORBIS; **Page 109:** NATO logo used by permission of NATO; **bottom:** © NATO; **Page 110:** map courtesy of Katie Pritchard; **Page 111:** courtesy of Katie Pritchard; **Page 112:** *The World Factbook*; **Page 113: top:** © AP Photo/Hussein Malla; **middle:** Organization of American States; **Page 114: top left & right:** Copyright © African Union, 2003. All rights reserved. Used by permission; **middle right:** U.S. Air Force photo by Tech. Sgt. Jeremy T. Lock; **flags at bottom:** *The World Factbook*; **Page 115:** flags: *The World Factbook*; **bottom:** © European Communities, 2009; **Page 116: top:** © European Communities, 2009; **bottom:** Roberto Stuckert Filho/PR/ABr; **Page 117:** WTO logo used with permission; **Page 120:** map courtesy of Katie Pritchard; **Page 121:** Government of Argentina

Part 2 opener: map courtesy of Katie Pritchard

CHAPTER 7

Page 126: map courtesy of Katie Pritchard and NOAA; **Page 127:** © NATO; **Page 128:** NASA/Goddard Space Flight Center Scientific Visualization Center; **Page 129:** map source: *The Cambridge Modern History Atlas 1912*, courtesy of the University of Texas Libraries, Perry-Castaneda Library Map Collection; **Page 130: top:** U.S. Marine Corps photo by Lance Cpl. Kelly R. Chase; **bottom:** © Shutterstock, Inc.; **Page 131: top:** map courtesy of Katie Pritchard; **bottom:** all images © 2007 JupiterImages Corporation; **Page 132: top:** photo by M.B. Marcell (ca. 1911), from Library of Congress; **bottom:** U.S. Air Force photo by SSGT Jacob N. Bailey; **Page 133: top:** Dept. of Defense photo by U.S. Navy; **bottom:** U.S. Navy photo by Mass Communication Specialist 3rd Class Kathleen Gorby; **Page 134:** U.S. Navy photo by Mass Communication Specialist 3rd Class Geoffrey Lewis; **Page 135:** Library of Congress; **Page 136:** art by John C. McRae (ca. 1620), from Library of Congress; **Page 137:** © Shutterstock, Inc.; **Page 138: middle:** photo by The New York Times (ca. 1954), from Library of Congress; **bottom:** map courtesy of Katie Pritchard; **Page 140:** U.S. Dept of Agriculture, from

Library of Congress; **Page 141:** © 2007 JupiterImages Corporation; **Page 142: top:** map courtesy of Katie Pritchard & US Dept of Defense; **bottom:** © Shutterstock, Inc.; **Page 143:** U.S. Air Force photo by A1C Tanya M. Harms; **Page 144: top:** created by Acme Litho. Co., New York (ca. 1910), from Library of Congress; **bottom:** created by Leslie-Judge Co., New York (1917), from Library of Congress; **Page 145:** created by United Cigar Stores Company (1918), from Library of Congress; **Page 146: top:** U.S. Government Printing Office (1943), from Library of Congress; **bottom:** © Shutterstock, Inc.; **Page 147: top:** Illinois Co., Chicago (1917), from Library of Congress; **bottom:** American Lithographic Co., New York (1918), from Library of Congress; **Page 148: middle:** © Shutterstock, Inc.; **bottom left:** Library of Congress; **bottom middle:** Brady-Handy Photograph Collection, Library of Congress; **bottom right:** official White House photo; **Page 149: left:** official White House photo; **left center:** © European Community; **right center:** official White House photo; **right:** Dept. of Defense photo

CHAPTER 8

Page 150: map courtesy of Katie Pritchard and NOAA; **Page 152: left:** originally published by Thomas B Noonan, from Library of Congress; **left center:** Library of Congress; **right center:** Library of Congress; **right:** Engraving by W. Holl after painting by Franz Hals, from Library of Congress; **Page 153:** CIA map; **Page 155: top:** *Blue Marble: Next Generation* image produced by Reto Stockli, NASA Earth Observatory (NASA Goddard Space Flight Center); **Page 157: left:** National Archives & Records Administration; **right:** National Archives & Records Administration; **Page 158: top:** Farm Security Administration, Office of War Information Collection 12002-27, from Library of Congress; **bottom:** maps courtesy of Katie Pritchard; **Page 159:** maps courtesy of Katie Pritchard; **Page 161:** created by James Montgomery Flagg (1918), from Library of Congress; **Page 163:** Library of Congress; **Page 164:** map by Katie Pritchard; **Page 165:** Library of Congress; **Page 166:** © European Communities, 2006; **Page 167: top:** © European Union, 2011; **bottom:** Bundesregierung/Laurence Chaperon; **Page 168:** © Nejron Photo, 2012. Used under license of Shutterstock, Inc.; **Page 169:** © JupiterImages Corporation; **Page 170: left:** Farm Security Administration—Office of War Information Photograph Collection, from Library of Congress; **left center:** Library of Congress; **right center:** National Archives & Records Administration; **right:** Dept. of Defense photo; **Page 171: left:** © European Union, 2011; **center:** © European Communities, 2009; **right:** © European Communities, 2006

CHAPTER 9

Page 172: map courtesy of Katie Pritchard and NOAA; **Page 175: top:** © 2008 JupiterImages Corporation; **bottom:** map source: *The World Factbook;* **Page 176:** map source: *The World Factbook;* **Page 177: top:** maps: *The World Factbook;* **bottom:** map source: *The World Factbook;* **Page 179: middle:** photo © 1941 by J. Russell & Sons, from Library of Congress; **bottom:** map source: *The World Factbook;* **Page 180: right:** map source: *The World Factbook;* **left:** map source: *The World Factbook;* **Page 181: bottom:** source: *Nuclear Weapons and NATO: Analytical Survey of Literature* by U.S. Dept. of the Army, courtesy of University of Texas Libraries Perry-Castaneda Map Collection; **Page 182:** map source: *The World Factbook;* **Page 183:** map source: *The World Factbook;* **Page 184:** maps courtesy of Katie Pritchard; **Page 185:** map by U.S. Central Intelligence Agency, courtesy of University of Texas Libraries, Perry-Castaneda Map Collection; **Page 186: left:** Dept. of Defense photo by Tech. Sgt. Cedric H. Rudisill, US. Air Force; **left center:** © NATO; **right center:** © NATO; **right:** photo from Official Russian Presidential Press and Information Office; **Page 187: bottom:** © NATO; **Page 188: top:** © Shutterstock, Inc.; **bottom:** © 2008 JupiterImages Corporation; **Page 189:** © 2008 JupiterImages Corporation; **Page 190: top:** © 2008 JupiterImages Corporation; **bottom:** from *Former Yugoslavia: A Map Folio* (1992) by CIA, courtesy of University of Texas Libraries; **Page 191: left:** White House Photo Office Collection (1971), from Library of Congress; **right:** © Lucas Jackson/Reuters/Corbis; **Page 192:** CIA map, courtesy of University of Texas Libraries; **Page 193:** map by Katie Pritchard; **Page 194: left:** George Grantham Bain Collection, Library of Congress; **center:** National Archives & Records Administration; **right:** © NATO; **Page 195: left:** © NATO; **left center:** © European Communities, 2007; **right center:** © NATO; **right:** © Shutterstock, Inc.

CHAPTER 10

Page 196: top: map courtesy of Katie Pritchard and NOAA; **bottom:** created by Strobridge Lithography Co. (1895), from Library of Congress; **Page 197: top:** © 2007 JupiterImages Corporation; **bottom:** adapted from *Blue Marble: Next Generation* image produced by Reto Stockli, NASA Earth Observatory (NASA Goddard Space Flight Center); **Page 198:** created by Strobridge Lithography Co. (ca. 1896), from Library of Congress; **Page 199: top:** © Shutterstock, Inc.; **bottom:** map source: *The World Factbook;* **Page 200: top:** created by W. Holland (1803), from Library of Congress; **bottom:** map source: *The World Factbook;* **Page 201: top:** scanned from Helmolt, J.F. ed. *History of the World* (New York, Dodd, Mead & Co., 1902); **top middle:** © Shutterstock, Inc.; **bottom middle:** engraving by A. Muller (1879), Library of Congress; **bottom:** scanned from Helmolt, J.F. ed. *History of the World* (New York, Dodd, Mead & Co., 1902); **Page 202:** from the George Grantham Bain Collection, Library of Congress; **Page 203: top:** lithography by M.A. Striel'tsova (ca. 1918), from Library of Congress; **bottom left:** *New York Times,* 1919, Library of Congress; **left center:** *Tsar Nicholas II* (1915) by Boris Kustodiyev; **right center:** Library of Congress; **right:** photo ca. 1909; **Page 204: left:** Library of Congress; **right:** photo from *Liberty's Victorious Conflict: A Photographic History of the World War* by The Magazine Circulation Co., Chicago, 1918; **Page 205:** map source: *The World Factbook;* **Page 206:** from New York World-Telegram & the Sun Newspaper Photograph Collection, Library of Congress; **Page 207:** U.S. Signal Corps photo, from Library of Congress; **Page 208: top:** photo by U.S. Office of War Information Overseas Picture Division, Library of Congress; **bottom:** map source: *The World Factbook;* **Page 209:** photo by U.S. Office of War Information Overseas Picture Division, Library of Congress; **Page 210:** © Shutterstock, Inc.; **Page 211:** © 2007 JupiterImages Corporation; **Page 212:** official White House portrait; **Page 213: top left:** Library of Congress; **top center:** U.S. Signal Corps photo, from Library of Congress; **top right:** photo from

Credits

IMAGE CREDITS

Franklin D. Roosevelt Library, Library of Congress; **bottom left:** White House Photo Collection, Library of Congress; **bottom left center:** © Bettmann/Corbis; **bottom right center:** © Bettmann/Corbis; **bottom right:** White House Photo Collection, Library of Congress; **Page 214:** White House Photo Collection, Library of Congress; **Page 215:** photo by Earle D. Akin Co, 1909, from Library of Congress; **Page 218:** map courtesy of Katie Pritchard; **bottom:** photo from Official Russian Press and Information Office; **Page 219: top:** © NATO; **middle left:** © NATO; **middle right:** photo from Official Russian Press and Information Office; **bottom:** photo from Official Russian Press and Information Office; **Page 220:** map from U.S. Dept. of Energy; **Page 221:** © NATO; **Page 222:** Produced by the Office of The Geographer and Global Issues, Bureau of Intelligence and Research, US Dept. of State, courtesy of University of Texas Libraries; **Page 223: top and middle:** © Shutterstock, Inc.; **bottom:** cover of *The Great Train Robbery* by Scott Marble, 1896, from Library of Congress; **Page 224: left:** George Grantham Bain Collection, Library of Congress; **right center:** U.S. Signal Corps photo, from Library of Congress; **right:** © NATO; **Page 225: left:** © European Communities, 2009; **left center:** © European Communities, 2009; **right center:** © NATO; **right:** © NATO

CHAPTER 11

Page 226: map courtesy of Katie Pritchard and NOAA; **Page 227: left:** *Blue Marble: Next Generation* image produced by Reto Stockli, NASA Earth Observatory (NASA Goddard Space Flight Center); **right:** NASA/Goddard Space Flight Center Scientific Visualization Studio; **Page 228:** © Regien Paassen, 2012. Used under license of Shutterstock, Inc.; **Page 229:** © Pichugin Dmitry, 2012. Used under license of Shutterstock, Inc.; **Page 230:** all images: © 2007 JupiterImages Corporation; **Page 231:** ca. 1915, Library of Congress; **Page 232:** © Shutterstock, Inc.; **bottom:** © Debra James, 2012. Used under license of Shutterstock, Inc.; **Page 233: top:** © Shutterstock, Inc.; **bottom:** © 2007 JupiterImages Corporation; **Page 234:** © Gavran333, 2012. Used under license of Shutterstock, Inc.; **Page 235:** © 2007 JupiterImages Corporation; **Page 236: top:** stereograph (1919), from Library of Congress; **bottom:** lithography by Cincinnati Lithography Co., from Library of Congress; **Page 237:** all images © Shutterstock, Inc.; **Page 238: left:** Dept. of Defense photo by Robert D. Ward; **center:** Dept. of Defense photo by Cherie Cullen; **right:** Dept. of Defense photo by Cpl. Mark Doran, Australian Defense Force

CHAPTER 12

Page 240: map courtesy of Katie Pritchard and NOAA; **Page 241:** photo ca. 1867, gift of Oliver Wendell Homes, from Library of Congress; **Page 242:** map by CIA, courtesy of University of Texas Libraries; **Page 243:** all maps: from CIA, courtesy of University of Texas Libraries; **Page 244: top:** map courtesy of Katie Pritchard; **bottom:** Library of Congress; **Page 245: top:** map source: *The World Factbook*; **bottom:** photo from the Frank & Frances Carpenter Collection, Library of Congress; **Page 246:** © 2008 JupiterImages Corporation; **Page 247: top:** © Jose Miguel Hernandez Leon, 2012. Used under license of Shutterstock, Inc.; **bottom:** Library of Congress; **Page 248: top:** scanned from Helmolt, J.F. ed. *History of the World* (New York, Dodd, Mead & Co., 1902); **bottom:** courtesy of Brazilian Embassy; **Page 249: top left:** Library of Congress; **top left center:** Fabio Rodrigues Pozzebom/ABr; **top center:** courtesy of Secretaria de Imprensa, Brasil; **top right center:** photo by Warren K. Leffler, from Library of Congress; **top right:** Government of Argentina; **bottom:** photo ca. 1900, from Library of Congress; **Page 250: top:** from *Judge, February 15, 1896*, Library of Congress; **bottom:** photo ca. 1900, from Library of Congress; **Page 251: top:** photo by Elias Goldensky (1933), from Library of Congress; **bottom:** photo by Warren K. Leffler, from Library of Congress; **Page 253:** © Shutterstock, Inc.; **Page 255:** map courtesy of Katie Pritchard; **Page 256:** Government of Argentina; **Page 258:** maps courtesy of Katie Pritchard; **Page 259:** all photos courtesy of Secretaria de Imprensa, Brasil, except the far right photo, which is courtesy of Wilson Dias/ABr; **Page 260: left:** painting by Ricardo Acevedo Bernal; **left center:** The White House Historical Association (White House Collection); **right center:** National Archives & Records Administration; **right:** Library of Congress

CONCLUSION

Page 264: top: map courtesy of Katie Pritchard; **Page 265: top:** courtesy of Katie Pritchard; **bottom:** © Shutterstock, Inc.

Index

A

Aborigines, 230, 236
    Stolen Generation, 236
Abortions, 29, 30
Afghanistan, 39, 56, 57, 167
    Taliban, 57
    USSR invasion of, 211, 214–215
Africa
    colonization, 156
    population, 17
    Nigeria, 17
African Union (AU), 114
    members, 114
    military, 114
Aging population, 24
Agriculture, 20–21, 69
    industry vs., 22–23
    production, 20–21
AIDS, 3
Albania, 29
American pop culture, 143
    banning of, 143
American Revolution, 66, 83, 129
Amnesty International, 119
Anarchy, 46, 47
    Somalia, 47
ANZUS. *See* Australia, New Zealand, United States Security Treaty.
APEC. *See* Asia-Pacific Economic Cooperation.
Arab League, 112–113
    members, 112
    Muammar Qaddafi, 112
Arab Revolution, 56, 144
Arab Spring, 53, 56
Armed forces, 162
Armenia, 29
ASEAN. *See* Association of Southeast Asian Nations.
ASEAN+3, 105
Asia
    Australia ties, 233–234, 235
    population of, 16
    takeover by Japan, 234
Asian population, Australia, 236
Asia-Pacific Economic Cooperation (APEC), 107
Association of Southeast Asian Nations (ASEAN), 105, 106, 236
    East Asia Summit, 106
AU. *See* African Union.
Australia, 30, 52,
    Asian trade, 233–234
    Asians, treatment as immigrants, 236
    China, 237
    climate, 228
    early history, 228
        convict colonies, 228
    East Asia Summit and, 236
    foreign policy, 234–235
    gross domestic product, 233
    Howard, John, 234
        immigration, 235–236

Australia (continued)
  indigenous population, treatment of, 230
    Aborigines, 230
  Iraq, 235
  Japan, 237
  Malaysia and, 235
  military ally, 231–232
  opposition to Iraq invasion, 231
  peacekeepers, 235
    Indonesia, 235
    Solomon Islands, 235
  physical characteristics, 227–228
  population, 229, 235
  primary products, 232–233
  raw commodities, 233
  regional sheriff, 234
  Rudd, Kevin, 235
  standard of living, 229
  Tasmania, 230
  terrorist threats, 235
  United Nations, 235
  United States presence in, 232
  urbanization of, 229
  whites only, as immigrant policy, 236
Australia, New Zealand, United States Security Treaty (ANZUS), 232, 237
Austria, 163
Ayatollah, the, 51
Azerbaijan, 29

B

Bahrain, 28, 50, 85
Belarus, 28
  oil economics, 188
Belgium 50
Bhutan, 50
Birth control, 23
Birth rate, 19, 20
Bolivar, Simon, 248, 260
Bolivia, Evo Morales, 254
Bolshevik Revolution, 204
  Lenin, Vladimir, 204–205
Border controls, European Union, 165

Bosnia, 29, 39
Brain drain, 137–138
Brazil, 24, 76, 79, 156, 245, 258
  landlessness, 248
  Landless Workers' Movement, 248
  squatters, 248
  Rouseff, Dilma, 248, 249, 254
BRICs, 116–117, 222
  members, 116, 117
Britain, convict colonies, 228–229
Bronze Age, 5
Bulgaria, 36
Burma, 56
Burquas, 163
Bush, George W., 235

C

CAFTA. *See* Caribbean Area Free Trade Agreement.
Cameron, David, 166
Canada, 65, 135, 166
  French, 127
  military, 132–133
Capitalism, 61, 63
China, 65
  Adam Smith, 66
  contradictions re, 63
  corporation, 66–68
  government intervention, 63
  human nature and, 63
  nationalization vs., 69
  private ownership, 63
Caribbean, 243
Caribbean Area Free Trade Agreement (CAFTA), 259
Castro, Fidel, 49, 65, 78, 249, 251, 261
Castro, Raul, 261
Catherine the Great, 200
Catholic Church, 31, 51
  Polish emigrants, religious issues, 163
  Pope, 51
  Vatican City, 51
Central America, 243
  country listing, 243
Central economic planning, 209
Chavez, Hugo, 78, 249, 254, 256

Chechnya, 43, 192
   Russia and, 43
Chile, 24, 68, 85
China, 5, 24, 28, 29, 30, 31, 36, 39, 40, 50, 52, 56, 62, 68, 69, 73, 74, 75, 76, 78, 79, 82, 83, 84, 85, 86, 92, 93, 146, 233
   capitalist reforms, 65
   economic partnerships, 221–222
   GDP, 131
   Hu Jintao, 65
   Kosovo, 192
   One Child Policy, 30, 31
   Opium Wars, 83
   relationships with Australia and United States, 237
   support of Kosovo, 192
   Tibet and, 45, 192
   trade with Latin America, 257
Christianity, 152
Churchhill, Winston, 179
Cinco de Mayo holiday, 241
Cinema recommendations, 149, 171, 195, 225, 239
Civil War, Russia and, 205
Civilization, 4, 5
   China, 5
   communication, 6
   Indus Valley, 5
   industrialization, 6
   Mesopotamia, 5
   population growth, 5
   transportation, 6
   urbanization, 5–6
Classic pyramid, 26–27
Climate, Eastern Europe, 173
Clinton, President William, 39
Coal, consumption of, 3
Cocaine production, 3, 253–254
   United States response to, 253
      Plan Columbia, 253
Cold War, 177–178
   alignment of countries, 82
   buffer zone, 178
   Latin America, 251–252
   Non-Aligned Movement, 82
Colonial period
   demise of, 83–84
   industrialization, 83
   technologies, 82–83
Colonies, 45
   French Guiana, 45
   Greenland, 45
   Western Sahara, 45
Colonization, 45, 155
   Africa, 156
   Brazil, 156
   decline of, 157
   French Guiana, 45
   Great Britain, 156
   Greenland, 45
   India, 156
   languages, 156
   Netherlands, 155
   New World, 155
   Portugal, 156
   Spain, 156
   Western Sahara, 45
Columbus, Christopher, 244
Column pyramid, 26
   country stability, 27
   replacement level, 27
Command economy, 62
Communication, 6
   internet usage, 6
   Skype, 6
Communism, 46, 48–49, 61, 62–63, 64, 66
   China, 62
   command economy, 62
   contradictions re, 62
   Cuba, 49, 62, 65
   demise of, 56
   economic system, 48
   Engels, Friedrich, 48
   Lenin, Vladimir, 48–49
   Mao Ze Dong, 48, 49
   Marx, Karl, 48
   North Korea, 49
   political system, 48
   reality of, 50
   Ronald Reagan's view on, 212
   socialism vs., 65

Communism *(continued)*
    soviets, 48
    Stalin, Josef, 48
    USSR, 48
    Vietnam, 62
Communist revolution. *See* Bolshevik Revolution.
Congo, 39
Conservative, 46
Constitutional monarchy, 50, 56
Continental powers, 160
Core countries, 77–78, 84
    China, 84
    France, 84
    India, 84
    Japan, 84
    multinationals, 84
    Russia, 84
    Spain, 84
    United Kingdom, 84
    United States, 84
Corporate earnings, 88
Corporate favoritism, 139–140
Corporations, 66–68, 134–135
    Exxon, 134, 135
    General Motors, 134
    listings, 134
    multinational, 67
    WalMart, 134
Correa, Rafael, 261
Costa Rica, 53
Crimea, 187, 222–223
    Russian takeover of, 188
Cuba, 49, 62, 65, 68, 113, 251
    Castro, Fidel, 49, 65, 249
Cultural bias, male vs. female, 29–30
Cultural entities, 112–114
    African Union, 114
    Arab League, 112–113
    Organization of American States, 113
Cultural imperialism, 143–144
    American pop culture, 143
    ideology, 143
Cultural lag, 21

Culture
    commonality of, 41–42
    Eastern Europe, 174
Cyprus, 44
Czech Republic, 44, 209
    joining NATO, 183
Czechoslovakia, 44, 56, 209
    dissent within, 212
    NATO, 183

D

Danish cartoon, Prophet Mohammad, 163
Dark Ages, 154
Death rate, 19–20, 21
Defense pacts, 107–112
    North Atlantic Treaty Organization, 109–110
    Shanghai Cooperation Organization, 111
    United Nations, 108–109
    Warsaw Pact, 111
Democracy, 49–50, 56, 135
    Canada, 135
    constitutional monarchy, 50
    direct, 49–50
    forcing of, 145
    French Revolution, 135
    Middle East, 144
    representative, 50
    United States, 56, 135
Democratic Party, 66
Democratic Republic of Congo (DRC), 95
Democratic socialism, 64
Demographic Transition model, 18–25
    Stage Four, 24–26
    Stage One, 19–20
        life expectancy, 20
    Stage Three, 22–24
    Stage Two, 20–23
    Stage Five, 25
Demographics, 88
    Japan, 88
    Russia, 88
Denmark, 50
Developed countries, 81, 95

education, 89
health, 89
middle class, 90
military technology, 92
political stability, 91
risk-taking, 89
Developed world, military technology, 92
Developing countries, 81, 95
China, 93
health, 90
Pakistan, 93
political stability, 91
wealth disparity, 91
Devolution, Soviet Union, 182
Dictatorships, 54, 56
Hussein, Saddam, 54
Iraq, 54
military governments vs., 54
Mugabe, Robert, 54
Zimbabwe, 54
Direct democracy, 49–50
Switzerland, 50
Domestication
concept of, 5
food supply, 5
tool development, 5
Dominican Republic-Central America Free Trade Agreement (DR-CAFTA), 103
Dowry, 29
DR-CAFTA. See Dominican Republic-Central America Free Trade Agreement.
Drug exportation, 253

E

Earthquakes, 3
East Asia Summit (EAS), 106
East Timor, 43
Eastern Europe
access to bodies of water, 174
buffer zone, 173, 178
climate, 173
Cold War, 177–178
cultural influences, 174
Czech Republic, 183
devolution of, 173, 176
Estonia, 183
history, 175
Hungary, 183
Iron Curtain, 179
Latvia, 183
Lithuania, 183
missile defense shield, 189
NATO, 181–182, 183, 218
Ottoman Empire, 175
Poland, 183
religions, 175, 176
Russia, 175–176
transition of, 173
Turkey, 175
Ukraine, 184–185
USSR, 177
collapse and, 182
takeover, 178–179
Velvet Revolution, 185
Warsaw Pact, 181–182
World War I, 176–177, 193
World War II, 177, 193
Yugoslavia, 190–192
Economic activities, 69–74
primary, 69
quaternary sector, 71–72
secondary, 70
sectors, 72–74
tertiary level, 70–71
Economic development, 86–92
demographics, 88
GDP, 88
labor productivity, 87
negative trade balance, 88
technology, 86–87
Economic distribution
core countries, 77–78
peripheral countries, 77–78
Wallerstein, Immanuel, 77
Economic entities, 102–107
Asia-Pacific Economic Cooperation, 107

Economic entities (*continued*)
   Association of Southeast Asian Nations, 105
   Dominican Republic-Central America Free Trade Agreement, 103
   European Union, 104–105
   Free Trade Area of the Americas, 103–104
   MERCOSUR, 105
   North American Free Trade Agreement, 102–103
   Organisation for Economic Co-operation and Development, 107
   Union of South American Nations, 105
Economic sectors, 72–74
   China, 73
   Egypt, 73–74
   India, 73
   labor cost, 73
   Turkey, 73
   Vietnam, 73
Economic systems, industrial revolution, 66
Economic Union
   Russia, 221
   Treaty of Paris, 158
Economies, types of, 62–66
   capitalism, 63
   communism, 62–63
   socialism, 63–66
ECSC. *See* European Coal and Steel Community.
Education, 21, 89
Egypt, 51, 53, 56, 57, 68, 73–74
   emigrants, 164
   Mubarak, Hosni, 51, 53
Emancipation Reform of 1861, 201
Emigration, 25
Emperor of Japan, 50
Engels, Friedrich, 48, 68, 204
English, 127
Equatorial Guinea, 76, 77
Estonia, 183, 185
Ethnicity, Australia, 228–229
EU. *See* European Union.
Eurasia, population, 16
Eurasian Union, 223
Europe's Continental Divide of Power, 160
Europe, population, 17

European Coal and Steel Community (ECSC), 158
European Union (EU), 104–105, 156–162, 186
   armed forces, 162
   border controls, 165
   central powers, 160
      France, 160–161
      Germany, 160–161
      United Kingdom, 161
   Continental Divide of Power, 160
   continentals, 160
   cultural issues, 163–164
      Catholic church, 163–164
      Islam, 163
   dissent re, 160
   eastern expansion, 160
   foreign policy, 162
   free movement of peoples, 159, 161
   free trade block, 158
   future of, 168–169
   Greece, 166
   gross domestic product, 161
   history of, 158
   immigration, 162–163, 164–165
      priority by country, 164
   judicial system, 161
   NAFTA vs., 159
   political shift, 165–166
   population declines, 165
   sanctions, 162
   soldiers, 142
   ultra-conservative movement, 163
   Velvet Revolution, 185
Exxon, 67, 84, 134, 135

F

Failed states, 95
   Democratic Republic of Congo, 95
   Haiti, 95
   North Korea, 95
   Pakistan, 95
   Somalia, 95
   Zimbabwe, 95
Famine, 201

Fascism, 54–55
    Hitler, Adolph, 55
    Mussolini, Benito, 55
Fertility rate, 23–24
Fiji, 53
Final sale of the commodity, 74
Financial entities
    BRICs, 116–117
    Group of Eight, 115
    Group of Seven, 114–115
    Group of Twenty, 115–116
    International Monetary Fund, 118
    Nongovernmental organizations, 119
    World Bank, 118–119
    World Trade Organization, 117–118
First world countries, 82
Fishing, 69
Food, supply of, 5
Forced collectivization, 209
Foreign deployment, United States Military, 142
Foreign policy
    awareness of, 144–145
    European Union, 162
    judgment calls, 141
France, 25, 35, 65, 68, 75, 84, 127, 160–161, 163, 164
    Francois, Hollande, 167
    GDP, 131
    Germany, relationship, 166, 167
    immigration issues, 162–163
    invasion of Russia, 200–201
    Sarkozy, Nicolas, 166
Free movement of peoples, 159,
    European Union and, 161
Free trade, 101
Free Trade Area of the Americas (FTAA), 103–104, 258
Free trade block, 158
Free trade self-righteousness, 140
Freedom House, 119
Free-trade, Latin America's opinion re, 257–259
French
    Canada, 127
    Guiana, 45
French Revolution, 52–53, 66, 135

FTAA. *See* Free Trade Area of the Americas.
Fur trade, 200

G

G-20. *See* Group of Twenty.
G-7. *See* Group of Seven.
G-8. *See* Group of Eight.
Gallipoli, 231
Gates, Bill, 89
GDP. *See* gross domestic product.
Gendercide, 29
General Motors, 134
Genocide, 39, 40–41
Geography, 8–9
    cultural traits, 8
    physical traits, 8
    scale of, 10–11
Georgia, 29, 222
    Rose Revolution, 56
Germany, 36, 47, 74, 75, 160–161, 167, 177
    France, relationship, 166, 167
    GDP, 131
    Hitler, Adolph, 177
    invasion into Russia, 208
    Merkel, Angela, 166, 167
    Russia non-aggression pact, 207
    Russia peace treaty, 205
    Schroeder, Gerhard, 167
Glasnost, 213, 215
Global warming, 140, 142, 221
Globalization, 3
Good Neighbor Policy, 251, 260
Gorbachev, Mikhail, 212, 213–214
    policies of, 213–214
        glasnost, 213, 215
        military spending, 213–214
        perestroika, 213, 215
Great Britain, 68
Great Depression, 85, 130
Greece, 166
    western philosophies, 152
Greenland, 45
Greenpeace, 119

Gross domestic product (GDP), 74–77
   Brazil, 76
   China, 74, 75, 76, 131
   corporate earnings, 88
   definition of, 74
   Equatorial Guinea, 76, 77
   European Union, 161
   exclusions, 75
   final sale of the commodity, 74
   France, 75, 131
   Germany, 74, 75, 131
   India, 76
   Iran, 76–77
   Japan, 74–75, 131
   Mexico, 75
   military expenses and, 92
   oil exports, 77
   Oman, 76, 77
   OPEC, 77
   per capita, 76–77
   positive trade balance, 88
   Saudi Arabia, 76
   United States, 74, 131
   wealth disparity, 76
Group of Eight (G-8), 115
Group of Seven (G-7), 114–115
Group of Twenty (G-20), 115–116
Growth rates of populations, 18
Guatemala, 68
Gulf Stream, 153, 154
   North Atlantic Drift, 153, 154
Gun powder, 82, 83

H

Haiti, 95
HDI. *See* Human Development Index.
Headscarves, 163
Health care, 89–90, 217
Hitler, Adolph, 54, 55, 177, 207
   Stalin, Josef and, 207
Hollande, Francois, 167
Holocaust, 39
Homo sapiens, 4
Homogeneous traits, regions and, 11

Howard, John, 234, 235
Human Development Index (HDI), 93–94
   trends, 94
Human rights groups, 40
Human Rights Watch, 119
Hungary, 209
   dissent within, 212
   NATO, 183
Hunter-gatherers, transition from 20
Hussein, Saddam, 54, 142
Hypocrisy, democratic practices and, 146

I

Ice-free zones, 221
Ideology of cultural imperialism, 143
IMF. *See* International Monetary Fund.
Immigration, 25, 138, 162–163
   European Union 164–165
   France, 162–163, 164
   Italy, 164
   priority by country, 164
   Spain, 164
Imperial control, 155
Imperialistic motives, 141
Import substitution, tariffs, 85
India, 24, 28, 30, 52, 56, 68, 73, 76, 78, 83, 84, 85, 86, 92, 156, 222
   dowry, 29
   Latin America, 257
Indonesia, 43–44, 57, 85
Indus Valley, 5
Industrial Revolution, 17, 66, 130
   communism, 66
   Marxism, 66
   socialism, 66
   work laws, 66
Industrialization, 6, 83
   agriculture vs., 22–23
   China, 83
   core countries, 84
   India, 83
   inventions, 6
   Japan, 83
   naval presence, 83

Russia, 83, 209–210
United Kingdom, 83
Information
   production of, 130
   technology, 71–72
International Monetary Fund (IMF), 118
International Red Cross, 119
Internet usage, 6
Interstate Highway System, 138
Intolerance
   China, 146
   Saudi Arabia, 146
   The Vatican, 146
Inventions, 6
Inverted pyramid, 26–28
   population decline, 28
Iran, 36, 44, 51, 52, 56, 57, 77, 136
   Ayatollah Khomeini, 51
   Latin America trade, 257
   Revolution of 1979, 51
   Shah of, 52
Iran/Contra scandal, 252
Iraq, 39, 40, 54, 56, 142, 167
   Hussein, Saddam, 142
Iraq War, 141, 231, 235
Iron Curtain, 179, 208
Islam, 56. *See also* Muslim.
   Hindu vs., 53
Israel, 42, 44, 121
Italy, 25, 36, 164
Ivan the Great, 199
Ivan the Terrible, 199
Japan, 25, 30, 50, 53, 56, 68, 74, 75, 83, 84, 86, 88, 222, 233
   Emperor, 50
   GDP, 131
   Russia vs., 202–203

J

Jintao, Hu, 65
Job specialization, 21
Judicial system, 161
Junta, 53
   Egypt, 53

K

Khodorkovsky, Mikhail, 217
King Abdullah, 65
Kirchner, Cristina, 261
Koranic law, 52
Kosovo, 43, 44–45, 192, 193
   recognition of, 192
Kuwait, 50
Kyoto Protocol, 142

L

Labor cost, 73
Labor productivity, 87
   effects of, 88
Landless Workers' Movement, 248
Landlessness, 246–249
Languages, 127, 156
   English, 127, 156
   French, 127
   Latin America, 244–245
   Portuguese, 156
Latin America
   anti-free trade, 257
   Barack Obama, 254
   Catholicism, 245
   China, 252, 257
   Christopher Columbus, 244
   common culture, 244–246
   Cuba, 254
   definition of, 242
   drug production, 253–254
      countries, 255
      United States intervention in, 254–255
   free trade, 258
   India, 257
   Japan, 257
   language
      Portuguese, 244
      Spanish, 244
      Treaty of Tordesillas, 244
   Mexico, 242
      original size of, 245
   nationalization, 257

Latin America *(continued)*
   origins of name, 241
      Maximilian, 241
      Napoleon III, 241
   partition of, 244–245
      Pope's involvement, 244–245
   population density of, 246
   regions, 242–244
      Middle America, 243–244
      South America, 242
   relationship with United States, 249–252
      anticommunist polices, 251
      Cold War activities, 251–252
      Good Neighbor Policy, 251
      military support, 251
      Monroe Doctrine, 249
      Roosevelt Corollary, 250
   Russia, 257
   Simon Bolivar, 248
   socialist programs, 254
      countries, 254
      popularity of, 255–256
      Venezuela, 254
   United States backyard, 252
   United States interests, 257
   urbanization, 246–247
      Mexico City, 246
      pull factors, 246
      push factors, 246
   USSR influence on, 252
   Venezuela, 256
   wealth disparity, 247, 255
Latvia, 183, 185
   oil economics, 189
Law of the Sea Convention, 142
LDC. *See* less-developed countries.
Least economically developed countries (LEDCs), 81
LEDCs. *See* least economically developed countries.
Left leaning political thinking, 46
Lenin, Vladimir, 48–49, 53, 64, 66, 177, 204–205
   death of, 206
   political support, 205
   Russian involvement in WW I, 205
   successor to, 206

Less-developed countries (LDC), 81
Liberal, 46
Libertarian, 47
   Paul, Ron, 47
Liberty
   individual, 135–136
   Iran, 136
   Malaysia, 136
   Russia, 136
   Singapore, 136
Libya, 39, 53, 142
   emigrants, 164
   invasion of, 110
   Muammar Qaddafi, 39, 53, 142
Liechtenstein, 44
Life expectancy, 20
   Russia, 217
Lithuania, 183, 185, 189
Logging, 69
Luxury items, taxes, 65

M

MAD. *See* Mutually Assured Destruction.
Madura, Nicolas, 65, 261
Mail-order brides
   Burmese, 30
   Thailand, 30
Malaysia, 50, 136
Manifest destiny, 130
Mao Ze Dong, 48, 49
Maori, 230
Maritime nations, 153
Marshall Joseph Tito, 191
Marshall Plan, 181, 208
   Eastern Europe and, 181
Marx, Karl, 48, 66, 204
Marxism, 66
Maternity leave, 65
Maximilian, 241
McDonalds Restaurant, 71
Medvedev, Dmitry, 219
MERCOSUR, 105
Merkel, Angela, 166, 167

Mesopotamia, 5
    population, 17
Mexico, 30, 75, 85, 157, 243, 258
    Cinco de Mayo holiday, 241
    landlessness, 249
    Maximilian, 241
    Napoleon, III, 241
    PRI political party, 249
Microsoft, 67
Middle America, 243–244
    Caribbean, 243
    Central America, 243
    Mexico, 243
Middle East
    democratic movement, 144
    economic diversification, lack of, 75
Migration, 4
    Homo sapiens, 4
Military
    Canada, 132–133
    expenditure by country, 133
    United States, 132–133
Military attack, Yugoslavia, 38–39
Military dictatorship, 56
Military expenses, GDP and, 92
Military governments, 53
    Arab Spring, 53
    dictatorships vs., 54
    Egypt, 53
    Fiji, 53
    junta, 53
    Libya, 53
    Sudan, 53
Military technology, 92
    China, 92
    India, 92
    Pakistan, 92
Milosevic, Slobodan, 38–39, 191–192
Mining, 69
Missile defense shield, 189–190
    NATO, 189
    Russia, 189–190
Mobility, 138–139
    Interstate Highway System, 138

Monarchies, 52–53
Mongols, invasion of Russia, 199
Monroe Doctrine, 249, 260
    renouncement of, 252
Monroe, James, 249, 260
Morales, Evo, 254, 261
Morocco, 56
    Western Sahara, 45
Mosaddegh, Mohammad, 78
Mubarak, Hosni, 51, 53
Mugabe, Robert, 54, 95, 162
Multinational corporations, 66–67
    Exxon, 67, 84
    growth of, 66–67
    Microsoft, 67
    Nintendo, 67
    Pepsi, 67
    state vs., 67–68
    Walmart, 84
Muslim religion issues, 163, 175
    Austria, 163
    burquas, 163
    Danish cartoon, 163
    France, 163
    headscarves, 163
    Switzerland, 163
Muslim states, 52, 57
    Egypt, 57
    Indonesia, 57
    Nigeria, 57
    Pakistan, 57
    Saudi Arabia, 57
    sharia law, 52
Muslims, 175
Mussolini, Benito, 55
Mutual defense clause, 109
Mutually Assured Destruction (MAD), 214

N

NAFTA. *See* North American Free Trade Agreement.
NAM. *See* non-aligned movement.
Napoleon III, 241
Napoleon, invasion of Russia, 200–201

Nation, 41–43
   Chechnya, 43
   common culture, 41–42
   Palestine, 43
   sans state, 42
   state vs., 41
   Tibet, 43
Nation development summary, 95
   failed states, 95
Nationalization, 68–69, 78, 85, 257
   Barack Obama, 69
   capitalism vs., 69
   Chile, 68
   China, 69
   Cuba, 68
   Fidel Castro, 78
   Guatemala, 68
   Hugo Chavez, 78
   Mosaddegh, Mohammad, 78
   oil, 220–221
   OPEC, 85
   Russia, 69, 85
   Saudi Arabia, 85
   Suez Canal, 68
   trend of, 68
   Venezuela, 68, 85
National health care, 66
   Obama-care, 66
Nation-state, 42
NATO. *See* North Atlantic Treaty Organization.
Navies, development of, 83
Negative trade balance, 88
Neolithic Revolution, 4
Netherlands, 50, 155
   Catholic Church, 163
   Polish emigres, 163
New World
   colonization of, 155
   Mexico, 156
New Zealand
   climate, 228
   indigenous peoples, Maori, 230
   nuclear-free zone, 232
   population, 235
NGOs. *See* nongovernmental organizations.
Nicaragua, 252, 261
Nieto, Enrique Pena, 262
Nigeria, 52, 57
   population, 17
1905 Russian Revolution, 208
Non-Aligned Movement (NAM), 82
Nongovernmental organizations (NGOs), 119
   Amnesty International, 119
   Freedom House, 119
   Greenpeace, 119
   Human Rights Watch, 119
   International Red Cross, 119
North America
   borders, 127
   Canada, 127
   corporations, 134–135
   democracy, 135
   disadvantages of, 139–146
      corporate favoritism, 139–140
      cultural imperialism, 143–144
      forcing of democracy, 145
      foreign policy judgment calls, 141
      global warming, 140, 142
      hypocrisy, 145
      imperialistic motives, 141
      intolerance, 146
      inward view, 144–145
      nuclear hit option, 141–142
      projection of power, 142
      resources per capita usage, 140
      self-righteousness, 140
      treaty disdain, 142
   individual liberty, 135–136
   language, 127
   mobility, 138–139
   opportunities, 137–138
   regional advantages, 128–138
      American Revolution, 129
      economic growth, 129–130
      GDP per capita, 132
      industrial revolution, 130

    information age, 130
    manifest destiny, 130
    military, 132–133
    physical distance, 128–129
    physical resources, 128
    service economy, 130
    technology, 130
  tolerance, 136
  United States, 127
North American Free Trade Agreement (NAFTA), 102–103, 259
  European Union vs., 159
North Atlantic Drift, 153, 154
North Atlantic Treaty Organization (NATO), 38, 39, 40, 109–110, 133–134, 181–182
  Eastern Europe, 183, 218
  Estonia, 185
  Latvia, 185
  Lithuania, 185
  Missile defense shield, 189
  mutual defense clause, 109
  Russia, 185
  Serbia, 192
  Shanghai Cooperation Organization vs., 112
  soldiers, 142
North Korea, 39, 44, 49, 95, 121
  South Korea vs., 44
Norway, 50, 65
NPT. *See* Nuclear Non-Proliferation Treaty.
Nuclear hit option, 141–142
Nuclear Non-Proliferation Treaty (NPT), 120
Nuclear weapon owners, 119–121
  India, 120
  Israel, 121
  North Korea, 121
  Nuclear Non-Proliferation Treaty, 120
  Pakistan, 120
Nuclear-free zone, New Zealand, 232

O

OAS. *See* Organization of American States.
Obama, Barack, 69
Obama-care, 66

OECD. *See* Organisation for Economic Co-operation and Development.
Oil economics
  Belarus, 188
  Latvia, 189
  NATO, 188
  Russia, 188–189, 220–221
    nationalization, 220–221
    privatization of, 220
  Ukraine, 188, 189
Oil exports, GDP and, 77
Oligarchs, 216–217
  Yukos Oil, 216
Oman, 76, 77
One Child Policy, 30, 31
One-party state, 51
  China, 51
  Egypt, 51
  USSR, 51
OPEC. *See* Organization of the Petroleum Exporting Countries.
Opium Wars, 83
Opportunities in North America, 137–138
  brain drain, 137–138
  immigration, 138
  risk taking, 138
Orange Revolution, 56, 186
  Yanukovych, Victor, 186
  Yushchenko, Victor, 186
Organisation for Economic Co-operation and Development (OECD), 107
Organization of American States (OAS), 113
  Cuba, 113
  members, 113
Organization of the Petroleum Exporting Countries (OPEC), 85, 222
  GDP and, 77
Organized crime, Russia Mafia, 216
Ortega, Daniel, 261
Osama bin Laden, 142
Ottoman Empire, 36, 52, 175
Over-population, population vs., 16

P

Pact of Non-Aggression, 177
Pakistan, 57, 92, 93, 95, 120
Palau, 43
Palestine, 42, 43
Paul, Ron, 47
Peasantry, 201
Pepsi, 67
Perestroika, 213, 215
Peripheral countries, 77–78, 79, 84–85
    Colonial period, 82–83
    evolution of
        Bahrain, 85
        Brazil, 79
        Chile, 85
        China, 78, 85
        India, 78, 85
        Indonesia, 85
        Mexico, 85
        South Africa, 79, 85
        South Korea, 85
        Turkey, 79, 85
        UAE, 79, 85
    history of, 82–86
    import substitution, 85
    nationalization, 78, 85
    specialization, 86
Peter the Great, 199–200
    continental expansion, 200
    westernization, 199–200
Philippines, 56
Plan Columbia, 253, 254
Poland, 209
    dissent within, 212
    emigres, Netherlands, 163
    joining NATO, 183
Political entities, 45
    Scotland, 45
    Tibet, 45
Political ideologies, 152
Political spectrums
    anarchy, 46, 47
    capitalism, 46
    communism, 46, 48–49
    conservative, 46
    democracy, 49–50
    dictatorships, 54
    fascism, 54–55
    left leaning, 46
    liberal, 46
    Libertarian, 47
    military governments, 53
    monarchy, 52–53
    one-party state, 51
    right leaning, 46
    theocracy, 51–52
Political stability, 91
Pope, the, 51
Population
    Africa, 17
    age, 21–22
    Asia, 16
    birth rate, 19
    death rate, 19
    decline of, 28
        Belarus, 28
        Europe, 165
        Russia, 28
        Ukraine, 28
    Demographic Transition model, 18–25
    density, 155
    Eurasia, 16
    Europe, 17
    explosion, 21
    future growth patterns, 30–31
        Australia, 30
        China, 30, 31
        India, 30
        Japan, 30
        Mexico, 30
        religious influences, 31
        Russia, 30
        South America, 30, 31
    growth of, 5, 15–16, 18
    Industrial Revolution's impact on, 17
    issues, 217
    listing by country, 16

loss, 25
Mesopotamia, 17
over-population vs., 16
regions, 16–18
skewed sex ratios, 29–30
South American, 17
United States, 17
world, 15–16
Population Momentum, 28–29
China, 28
India, 28
Population pyramids
classic, 26–27
column, 26, 27
inverted, 26–28
Portugal, 156
Brazil, 245
Positive trade balance, 88
Poverty levels, 138
PRI political party, 249
Primary economic activities, 69
resource extraction, 69
Prime minister, political power of, 50
Private ownership, 63
Privatization, 68–69
China, 68
India, 68
Japan, 68
United States, 68
USSR, 68
Processing raw materials, 70
Projection of power, 142
EU soldiers, 142
Iraq, 142
Libya, 142
NATO soldiers, 142
Osama bin Laden, 142
United Nations soldiers, 142
United States military, 142
Prophet Mohammad, 163
Protectionism, 102
Puerto Rico, 45
Pull factors, 246
Push factors, 246

Putin, Vladimir, 65, 186, 190, 217
economic stability, 219
nationalism, 219
political consolidation, 219

Q

Qaddafi, Muammar, 39, 53, 112, 113, 114, 142
Quaternary sector, 71–71
India, 92
information technology, 71–72
Queen of England, 52

R

Racism, 236
Rasputin, Gregory, 203, 204
Reagan, Ronald, 212, 252
arms race, 212
communism, views on, 212
Reciprocity, 38
Yugoslavia, 38–39
Red Crescent, 119
Red Cross, 119
Regional geography, 263
Regions, 9–10
homogeneous traits, 11
scale of, 10–11
Religion
Catholicism, 31
Eastern Europe, 175, 176
Islam, 31
theocracy and, 51
Replacement level, 24, 27
Representative democracy, 50
United States, 50
Republican Party, 66
Resource extraction, 69
agriculture, 69
fishing, 69
logging, 69
mining, 69
Resources used per capita, 140
Revolutions, 66

Right leaning political thinking, 46
Risk-taking, 89, 138
Romania, 36
Romanov dynasty, 199
    Anastasia, 206
    assassination of, 205–206
    Peter the Great, 199–200
Roosevelt, Theodore, 250, 251, 260
Roosevelt Corollary, 250, 260
Rose revolution, 56
Rouseff, Dilma, 248, 249, 254, 261
Rudd, Kevin, 235, 236
Russia, 25, 28, 30, 39, 40, 56, 65, 68, 83–85, 88, 136, 176–177, 185
    absorption of Crimea, 188
    Bolshevik Revolution, 204
    Catherine the Great, 200
    Chechnya and, 43, 192
    China, 222
    civil war, 205
    climate, 198
    continental expansion of, 200
    creation of Soviet satellites, 209
    Crimea, 192, 222–223
    deaths suffered by, 208
    early history, 199–201
        Ivan the Great, 199
        Ivan the Terrible, 199
        Mongolian invasion, 199
        Romanovs, 199
    Eastern Europe
        effect on, 175
        takeover of, 208
    economic collapse, 215–216
    economic partnerships, 221–222
    economic stability, 219
    Economic Union, 221
    Emancipation Reform of 1861, 201
    environmental concerns, 217–218
    Eurasian Union, 223
    famine, 201
    fur trade, 200
    Georgia, 222
    German invasion, 208
    German peace treaty, 205
    Germany non-aggression pact, 207
    global warming's impact on, 221
    government corruption, 216
    health care, 217
    ice-free zones, 221
    industrialization, 209–210
    influence on world, 218
    Iron Curtain, 208
    Japan and, 202–203
    Kosovo, 192
    Lenin, Vladimir, 177
    life expectancy, 217
    Medvedev, Dmitry, 219
    military, 220, 222
    missile defense shield, 189–190
    modernization of, 207
    Napoleon's invasion of, 200–201
    nationalism, 219
    1905 Revolution, 203
    oil, 188–189, 220–221
        nationalization of, 220–221
        privatization of, 220
    oligarchs, 216–217
    organized crime, 216
    Pact of Non-Aggression, 177
    peasants, 201
    Peter the Great, 199–200
    political consolidation, 219
    population issues, 217
    Putin, Vladimir, 21, 65, 186, 190, 217, 219
    Rasputin, Gregory, 203
    retribution against West, 189–190
    Romanov Dynasty, 199–200, 205–206
    serfs, 201
    Soviet satellites, establishment of, 209
    Stalin, Joseph, 177
    Tsars, 52–53
        abdication of, 204
        Alexander II, 201
        Tsar Nicholas II, 203
    Ukraine, 185–188
    World War I, 203
        withdrawal from, 205

World War II, 208
Yeltsin, Boris, 219
Russian Mafia, 216
Russian Revolution, 52–53, 66
Russo-Japanese war, 202
Rwanda, 40

S

Sahel, 52
Sailing technologies, 82
Sanctions, Zimbabwe, 162
Santos, Juan Manuel, 261
Sarkozy, Nicholas, 166
Saudi Arabia, 56, 57, 64, 65, 76, 85, 146
 King Abdullah, 65
Scale
 geography and, 10–11
 regions and, 10–11
Schroeder, Gerhard, 167
SCO. *See* Shanghai Cooperation Organization.
Scotland, 45
SDI. *See* Strategic Defense Initiative.
Second world countries, 82
Secondary economic activities, 70
Secular state, 51
 Catholic Church, 51
Serbia, 29, 44–45, 192
 attack on, 39
 Milosevic, Slobadan, 191–192
 NATO, 192
Serfs, 201
 demise of, 83
Service economy, growth of, 130
Service sector, 70–71
 McDonalds Restaurant, 71
 Walmart, 71
Sewage treatment, 21
Sex ratios, skewering of, 29–30
 abortions, 29, 30
 Albania, 29
 Armenia, 29
 Azerbaijan, 29
 Bosnia, 29

 China, 29, 30
 cultural bias, 29–30
 gendercide, 29
 Georgia, 29
 India, 29, 30
 mail-order brides, 30
 Serbia, 29
 societal behavior, 30
 South Korea, 29
 Vietnam, 29, 30
Shah of Iran, 52
Shanghai Cooperation Organization (SCO), 111, 222
 NATO vs., 112
 signed treaties, 111–112
Sharia law, 52
 Koran, 52
 Nigeria, 52
 Sahel, 52
Singapore, 136
Skype, 6
Slavery, demise of, 83
Slim, Carlos, 262
Slovakia, 56
Smith, Adam, 66
 Wealth of Nations, 66
Social democracy, 64
Socialism, 63–66
 Canada, 65
 China, 65
 communism vs., 65
 contradictions re, 64
 Cuba, 65
 democratic, 64
 France, 65
 Norway, 65
 Russia, 65
 Saudi Arabia, 65
 social democracy, 64
 state control, 64
 state taxes, 64
 Sweden, 65
 United States, 64, 65
 Venezuela, 65, 254
Somalia, 47, 95

South Africa, 79, 83
South America, 30–31
    population, 17
South Korea, 29, 85, 86
    North Korea vs., 44
South Sudan, 44
Sovereign state, 36
    definition of, 37
Sovereignty, 37–38
    Afghanistan, 39
    Bosnia, 39
    Chechnya, 43
    China, 39, 40
    Congo, 39
    debate re, 40–41
    human rights groups, 40
    Iraq, 39
    issues, World Bank, 119
    Libya, 39
    North Korea, 39
    reciprocity, 38
    recognition of, 38
    redefinition of, 39
    Russia, 39, 40
    Rwanda, 39
    Sudan, 39
    Syria, 39
    Tibet, 43
    Zimbabwe, 39
Soviet rule, challenges to, 183
Soviet satellites, 180
    creation of, 209
    Czech Republic, 209
    Hungary, 209
    Poland, 209
Soviet Union, 48, 50, 56
    collapse of, 182
Spain, 50, 84, 156, 164, 245
    control of Latin America, 245
Specialization, 86
Stage Five Demographic Transition Model, 25
    emigration, 25
    immigration, 25
    Italy, 25

    Japan, 25
    population loss, 25
    Russia, 25
    Sweden, 25
Stage Four Demographic Transition Model, 24–26
    France, 25
    Japan, 25
    population age, 24
    United States, 25
Stage One Demographic Transition Model, 19–20
    death rates, 19–20
    infant mortality, 20
Stage Three Demographic Transition Model, 22–24
    agriculture vs. industry, 22–23
    birth control, 23
    Brazil, 24
    Chile, 24
    China, 24
    fertility rate, 23–24
    India, 24
    replacement level, 24
Stage Two Demographic Transition Model, 20–23
    agricultural production, 20–21
    cultural lag, 21
    education, 21
    heath care, 21
    hunter-gatherers, 20
    job specialization 21
    population age, 21–22
    population explosion, 21
    sewage treatment, 21
    water resources, 21
Stalin, Josef, 48, 54, 177, 206–207
    dictatorial powers, 206
    Hitler and, 207
    modernization of Russia, 207
    psychosis of, 206
Star Wars. *See* Strategic Defense Initiative.
State of Iran, 44
State
    Bulgaria, 36
    China, 36
    colonies vs, 45
    control of, 46–56

definition of, 35
France, 35
Germany, 36
Iran, 36
Italy, 36
multinational corporation vs., 67–68
North Korea, 44
Ottoman Empire, 36
recognition by others, 44
Romania, 36
South Korea, 44
sovereign, 36
territories, 45
State recognition
Cyprus, 44
Czech Republic, 44
Iran, 44
Kosovo, 44–45
Liechtenstein, 44
Serbia, 44–45
Taiwan, 44–45
Turkey, 44
States
China, 43
East Timor, 43
failed, 95
growth in, 56
Haiti, 43
Indonesia, 43–44
Israel, 44
Kosovo, 43
Palau, 43
Palestine, 43, 44
as political entities, 45
Puerto Rico, 45
recognition of, 43–45
United Nations, 43
Vatican City, 43
South Sudan, 44
Sudan, 44
Taiwan, 43
Transnistriia, 43
Strategic Defense Initiative (SDI), 214

Subsidies, 102
Sudan, 39, 53
Suez Canal, 68
Supranationalists, 101
Sweden, 25, 65
Switzerland, 50, 163
Syria, 39, 56

T

Taiwan, 44–45, 86
Taliban, 57
Tariffs, 85, 102
Tasmanians, 236
Taxes, 64, 65
luxury items, 65
Saudi Arabia, 64
Sweden, 64
United States, 64
Venezuela, 64
Technology, 86–87
growth, 130
gun powder, 82, 83
sailing, 82
Tertiary level activities, 70–71
Thailand, 50, 56
bride, 30
Theocracy, 51–52, 57
Iran, 51, 57
Muslim states, 52
religion, 51
secular, 51
Taliban, 57
Third world country, 81–82
Tibet, 43, 45
China and, 192
Tierra del Fuego, 33
Tito, Marshall Joseph, 191
Tools, development of, 5
Trade balance, 88
Trade blocks, 101, 159
Transnistriia, 43
Tansportation, 6
Travel, speed of, 3

Treaty disdain
    Kyoto Protocol, 142
    Law of the Sea Convention, 142
Treaty of Paris, 158
    European Coal and Steel Community, 158
Treaty of Tordesillas, 244
Tsar of Russia, 52–53
    Tsar Alexander II, 201
    Tsar Nicholas II, 203
        abdication, 204
        arrest of, 205
        assassination of, 205–206
Tunisia, emigrants, 164
Turkey, 55, 56, 73, 79, 85, 175
    Islam, 56, 175
    Muslims, 175
Tymoshenko, Yulia, 187

U

UAE, 79, 85
Ukraine, 28, 184–188
    Crimea, 187
    disintegration of, 193
    NATO, 187
    oil economics, 188, 189
    Orange Revolution, 56, 186
    political affiations, 186–187
    protests, 188
    revolutions, 56
    Tymoshenko, Yulia, 187
    Western influence on, 187
Ultra-conservative movement, 163
UN. *See* United Nations.
UNASAR. *See* Union of South American Nations.
Underdeveloped nations, 81
Union of South American Nations (UNASAR), 105
United Federation of Russia, 215
    Yeltsin, Boris, 215
United Kingdom, 45, 50, 56, 83, 84, 161
    Bermuda, 45
    Cameron, David, 166, 167
    convict colonies, 228
    Scotland, 45
    United States, relationship, 166
United Nations (UN), 11, 41, 43, 50, 93 108–109
    effectiveness of, 108
    Human Development Index, 93–94
    Permanent Security Council, 108–109
    soldiers, 142
    United States, 141
United States, 25, 50, 52, 53, 64, 65, 68, 74, 84, 127, 135
    American Revolution, 135
    arms race with USSR, 212
    Democratic Party, 66
    foreign policy, 141, 144–145
    Gross Domestic Product, 131
    government services debate, 66
    Latin America, relationship with, 249–253
        Good Neighbor Policy, 251
        Monroe Doctrine, 249
        Roosevelt Corollary, 250
    military, 132–133
    national health care, 66
    NATO, 133–134
    population, 17
    projection of power, 133–134
    Republican Party, 66
    soldiers in foreign countries, 142
    United Kingdom, relationship with, 166
    United Nations vs., 141
    Venezuela vs., 256
Uranium, export to China, 233
Urbanization, 5–6
    landlessness, 246–249
    pull factors, 246
    push factors, 246
US's Backyard, 252
USSR, 48, 51, 65, 68, 177
    Afghanistan invasion, 211, 214–215,
    arms race with United States, 212
    central economic planning, 209
    collectivization, 209
    dissent within, 212
    economic collapse of, 211–212
    exports, 210
    Gorbachev, Mikhail, 212
    industrialization, 209–210

Latin America, influence on, 252
military spending limits, 213–214
Reagan, Ronald, and, 212
restructuring of, 215
Soviet satellites, 180
Strategic Arms Limitation Talks, 214
takeover of Eastern Europe, 178–180
United Federation of Russia, 215
See also Russia.

V

Vatican, 43, 51, 146, 244
Velvet Revolution, 185
Venezuela, 8, 64, 65, 68, 85, 254
    Chavez, Hugo, 249, 254, 256
    Madura, Nicolas, 65
    United States vs., 256
Vietnam, 29, 30, 56, 62, 73

W

Wallerstein, Immanuel, 77
Walmart, 71, 77, 84, 134
Warsaw Pact, 111, 181–182
Water resources, 21
    Western Europe and, 153
Wealth disparity, 76, 91
    Latin America and, 247
Wealth of Nations, 66
Western Europe
    colonization, 155
    commonalities, 152
    competitive states, 154
    decline of, 156, 157
    education of, 154
    European Union, 157–162
    geography, 153
    Gulf Stream, 153, 154
    history, 154–157
    imperial control, 155
    maritime powers, 153
    political ideologies, 152
    population density, 155
    quality of life, 152
    states of, 152
Western philosophies, 152
Western Sahara, 45
Work laws, 66
World Bank, 118–119
    sovereignty issues, 119
World population, growth of, 15
World systems theory, 77
    economic distribution, 77–78
World Trade Organization (WTO), 11, 67, 68, 117–118
World War I, 176–177, 193
    Russia, 176–177, 203
World War II, 177, 193
    Russia, 208
WTO. *See* World Trade Organization.

Y

Yanukovych, Victor, 186, 188
Yeltsin, Boris, 215, 219
Yemen, 56
Yugoslavia, 38–39, 56, 190–192
    attack of, 38–39
    disintegration of, 191–192
    Kosovo, 192
    Milosevic, Slobadan, 191, 192
    religious mix, 191
    Serbia, 192
    Tito, Marshall Joseph, 191
Yukos Oil, 216
Yushchenko, Victor, 186

Z

Zimbabwe, 39, 54, 95, 162
    Mugabe, Robert, 95, 162